Nul Points

Tim Moore's writing has appeared in the *Daily Telegraph*, the *Observer*, the *Sunday Times* and *Esquire*. His books include *French Revolutions, Do Not Pass Go* and *Spanish Steps*. He lives in west London with his wife and three children.

By the same author

Frost on My Moustache
Continental Drifter
French Revolutions
Do Not Pass Go
Spanish Steps

Nul Points

Tim Moore

JONATHAN CAPE
LONDON

Published by Jonathan Cape 2006

2 4 6 8 10 9 7 5 3 1

First published in Great Britain in 2006 by Jonathan Cape
Random House, 20 Vauxhall Bridge Road,
London SW1V 2SA

Random House Australia (Pty) Limited
20 Alfred Street, Milsons Point, Sydney,
New South Wales 2061, Australia

Random House New Zealand Limited
18 Poland Road, Glenfield,
Auckland 10, New Zealand

Random House (Pty) Limited
Isle of Houghton, Corner of Boundary Road & Carse O' Gowrie,
Houghton 2198, South Africa

Random House Publishers India Private Limited
301 World Trade Tower, Hotel Intercontinental Grand Complex,
Barakhamba Lane, New Delhi 110 001, India

The Random House Group Limited Reg. No. 954009
www.randomhouse.co.uk

A CIP catalogue record for this book is available from the British Library

ISBN 9780224077804 (from Jan 2007)
ISBN 0224077805

Mixed Sources
Product group from well-managed
forests and other controlled sources

Cert no. TT-COC-2139
www.fsc.org
©1996 Forest Stewardship Council

Typeset by Palimpsest Book Production Limited,
Grangemouth, Stirlingshire
Printed and bound in Great Britain by Clays Ltd, St Ives plc

Acknowledgements

Thanks to Birna, Jane Awdry, Andreas Schacht, Martin Faulkner and Chris Barrow of doteurovision, John Thompson at *www.nul-points.net*, and the bewilderingly tireless compilers of *diggiloo.net* and *esctoday.com*. Also to OGAE Turkey, Frida Thorsen, Sissel Bryggman, Øistein Wickle, Alan McCarthy, Tinna Traustadottir, Cicely and Jack.

And I shouldn't forget all my nul-pointers, even those I sometimes wish I could.

To Çetin Alp

Nul Points

'Our next song for Europe is performed by Jane Alexander,' intones Terry Wogan, with a gentle reverence he won't be deploying too often on finals night two months hence, 'and it's called *Shame.*'

One walked out of the *Blockbusters* studio with three gold runs and an adventure break in North Wales under his belt, another was once asked out by Placido Domingo, a third competed with distinction as Sicily's representative at the 1983 Italian *Donkey Kong* championships. But of all my friends' most notable achievements, none is more impressive nor improbable than the feat whose perpetrator is now hunched and cringing on an adjacent sofa.

The lazy, pitiless jeers that have cannoned around this south-London front room for the past half-hour fade to avid silence; three of us lean forward and Jane sinks back, watching through face-clasped fingers as her rather younger self manoeuvres a pair of spinnaker-sized red lapels through the side curtains.

A Song For Europe is Eurovision's school of hard knocks, and reliving its videotaped 1989 incarnation, my wife Birna and I, and Jane's husband Chas, have been pulling no punches. Our hooted derision has seen off the snaggle-toothed puffball pixies and the hungover minicab controller; one especially vicious blast blew Jason Donovan's cousin clean out of the ugly tree.

And how we've thrilled to the period catwalk comedy that is such a treasured Eurovision rite: four acts in, the have-your-eye-out shoulder pads aren't quite the mirth-magnet they were, but the back-combed, sprayed-up, cliff-fringed tonsorial splendour is still reliably reducing us to exhausted, whimpery croaks: 'The hair . . . *the hair.*'

Given what Terry's introduced before, and most of what he's going to introduce after, there seems no real justification for our hostess's embarrassment, though I don't imagine that jacket is too near the front of the current Alexander wardrobe. Jane quickly confirms what our eyes and ears have been telling us throughout years of friendship: she has a fantastic voice, and she looks great. For the next three minutes her performance thrills not only her front-room companions, but the fêted studio guest whose verdict Terry now requests.

'I hope that sounded as good at home as it did here,' enthuses Lulu, in breathy, eager Glaswegian lite. 'That really is my favourite. Wasn't she *terrific*?'

The audience expresses its loud consent, Birna and I yelp 'Boom-Bang-A-Bang!' in ragged unison, and Jane finally lets her hands drop from her face.

'Yeah, well, not that terrific,' she murmurs, wryly, 'or I'd have done better than third.'

Oh, come on! This is Eurovision, or very nearly, an institution watched by half the world since telly began: you've played a part in the greatest show on earth! And how about that Lulu stuff? Lulu! A bona fide Eurovision legend, back in the days before we all started to . . . well, you know . . . like we just did . . . to, ah, everyone except you.

'Um, thanks,' says Jane.

Drafted in at very short notice when *Shame*'s intended performer bottled it, *A Song for Europe* – the national qualifier held to select Britain's Eurovision entry – gave Jane a free roll of the fame dice, after a vocal apprenticeship served out in clubs and bars. 'You think: Well, this could be the big moment,' she sighs, as Live Report stroll out to reprise their winning entry. 'Sitting in our little dressing rooms I'm sure we all thought it. Look at these guys – they went off to the final and nearly won.'

No shame in coming third to them, particularly when the well-stocked internet archives I find myself consulting the next morning reveal that with 47,664 televotes, Jane ended up just a couple of thousand shy of the puffball pixies who somehow finished second. But Eurovision wouldn't be Eurovision without its sorry, hopeless losers, and as a child of the Wogan generation I can't resist a gloating peek at the wrong end of the *Song For Europe* scoreboard: no shame in third, but perhaps – snigger – just a smidge in last.

So there's Danny Ellis, whose performance lured just one viewer to the phone for every twenty who dialled up in support of Live Report. *Just for the Good Times*, eh Danny? Whoops!

I enlarge the muddy screenshot beside his score: it's the minicab controller, focus of some of our lairier jeers. Suddenly it isn't quite so funny. My unappealing smirk withers, like a bully's at the inquest of his taunted victim. Eighth out eight; Danny's dreams of stardom stillborn – from wannabe to never-was in three minutes. Viewed in guilty hindsight, there's an earnest fragility in those pasty, nondescript features, a poignant, unschooled haplessness in that slightly bouffant centre parting and the night-out-at-Harvester jacket.

If *A Song for Europe* was an unexpected opportunity for Jane, for Danny it must have seemed the biggest break since half of Beachy Head fell off. Out of the blue you're offered a shot at the big-time, then live before the Saturday-night prime-time millions, you unload straight into your foot.

It hardly bears thinking about, so of course for the rest of that day I do little else. I'm still doing it long after the online revelation of Danny's happy ending: the Florida home shared with wife and daughter, the voice seminars and workshops, even the release of a recent album, albeit one that expresses his journey to joy through the teachings of Prem Rawat. And I'm doing it because it's just not possible to dwell on Eurovision misfortune without pondering the fate of those who finished not just last, but least, and whose reward was a flatly derisive soubriquet that has come to exemplify ignominious ineptitude. The gold standard of catastrophic failure, the benchmark of badness, it's a catchphrase that sits alongside *Waterloo*, Bucks Fizz and that German girl on a stool with her big white guitar in our shared Eurovision memories, a catchphrase whose universality, as I swiftly discover, has now attracted the Oxford University Press lexicographers.

> **nul points** n. *a score of zero in a contest; a verdict of abysmal quality. A facetious British usage inspired by the Eurovision Song Contest.*

Ah, that facetious British usage, and oh, its inspiration.

Here, in the land that Katie Boyle first taught us to know as la Royaume Uni, we gave birth to the pop song, nurtured it to wise maturity. Pop was our gift to the world, and on a Saturday night each May, we'd settle smugly down on the sofa to watch our hapless continental brethren try and return the favour. At 8 p.m., Terry Wogan would welcome us with a complicit chuckle to Zagreb's Vatroslav Lisinski Hall, or the Palais de Centenaire in Brussels, and an evening of unfailingly hilarious schadenfreude would unfold. We gave them toe-tappers, they gave us thigh-slappers. La, la, la, ding, dang, dong, ho, ho, ho.

The Eurovision Song Contest entertained us in ways it was never supposed to: we tittered at its kitsch inanity, its stubborn reinforcement of the crudest national stereotypes, at a scoreboard shamelessly corrupted by cross-border amity and hatred. A ludicrous, lamé farce, three hours of Austrian power ballads, hand-jiving Latvians and Maltese electro-folk. A towering cathedral of cheese, constructed entirely without cheddar.

What is it pride comes before? We found out on 24 May 2003, live from the Skonto Arena in Riga. Tackling our nation's chosen song for Europe, chirpy Scouse duo Jemini launched into *Cry Baby* half an octave south of the backing track, then spent three agonising minutes failing to find their way back. Don McLean's was not the last word on the subject – this was the day the music died.

The incompetent delivery of awful songs had been luring us to the sofa for years. That yodelling, sequinned Hungarian; the Travolta-maned Turkish rasper in his tieless white three-piece, those bearded, whistling Danes: no ESC was complete without its daft, deluded musical martyrs, trampled in the stampede towards our continent's lowest cultural dominator. But this . . . well, this was never supposed to happen.

'Here are the results from the Icelandic jury,' announced a shaky Nordic voice. No mention of la Royaume Uni in the faltering list that followed, nor from Austria, nor Ireland, nor Turkey. Terry Wogan's chortling contempt rang dismally hollow for the rest of the evening; that British usage would, henceforth, be rather less facetious. Nul pwah, since student days in everyday use as a response to acts of slapstick clumsiness, was quietly dropped from my vocabulary.

Eurovision was one of the rare international competitions the British had never entered as underdogs; I wasn't quite sure how to recalibrate my scornometer. Watching a Frenchwoman totter around the 2004 stage in six-foot stilts, I understood that sober respect for the contest as a whole might, as the football fraternity would have it, be too big an ask. But the minimum requirement, surely, was humbled compassion for the scoreboard-proppers, those whose injury we had for years delighted in supplementing with insult. The old reflex had been there when I barked a jeer at the dunce in *A Song For Europe*'s class of '89, but its hooted follow-up had died in my throat and now, in a spirit of penance and forgiveness, I had done my bit towards the rehabilitation of Danny Ellis.

And his, I now reminded myself, was a blow softened by 6,777 telephonic messages of support, a solace of sorts on that long journey to joy. But to win the national qualifier and get to the final, to jump with all your eager might on the gilded springboard to ABBA-land and feel it shatter, to have so far to fall with nothing to cushion your landing, to awake after the worst night of your life and find sympathy boiled down to poorly stifled sniggers in the hotel lobby . . . to max out at the

Eurovision Song Contest is to find yourself atop the lonely, windswept summit of Mount Fiasco.

Even the most disastrous humiliations of my life barely register on the nul points Richter scale. The mind alights reluctantly on the occasion I lavishly succumbed to sea-sickness while taking off my polo-neck in a cabin full of Norwegians; on my blared enquiry as I cheekily leafed through a female friend's diary in front of a large group of associates: 'So who's this "P" you've been meeting every month, eh?' And then there was the moment, in distant early childhood, when Mrs Hoyle forced a Breton fishermen's jersey over my pudding-bowled head and shoved me out from the wings to stand in for her bed-bound protégée at the Silverdale Primary annual pageant. It is difficult even now to relive the centre-stage horrors I suffered thereafter, a half-dancing, half-singing study in blinking, craven, spotlit bewilderment as the chorus line behind rollocked their way through *All the Nice Girls Love a Sailor*. Thirty-five years on, the memories are still weighing my head down below the public-performance parapet. We've all cocked up at the karaoke, but who can conceive of the monumental indignities sustained by the nul-pointer who stands up to be counted by all the peoples of Europe, and then isn't?

These performers didn't just walk on to that one stage and bomb; in appealing to each and every Eurovision jury they effectively entered two dozen separate contests around the continent, sang their little song, the repository of all their hopes and dreams, then had to sustain those brittle Eurosmiles as duck after duck after duck popped up on the giant scoreboard, a deck of portholes stretching along its busy superstructure. Did they like me in Germany? *Nein*. Latvia? *Ne*. Right across the continent, from Reykjavik to Riga, Lisbon to Limassol, they'd watched and listened, then yawned, cringed, guffawed. Heady excitement curdled into towering, grandiose humiliation, before a crowded auditorium and half a billion live viewers. All nudging each other with the same pitiless rhetorical query: how about that Norwegian pillock, eh?

Well, now that I mention it: how about that Norwegian

pillock? It's a Saturday night in mid-adolescence, and I'm sprawled and smirking on the sofa, already enjoying Eurovision for all the wrong reasons. And here he comes, the majestic wrongest of all those wrongs, some straw-haired ninny in bad shades and braces, prancing his way to infamy. No one forgets their first nul-pointer.

Though in doing so I'm dimly aware of slipping further into the realms of obsession, it doesn't take long to put a name to that fuzzy, half-remembered face. Jahn Teigen, 1978, the nul points granddaddy, the reason Norway now has those two words branded across its buttocks. 'Eurovision's most notorious flop,' begins the BBC's brutally terse biography, 'Teigen sang *Mil Etter Mil* while twanging his braces and kicking his legs.' A small picture portrays a man in red trousers energetically thus engaged. 'He went on to run Norway's only private pub-brewery and a naturopathic pharmacy.'

Now there's a sentence you don't just read once. Running widened eyes across it a third time, the Jemini-flavoured contrition with which I'd recalled my unedifying part in Jahn Teigen's downfall is swept aside by a surge of more stirring sentiment. Yes, I was there when Jahn was thrown down the nul points mineshaft, cackling harshly as his screams faded to an echo; now, though, all these years later, I'm here again as in weary triumph he hauls himself out, this time awed to respectful silence by those heroic powers of recuperative reinvention. From pan-continental laughing stock to hippie publican, here was a survivor with an extraordinary tale to tell. Little red-trousered man on my monitor, I salute you.

It's only as I scroll down the page that whimsical curiosity hardens into excited, righteous, torso-tautening determination. For below Jahn's entry is a roll-call of the nul points fallen, some names distantly resonant, others no more to me than unknown warrior-minstrels left face-down in the Eurovision no man's land. Remedios Amaya, Tor Endresen, Seyyal Taner, Gunvor Guggisberg . . . on it goes, from Jahn to Jemini, from Oslo to Istanbul, fourteen sacrificed reputations remembered on the entertainment world's most luridly desecrated memorial. Fourteen hands to shake, fourteen stories to hear, fourteen shaming wrongs to right.

So headily mesmeric is this fledgling vision that it's hardly a surprise to encounter its mission statement twice in the course of a single evening's telly-watching. I first hear Jeremy Clarkson employ those two evocative words during some lavish vehicular dismissal, and then, rather more divertingly, Doctor Who, taunting the Daleks as they fail to broach the Tardis forcefield: 'Is that it? Useless! Nul pwah!' And this from one who can draw his insults from right across the space-time continuum: as a pan-galactic benchmark of arrant, ignominious failure, it shall endure until the end of history. Unless . . . yes, unless I travel back through the colourful sands of Eurovision time, scrubbing away the stigma of a nul points past with fourteen heartwarming tales of life after scoreboard death, castrating that brutal phrase – snip, slash – of its malevolent might.

So let me come to you, strange Jahn and your thirteen persecuted apostles: I wish only to cleanse myself and my nation of the guilty stain of facetious usage, to share your pain and hail your salvation, to hear where you are now, and, um, why you were then. I shall travel to your homes in Eurovision's loneliest outposts, offering escape from exile on that light-entertainment Elba, years after finally facing your Waterloo. How could you ever refuse? You'll feel like you win when you lose.

On 12 February 1950, representatives of twenty-three broadcasting organisations from around the continent gathered in a Torquay conference room to hammer out a system of technical co-operation. It can't have been a long meeting – with peace not yet five years old, technical co-operation meant establishing who'd hold the ladder and who'd twiddle the bent coathanger on the roof – yet the gathering was significant as the first held by the European Broadcasting Union.

By the time Swiss TV director Marcel Bezençon rose to address his fellow delegates in Monaco five years later, the EBU and its realm had conspicuously evolved. The Union now found itself at the helm of a pioneering network of pan-continental communication channels, capable of transmitting simultaneous footage right across Europe for the first time; though only 5 per cent of European households had access to a television in 1955, the projections accurately predicted a rapid surge in ownership.

And if the EBU had at last fashioned the infrastructural means to join hands, eyes and ears across its borders, it would now be doing so in pursuit of a sombrely urgent end. The continent that had, a short decade earlier, been the crucible of history's bloodiest war now found itself in the no man's land of a stand-off that threatened to end in unthinkable apocalypse. The Warsaw Pact had just been signed and, as the looming Suez Crisis would emphasise, the US now considered the old European powers a tiresome irrelevance. The Cold War battle lines were being drawn, and Europeans watched in ratcheting terror as they were drawn right across their front gardens.

As the Soviets crowded Europe's eastern borders with mid-range thermonuclear missiles, by 1955 the forces encroaching from the west carried a rather more subtle threat. That year saw the British release of *Blackboard Jungle*, a transatlantic depiction of teenage discontent whose screenings incited audiences to trash the local Odeon before nipping down the shops for a copy of the theme tune; Bill Haley's *Rock Around the Clock* topped the year-end UK charts. American Forces Radio was becoming the station of choice for millions across the continent, and with the first transatlantic phone cable nearing completion there were loudly voiced fears of a cultural takeover.

Perhaps raising his voice above disgruntled reminiscences of sodding Torquay in bloody February, Marcel explained that the EBU was not in Monaco for a publicly funded piss-up down the casino. The vision that haunted him was of a newly united Europe destroyed in tender infancy, if not through annihilation in the nuclear crossfire, then by stealthy annexation into the American empire. There wasn't much he could do about the first, perhaps, but in the EBU's new pan-European broadcast network he saw a powerful weapon in the fight to bolster the continent's cultural identity.

The technology had already been successfully trialled: on 6 June 1954, three million viewers across Europe had been triumphantly welcomed to a yodel-float drive-by, live from the Montreux Narcissus Festival. The summer season of transmissions that ensued – a party for refugee children in Holland, an athletics meet in Glasgow, Pope Pius XII's thoughts on the mixed blessings of television, in Latin – had been bracketed together by the EBU as 'the Lille Experiment', in recognition of the control centre's location. It took *Evening Standard* journalist George Campey to come up with a blanket term less suggestive of some diabolical instrument of subliminal indoctrination. '"Eurovision" is a system for the exchange of television programmes between the countries of western Europe,' he declared, and a nickname was born.

The triumph of these eclectic summer broadcasts convinced Marcel that an annual flagship event offered the most effective means of spreading unity through Eurovision. Around the Monaco conference table he outlined the options. Unless Esperanto belatedly took off in a big way there were clear drawbacks with anything overly reliant upon the spoken word. Physical competition was one obvious answer, but logistical difficulties precluded a major annual sporting tournament (the quadrennial, Marcel-inspired European football championships were launched in 1960), and it would be a decade before some oaf-rich EBU committee concocted *Jeux Sans Frontières*.

Marcel's conclusion was that European harmony might be

best celebrated – and the burgeoning threat of US cultural imperialism best forestalled – via the fearsome rallying might of light entertainment. His first suggestion, a 'Eurovision cup for amateur entertainers', lost out in the show of hands – if that Dutchman hadn't been asleep, we'd have spent those springtime Saturday nights watching Björn saw Agnetha in half while Brotherhood of Man circled the stage on a motorcycle pyramid; how rewarding to picture Jahn Teigen as the madcap MC, hooting Norwegian one-liners through a megaphone.

Instead the delegates plumped for Marcel's plan B, inspired by the San Remo Song Festival, a glitzy extravaganza that for five years had been drawing big names to the Italian Riviera. The framework was laid out for a contest 'to promote high-quality original songwriting in the field of popular music', one wherein all EBU nations would sublimate their rivalries in ritualised artistic combat. 'After centuries of taunting, discordant chants,' he may have declared, 'let all of Europe sing together in harmony! Um . . . and in Switzerland, because it was all my idea.'

No one was about to argue with a man who had written a fond memoir of Mussolini's adventures in pre-war Switzerland: on 24 May 1956, Thursday-night viewers across the continent watched the monochrome figure of Jetty Paerl take to the stage of Lugano's Teatro Kursaal. She burst into *De Vogels Van Holland* not a moment too soon: the next day *Blue Suede Shoes* broke into the UK top ten, and before the weekend was out the Americans had detonated the first aerial H-bomb out at Bikini Atoll.

As a centralised European committee, the EBU did its best to strangle the new baby with red tape. Of the ten nations who had agreed to participate in what was more precisely the first Eurovision Grand Prix - still the preferred term across the continent – three (including the United Kingdom) were disqualified for registering after an obscurely declared official deadline. Abruptly faced with a humiliatingly truncated show, the organisers demanded that each surviving nation perform two songs – a convenience for the Belgians and Swiss, who were thereby able to appease the bulk of their linguistically disparate populations, but not for the Luxembourgeois: when Michel Arnaud took to the Teatro Kursaal stage for the second time, he did so in a different jacket that wasn't fooling anyone.

Alongside mindless bureaucratic pedantry, another of the themes that now define Eurovision was apparent in that debut year. More at home on the spine of an *Observer* handbook than circling the label of a chart-topping 45, Jetty's *The Birds of Holland* established an enduring tradition of musically saluting our continent's fauna in general and its avian diversity in particular; Switzerland's other entry, translated as *The Old Carousel,* was meanwhile the first in what for two decades would be an almost annual celebration of fairground infrastructure and accessories. When Europe was required to embody itself on the back of a banknote, it came up with a series of bridges; asked to do so lyrically, its default choice in those early years was a puppet, a small boy or a flock of starlings. The Eurovision success of Father Ted's *My Lovely Horse* came as no surprise to seasoned contest-watchers.

Thus was born the trivial banality that in 1982 inspired the French to announce a unilateral Eurovision boycott. 'This so-called pop-music competition,' declared their minister of culture, 'is nothing more than a monument to drivel.' More than a little rich, for prominent amongst the many Gallic dedications decorating that metaphorical edifice is the name of Jean-Paul Mauric. On 18 March 1961, lounge-suited Jean-Paul strode out on to the stage at the Palais des Festivals in Cannes to deliver his nation's entry, *Printemps,* a song whose opening line was to have unfortunate and enduring repercussions for Eurovision watchers in the decades ahead. 'Bing et bong,' Jean-Paul stridently declared, arms splayed, neat quiff tilted slightly aloft, 'et bing et bong et bing.'

Yet by then the contest was well established as an institution, drawing TV audiences that no non-sporting event could match. In 1970, more than 180 million viewers tuned in; that year Brazil and Chile watched live on satellite, with Japan and much of southern Asia following the year after. The competition that started life as a rather drab parade of cocktail-bar crooners had developed into an extravagant showdown between some of the era's greatest pop performers in all their period finery: Sandie Shaw's barefoot victory in 1967 heralded the end of the ballgown-and-tuxedo era. *Puppet on a String* ended the year as the UK's best-selling single, topping charts right across the continent. Eurovision has always dragged its cultural anchor, but having belatedly acknowledged the all-conquering rise of commercial pop, the contest now swiftly established itself as the phenomenon's mightiest kingmaker.

For an insight into the contest's significance at this time, we need look no further than the experience of its most notable runner-up. When Spain's *La La La* pipped *Congratulations* by a single point in the 1968 final, frilly-shirted Cliff Richard – comfortably the biggest star to have stood on a Eurovision stage – was apparently driven to such entertaining extremes of embittered fury that he ended the evening locked in the Albert Hall gents. Five years later, he arrived in Luxembourg equipped for the worst: by the time *Power to All our Friends* had come home third, Cliff was already slumped in a Valium-induced backstage slumber.

'A dull song,' he muttered, prodded awake to give an opinion of Anne-Marie David's victorious offering – more gracious than he'd been in 1968, when confessing a desire to congratulate Spain's Massiel by 'shaking her warmly by the throat'. Three decades on he had still to forgive or forget. Halfway through the 1997 final, sporting that alarming Yorkshire Ripper beard grown for his musical *Heathcliff*, up popped Cliff between acts to deliver a snatch of *Congratulations*, rounding it off with an arms-folded, pursed-lip glare into the camera: 'Good luck if any of you tonight sell as many as that one did,' he hissed, 'even though it didn't win.'

With this sort of high-octane action taking place up the top of the scoreboard, there was as yet little interest in the bottom. Few even noticed when Belgium's Fud Leclerc started the no-ball rolling in 1962, the first of four acts that year to go home pointless. (Fud's undoing was very probably his technique of substituting volume for precision during *Ton Nom*'s more challenging high notes, but in all honesty the four-time veteran had been skirting the Eurovoid for many years. The decision to announce only the winner in 1956 may have spared Fud's blushes: it's not easy to imagine any orthodox judge putting his or her tick beside *The Drowned Men of the River Seine.*)

Back in 1962, the international juries had a modest ninety-six points to distribute amongst the acts: between Fud's dud and Domenico Modugno's 1966 nul-pointer *Dio Come ti Amo*, no fewer than sixteen entrants had sung for their supper and gone hungry. (In 1958, Domenico confidently crooned his way through *Volare* and came only third; after a further failure before that 1966 nadir he must have been wondering what he had to do to win, though calling his entry something other than *God How I Love You* might have been a start.) The ducks were running amok on the scoreboard, but it took a four-way tie at the top of the table in 1969 for the EBU to admit the scoring system's flaws.

Ever reluctant to challenge bureaucratic stereotype, Marcel's boys essayed seven alternative procedures before settling upon the one in place today. The current Eurovision rule book runs to twenty-three pages, each dense with arcane meandering: 'If it is necessary to ask for a stand-by jury, the reason(s) must be notified in writing to the Permanent Services by a notary. Upon request, the Reference Group is authorised to make an exception to the televoting rule for a country where telecommunications penetration is less than 80 per cent . . . Four members of each stand-by jury must be representatives of the public in the country, the other four being music professionals . . . There should be an equal number of men and women on each jury, with four jurors aged below thirty and four above thirty years of age . . . A song may be presented by a maximum of six artists, who must all have attained an age of at least sixteen years in the calendar year of the final . . . Upon request, the producing organisation shall provide a comprehensive drum kit and/or a grand piano . . .' If a camel is a horse designed by a committee, the Eurovision is a song contest designed by a puffin.

How fondly I recall the voting system that endured from 1971 to 1973, under which two jury members from each nation – one under twenty-five, one over – were required to award every song a number of points from one to five. Overawed by the attention of a live audience that now topped 250 million, outshone by the garish period splendour of their own outfits, the decisions proved predictably wayward. In 1971, the grim Luxembourg duo truculently dispensed a total of forty-two points (the absolute minimum being thirty-four); the bug-eyed, yammering French pair, noisily straddling that drivel monument, lavished 107 points on the seventeen songs.

Throughout those years, of course, it was impossible to score zero, and it hasn't been much easier under the procedures in place since 1975. The fourteen nul-pointers I'd found listed and had now pledged to visit were those who had met their fate in the years that followed, and doing the maths I understood what made them special. With each jury now required to vote for its ten favourite songs, awarding them twelve points down to one in order of declining preference, Jahn's nineteen fellow competitors were competing for 1,160 points; in 2003, Jemini shared the Skonto Arena stage with twenty-five other acts, giving a total of 1,508 points up for grabs. Failure to persuade a single nation, not Bosnia, not Belgium, that your song merits even one lonely point, is a rare and remarkable achievement. Fittingly, it took a rare and remarkable performance to secure the modern era's debut whitewash.

It was perhaps Jahn's misfortune to enter a contest already in steep decline as a showcase for pop-musical excellence. ABBA's triumph was at once the ESC's finest hour and its kiss of death: having made global stars of these virtual unknowns, Eurovision thereafter found big-name international performers conspicuous by their perennial absence. Why run the just-ask-Cliff risk of being humiliated by a Spanish nobody, when even victory might achieve nothing more than unflattering comparison with the masterful winner-of-winners, *Waterloo*?

By the tail end of the seventies, we'd stopped expecting Eurovision to fulfil Marcel's original brief: the songwriting could now rarely be described as original, nor high-quality. No winner has topped the UK charts since 1982, and none since Céline Dion (a Canadian singing for Switzerland in 1988) could claim to have converted Eurovision victory into enduring celebrity. Yet we haven't stopped watching.

Yes, for the nations welcomed more recently into the Eurovision fold – Israel in '73, Greece in '74, Turkey in '75 – geo-political symbolism was enough to guarantee huge audiences. For them, as for the former Soviet satellites who since the mid-Nineties have annexed such vast swathes of the scoreboard, the ESC retains its significance: a pan-national pageant inaugurated to unite a troubled, riven continent, to bring together half a billion people in a march towards peace and brotherhood, a march led by two cat-suited Cypriots and a spangled Finnish accordionist.

But what lured two-thirds of all Belgians to their tellies on 24 May 2003? Why did more Swedes watch Afrodite finish eighth at the Saku Suurhall in Tallinn in 2002 than saw their national team's extra-time exit from that year's World Cup? And how were 54 per cent of all available UK viewers persuaded to tune in to the 2004 Eurovision voting – the highest 11 p.m. audience share recorded that year?

It's partly the hypnotic draw of the scoreboard, the numerical nip-and-tuck played out on that giant electronic abacus with all the allure of a general-election night on fast-forward. Even as the ESC's artistic appeal eluded me, I'd found deep satisfaction in the voting charts, a satisfaction redoubled with the discovery of those online troves of psephological analysis: running a finger along rows and down columns, fifty years of glory and hatred distilled to calm statistics.

And it's partly that, as the quality threshold was lowered, so we got our kicks watching those who tripped over it most spectacularly. With the winning songs ever more blandly forgettable, it was the mad, bad losers who made the deepest impression. As the original reality-talent show, Eurovision was first to demonstrate a sad but universal truth: a good song sung well might win over the judges, but nothing puts more bums on sofas than a farcical no-hoper.

In this ridicule-ready environment, so profound was the impact of Jahn Teigen's performance that it is credited with spawning the unkind epithet that would attach itself to all those who repeated his unfortunate feat. In eloquent judgement of Eurovision's failure to foster continental unity, the phrase is in truth no more than pseudo-Gallic nonsense: to me it's *nul points*, to others it's *nil points*, to the French it's *nul point*, not a single point. More arrestingly still, the words have never been heard on a Eurovision stage: jury points are announced from one to 12, and no compere has ever done a bilingual run-down to those depths of the scoreboard. Like 'Play it again, Sam', 'Beam me up, Scotty' and 'Look, Cliff, just open the bloody door,' it's an entirely confected catchphrase.

Though as I set about tracking down my luckless fourteen, I had a feeling that mightn't be much of a comfort to them.

22 April 1978
Palais des Congrès, Paris
Jahn Teigen
Norway
Mil Etter Mil

Awed perhaps by the contest's magnificent foolishness, perhaps by the soothingly bounteous statistical data accumulated in its name over six decades, the brotherhood of Eurovision obsessives is populous and ever-swelling. Theirs, happily, is no jealously guarded passion: after no more than a tentative paddle into the vast ocean that is the pool of their online knowledge, I'd discovered that two contestants have been the grandchildren of Nobel laureates, that Iceland and Greece have both entered songs entitled *Socrates*, that when ABBA triumphed at The Dome in Brighton, they did so without a single vote from the UK jury.

I chanced upon Andreas Schacht while delving a little deeper into the life of Olivia Newton-John's prizewinning forebear, a theoretical physicist whose pioneering work in quantum mechanics was paid fond homage in his granddaughter's 1974 Eurovision entry, *Long Live Love*. A respected authority on the contest and the curator of an unrivalled video archive, Andreas was also German: a winning combination, which meant that less than two weeks after making email contact, my morning cup of in-bed tea was interrupted by the arrival of a modest but very heavy box, postmarked Bremen. Within were two clear plastic cylinders, each carrying over fifty carefully hand-labelled DVDs, together comprising every Eurovision final from 1978 until the present day. I dashed back upstairs, slotted the top disk in the bedroom DVD player, threw the still-warm duvet over myself and hit 'play'. It was the first act of a televisual labour that would enthral, amuse, madden and distress in roughly equal measure.

Marked 'Norway 1978', the first show is introduced by a title sequence so warped and blotched, so sonically wayward as to be almost unintelligible. There's a flash and a fizz, as if someone's just banged the top of the telly, and the modestly enhanced image allows first a stage, then a presenter, to take shape in the bath of melted colours. An earlier straw poll amongst family and friends had revealed I wasn't alone in recalling the 1978 final, or at least the winners (Israel's Alpha Beta, with *A-Ba-Ni-Bi*) and our splits-leaping brace-twanger, but now I'm questioning my powers of recall. Of course Eurovision was always a bit of a shambles, but was any audience ever that modest, any set that flimsy, any host that uncomfortable?

It's only when the scoreboard hardens into focus, displaying a parade of circle-topped As and crossed Os, that I begin to grasp what's happening. Stein Ingebritsen vacates the tiny stage to make way for Britt Andersen singing *Hør Hva Andre Har Fått Til*, and I'm belatedly certain. This isn't the 1978 Eurovision final at all, but what can only be that year's Norwegian preselection show, broadcast earlier to decide the nation's entry in the manner of our own *A Song For Europe*. I sift through Andreas's labelled DVDs: as a bonus I'm obliged to describe as special, I find he has sourced and digitised recordings of several such domestic qualifiers, from all around the continent.

Whatever the production values currently on display might suggest, in the weeks ahead I'm to discover that the homegrown show Norwegians call the Melodi Grand Prix means almost as much to them as the Eurovision final itself. Over many decades, the 'MGP' qualifier has become established as a mighty cornerstone of state broadcaster NRK's light-entertainment calendar: the country's leading vocalists put themselves down for it year after year. Part comforting family-TV ritual, part patriotic duty, it still dependably attracts a dumbfounding 80 per cent of the national audience.

Sitting up in bed as the NRK presenter drones gormlessly through his next introduction, I feel my features crease in befuddlement. How could *Mil Etter Mil* have triumphed in any sort of musical contest, let alone a major nationwide event such as this? It seemed an affront to reason. I'd never entertained the possibility that anyone with a nul-points pedigree might ever have been a professional musician: the Eurovision selection process as I'd imagined it involved a work-experience TV researcher being sent out into the Oslo streets one lunchtime, returning half an hour later with an eager but slightly confused busker. Was I really going to sit here in bed and endure seven songs that a jury of Norwegian impresarios and music executives had adjudged worse than *Mil Etter Mil*? How, oh Saint Jahn of the Bad Noises, how could this be so?

That it just might becomes apparent as the compere falteringly welcomes one hopeless hopeful after another. All the decade's contemporary clichés are here: the footballer, the porn star, the towering Crimplene berk. Didn't anyone not look daft or sinister in the seventies? Not in Norway they didn't. Checked cheesecloth, chrome bar stools, one hell of a lot of royal blue. Ringmaster suits with lurex lapels and limb-swallowing sleeves and trouser legs. Girls with pie-crust collars, puff sleeves and vast beaks – their lips move and sounds emerge, but all I hear is four and twenty blackbirds baked in a pie. There are a great many Benny-from-ABBA beards, scourge of Scandinavian manhood for over thirty years. After one particularly harrowing close-up, the camera abruptly recoils to a distant wide shot and stays there.

And my word, they're a miserable bunch: one woman, arms hanging limply by her sides, exudes all the expressive physical dynamism of an unplugged standard lamp. Sometimes the tempo is so stubbornly lethargic that only by succumbing to the lure of fast-forward search do I appreciate that a performer is actually dancing. And those omnipresent brass-heavy oompah arrangements don't help, especially when blended with the 'happening sounds' of bongos and *Shaft*-style wah-wah guitars. Eurovision's pop-cultural clock has always run a couple of years slow, but this is ridiculous: *Shaft* came out in 1971.

Jahn Teigen is up last, and before the conductor raises his baton it's plain that we're looking at the Melodi Grand Prix winner, the man who will go on to represent Norway in the Eurovision final. (In the event he romps home by a margin of minus five: under a voting regime impressively daft even by Eurovision standards, the song with the fewest points wins. The EBU must be flicking their own noses for not thinking of it first.) In a collarless granddad shirt and drainpipes Jahn is hardly surfing the crest of fashion's post-punk zeitgeist, but beside the loon-panted satinette stylings of his rivals, it's a look that's both acceptably contemporary and perhaps just a little street. Almost alone amongst the male contestants, Jahn's hair falls no further than his (absent) collar; his chin and long cheeks are bare.

Showbiz it isn't: Jahn's appearance and demeanour are that of a laidback teacher cementing his popularity with a slightly risqué monologue at the end-of-year show. But if he's hardly made an effort, it's because he doesn't need to – all the spangles and glitter that have gone before are now exposed as desperate, clumsy attempts to bolt on personality where none existed, to paint lipstick on a performing corpse. Jahn cracks a lazy, gap-toothed smile at the audience, and tosses an amused and knowing glance into the camera. Without having opened his mouth, he's exuding a cocky yet winning self-confidence so conspicuously absent from the previous performers, all cruelly stripped of charisma at birth. And then he starts to sing.

My recent nul-points experience, I remind myself as he does so, is restricted to five downloaded seconds of Jemini's *Cry Baby*. Yes, if pressed I could recall watching four or five other contests over the decades when the voting had ended with at least one zero on the scoreboard, but put the performers in an identity parade and I'd only have picked out Jahn. And that, of course, was solely down to the unforgettable visual aspects of his performance. It was over a quarter of a century since I'd last heard *Mil Etter Mil*. Ask me to hum it and you might just as well as have asked a cat (ideally not the one responsible for *Cry Baby*'s opening bars).

Taking all this into account, I'm perhaps more surprised than I should be at what now unfolds. *Mil Etter Mil*, a song whose reputation alone still reduces good people to hooting, jeering malevolence, fails to plumb the predicted depths. No Alpine horn solo, no diddle-daddle *Birdie Song* chorus; the non-negotiable jazzed-up orchestration aside, *Mil Etter Mil* proves itself a simple, pleasing composition, whose more muscular middle eight recalls that of Marvin Gaye's politico-soul classic *Abraham, Martin and John*.

The lyrics, too, seem appropriately undemanding: to learn that I've correctly translated the title as *Mile After Mile* is no cause for linguistic celebration, or at least shouldn't be. I'd imagined the extensive journey of which Jahn sang (the rarely encountered Norwegian mile is equivalent to 10 kilometres) as a metaphorical expression of the lengths lovers will go to meet, but a quick pause to consult the dumbfoundingly authoritative database of Eurovision lyrics on diggiloo.net reveals an unexpected complexity of sentiment. 'The water is trickling into your shoes,' reads the on-screen translation, 'your longing drives you towards a light that you see, but I can't, mile after mile after mile.' Bong-a-doo-la it isn't.

The disk ends, and returns to Andreas's impressively animated menu screen. I've just spent over an hour watching flared Norwegians fail to qualify for a twenty-six-year-old Eurovision Song Contest. Is that really an OK thing to be doing? Figuring that the only way is up – in terms of spectacle, entertainment and my own self-esteem – I press eject and stick in the DVD of the 1978 final. The genuine, international Eurovision final.

By hallowed Eurovision tradition, France's 1977 victory – a triumph that remains their most recent – had won them the honour of hosting the following year's contest. The opening titles scroll across a floodlit Eiffel Tower in swift evocation of Eurovision's fastidious dismissal of all but the very crassest national clichés: Notre Dame, l'Arc de Triomphe . . . could we be in Paris? We surely could! Not that I'll be learning so from the commentary, which in Andreas's archived recording is coincidentally provided (apparently from a phone box full of crisp packets) by Norwegian state broadcaster NRK. All I'll glean from their man in the hours ahead is that he's rather provocatively referring to the UK as 'England'.

In 1978 England, and perhaps even Britain, looked out over a post-punk musical landscape. Not so the dinner-suited audience at the Palais des Congrès on the night of 22 April. Plastic Bertrand might have released *Ça Plane Pour Moi* over a year earlier, and been Belgian rather than French, but the continental music scene in general and Eurovision in particular remained resolutely pre-punk (young Plastic reminded us all of his never-say-die adherence to solvent-fuelled anarchy when he represented Luxembourg at the 1987 Eurovision, finishing second last with *Amour, Amour*). Here, in 1978, it was *New Avengers*-style brass and white suits. All three-piece, tieless and aggressively starched.

'Ah: dear old Eurovision!' sighs the pompous old on-stage compere in fruity, faultless English. Only twenty-two years since its birth, and already the contest has become part of the cultural furniture. Yet there's an innovation this year: the first ever co-host, a toothsome dolly-bird who alongside her leathery beau forms a winningly traditional Gallic combo. 'This contest,' he continues grandly, 'is intended to encourage high-calibre songwriting, by allowing composers the opportunity of comparison on an international scale.' You can sense the French scriptwriters fighting a doomed rearguard battle against the gathering forces of puerile pop idiocy, and the towering monument to drivel they were so busily constructing.

Jahn is second out, following a hunched but lively little Irishman in a cravat who repeatedly bellows *I Was Born to Sing* through his beard. ('How wrong can you be?' asked Clive James in his *Observer* TV review.) Colm Wilkinson's performance is more irrepressibly physical than you'd have thought possible for any song orchestrated by a bow-tied conductor, but watching it backstage Jahn might have felt himself unwisely inspired.

In place of the usual 'postcards from abroad' I so fondly recalled, the '78 between-act slots simply follow the next performer's progress from green room to stage. So here's Jahn, goofing around, waving at invisible associates, walking into walls. By the standards of what's to follow, it's difficult to criticise his outfit: it isn't a white suit, and it doesn't involve huge triangles of shirt collar folded out over huger still lapels. With a narrow tie down at halfmast, an upturned shirt collar and a pair of bright red drainpipes, he could have been fronting some power-pop outfit of the sort then so prevalent (in la Royaume Uni, at least).

Or almost. Something bad has happened to Jahn's fringe, which since the Melodi final he's had centrally parted in the manner that would see footballers through the coming decade. Below it are a pair of graduated-tint aviator shades, eyewear of choice for a generation of mid-Atlantic tosspots. And though the large golden rose pinned over his left nipple adds an entertainingly surreal touch, no one's looking at that. Already I'm transfixed by the prominent silver braces, and more particularly the way Jahn (or Yarn, as the NRK man has now taught me to call him) is tentatively, ominously fingering their straps. Why has he done all this? No one, I think, will ever understand what inspired these catastrophic sartorial relapses. (Even as I lie there shaking my head, a terrible image takes shape within it: it is two months after Jahn Teigen's Parisian meltdown, and here's an anxiously excited fourteen year old filing into the Hammersmith Odeon for his first experience of amplified live music – the Boomtown Rats. But what's this? On his back, a jacket of blackest, newest C&A velvet; around his neck, an orange woollen tie.)

Carsten Klouman raises his baton; the NRK commentator emits the words *'Mil Etter Mil'* in a hoarse, portentous, a-nation's-hopes-are-with-you murmur; and as a brass fanfare blasts waywardly out Jahn dashes from the wings, past three female backing singers, reaching the mike just in time for his opening line. This passes without incident, but at the end of the second it's starkly apparent that in addition to the handicap of his braces, and what he's about to do with them, Jahn is also likely to be rather hamstrung by his mother tongue's capacity to alarm.

'*Krrrrrroppp!*' he exclaims, with tongue-thrumming, phlegm-loosening relish, raising his eyebrows in amused recognition of the effect this extraordinary syllable will be having south of Oslo. Across the continent people look up in shellshocked silence from lap-bound plates of dumplings, chips or gnocchi: are 400 million of us about to see a Eurovision performer choke to death live on-stage?

Foreigners were funnier in 1978. In the quarter-century since, cheap travel and billion-channel TV has dulled the once irresistible comic effect of someone saying something – anything – in a different language. And the more different the language, the funnier. In all the earlier shows I'm to watch, every Izel, Lars or Jarkko who takes the stage does so to a faint but clearly audible audience frisson. This one's going to be a cracker . . . look, even the conductor's called Onno Tunk!

This golden age was inaugurated after Sweden's Ingvar Wixell controversially entertained the 1965 audience with the English-language *Absent Friend* ('We ought to walk behind the hedge, where the cowslips grow'). Reminded of the contest's statute-enshrined intent to prevent American culture annexing a weak and vulnerable post-war Europe, the EBU's response was a rule obliging performers to sing in their native tongue. This latest addition to Eurovision's Bumper Book of Clauses persisted until 1973, with ABBA the most obvious beneficiaries of its abandonment. Five years later it was abruptly reinstated. ABBA had by then conquered the world, yet the EBU's pride in catalysing this achievement was tainted with guilt: the band had done so in the language of American Forces Radio.

With Eurovision's eastward expansion in the early 1990s, juries confused by the Estonian and Slovakian choruses tumbling about their booths began comfort-voting for any song performed in English, and in 1999 the language rule was discarded for good (by 2005 even the Germans were plumping for pop's lingua franca). Too late for Jahn. If in 1978 he'd been allowed to perform the English-language version of *Mil Etter Mil* he later recorded, 'kropp' would have been translated into 'body'; perhaps that alone might have been worth a point from someone, somewhere.

As it is, the peculiar noise he's just made seems to galvanise Jahn in the most dangerous manner. Now that he's got our attention, he isn't about to let go. He strokes his chest like a stripper; he spreads his legs and throws back his head. It's a big performance, much too big for the song. Lost under a thick layer of cloying, silly brass fills and trills, *Mil Etter Mil* is reduced to a period quiz-show theme. Our eyes say Aerosmith, our ears say *Sale of the Century*.

We're about halfway through when Jahn clamps his eyes shut, and with the mike held tight in both hands winds up an ambitious bray of vibrato. In terms of his vocal routine, this is the triple-axel-with-toe-loop moment: in the national qualifier he'd just about pulled it off, but here it's arse-on-the-ice time. What was intended as a hairy-chested Led Zep roar comes out as a thin, wandering shriek that shares its pitch and intonation with the noise my eleven-year-old son makes while narrowly averting some Nintendo disaster. Another big tick on the nul-points checklist.

The song is winding down when Jahn abruptly casts aside the rock-god mannerisms. All that remain are a dozen-odd plodding repetitions of the phrase '*mil etter mil*', but after only two of these our man succumbs to ennui, which he proceeds to tackle in a fashion few would have dared predict. The whiff of anarchy has been in the air since Jahn emerged from the wreckage of that set-piece rock-scream with a nothing-to-lose gleam in his eye, and now it's as if he's suddenly undergone a liberating, joyous epiphany. If Jahn's undone tie and drainpipes are the Eurovision equivalent of safety pins and bondage trousers, then what follows is the

Eurovision equivalent of the Sex Pistols calling Bill Grundy a dirty fucker on live television.

Jahn's gaze darts restlessly about the auditorium: just a moment, he's thinking, this whole thing is idiotic bollocks! What am I doing up here? And why are you watching me do it? Well, I'll give you all something to remember. Oh, yes. I hope you're ready, but I don't care if you're not. This is for Annie Palmen, Conchita Bautista, Fud Leclerc – this is for every Eurovision martyr who's come up here, made a twenty-four-carat twat of themselves, and gone away with a fat fuck-all!

And plunging both thumbs eagerly under his brace straps like a music-hall costermonger, Jahn stretches them right out and back, to the beat, first together, now alternately, now with a bandy-legged, knees-up accompaniment. His features spread into a fatuous, complicit grin, as if this is a karaoke bar and we're the pissed-up mates who've dared him to get up there.

After those first eager twangs his Lambeth Walk seems to lose a little of its vigour, and by the time a building orchestra crescendo alerts him to the song's proximate finale, he's doing no more than idly milk himself. Yet I know he's not finished. The intervening years, all twenty-six of them, have not eroded the memory of what is to come.

Turning sideways, Jahn bends his knees, swings back his arms and propels himself upwards into a spread-legged scissors leap of the type trademarked by Pete Townshend. It proves a deficient homage: at the jump's freeze-framed ceiling Jahn's feet are at least forty degrees shy of the intended 180, and only about two foot off the ground. And though his landing is clearly intended to coincide with the final beat, he's come back to earth and stretched out an arm to thank them well before the orchestra honks and parps its last. Perhaps most crucially of all, Jahn has not been talking 'bout his generation, but 'bout water trickling into someone else's shoes. Less of The Who, and more of The Why. In ten dumbfounding seconds, Norway's Jahn Teigen has guaranteed himself nul points and a place in modern cultural history.

Subsequent research pinpoints that brace-snapping/splayed-leap combo as the widely accepted sealer of Jahn's fate. The tiny clip that graces the BBC's online Eurovision archive distils his performance to those two actions alone. Norwegian Eurovision websites speak prominently of Jahn's '*splitthopp*', and expand my knowledge of their venerable tongue to include the useful phrase '*konstante ablegøyer*', which I shall be sure to employ the next time I suspect anyone tall and blond of twanging to excess.

Short of arson or puppy-juggling, it's difficult to imagine what else Jahn could possibly have done to alienate the jurors more comprehensively, yet he strides off stage with a winner's swagger. Most subsequent artistes exit too drained even to spare a nod as the next act passes them in the wings, but Jahn marches straight up to the Brotherhood of Man Italians standing in wait and kisses each of its female components full on the lips. I can only imagine what effect his only-here-for-the-beer demeanour is having upon the dumbstruck NRK commentator, but for my part I'm thinking: Way to go, Yarn. Ridicule is nothing to be scared of.

Of the eighteen songs that follow *Mil Etter Mil*, many – perhaps even most – prove handsomely inferior. In accordance with Eurovision tradition the vast bulk are utterly forgettable, and those that aren't you wish were. Spain's attempt at a flamenco waltz is as bad as it sounds; ditto France's *There Will Always Be Violins*. Cheryl Baker, whose detachable skirt will help Bucks Fizz to the Euro crown three years later, pre-blots her copybook with a full-on hello-Mum as she walks out with CoCo. Greece has Zorba the geek and his mother in a bowler hat and cane; entitled *Charlie Chaplin*, their composition is a painful monstrosity, but no one's going to send that poor, dear woman back to her village taverna without a point. She ends up with sixty-six. Germany offer a poor man's *Money Money Money*; Belgium a dead man's Charles Aznavour.

The aesthetically petrifying Danes – back after a twelve-year absence with four Rod Stewarts and a big drum with a heart on – are filling the screen when my nine-year-old daughter puts her head round the door. A forty-year-old father of three watching the 1978 Eurovision final in bed at lunchtime: I think I'd rather have been caught with a drugged goat in a wig. But fashion's silly wheel has creaked full-circle, and she appraises those spike-topped blond mullets with a succinct murmur that desecrates the harrowed, never-again oath sworn by those of us trousered throughout early adolescence by Clockhouse Kids: 'Cool.'

Luxembourg, the perennial mercenaries, have hired Spanish-born, German-based Baccara, who perform a shamelessly transparent variant on the ultimate period boast that made their name: *Yes Sir, I Can Boogie*. Worst of all, and most comfortably sub-Jahn, are the flat-capped, white-suited Austrians humming their way through *Mrs Caroline Robinson*.

Leathery jazz lords Stephane Grappelli and Oscar Peterson provide the interval entertainment (you can just imagine the French director blowing out a huge cloud of Gitanes smoke in the control room and sighing, 'Now *that's* music'), and the disk ends. It says something about the nature of ESC obsession that of the two DVDs allocated by Andreas to each contest, the second is wholly dedicated to the voting. I'd originally imagined that for the obsessives it was all about the music; perhaps there'd be a shot of the final totals, but no more. But when you're into Eurovision, it seems, you're into the whole package: it's apparently unthinkable to separate the songs from the scoring.

As I was learning, the ESC's inner circle of diehard fandom is an unlikely fraternity of cardiganed stat-fiends and boa-toting champions of kitsch. For the former, there are far more numbers to stick in the cruncher than just the winning total: fondly tended online archives are devoted to percentage accrued of the available maximum votes (Brotherhood of Man still top this league with 80.4 per cent), to the triumphant entry's place in the draw (Jahn was second out, a slot which has yet to produce a winner), to the weighting attached to language (though thirty-one tongues have been heard on the Eurovision stage – one of them a fantasy creation unknown outside the lyrics to Belgium's 2003 entry – English and French account for over two-thirds of victories). And then, of course, there's the rather more universally provocative issue of who voted for who.

The scoring controversies that so dependably besmirch the Eurovision experience have dogged the contest from birth. These days Luxembourg can lay claim to the world's highest per capita gross national product (source: my son), but so cash-strapped was the pocket duchy's state broadcaster back in 1956 that it balked at dispatching the requisite pair of judges off to Lausanne. The hosts nobly volunteered to cast votes on Luxembourg's behalf, and whilst it may be unfair to make a connection between this, the existence that year of a secret ballot, and Switzerland's triumph, there you go – I've just done exactly that. (The year after, with voting now made public, the Swiss stumbled in second last.)

But even as the scope for self-serving corruptibility was diminished, and with the advent of mass televoting ultimately snatched away, so the dependably corrosive influence of cross-border friendship rose to warp the scoreboard in its stead. Scandinavian back-scratching, a blight throughout the contest's early years, reached its shameful zenith in 1963 when the Norwegian jury foreman interrupted Switzerland's triumphant celebrations to furnish a flummoxed Katie Boyle with his revised votes: after a recount, victory was handed to Denmark. An EBU inquiry inexplicably cleared all those involved, but there were loud audience jeers in 1966 when Sweden's starkly idiotic flute-playing swineherd claimed second place despite harvesting just one point from the non-Nordic jurors. By a similar token, Spain and Portugal have had a bit of thing going on over the years, and it's hard to ignore Luxembourg's embarrassment of kindly minded neighbours when asked to explain the five victories that have established the principality as Eurovision's second most successful nation.

Since phone voting enfranchised the European public in 1997, neighbourly and expatriate bias has run idiotically amok. In the seven years before that first televote, no German jury had awarded Turkey a single point, but when the 2.5 million Germans of Turkish origin were allowed their telephonic say, the aggregate haul over the three years that followed was thirty-six points, the maximum available. After an abysmal run of results, in 2005 the Swiss imaginatively signed up a team of Estonian pop mercenaries: without quite repeating the 1988 victory of Swiss-for-a-night Canadian Céline Dion, thirty-two Baltic-sourced points helped Vanilla Ninja secure Switzerland's first top-ten finish in over a decade.

But friendship is fleeting; a grudge is for ever. Those who find it hard to imagine the contest's devotees arguing over much beyond chorus structure and heel height may be as alarmed as I was to find online Eurovision chatroom topics headed 'Fuck the Nationalist Greek nation' and 'This is the ESC, not the Macedonian independence front'. Every Eurovision entry lugs its baggage out on to the stage, and sometimes there's so much on the trolley the jurors can't see over it.

Repeated Irish triumphs in the eighties and nineties are commonly attributed to the magic combination of singing in pop's lingua franca whilst keeping their diplomatic noses clean. For here in la Royaume Uni, we continue to reap a poisoned scoreboard harvest seeded by centuries of international plunder: if we've stolen your cod, or your antiquities, or that big rock with the monkeys on, you're still letting us know, with an O.

Most notorious, though, is the eastern Mediterranean hate triangle viciously etched across every Eurovision scoreboard. The Turks and the Greeks refused to enter the contest together before 1978, and for almost two decades thereafter exchanged zeroes with bitter ceremony. Cyprus first competed at the finals in 1981, but it would be twenty-three years before an Ankara jury awarded the islanders a single point, by which time its Athenian counterparts had lavished 191 upon them. Marcel Bezençon conceived Eurovision as a healer of European rifts; at times he must have sat through the voting glumly, asking himself if it was crowbarring old enemies ever further apart.

Though deception, venality and empurpled spite all have their role to play, it would be remiss to discuss the workings of any European bureaucracy without mention of good old-fashioned administrative incompetence. The 1977 victory by which Marie Myriam brought Jahn and his fellow performers to Paris was secured amidst such a relentless farrago of voting ineptitude – Greece awarded four points to two nations, the Israelis to none, and the French jury foreman contrived to short-change or over-indulge Portugal, Italy, Belgium and Austria – that a subsequent audit adjusted the final totals of precisely half of the eighteen competing nations.

Acknowledging this, the Parisian compere's introduction to our scoreboard vigil is prefaced by an extraordinary pledge that justice must and shall be seen to be done. 'On such an international level,' he intones gravely, 'one is never too strict.' This statement raises a great many more fears than it lays to rest: it's a frank admission that when nation goes against nation, no matter how silly the scenario, chicanery is inevitable. (Backstage in 1993, the head of a sadly unnamed delegation was overheard offering to swap maximum points with any interested counterparts.)

For almost an hour my TV screen is filled by a huge scoreboard, its digits formed from lightbulbs in the fashion formerly associated with Wimbledon. This was an era when live jury contact meant a screeching, crackling, over-amplified phone conversation with unseen foremen across the continent; for me, the golden age. 'This is Dublin calling,' thunders an echoing voice, and we're off.

Despite knowing what I know, I'm oddly nervous. Oslo is next on the line – blithely distributing points in happy ignorance that they'll receive none in return. Tragically, Norway's own votes help secure their humiliation: the two points they award Finland prove to be all that prevent Jahn's ignominy being shared and halved with Seija Simola.

Next up Rome, then Helsinki. I find I'm willing those double zeroes alongside Norvège to do something, to wake up and snap out of it. Four rounds down, and only Denmark's Rods and those godawful Austrians are with Jahn; after two more he's alone. Guten abend, bonsoir, shalom. *Mil etter mil, nil etter nil.* With half the votes in, the NRK commentator seems prepared for the worst. He settles into a routine of simply translating French numbers into Norwegian; the words 'Jahn' and 'Teigen' do not once escape his lips. His boy is taking one hell of a beating tonight. Sweden are the last to vote, and perhaps he's confident that they'll step in with a late quid pro quo. When they don't, he simply switches the mike off. It's left to our hostess to wish the Israeli winners a long and successful career. (The many Arab broadcasters screening the 1978 contest had stuck in a three-minute ad break while Alpha Beta performed; when Israel's votes began to pile up, most simply pulled the plug. Jordan prematurely ended their transmission with a lingering still shot of a vase of daffodils.)

One nul-pointer down, thirteen to go. Am I really prepared for all this human tragedy? Much as I admire Jahn's cockily defiant stage exit, it's awful to think that the clumsy leap that preceded it hadn't just squashed his Eurovision chances, but flattened what judging by his apparent age – he's got to be pushing thirty – must surely have been a long career in music.

Except, rather splendidly, it hadn't. That evening I dispatch a missing-persons APB to my growing band of Eurovision oracles, and by morning there's a reply from Andreas in my inbox. As I read, trepidation melts into relief, and then tickled delight. 'Teigen is still releasing CDs and presenting shows on Norwegian TV,' it begins. 'He is still signed to Global Music in Norway. Should be quite easy to contact.'

So indeed he proves to be. A quick call and a bit of web trawling and I'm sending an email off to Frida Thorsen, who I've found named as Jahn's manager. He's still got a manager! Her almost instant reply heartens and intrigues in equal measure. 'Jahn has in the past three years directed Teigenstudio, where he is recording new talents in the music industry,' begins Frida. 'In the last year he has released two albums as well, the last one was a greatest hits album called "Fra Null Til Gull" ("From Zero to Gold"), it has nearly sold to platinum here in Norway. Jahn is also travelling around talking about his zero-point experience to groups and companies around Norway. He can meet you on 21 or 22 January.'

If Jahn Teigen has had to put up with a lot of laughs since 1978, fantastically it seems that the last is his. I don't know how many units you need to shift in Norway to go platinum.

Maybe it's 104. But the bottom line here is that two and a half decades after he made a name for himself as the world's most hapless performer, the man who launched an international catchphrase for ineptitude and arrant failure is still making music and selling records. More than that, he's willing to meet me to talk about it. My phobic dread of a song that I'd begun to think of as catastrophe's theme tune instantly evaporates. I'm so happy that I locate and download the original studio recording of *Mil Etter Mil*, and begin to fall slightly in love with it.

I have by now established that the Melodi Grand Prix is merely the last stage of the Norwegian selection process: just to get down to that last eight, *Mil Etter Mil* had first dispatched no fewer than 640 rivals. Those whose experience of the song is limited to its Eurovision variant will respond to this statistic with a haunting screech, and rightly so. However, I urge these people to unclamp those clawed, bloodless hands from their own throats and give the original a listen. Unburdened by cloying orchestration, the song is allowed to breathe. Its chopped chords give Jahn the space to let the soft, simple melody almost take care of itself; no massed brass for him to shout over (though naturally enough, he does a bit anyway).

This is the song that the Norwegian judges heard and championed; the song that's the one notable absence from the www.nul-points.net chart of Eurovision's all-time worst entries. Though too down-tempo ever to have won the contest, it's a distinctive and likeable tune. After three listenings I'm humming it. After four I retrieve my Fender Bullet case from under the matrimonial bed for the first time in a great many years, and within half an hour I'm enthusiastically strumming along from start to finish. I even join in with Jahn's *krrrrropp*.

It's a eureka moment: sitting there, Fender in lap, I can think of no more appealing way to win over a nul-pointer than by offering to perform their song as they first heard it, with simple dignity, me on guitar, them on vocals, putting the warped record straight. Yes! Why stop with Jahn? It's the work of an excited moment to imagine myself hauling that knackered flight case all round Europe, airport, hotel, gig, airport, hotel, gig – you know: on tour. Eyes alight, I snatch the Fender up and clamp my left-hand fingertips to the neck: *C, A minor, D7, G, mil etter mil etter mil . . .* Within two days Birna is asking me to shut up. Within two weeks I'm queuing up at the SAS desk at Heathrow's Terminal 1, Fender by my side, hoping that Jahn will appreciate the lurid red cords I'm wearing in genuine, heartfelt homage.

'What you got there?' trills the check-in girl, eyeing up my flight case. Nowhere like a strip-lit departure hall at dawn for a brutally effective wake-up call.

'A guitar,' I mumble, feeling suddenly foolish and fraudulent. 'An electric one.' The case's inset Fender logo harbours the thickly dusted legacy of that under-bed exile; the fingers clasping its handle are now cramped and tender from the forgotten rigours of chord-craft. From final exams until fatherhood, my Fender had lain undisturbed. Even since it had been withdrawn only as an occasional family-singalong prop; indeed very occasional – with their father lacking the technical wherewithal to adapt his *Teenage Dirtbag* to a register appropriate for the infant vocal range, the children swiftly tired of my solo instrumentals. The two performances listed on my live-music CV were both as bassist, on grounds agreed by all fellow members of Rough Justice that four strings gave me 50 per cent less to cock up. Fifteen summers had passed since the last of these performances, at a social club in north Oxford.

I spot the Fender from afar, circling a distant carousel, as I traverse the unpeopled wooden vastness of Oslo's handsome new airport. During the flight my misgivings had been efficiently contextualised: whatever performing indignities I had suffered or was about to, they could never compete with those endured by Jahn Teigen, unless maybe he threw herrings at me. When we'd done with the bad times, and the good times, he and I were going to stand side by side in Teigenstudio and make sweet, sweet music until the water trickled into our shoes.

'Hallo please?'

I'm already past the customs post – two more paces and it's through the automatic doors, out amongst the namecard-toting chauffeurs and welcoming family groups. I turn to find myself being idly beckoned by a ruddy-faced customs officer in a shapeless pullover, his status betrayed only by the ID card dangling askew round that chubby neck. 'English?' he asks when I'm standing before him; I nod. He tilts his round, red head at the Fender. 'You play music?'

'Well, yes and no.'

This is a very poorly selected response, one certain to intrigue even the least circumspect controller of borders, and as soon as those four words escape my mouth I accept that my attempt on the Heathrow to Oslo Central commuting record is at a premature end. Neither am I helping my case when, during the explanatory blather unleashed by this opening gambit, I find myself repeatedly invoking the name of Norway's godfather of nul.

'You meet *Jahn Teigen*?' The significance with which he loads these latter words causes belated consideration of the pub-brewery business, particularly in conjunction with the lost weekend hinted at in a bullet-point online biography: 'Jahn had a "down" period in the eighties and early nineties. He got divorced and his musical career was close to nothing. He has now many marks and scars after all the battles and "pranks".'

The official's benign, fleshy features harden, and he embarks on a painstaking hunt for whatever 'pranks' I might be hoping to share with Jahn. A diligent rummage through my guitar case, and in particular the dusted ephemera clogging a compartment intended for plectrums and spare strings, brings his reward: a small, clear-plastic zip-lock bag. He withdraws this with a conjuror's triumphant flourish, one that withers as together we contemplate its unavoidable emptiness. With diminished portent he parts its fastening, sniffs its minuscule interior, holds it up to the light. 'You keep something in here?' I have no idea. There are things in that case that have lain undisturbed for over two decades. Still, it seems important to say something.

'Buttons.'

'Party buttons?'

The involuntary spasm of mirth this rhetorical query elicits is still creasing my features when a plump, probing hand locates and holds aloft a second bag. It is identical to the first in every way but one: tiny but stark in a wrinkled corner nestles a dark granule.

'And this?'

Buttocks, I think, then repeatedly mutter. Half the size of an ungenerous chocolate chip it may be, and of a modest potency further depleted over many forsaken years in that rock 'n' roll time capsule, yet we both instantly understand that this stupid brown speck will account for several forthcoming hours of our lives. For the customs officer, these are largely devoted to a forensic examination of my possessions; for me, they're spent alone in a stainless-steel chamber, honing that buttocks mantra to reedy perfection.

Our paths next memorably converge when my now latex-gloved custodian enters the cell and tonelessly asks me first to strip, and having done so to spread my legs and jump up and down. When my bare feet hit the cold floor for a fifth time without an intimately secreted stash of party buttons being thus dislodged, I am told to dress, then once more left alone with my wayward thoughts and the hand-etched footballing allegiances of previous British occupants. What would Jahn do? Giggle less hysterically, perhaps, and certainly cut that pitiful whimpering right out.

A long hour later, two very young policemen, one of either sex, gently ease the cell door ajar and usher me outside. 'Your drug was too small to register in our machine,' murmurs the shaven-haired male, in a remorseful tone that correctly warns me not to get my hopes up, 'so you have been charged with holding hashish resin, quantity under 0.1 grams.' He essays a bracing smile, and holds out a chewed ballpoint. 'Write your name here to accept the penalty of 350 Norwegian kroner.'

A moment afterwards I'm being conspicuously escorted towards the arrivals-hall cashpoint, through a curious throng of meeters and greeters. 'I am sorry your visit to Norway has started like this,' says the female officer as I shakily stab in my PIN number, 'but we hope you can still have a good time here.' Just over an hour later I'm hauling the now hated Fender into downtown Oslo's Hotel Munch, my face a violated homage to that artist's most celebrated work.

For an hour I gaze down at the clean, cold streets from my modest fifth-floor room, trying to square the ignominies of my arrival with the almost mocking tranquillity of the bright, pleasant metropolis laid out below. The United Nations recently declared Norway the world's best place to live, and down there is its capital, a city that I'm trying to remind myself I'd grown quite attached to during a couple of long-ago visits.

But by the time my mobile rings I've successfully recovered a little of the morale displaced during those naked, cell-bound star jumps, and with it a little of my affection for Oslo and its people. The odd consolation has even introduced itself. Jahn's p.m.-focused work schedule means that despite the unforeseen delay, I'm still early. And when we did meet, I now had an ice-breaking, life-on-the-road, us-against-The-Man anecdote to win him over with. Marks, scars, battles, pranks – been there, done that, taken off the T-shirt.

'Tim?' It's Jahn's manager-cum-PA, Frida, who had organised our meeting with calm efficiency. 'Jahn was working a little bit late last night, presenting an award for young musicians . . . you know, because a lot of his fans are a bit older, he really enjoyed it. Maybe he enjoyed it too much! We'll meet him at his studio.'

Frida very kindly picks me up from the hotel at the wheel of Jahn's plush new Audi estate – the first indicator that all that talk of post-nul-points success is more than bluster.

A close-cropped blonde in her mid twenties, Frida's businesslike appearance is matched by a complementary driving style. As she pilots us calmly through Oslo's compact low-rise heart, I pick out statues and parks familiar from previous trips; even the kebab shop where in this ferociously expensive city I'd regularly refuelled for next to nothing (at time of writing, the Norwegian nothing was trading at £3.12). Then the museums and offices part around us, and we're facing the prim but cosy suburbs that tumble down the opposite hills into a harbour as vast and comely as Sydney's, its sun-dappled waters home to bright white cruise liners and tall ships.

Frida calls her boss as we pull up outside his studios at the bright and windy periphery of Aker Brygge, Oslo's gentrified, beautified docklands. Even with half an Audi between us I pick up the disoriented grunt that suggests Jahn is not yet even half awake. 'OK,' says Frida when the brief call ends. There is no surprise or disappointment in her tone, just the brisk common-sense one imagines is a prerequisite for making sense of Jahn Teigen's life. 'We are early, so I show you around here, and afterwards we go to meet him somewhere for coffee.'

Teigenstudio, upstairs next to a ballet academy in an old harbour administrator's building, is not quite as I'd anticipated. The young musician's award last night, along with the stuff in Frida's email about helping new talents, had led me to expect a School of Rock, but one run (by Frida) with earnest Scandinavian professionalism. In one room, beanpole youths would be working, with the straight-faced, straight-backed diligence of a young Björn Borg hitting balls at a wall, through a barber shop rendition of *Dancing Queen*. I'd put my ear to a door marked LYRICS (ADVANCED), and hear: 'Listen, I don't care if we're here till midnight: no one leaves this room until we've got three more rhymes for "harpoon".' Perhaps after lunch the great man himself would drift in for an impromptu masterclass: 'No, no, no: it's *krrrrrroppp*! OK, let's take it again, from the bridge.'

None of this is implied by our sombre, foot-echoing progress along corridors bookended by self-slamming fire-doors, a journey I attempt to enliven with an account of my expensive and trouserless airport adventure. It doesn't quite hit the spot: Frida's half-chuckle is expelled with a pained reluctance that suggests a professional life blighted too often by variations on this tawdry theme.

'Anyway,' I falter, as we enter a long, high-ceilinged hall of a room, with a desk at either end, 'so nothing kind of, you know, falls out, and then I'm, um . . . yeah.' Before me, stacks of framed gold and platinum discs lie against a wall fulsomely decorated with album covers; the most recent of these is a compellingly frank study in degeneration. Jahn's long face is deeply scored with Keef crevasses, running east to west across the forehead, and most dramatically north to south from eyes to jaw; old-lady pinch-lines purse down into a narrow top lip. The hair – rock-long, blondish and swept back carelessly over Jahn's head and behind his ears – imparts a look of dishevelled insouciance: here is a man who has been round the block a few times, and got lost more than once while doing so. Jahn's countenance and certain aspects of his lifestyle had drawn online parallels with Iggy Pop's, but though at fifty-four he's three years Iggy's junior, he looks more like his dad. Like Iggy's pop. I suppose there are going to be a lot of moments like this in the months ahead. I'd better get used to it.

'Jahn needs to be respected,' says Frida, catching my wide-eyed, slack-jawed gaze and returning it with a level, admonitory glare. 'He's a star, he makes gold records, he does a lot of shows, maybe three every week in summer.' (As I know from long Icelandic experience, Scandinavians tend to hibernate.) She scans the album covers with an air of dour reverence.

Does he have a foreign fanbase? I enquire, still unconvinced that the modest domestic market could keep Jahn in new Audis. Frida considers briefly. 'We have a connection with Malta.' I nod slowly; perhaps it's an odd Euro variant on those obscure British bands who somehow crack Japan. 'A Norwegian tour operator had contacts with Malta's tourism and culture officials, and they came to a travel fair in Norway and saw Jahn, and how huge he was for people here.'

I pause before a large, soft-focus print of a baby-faced Jahn cheek to cheek with a woman I recognise as his ex-wife and sometime Eurovision collaborator, Anita Skorgan. 'What you will see is how interesting Jahn is, how different,' says Frida, 'how he connects with people, what a star he is.' A pause. 'He has thirty-eight albums in total, and two million sales.' It works: I'm flabbergasted, to the point of impertinence.

We stroll along the album wall. Jahn in a yellow jumpsuit, holding an artist's palette; Jahn in a flasher's mac; Jahn – *Jahn?* – battering a large fish and a pint of beer with a huge club, his face semi-mummified in tape. 'This was Prima Vera, a kind of insane group, a kind of Monty Python thing he was in for many years. Some songs, some funny scenes. You call them sketches?'

'Jahn Teigen, man of a thousand faces,' read a newspaper headline that Birna and her Norwegian-Icelandic dictionary had translated at my request, and which now recurs to me, along with its memorable sub-heading: 'national clown who ate bouquet of flowers'.

As we walk on, I become aware of a muffled Prima Vera-style commotion coming from behind the wall. 'It's the studio,' Frida explains, dismissively. Inside, I can only assume, are some of the livelier 'new talents in the music industry' that Jahn has taken under his wing. 'I work for a real perfectionist,' she continues, improbably, raising her voice in a doomed bid to drown out the multiplying thumps and guffaws. Frida indicates the pile of gold discs: 'These are still like this because Jahn can't decide how they must go up, in what sequence.'

I bend down to inspect the top one, and in doing so am caught square on the side of the head by the studio door. A young man dressed in joke-shop homage to Elvis Presley's Vegas phase – black wig, white jumpsuit, wraparound shades – emerges on his knees, along with a ragged chorus of background jeers that fade to a muted hubbub as the soundproof door slams behind him. He rises with some difficulty, pulls off his eyewear, scans the room with a red-eyed gaze of blank confusion, then palms my doubled form haphazardly aside before staggering at unwise speed towards the exit.

'Yes,' says Frida, by way of explanation and apology. 'It is OK with you if I smoke a cigarette?'

She's extinguishing it when Elvis reappears, his breathing heavy and uneven. 'English!' he shouts, interrupting our converstion on Norway's place in Europe. 'Tell me, tell me, what is your team?' His response to my answer is one of lethargic hysteria. 'Tot-ten-ham, Tot-ten-ham, ha, ha, ha. Ha ha ha! Gary Mabbutt!' An unexpected reference to a defender whose playing days ended when young Elvis here was nothing but a hound pup. 'Ha ha ha!' He throws open the door, which rebounds violently off his misplaced white brothel creeper. Re-entry to the studio is eventually completed at the third attempt; we are allowed a glimpse of shirtless male revelry before the door slams shut once more.

'What, um, kind of band are they?'

Frida ineffectively stifles an exasperated sigh. 'There's a tradition in Norway that on some occasions, people want to make a record.' Occasions? Like, occasions when you want to be a rock star? 'Maybe when you leave a job.'

The door opens an inch: 'Tot-ten-ham! Osvaldo Ardiles! Steffen Iversen!'

With a brittle smile Frida leans over and heaves it shut. 'Or before you . . . get married.'

And so it emerges, in Frida's rather craven confession, that the main business undertaken here at Teigenstudio is the digitised recording of stag-party karaoke sessions. I press my head to the door: isn't that Wet Wet Wet? The game's up; Frida shrugs. 'You pay, you choose. For 2,500 kroner you select the backing track and record your CD. Sometimes in the summer we have ten of them in a day, and it's too much.' She shivers in haunted recollection, but having done the maths – ten times 2,500 kroner is the thick end of £2,000 – I tell her I'd put up with a lot worse for that sort of return.

Perhaps consoled by this, and maybe relieved that the loud, drunk cat is out of the studio bag, Frida seems to mellow as we heave open the fire-door and walk back down the corridor. 'Jahn is very down-to-earth,' she says, almost tenderly. 'Sometimes people want to book him to sing with them, and if he can do it, he does.' I nod happily, then recognise that this is the ideal moment to bring up my planned duet. Except it isn't. 'We can maybe ask him,' says Frida, with a politely regretful air that squashes my hopes more completely than a furious volley of outraged invective.

'These days Jahn likes to talk more than sing,' she explains, as we walk out into the waning light of a Nordic winter afternoon. 'About his philosophy on life, about being positive. He goes straight to people's hearts.' Still a little crestfallen, I ask if she means those life-after-nul-points corporate lectures. 'Yes, for business, or like last week, at a silver wedding. Jahn reaches out to all people, all ages. People connect with him.' With a blip and a click she unlocks the big Audi, and in we get. 'He has families to watch him at the summer music festivals, and then at these clubs, well . . .' She smiles indulgently. 'So many drunk people try to climb up on-stage to be with him. Sometimes he needs five security guys.'

A moment later we're pulling to a halt in a car park further down the waterfront. 'Jahn is at this place most days,' says Frida as we walk out of the frail, dying sun and into a wind funnelled to painful bitterness down a tight, shadowy street of bars and designer shops. 'Ah! I see him. Outside that café with his . . . people.'

A small coterie of twenty and thirty somethings, all in artfully weathered retro streetwear, is huddled beneath the radiant glow of a stainless-steel patio heater. At the group's centre, blanket over his lap like a cruise-ship pensioner in a deck-chair, sits a cadaverous figure in bug-eyed red sunglasses, fag propped between his thin, dry lips. Emerging beneath the blanket, two tightly denimed legs end in a pair of scuffed trainers. Above it is the top half of a shapeless and very long coat, concealing a suit jacket that the wearer later tells me, with quiet pride, was his father's.

We approach; that long face spreads into a smile that somehow sparkles despite opening up a whole new set of parched flesh valleys. 'In Malta they have a law against smoking in bars, but not like here everyone ignores it,' says Jahn Teigen, his voice low and engagingly assured. 'You know, I bought a book in Malta,' he continues seamlessly, 'with one sentence for each day. And on my birthday, 27 September, it said, "You are a god, but you don't know it."'

Holding that twinkly, wrinkly beam Jahn stands; the cronies melt away and Frida and I follow the slight figure inside. He is offered a prime table – apparently kept on hold for his personal use – and a waitress glides up. Jahn orders a coffee and a water; I brace myself with a beer; all three arrive almost immediately. Bending to raise the former to his lips, the red-framed shades slip down his thin nose, as they will throughout our meeting; he pushes them back in place with a twisted, ancient index finger. As a chain-smoking serial gesticulator, Jahn has his hands on permanent display, and both sprout digits as gnarled and swollen as bonsai oaks. He seems to have far too many knuckles, each the size of an Adam's apple. 'His arthritis is bad,' the peerlessly named president of Jahn's fan club, Øistein Wickle, will later tell me, 'but he never talks about it.'

I'm wondering whether to kick off with my strip-search icebreaker when Jahn starts to talk. What follows is a lecture more than a conversation, but if it's one he's given before then practice has not made perfect. 'You know, we can blame the Swedish. Some centuries ago the Swedes sent their stupidest king to rule Norway . . .' He begins to move ashtrays around like a demented cup-and-balls street trickster, in apparent representation of shifting alliances amongst Scandinavian nation states in the fourteenth century. I have no idea what he's on about, other than possibly pre-empting my theories about trans-Nordic Swedish-envy, but it's an undeniably diverting performance. Jahn, I can already sense, is an it's-the-way-I-tell-'em entertainer.

With difficulty I steer him back to the beginning. 'OK,' he croaks, expansively. 'So Eurovision was a dream for me since I was a young boy. I remember watching in 1963 and seeing Anita Thallaug sing for Norway, and in this year Denmark won. This was exciting.' That it certainly was, I say, but Jahn doesn't seem too interested in my account of the scandalous voting antics by which his countrymen deprived Switzerland of victory that year, and it seems a bad idea to mention that Anita's *Solhverv* delivered Norway its first nul-points finish. 'I thought this was a great possibility to be big outside Norway, and I really believed I would do it one day.'

The son of a barber, Jahn was born in 1949 in Tønsberg, a modest industro-maritime town of refineries and trawlers a couple of hours south down-fjord from Oslo. 'You have to imagine this, and I think you can: in the sixties, Norway was very grey. No live rock music, no Norwegian pop stars, nothing like this.' The teenage Jahn, humming the Beatles (and, um, Frankie Valli) as he watched the ferries from Oslo steam past en route to more colourful lands, knew that Tønsberg wouldn't hold him for long.

By sixteen he'd already formed his first band, the Enemies, and a year later Jahn jumped on one of those ferries and went off to Copenhagen, blagging his way into a clerical job in a music management office. 'I was there when this beat band from Manchester phoned up: the Red Squares, really big in Denmark and Sweden then.' Indeed: subsequent research reveals damp-seated, screaming idolatry at their gigs. 'I was thinking: They could come to Norway. I had no authority at all, but there was no one else in the office to hear, so right there on the phone I booked them to do a tour of my country.' His voice is animated with excited reminiscence; for a seventeen year old from the Norwegian woods, this must have been quite a moment.

Yet it was quickly trumped, then trumped again. Jahn was drafted in as a roadie, and when the Red Squares' bassist abruptly quit, the band asked him to step in. 'I had to think for some time, because I was actually still in the Enemies,' he says, but any recriminations must have been shortlived: within eighteen months the Red Squares were in London, recording at Abbey Road. 'We were there at the same time as the Beatles. Incredible! I was always bumping into them.' Jahn slowly shakes his head; thirty-seven years on, he still can't quite believe it.

For both bands, those Abbey Road sessions marked the beginning of the end. Looking around afterwards, I can find evidence of only one single (*Five Times I've Said Goodbye*) released during Jahn's tenure with the Red Squares, and when work-permit problems made life difficult in their Danish power base, the band rolled the dice one last time and decamped to Israel. A bold and swiftly disastrous move: in December 1969, the Red Squares split up and went home, leaving their bassist in Jerusalem.

But Jahn's blue touch paper had been lit. Two years before he'd been marooned in the deafening silence of small-town Norway, and now, though not yet 20, he had known what it was to be screamed at by girls, to unzip beside Ringo at the Abbey Road urinals. It might be the end for the Red Squares, but for him this could only be the start. 'I had begun to believe that everything was possible,' he smiles. 'The happiest parts of my dream were already coming true.' But Jahn didn't get wherever he was today by submitting to the obvious: he joined a local group, The Lions of Judea, and stayed in Jerusalem for over a year.

Having conspicuously failed to break out of (or even into) the Israeli market, Jahn Teigen returned home to find that shifts in the European music zeitgeist had been felt even in Oslo. It was now 1971, and close-harmony beat groups on the Red Squares model were finished: things were getting rockier, hairier and generally more flared. If you couldn't tell as much from its name, Arman Sumpe Dur Express represented a bearded, floral and album-oriented departure for the ooh-baby bassist, one best described in the pages of www.progrock.no.

Within a year the band metamorphosed into Popol Vuh, but back in the mid seventies you had to be pretty quick off the mark when naming yourself after the creation story of the Maya, and the pre-existence of a German Popol Vuh forced a rebrand to Popol Ace. With its epic tone and hobbity subculture, prog rock has always struck an almost deafeningly resonant chord in the land of trolls and Vikings, and as lead vocalist of Popol Ace, Jahn enjoyed his first big album hits.

Dragons-on-Mars fantasy-art album covers, checked-cheese-cloth Open University chic, lashings of Gothic script: Popol Ace went the whole nine yards, and not just when ordering their trousers. (It is to Jahn's enduring credit that throughout these testing years, he never went beyond a Shakespeare goatee and a Conan-the-Barbarian centre parting.) They were playing to crowds of 40,000 throughout Scandinavia, and, perhaps uniquely for a symphonic-progressive rock band, given their own national TV series (and having seen their album covers, how I'd loved to have watched that). Within a couple of years, Jahn had conquered his homeland. What else was there to do?

His record company thought they knew. When a British band outgrows its domestic market, it looks to crack America; for a Scandinavian group, the next step is Europe. With this in mind, Popol Ace's 1975 album 'Stolen From Time' was painstakingly recorded on a vast budget and accompanied with a set of lavishly produced promo videos. Musically the principal influence was Genesis, and when the public-school prog-rockers toured Norway that year Jahn made it a priority to meet up.

'After their concert we found them in a bar,' he says, beginning to smirk oddly. 'I was talking to Michael Rutherford and then our new Popol Ace video comes on the TV in the bar: he watches it and hears me singing, and says, "You know Peter Gabriel is leaving, and we need a singer. What kind of contract do you have with your band?"'

I look at Jahn; the look quickly settles into a frozen gawp of astonishment. As if to show he is not shirking my impertinent stare, Jahn doffs his shades. 'Yes: I was asked to join Genesis. And I said no.' My gawp hardens further, evolving helplessly into one of frank incredulity. 'Well, how would you think?' And with that he launches into one of his trademark vignettes, opening an imaginary newspaper with theatrical gusto and reading from it very loudly: 'Oh, I see Peter Gabriel has left Genesis . . . and the new singer is . . . *Norwegian*?' So strident is the incredulous bark of disdain employed for this last word that a woman walking past the window outside turns to see what the fuss is about. 'You know, sometimes it's just not the right time to take a chance like that.' And so began the grim process that was to end with 'No Jacket Required'.

'Stolen From Time' predictably bombed abroad; Popol Ace predictably split. Jahn was already setting up Prima Vera with his friends Herodes Falsk and Tom Mathisen; at the same time, though he's now reluctant to talk about it, Norway's overlord of prog-rock formed the Norsk Punklag, or Norwegian Punk Union. Needing a cover story to deflect attention from a recent career that had embodied everything punk was so eager to vomit upon, Jahn held a press conference to announce his redrafted CV: having been thrown out on to the streets at the age of thirteen, he told gathered journalists, he had spent the balance of his adolescence in a brutal children's home. No one believed him – an authority on Norwegian punk dismisses the band as 'counterfeit' and 'irrelevant' – and in partial consequence no one bought Norsk Punklag's only single: *You Are a Pig* b/w *I'm Just Sitting Here Bored*.

Prima Vera was never a full-time job for Jahn, but around this time the absurdist partnership occupied much of his creative energy. 'Green tights and dinner jackets!' emailed one Norwegian Eurovision fan when I posted a message requesting an encapsulation of their appeal; clearly it's difficult to explain to a non-Norwegian why Prima Vera have notched six top-ten albums, so difficult that Jahn can't even bring himself to try. Nonetheless they've apparently managed to outrage the Norwegian royal family and the nation's religious authorities on a regular basis, which isn't bad going for a Eurovision performer. 'Prima Vera have amused and offended our country for years,' concluded a review of a recent retrospective, and of that Jahn Teigen can be justly proud.

'You can say I was not a typical Norwegian artist,' he says, with a smile, and it's certainly difficult not to admire the man's capacity for shameless reinvention: from prog-rock to Python to punk to the Palais des Congrès, all in the space of a year. Considering it afresh, his *Mil Etter Mil* outfit was the perfect synthesis of this progression – the half-mast narrow red tie and drainpipes, the braces, the centre parting and aviator shades, the gold rose. If the brace-twanging was Pythonesque in its silliness, then the leap that followed it was half rock-god, half pogo.

In fact, *Mil Etter Mil* wasn't his first Melodi Grand Prix entry at all: he'd tried three times before, most memorably in 1976 when performing *Voodoo* dressed as a skeleton. Eurovision, and its tantalising promise of global stardom, was becoming an obsession. 'We all saw what ABBA did after *Waterloo*,' he says. 'In my part of the world Eurovision was really the only way to get an audience in other countries.' When I ask if he ever felt uneasy mixing Eurovision with punk, prog and Python, he shoots back: 'You are going to start talking about credibility. I hate this terrible word! What an arrogant concept!'

Jahn first heard *Mil Etter Mil* in 1977. Written by Kai Eide and Brit expat songwriter David Cooper in the latter's Oslo flat, Jahn recalls it as 'a nice, sweet song, a little like Creedence Clearwater Revival.' I stifle a gulp of misapprehension: is my beloved *Mil Etter Mil* at the top of a slippery slope into blando Yankrock? If so, it's clearly too late. Six long months later, watching Live8 unfold over a great many sofa-bound hours, I'm possessed of a powerful desire to see Jahn Teigen hold his microphone out to a swaying, singalong crowd of uncountable thousands, stretching to the horizon on all sides: *'C'mon, London! Mil etter mil etter mil . . .'*

Inevitably, the pared-down three-piece original didn't appeal to the NRK executives responsible for the Melodi Grand Prix. I'm mightily relieved to hear Jahn decry the reworked orchestral version: 'From the opening it was awful . . . it had *nothing*. As an artist, that's hard, to do a good song that has been destroyed like this.'

Telling him how much I've enjoyed playing along to that first version, and shooting a quick glance at Frida, I mention that I've brought my guitar along.

'Oh yes?' he says, in a tone that says, 'Oh no.'

'I could go to the hotel right now and get it: I'd really like us to play *Mil Etter Mil* together,' I say, trying to pretend he isn't glazing over before my eyes at this evidently underwhelming prospect. His gaze settles on my red trousers, and tightens into a small frown. Take the piss out of my outfit if you must, he's thinking, but I'm not having you take the piss out of my song.

'I'm not so sure about this idea,' he says, with an air of closure. But Jahn Teigen doesn't do haughty refusals too well, and a moment later his face lights up. 'Maybe instead we can do something more fun – in a studio! In Abbey Road, why not? Maybe we take these thirteen, fourteen zero-points songs, and record them again – the worst songs that are not the worst songs!'

He picks up a pencil and doodles on one of Frida's press releases. 'We can call this CD . . . "From Zeroes to Heroes"! No . . . we can call it just zero, like the Beatles had that album "1". Like this!' He draws a square the size of a beermat, and fills it with a big nought. 'It is the solution of the dream for everyone, because all these people have a strength inside them that comes from their suffering.' The gleam in his eye is zealous; perhaps just half a watt shy of manic. 'Charlie Chaplin, John Lennon . . . Sammy Davis Junior! They have suffered, just as the zero-points singers!' (Later I will try, without success, to rekindle Jahn's interest in – and indeed memory of – this appealingly unhinged project.)

It's the first time Jahn has acknowledged that to score nul points is to suffer, and perhaps recognising this he moves quickly to set his own looming experience apart. 'But after we won the Melodi, everyone was up. This was my fourth try to qualify, and I've done it! And *Mil Etter Mil* was already in the charts! Of course, everybody was confident. Everybody thought this could be my chance, Norway's chance.' And he's off once again on what Eurovision means to Norwegians. 'It's such a *strong* opportunity for us – to be noticed outside our small country. Here in Norway we don't have any self-confidence. We have this bully big brother next to us, and here in this contest is our chance to get one back.'

The bully, of course, is Sweden, and I'm therefore now treated to another dilatory diatribe against the Nordic region's most hated foisters of stupid kings. Jahn is hardly a lone voice in the considerable Norwegian wilderness on this issue: when in 1905 Norway held a plebiscite on ending its union with Sweden, the country voted in favour of dissolution by the impressive majority of 368,208 votes to 184.

The long tradition of Scandinavian jokes makes Norway's place in the regional hierarchy clear. The Swede is always depicted as rich and a little arrogant, the Dane as a decadent hedonist, leaving the Norwegian to assume the role currently played by the Welshman in the British Isle equivalents. (Being just that little bit too odd, the Finns and the Icelanders tend to get left out.)

Here is one instance. A Swede, a Dane and a Norwegian are shipwrecked on a desert island when a genie appears, granting each a wish. The Swede immediately demands to go home, proudly detailing the many lifestyle enhancements present in his open-plan, beech-floored residence. After he vanishes, the

Dane expresses his desire to be returned to his Copenhagen penthouse, fondly eulogising its yielding leather furniture, fridge full of brewed intoxicants and winsome female incumbent. In a flash, he disappears. The Norwegian, having pondered his predicament for some time, turns to the genie and says, 'It's miserable here now. I wish for my two friends to come back.'

It was different, as we have seen, in the contest's early years. During the sixties all Scandinavians felt as Jahn claims the Norwegians still do – uncertain outsiders, newly emerged from harsh rural poverty. They had to bury their old rivalries and band together, support each other. Yet in this alliance of equals, Sweden somehow managed once again to be the most equal. The nation sourced all its Eurovision points from the Nordic brotherhood in 1965, half in '67 and '68, three-quarters in 1969; Norway, having lavished a total of nineteen points on Sweden in these four years, received precisely two in return. Even in 1966, when the shamelessness of inter-Nordic voting patterns almost handed victory to Sweden's flute-playing swineherd, Norway's dutiful scratching of neighbourly backs went stubbornly unreciprocated.

Succumbing to the slightly autistic obsession with data that infects anyone over-exposed to the ESC, I'd trawled the 1966 stats: in that year Denmark garnered all its points from Scandinavia, and Sweden and Finland all but one. Norway's Åse Kleveland, though, had to look elsewhere for votes: of her 1966 total of fifteen, just three were secured from Nordic nations. (Good enough for third, mind you: Åse's reward for the best Norwegian result to date was a future career as the nation's Minister of Culture. Try to picture Sandie Shaw's bare feet under the cabinet table and you'll understand the fjord-wide chasm that separates the British perception of Eurovision from its Scandinavian counterpart.)

When *Waterloo* triumphed, the grumbles of discontent gave way to an open venting of seething historical enmities. Sweden, the 'bully big brother' who had dominated the region – economically, politically, culturally – for 400 years, was at it again: the history book on the shelf is always repeating itself. For the Swedes, ABBA's victory, and subsequent global success, underpinned their growing self-confidence, by inference amplifying the mewling whines of those parochial unsophisticates across that endless western border. Watching a Swedish TV channel in my hotel room (yes, yes), I was struck by the number of adverts broadcast entirely in English – an indicator of laid-back cultural relaxation unthinkable in Norway.

Waterloo buried the one-sided votes-for-Vikings alliance: in 1975 Sweden sourced less than a quarter of its votes from fellow Scandinavians, and in '77, '79 and '80 it was shunned by them completely. Only with the introduction of televoting in 1997 was this trend reversed: the intra-Scandinavian diaspora meant that all the thousands of Swedes living in Norway, and all the Icelanders in Denmark, could phone up and vote for themselves. In that first year of phone voting, Sweden and Iceland secured half their votes from Scandinavia, and Denmark a monstrous four-fifths. Yet somehow, the 1997 contest ended with the perennial exception to this rule anchored to the bottom of the scoreboard: la Norvège, nul points.

It's becoming rather easier to understand Jahn's reaction when, in 1985, Bobbysocks won Norway its first ESC . . . *in Sweden*: 'I was in the hall, but I had to leave before the voting was over – luckily not before it was clear Norway were going to win,' he told a journalist afterwards. (A shame: he'd have missed out on the Swedish compere's splendidly barbed congratulations. 'I'm so pleased you won,' she simpered, handing Bobbysocks their bouquet. 'Norway so often loses.') 'So when I got out on the street a lot of Swedes recognised me and asked me who was the winner. "Norway!" I shouted ecstatically, but the Swedes just laughed and said, "Sure, Teigen . . .". They refused to believe it was true. That night – and all the celebrations afterwards – I'll never forget.' To the extent that he cites Bobbysocks' *La Det Swinge* as his favourite Eurovision number of all time. Even though it's awful.

A world citizen as yet unburdened by the fallout of failure, Jahn arrived in Paris, light of head and fleet of foot, a week before the 1978 final. 'I did my best to turn the other artists into punks. It was a great time. Everyone liked me! The Israelis, you know, had all these bodyguards, and people were too scared to talk with them, but I just went straight past their guards and said: "*Mazel tov*!"' That year with The Lions of Judea wasn't all wasted, then. Jahn smiles, then stops. 'I was the clown there, but they all thought I could win. I remember the NRK boss in Paris coming into my dressing room twenty minutes before the show, really excited, saying, "Everyone likes you, everyone likes Norway – I just talked to some other bosses and they say we have a real chance! But quick, Jahn – you are on-stage in twenty minutes! You must change now!" And I tell him that no one tells me what to do, what to wear. This is my outfit, I tell him, these braces, this shirt, this is me.'

His expression morphs again, into an unsettling, narrow-eyed, narrow-mouthed glare of furious hatred. He raises one of those alarming fingers to my face and I become genuinely concerned: I'd always been aware that the questions I'm going to ask my nul-pointers could lead to confrontation. And indeed they will, but not just yet. For the moment, he's the director, and I'm Jahn Teigen. 'Mr Teigen,' he growls at me venomously, 'if you wear that on-stage tonight, I will personally make sure that you never appear on NRK again.' What I'd taken for the commentator's Nordic reserve was clearly nothing of the sort.

If Jahn doesn't regret his wardrobe (which he later tells me he still has somewhere), what of the performance? 'It was just three minutes. It's strange to think everyone is still so excited about it.' Bitter words on paper, but uttered in a tone of simple curiosity. 'I think you are talking about the jump, yes? I have seen that 6,000 times on TV.' Well, yes, the jump. And the brace-twangs. 'You see, I was just so *happy*, I couldn't not do these things. I always try to do something unexpected, to give people something to think about. If *Voodoo* had won in '76, I would have worn my skeleton suit to Eurovision. And no one thought it was so stupid at the time. All the other performers were clapping for me backstage. Even the NRK director was a little proud. I did the jump again in the green room, I remember, and we were all drinking champagne.'

It's a little awkward to sit there, knowing where the story's leading. 'After five or six countries gave us no points, I felt a little embarrassed, a little afraid.' But even as he says this, Jahn is allowing his lips to crack into a smile. 'Then someone in the green room shouts, "I hope Norway get zero points!", and there is a big laugh, and after this magic moment everyone is cheering for me!'

So hearty were the Jahn-based celebrations when this unlikely dream came true that the Israeli winners had to wait for over half an hour after the TV broadcast had finished before receiving their medals. 'Somehow, scoring my zero was like scoring a goal in the last minute. The situation had looked terrible, then suddenly it was saved.' Noughty, but nice.

'A lot of us went out into town, and we ended up in a club with a grand piano. I was playing *Mil Etter Mil* when Serge Gainsbourg came in, and joined in with me.' I'd spotted the world's Frenchest man in the Palais des Congrès audience – as composer of the excellent *Poupée de Cire, Poupée de Son*, he'd been a Eurovision winner back in 1965. The moment Serge offered his patronage, Jahn must have known that despite the NRK boss's pale-faced exit from the green room, coming rock bottom could turn out better than coming second last; perhaps even second. Or indeed first: *A-Ba-Ni-Bi* was by some distance the best song performed that night in Paris, but as I learn from my online Eurofriends, twenty-six years on, the band that performed it have long since dropped off the pop radar.

Waking up to find his hotel room bestrewn with comatose strangers ('I left them there to pay the minibar bill – I knew NRK wouldn't want to give me any money for it now'), Jahn set off for the airport not yet aware that this was the start of the most extraordinary day of his life. Outside Norway he was being derided as a buffoon or lambasted as a subversive ('some foreign journalists thought my whole performance was a protest against Eurovision,' he recalls), but at Oslo they were already rolling out the red carpet. 'A real red carpet at the airport! And when I go outside there is a group of Hell's Angels, who have come to escort me to my hotel. For the first two or three days it was nearly like the Beatles. Imagine my parents, to see the son of a hairdresser almost as famous as the king. I had so much love, I could feel the vibrations from people aged five to ninety. So *Mil Etter Mil* was now a really big hit in Norway.' Number one, indeed: having already clawed its way above *Mull of Kintyre* and three Bee Gees' singles in the top ten, in Eurovision week it leapfrogged the second of the two Bonnie Tylers.

Mil Etter Mil headed the charts for two months and stayed top ten for three more. 'And of course I called the next single *I Won't Give Up*, and that was in the charts for the rest of the year.' Jahn is savouring these heartwarming recollections, and so am I. On the plane to Oslo I'd suffered a destabilising crisis of confidence in my quest: what kind of sport was this, dragging underdogs back to their vomit, then making them eat it? How upliftingly splendid to sit here now, half a day and a strip-search later, hearing Eurovision's most notorious failure describe his majestic ascent from the nul-points flames.

'People were so happy for me – they said, "Here is our friend, he's our man, he's one of us",' says Jahn, who's clearly analysed in some detail the extraordinary national response to his humiliation. 'I am like this everyman who has been chosen to represent his country, maybe in running, and then at the final he falls over. Young people, old people, they were sad for me. That man,' and here Jahn exchanges waves with a lingering member of his coterie, who's been monitoring us with slightly sinister diligence from the other side of the café, 'he was eight, and he cried. And his grandparents. They say, Jahn was just trying his best.'

This time, the sense of injustice was too deep to be effectively dispersed over Norway's smug neighbour. Jahn admits as much during the entertaining rant that now ensues. 'Everyone here was so proud of me when I came home, because the original song was fantastic, and because I was their friend. They were *so angry* at Eurovision. In fact, at everyone in Europe! People said: "Why do they smash us down like this? Fuck you, Europe! Stupid fucking idiots!"'

This seems the best moment, or at least the most exciting one, to bring up Eurovision's founding principle of continental fraternity, and in particular the extent to which the contest has apparently failed to foster it. 'Well, I voted No when Norwegians were asked to join the EU. Maybe not everyone can manage on their own, but we can.' Indeed: North Sea oil has foisted improbable wealth on Norway's four and half million 'blue-eyed Arabs', and inevitably reduced the security-blanket appeal of EU membership: of all the countries who have held referenda on joining the EU, Norway remains the only one to have voted No. Twice, indeed.

Yet in the 1994 poll, the Nei camp triumphed by only a tiny margin, and I wonder aloud if the lingering anti-European vitriol stirred up by Jahn's nul points could have tipped the balance: after all, far more Norwegians went out and bought *Mil Etter Mil* in two-fingered, anti-European pique than the 64,000 whose votes would have swung it for the Ja campaigners. Jahn has clearly come to this conclusion already. 'For sure! People still tell me they hate Europe because of what happened to me in Paris.' I'm impressed, even oddly empowered. A daft celebration of musical badness it may still be to some, but fifty years on Eurovision still has the power to change the course of geo-political history.

Up in his Oslo hotel room on 23 April 1978, Jahn wasn't looking that far ahead. 'I am by the window with people waving up at me down in the street, thinking: This is amazing – but what do I do next?' His eventual answer was the Toilet Tour, so named, says Jahn with a crooked smile, 'because *Mil Etter Mil* had gone down the toilet'. To endow the tour with a commercial rationale Jahn rushed out an album, entitled in the same spirit 'This Year's Loser'. 'It was almost a musical about that week – we sang words like "Sack that Jacques!", all to do with Paris. But in Norwegian.'

I've been aware that Jahn's surprisingly full-on nationalism sits uncomfortably beside a recorded output that to date had been vocalised almost entirely in English. From the Enemies to Popol Ace – via the Red Squares and even The Lions of Judea – he'd always sung in pop's lingua franca (though practice didn't necessarily make perfect: appraising Popol Ace's legacy, one prog-rock reviewer derided 'Jahn Teigen's hilarious English pronunciation'). Indeed, aside from collaborations with his fellow Prima Vera loon Herodes Falsk, *Mil Etter Mil* was only the second single he'd recorded in Norwegian – the first being *You Are a Pig* (or *Du Er Eit Svin*, as it was more familiarly known to phlegm-faced Oslo teenagers).

Was Jahn's sudden studio conversion to the mother tongue related to events in Paris? Perhaps a tacit acceptance that he would never now sell records outside his homeland? 'No,' he says, simply. 'I just wanted people here to understand every word. That seemed more important now.'

Launching himself into a maelstrom of mixed metaphors, Jahn rode the crest of the nul-points backlash for longer than he'd imagined possible. In a commendable display of sod-you defiance, in 1980 he entered the Melodi Grand Prix again, having sat out 1979 to allow his girlfriend and fellow Eurovision obsessive Anita Skorgan to enter, win and finish eleventh in Jerusalem. Dressed as a big-game hunter he finished last, but in 1982, his schmaltzy duet with Anita, *Adieu*, won over the nation and romped home.

Reselecting Jahn for Eurovision '82 after a second Norwegian nul-points showing the year before was, on the face of it, an act of reckless, fate-tempting bravado: just as they had done when keeping *Mil Etter Mil* in the charts for half a year, Jahn's countrymen were once more thumbing their cold noses at Europe. In fact, behind the scenes, Norwegian hands had been wrung until they bled.

It was difficult not to respect the Viking defiance that had inspired the Norwegians to send along a song they liked, without caring whether anyone else did. Let the rest sing A Song For Europe; their entries were always just A Song From Norway. But now we'd broken their spirit: in their desperation to avoid a much-prophesied hat trick of ignominy, NRK had secretly contracted an Anglo-French professor of linguistics for advice. His suggestion, which presumably didn't include the words 'Jesus! Not that tit in the braces again!', was to purge the lyrics of those abrupt consonants that dependably startled so many non-Scandinavians.

'He cut a lot of things,' recalls Jahn, 'and when I sang on-stage in Harrogate at the final I forgot some more, so the song was just two minutes, I think the shortest Eurosong ever.' Nonetheless, *Adieu* picked up forty more points in Harrogate than *Mil Etter Mil* had managed in Paris, and after recording a back-to-back MGP triumph with the ruthlessly Eurovision *Do-Re-Mi*, Jahn went better in 1983 – thirteen points better, good enough for ninth place and Norway's best finish for a decade. That was his final MGP victory, but far from his final appearance in the national qualifier. He now has fourteen under his belt: available, as Frida butts in to inform me, on a compilation CD entitled 'Jahn Prix'.

Never satisfied, ever restless, Jahn found his energy being channelled into whole new arenas. He had played Riff-Riff in *The Rocky Horror Show* in Oslo the year before, and now wrote the score for a musical, *The Phantom's Wedding*, which opened in November 1978 and played to full houses for months. He began working with his Prima Vera colleagues on a film script that would tell, in predictably Pythonesque terms, the story of the Viking monarch who encountered Christianity in Britain and returned to convert his heathen subjects. *The Saga of King Olaf the Holy* was eventually released in 1983, with Jahn naturally in the title role. 'We had Terry Jones here to help launch it,' he recalls, excitedly. 'In the first week it was the number-two movie after *Octopussy* in Norwegian cinemas.' Not in the second week, however: reviewers slated it with unusual vitriol, one damning the film as 'historically inaccurate, scandalous, daft and appalling'.

After such an enduring run of multi-artistic success, *King Olaf*'s crushing failure appears to have been a professional tipping point. Summarising his national standing at this time, Jahn says, 'I was the most known artist in the country, as a solo, a duo [he would marry Anita Skorgan in 1984], a trio [Prima Vera].' He smiles strangely. 'And then in 1983 . . . it all stopped.' His glasses slip down again, and he rams them forcefully back up his nose. 'Now I must go outside to smoke.'

Huddled under the patio heater, my steamed breath mingling with his Marlboro exhalations, I contemplate Jahn's extraordinary domestic achievements. One Norwegian Eurovision chat-roomer had hailed Jahn as 'our first real pop star', but I'd already learnt that there was a lot more to him than that. Musician, actor, comedian . . . having entertained his countrymen in all these guises for almost forty years, Jahn Teigen must surely be an institution. I gather as much when a passing young man who can't have been born when his parents first heard *Mil Etter Mil* marches straight up as Jahn lingeringly stubs out his cigarette. Having established my nationality, our new friend addresses me in an epic tone tremulous with emotion.

'You know this man? This is Jahn Teigen.'

Jahn smiles that special celebrity smile, gratitude and acknowledgement tempered with discomfort (the low-level, self-deprecatory type rather than Hollywood-strength that's-great-now-please-piss-off hauteur). 'This is my hero since I was a little boy. This is a great man.' I thought people only spoke like that when they were drunk. But he isn't. There are handshakes, and the hint of a welling tear; we stand to go back inside and our young associate departs across the windy granite piazza.

'It's strange to imagine the love I get from people.' Jahn half-sighs. 'Me, a little pimpled boy from Tønsberg.' The repeated failure of his bids for international glory might still incite the odd pang of regret, but in Norway at least, that ravaged face was now a cherished feature of the cultural landscape. Here it was never a question of rueing what might have been, but cosily luxuriating in what had been, and still was.

Comforted by this reiteration of his enduring popularity, Jahn seems suddenly reluctant to return to his account of the period when he did his best to destroy it. 'After 1983 . . . well, I took away many years,' he says, in a nonchalant murmur that seems to acknowledge the statement's inadequacy. We're into the dark heart of Jahn's career, and he isn't handing me a torch. Every time I raise a question relevant to the decade that follows, he calmly delivers a verbal whitewash of platitudes or fast-forwards to his mid-nineties renaissance.

My subsequent investigations fail to broach the wall of silence erected around the Teigen Slough of Despond. So stubbornly immune to salacious rumour-mongering are Jahn's countrymen – and so admirably keen to protect their prodigal son – that exhaustive Googling uncovers nothing more than euphemistic chat-room asides about 'economic difficulties, bad reviews, and problems with his new marriage', or Jahn 'looking more to express himself as a private person than as an artist'. The circumstances that led to our fresh-faced popster booking his extended break to Planet Odd, and the events that weathered him therein, emerge only months later, largely in interviews unearthed and translated by a kindly minded Norwegian associate (Lasse, son of Sissel, I salute you).

After his wedding-of-the-year marriage to a pregnant Anita, Jahn disbanded Prima Vera, returning to his home town Tønsberg to open and manage a naturopathic pharmacy. Six months afterwards, Anita gave birth to Sara – 'people offered 100,000 kroner to take pictures of our daughter,' he told one paper – but there was soon trouble ('because of another man') and in 1987 the couple divorced.

The year after, in a move hardly designed to turn his life around, he acquired the pub-brewery, Norway's first. I'm of course particularly keen to find out more about this intriguing venture: in an online set of Eurovision Top Trumps I'd come across, Jahn's micro-brewery earnt him an impressive 'Special Powers' score of 87 per cent (one less than his unkindly harsh Ugly Rating). But all that emerges is an obscure suggestion that a rock star with his own pub, and the on-premises equipment to keep it supplied, is going to find himself with many new friends, mostly of the wrong sort.

Whilst pointing his gnarled finger at love trouble, bankruptcy and pubs, Jahn has, quite typically, pinned most of the blame for a 'life that went to hell' on a carpenter. 'I was rebuilding my home after Anita moved out,' he told an interviewer, 'and then there was the restaurant I had in Tønsberg, The Three Little Pigs, and as well as the micro-brewery, I had three more houses and was building a fourth. And I think I had six cars.' Jahn's life had never been simple, but I'm astonished to learn of the remarkable lengths to which he went in his determination to over-complicate it. 'All that meant a lot of problems, and I met a woman from Tvedestrand, and that didn't work either.' Later, he talks of his sadness after she broke off their engagement; at twenty-four, she was half Jahn's age. 'Every day was a new nightmare. And then this carpenter came and almost destroyed my life.'

Seeking settlement for 5,000 Norwegian kroner (a little under £500) he was owed by Jahn, the tradesman initiated legal proceedings. Word of these led to a stampede of creditors: 'The snowball started rolling, lawsuit upon lawsuit,' he recalled. Only now did Norway's solitary gossip magazine (at best a reluctant dirt-disher – perhaps more of an *Um . . . Hello?* or a *Well, If You're Sure It's OK*) begin to suggest discreetly that the funny old world of the country's first pop star might be getting a little too funny. Jahn himself has mentioned some of the speculation in interviews: 'I heard rumours that I was a religious obsessive, that I was sick in the head, that I was selling drugs.'

He went off for long months, hiding with old friends in Israel, and then London, returning only when the case belatedly came to court. 'The trial was really painful. It almost killed me. Then Dag-Erik Pedersen called.' This name rings a faint bell in my brain's yawning sports department, and a quick online check confirms its owner as a noted cycling pro, winner of three Giro d'Italia stages in the mid eighties. In any other life story, you'd wheel out the phrase 'unlikely saviour'.

'Dag-Erik had heard I was down, and he says: "The tickets are ready. Come to Italy, you will be better here. The plane leaves 16.30." It was sad, but I felt I had to leave the country. I was only going away for a week, but then it became three months, then three years . . .'

Yet it would be inaccurate to date Jahn's recovery from the moment he stepped off the plane in Rome. As well as occupying his time in Italy with the recording and release of a universally panned album, 1991's 'Exile in Paradise', he also held a press conference outside the Colosseum during which he declared himself the reincarnation of Julius Caesar. Only in 1992, when he decamped to London for a further extended stay, did Jahn Teigen feel himself coming out of the woods.

So much I assume from the fact that this is the point Jahn chooses to resume our narrative, albeit with the arresting claim that while there he was asked to perform the lead role in *The Phantom of the Opera*. 'The composer personally wanted me for the part,' he tells me with teasing nonchalance. The composer being Andrew Lloyd-Webber? 'Of course. But there was a problem with one or two notes, so I decided not to go to the next audition. It was not part of my journey. I was going somewhere, but it wasn't there.'

I wonder later if his eight-year lost weekend was a delayed reaction to that night in Paris. Perhaps the strain of keeping a brave face finally got too much; the critical opprobrium heaped upon his King Olaf film ruptured the thick scar tissue sealing his nul-points wound, and out burst half a decade of pent-up self-loathing and inadequacy.

Certain Teigen musings on that night in April 1978 lend weight to this. 'If someone else had done that song, they would not have got zero,' he mumbles at one point. 'It was just because of me. The juries thought: this silly man is ruining our festival.' And he hints that even while surfing the great wave of national indignation unleashed by the 1978 result, there were times when he felt its mighty undertow pulling him down. 'The country really engaged with this injustice, they really took it personally for a long time. A guy from Belgium, or anywhere, he goes home after Eurovision, maybe he gets some points or none, but the next day it is all over, all forgotten. But not for me.' A persistent Jahn theme is moving forward, the onwards journey in life. Maybe he just had enough of his countrymen always looking back. Had enough of the gnawing fear that his enduring popularity might be based on pity.

Certainly there's an undeniable frailness, even a desperation, in those stubborn celebrations of his failure. The Toilet Tour, 'This Year's Loser', 'From Nothing to Gold' . . . Kai Eide, *Mil Etter Mil*'s co-composer, went on to form a blues outfit called

The Nil Club. All that, particularly seen in the light of Jahn's almost reckless determination to compete at Eurovision again, seems to suggest a man protesting his indifference too much.

Maybe somewhere in there is that pimpled boy from Tønsberg, belatedly coming to terms with a thwarted dream of global stardom. It's tempting to view the extended stays in Israel, London and Italy as the last, frail foreign forays of an aged Viking still bent on conquest, his spirit willing but his flesh weak. Jahn himself admits that though his early MGP appearances were intended as launch pads for overseas glory, in recent years he's only done the show 'to offer the Norwegian people a new song'.

Back in Oslo, Jahn started fumbling together his shattered career: having released no fewer than thirteen albums in the five years that followed *Mil Etter Mil*, in the five since his divorce he'd managed just two. His first break came courtesy of another member of Norway's hard-bitten Eurovision club. As Dollie Deluxe, Ingrid and Benedicte had earnt a par-for-the-course seventeenth place in the 1984 final; over the next eight years they devised and composed a musical entitled *Which Witch*, a knockabout romp of blasphemous adultery and fire-based slaughter set in medieval Norway. Jahn was persuaded to take the role of the executioner, and performed it with predictable relish. After 100 well-received performances at home, Norwegian corporate backers put up the finance for a run in London's West End; it opened – in the presence of A-ha – at the Piccadilly Theatre in October 1992.

The musical's heritage, and the on-stage presence of Jahn Teigen, proved too great a temptation for our critics. 'Nul Points for Norway' read the review headlines, and the show closed before Christmas. Even now it lives on as a benchmark of awfulness: 'right up there with *Which Witch* for connoisseurs of the truly bad musical', said the *Standard* of a recent West End attempt to put the life of Wallis Simpson into song; in 2002 the *Guardian*'s theatre critic reminisced on the 'excesses of incompetence that lent *Which Witch* a curious fascination'. Precisely the sort of stuff, you'd have thought, to send Jahn back to his pub-brewery with an unquenchable thirst, yet after

Which Witch enjoyed a long and successful additional run back in Norway, he felt himself reinvigorated.

'I did some children's TV, and then in the mid nineties I was asked to be the host for Norway's *Stars in Their Eyes*, which I worked on for three years,' he says quietly. We're back outside now, watching the tip of Jahn's latest Marlboro glow in the dwindling light. Did anyone try and 'do' him? 'A few times.' A crevassed grin. 'But of course it was just not possible.'

His TV work opened up a new, younger audience, who Jahn now blended with his older fanbase. 'We reformed Prima Vera, and sold 120,000 copies of a new album, made a new TV series, released a DVD, did a big sell-out tour.' His prog-rock pomp was revisited in the symphonic glory it had always screamed out for when the NRK orchestra remixed the greatest hits of Popol Ace. 'And then I thought: I have had reunions with Prima Vera and Popol Ace – but I haven't had a reunion with me!'

And so in 2004 he released a new album, 'Undressed With Myself', the one whose cover-portrayal of decrepitude had so shocked me back at the studio. Frida delves into her black satchel and delves out a copy. Looking at the cover again, and at the man huddled up beside me with a ciggie in his pinched and puckered gob, I'm reminded of jazz wit George Melly's unimprovable retort to Mick Jagger, after rock's most deluded narcissist dismissed his deepening wrinkles as 'laughter lines': 'Nothing's that funny.'

But Jahn is no Jagger. He knows what he looks like, and he's comfortable with it. The CD's inside sleeve is an untouched celebration of physical decline: a *Hard Day's Night* gallery that showcases Jahn's glaring, gurning, grinning visage in all its dilapidated glory. Almost simultaneous was the release of the zero-to-hero greatest-hits anthology Frida now hands me. Inevitably, the track list kicks off with *Mil Etter Mil*.

I listen to 'Fra Null Til Gull' a week or so later: a bit Leonard Cohen, a bit Bob Dylan, a lot Jahn Teigen. It can't have been easy to see the best-of retrospective rise to number four in the album charts, while the new material received a critical roasting and limped to a peak of twenty-one. No Teigen album had ever sold so badly. A quick spin suggests why this might be: downbeat to the point of torpor, it's uncomfortably suggestive of an anthology of Eurovision ballads from the late eighties.

But perhaps there's more to its failure than that. Following Jahn back towards the café entrance, I glance about at the huge scale of the refurbishment and regeneration happening all around. Here at the old docks, everything was being modernised, improved, overhauled; the route I'll take back to my hotel is circuitously routed around stadium-sized holes in the ground and crane-forest construction sites. With an enviable economic destiny assured by canny investment of their oil billions, maybe Norway is more confident now, more at ease with itself and its enhanced position in the world. No longer a nation of fishermen, with chips on their shoulders. See all this, Sweden? See all this, Brussels? We don't need you, any of you. We've done all this on our own. As one of the most conspicuous figureheads of Norway's parochial past, perhaps Jahn Teigen is being crowded out of its fast-paced, hi-tech future.

With his studio career winding down, so Jahn is now obliged to earn his crust from those stag-party karaoke recordings and what must be an increasingly debilitating schedule of live performances. 'But in this I also include my talks to businessmen and others,' he says. Ah yes! I've been wanting to hear about these, and it seems that Jahn has been wanting to tell me. Almost immediately he's prone on his banquette, those pipe-cleaner legs hanging limply off the end. 'This is my philosophy,' comes a voice from under the table. 'If you are in a home for old people, the people there want you to stay in bed. It's easier for them, and for you. This is a little similar to my zero-points situation. I could have given up, I could have stayed in bed. But if you stay in bed . . . *you die*!'

With far more vigour than I'd have thought possible, Jahn abruptly levers himself to his feet, and begins to wave his arms and jog on the spot. 'Everything starts with zero! Every day! Getting no points is like getting up in the morning, like coming out of an egg!' Single exclamation marks do not do justice to the animation of his physical performance and its associated utterances. The small number of our fellow patrons previously unaware of Jahn Teigen's presence amongst them is swiftly reduced to zero. He's suddenly everywhere, like the boy who was at both ends of the school photo. 'Some of us, we come out of the egg and we make noise. We make friction, we dare to do difficult things, we use energy, and maybe we make ourselves idiots. Like Eddie Eagle, your ski jumper, he dared! He was brave! And the people who aren't so brave, who don't want to take a chance or be an idiot, they like us. They love us!' I'm beginning to understand. Jahn is not a musician, but a performer, one who thrives on forcing people into a reaction – any reaction. Applause, tears, screams, abuse, jeering scorn: it's all grist to the strangely geared Teigen mill.

Not for the first time I'm reminded of my wife's uncle, who as a fifty-something Scandinavian rock survivor (he now owns and runs a Reykjavik recording studio) shares many of the bullet points on Jahn's CV. He's also a holder-forth, a showman, and as entertaining as he always is, on certain occasions – public occasions – it's sometimes a little too conspicuous.

Suddenly Jahn sits down, shuts up and fixes me with a look of troubled earnestness. 'You understand,' he says at length. 'This zero-points is . . . *An Experience*. It's something I created or gave birth to, but it's not simple to explain. Look at this cup!' Not hard: it's now being held aloft two inches from my nose. 'How do you make a cup? There's so much to it.'

We're on our way back out for what proves to be the final fag break when a pale, black-haired young woman with a fair bit of metal in her face shuffles listlessly up and mumbles something sullen at Jahn's shoes. 'My daughter,' says Jahn simply, once she's shuffled off again a moment later. 'All the attention has not been easy. People expect her to be a performer, like me, but that's not her. She works in the theatre as a hairdresser.'

'Like her grandfather in Tønsberg,' I offer, bracingly, as we watch her trudge away up the street alone, hooded top angled at the floor, arms wrapped defensively around her middle.

'You know I am in the Melodi Grand Prix again this year?' blurts Jahn, yanking our attention from this uncomfortable spectacle and its associated ruminations. It's a clumsy but highly effective diversion – I had no idea. 'You know Tor Endresen?' Not yet, I reply, though with reference to this man's experiences at Dublin in 1997 I soon will. 'He's a good friend, and he's entering again, so I thought I must also. I don't want him to catch me: he has nine Melodi entries, I think, and I have fourteen.'

And so a moment later, having been asked for my linguistic input, I'm squinting raptly at Jahn's scrawled English lyrics for *My Heart Is My Home*. A few weeks back this would have been at best an awkward scenario, but as it is I'm thrilled to a tizzy: what I say now will, however fleetingly, affect the lives of 400 million people.

'You seem to say "hate" quite a lot,' I offer at ruminative length. 'Maybe that's not really a great Eurovision word?' I'm about to suggest something more apposite, perhaps 'bomp' or 'laloo', or a cheeky '*krrrroppp*' for old times' sake, when I clock the intensity of Jahn's nodding.

'Yes . . . but the hate fits with the song.' Loudly, and without skimping on the gesticulations, he now performs the song. Weighty and anthemic, it most closely approximates to *We Will Rock You*.

'Well, that sounds a lot better than almost everything I've heard in the last few weeks,' I say when he sits down, and I say it with feeling and a clean conscience.

'Thank you,' Jahn rasps, clearly exhausted by his performance. 'You know, I have a concert tonight.' He suddenly looks even older, and only with difficulty do I stop myself grabbing one of those thin arms to steady Jahn as he rises. 'Maybe I have to go to sleep a little now.'

After an exchange of thanks and farewells, I turn to walk away across a square burnished by the low-angle Nordic sunset. All around me, Oslo is doing its low-key, Saturday-night warm-up: pallid, stringy skateboarders clattering off a banister, apple-cheeked families with ice-skates hung over their shoulders massing towards a new open-air rink Frida had mentioned. I look behind for a last glance at this nation's first pop star, and doing so suddenly remember the one thing I meant to say to him, or the one thing that wasn't a question. Jahn and Frida are now thirty yards away across the wide and windy plaza, but having spent half a day in such reckless, theatrical company I'm hardly scared to shout.

'I had to take my trousers off at the airport!' Jahn turns, and his furrowed brow furrows further. Frida leans towards his ear and says something into it. 'Yeah,' I call, my internal volume knob swivelling rapidly anti-clockwise. 'Yeah, Frida will tell you . . . pants down, drug-jumps, the works.' Jahn hoists an uncertain, placatory wave and I shuffle away, cringingly aware of how little I rock.

'So – you know Freddie Mercury?' says a voice from just behind me.

Here we go, I think, turning slowly around to face the fallout of my ill-chosen public pronouncement. With a chest-length ginger beard of galloping pubic frizz, my youthful interrogator clearly stands apart from his contemporaries, although just how far apart only becomes apparent during his reply to my monosyllabic expression of assent. 'So do you know his, ah, dead place?' It's a bad time to notice the many rather large pieces of food that have made their home deep in the young man's rampant chin furniture. Christ – is that half a lollystick? 'So do you know, one hundred per cent, he is dead?'

'Well . . .' I say, setting off a furious volley of impassioned, beardy nods.

'So do you know John Deacon? The house of Deacon, where Deacon is at home?'

It's at this point that I wonder if I'm falling victim to an elaborate sting organised by Norwegian eccentrics – both of them. Had I not many years ago spent a painful two days failing to master one of Mr Deacon's few prominent instrumental performances, it is probable that the name of Queen's bassist would mean no more to me than the name of Queen's florist. As it is, I did not allow a persistent indifference to their musical legacy to prevent the fostering of a mild but stubborn fixation with the band's most anonymous member.

The Queen-ish aspects of Jahn's new Melodi entry had set off a train of thought that, having rattled at merciful speed past youthful memories of the cover of *Crazy Little Thing Called Love* that was part of the Rough Justice repertoire, had mere moments ago pulled up to the buffers at Deacon Central. His, I long ago decided, was the most enviable of lives – being John Deacon meant enjoying huge wealth, seasoned with just the right amount of ego-fondling adulation. You'd get stopped in the street often enough to keep you smiling, and only then by apologetically nerdish anoraks rather than unhinged stalkers who'd hide under your shed, and then get immovably wedged and scratch a note blaming their slow deaths on you. And as one whose short on-stage career was largely occupied in finding the biggest speaker cabinet and hiding behind it, John Deacon had always been my live-performance idol: a non-singer blessed with the face of a lab technician, he was never expected to compete with the preening showmen around him.

Walking across the plaza it had begun to occur to me that being Jahn was a little like being John: yes, the money wasn't so good, and as I'd seen for myself the attention could become overbearing. But that top-of-the-range Audi estate told its story, and as far as the street-hassle went, all Jahn had to do was get on a plane. Any plane. Go anywhere else in the world and as long as you steered clear of any suspiciously blond tourists you'd be safe.

'That's quite extraordinary,' I say, oblivious now to the man's previously unsettling lunacy. 'I've been thinking about John Deacon for the la–'

'So do you know Creedence Clearwater?'

Well, that was too much. By the time he obscurely excused himself with a shriek of '*Errrta Kitt*!' I was 100 yards nearer my hotel.

4 April 1981
Royal Dublin Society
Finn Kalvik
Norway
Aldri i Livet

A determination to visit all my nul-pointers in chronological order, combined with Scandinavia's impressive early hat trick and the time of year, seemed to promise a forbiddingly dark, cold beginning to my tour. But excellently, in every way but financial, I soon learnt that one of the three Norsemen in question was looking up at a very different winter sky.

'If u really want to hook up with me,' wrote Finn Kalvik in reply to an email I'd sent to his website, 'I'm planning to go up to a good place in Thailand, a beautiful tiny island that would "freak u out" because of all its colourful fishes in the sea, and small beautiful beaches.'

After Jahn and his two million albums, here was an even more compelling post-nul turnaround: once we'd established phone contact, Finn explained in eager, boyish tones that South Seas island-hopping throughout the Norwegian winter was his long-established wont. 'Painting, scuba-diving, writing songs – that's my life out here.' Every time I called to arrange another detail – he was unfailingly helpful in providing travel assistance – he'd break off briefly to order a beer, or apologise for being distracted by some comely female presence.

'I'm really a lucky guy,' he mused in our last chat, the day before I left. 'I wrote these huge hits, and in the winter I leave Norway to live in all these exciting places. My view here . . . it's like a postcard or a commercial.' At fifty-seven, how much better could life possibly be?

It was under a month since Thailand's western coast had been so murderously battered by the tsunami, but Koh Samui – an offshore tourist magnet deemed by Finn more logistically sensible than the tiny island originally planned for our rendezvous – was on the east. All Finn had noticed, he said on the phone, were odd patterns in tourist numbers: in the days after the disaster the island had been crowded with holidaymakers diverted from Phuket, but now, with these gone, there was an eerie emptiness. Wholesale, knee-jerk cancellations meant that even unaffected areas were almost devoid of tourists, and despite the heart-punching expense involved, I'd had no trouble in bagging a last-minute flight.

My fellow passengers at Heathrow were an odd assortment of backpackers and beer-bellies, united by a shared love for indelible body art. Young couples with a dozen earrings each trooping into the 747 alongside balding, grizzled men of Kalvik vintage, lardy rejects off to punch way above their considerable weight with the economically disadvantaged female populace. Was that what had drawn Finn there? Despite the bar stool ogling, it didn't seem likely. His website photo depicted a svelte, tanned blond exuding good health and happiness, looking how Björn Borg might have done if he'd kept playing tennis, instead of designing underpants. Though two years older than Jahn, he appeared twenty younger.

There were dozens of young Scandinavians in the rows around, and with a now practised eye and ear I placed them all. The three blonde girls in front could only be Swedish – they wore immaculate matching sportswear, and did everything, even sleeping, in strict synchronisation. The two couples behind, their hackingly guttural enunciation emphasised by a debilitating intake of beer, were surely Danes. I passed the Norwegians on the way to the loo. There were five of them, all reading or watching their seat-back screens in straight-backed silence. With flags on their hats.

As we left Europe behind I plugged in my MP3 player and clicked forward to the now familiar introduction to their nation's 1981 Eurovision entry. *Aldri i Livet (Never in My Life)* was a self-penned, folk-pop love song, crisp and clear as a Norwegian summer's morning. The promo video I had fondly imagined over many listenings featured a rucksacked Finn striding alone across the lower slopes of a sunny green mountainside, perhaps pausing to refresh himself from a chuckling brook; it wasn't hard to transpose this solitary bucolic paradise from Scandinavia to a palm-fringed beach.

Again, there was nothing in the musical make-up to warrant its fate, and again I'd enjoyed learning the chords, clumsy as they sounded alongside Finn's delicate picking. Despite Jahn's fulsome pooh-poohing of my mooted duet, I'd still hoped to coax *Aldri i Livet*'s creator into a singalong: how could he object when we were sitting there side by side on the empty sand? It was a deflating moment when Thai Air advised me that the modest gap between arrival at Bangkok and the departure of my connecting flight to Koh Samui forswore anything beyond cabin luggage; the Fender hadn't come along for the ride.

My head filled with the impressively lush introductory backing vocals, then a brain-snagging keyboard hook, which segued into Finn's sonorous plucking as his sweet, choirboy tones picked up the melody. Nulpoints.net cited the song in describing what it called 'the scandalous treatment of Norwegian Eurovision entries from the mid-sixties to the mid-eighties'. So too did the EBU's veteran voting scrutineer Clifford Brown during a 1992 BBC documentary: 'On several occasions back then I chose Norway, because I thought theirs were very catchy, very beautifully orchestrated little songs.' However else it upset the Eurovision jurors, it can't have offended their ears.

It's two weeks earlier, and I'm in bed watching a logo jerkily rotate to the grandly ceremonial Eurovision fanfare, Marc-Antoine Charpentier's *Te Deum* being put to a use he probably didn't imagine when composing it in 1692. My Andreas-sourced commentary for the 1981 Dublin final is by France's TF1, which should at least give me the chance – as it transpires my last chance – to decode some of the voiceover asides. As well as the compere's utterances: thanks to Johnny Logan, the Irish are staging Eurovision for the first time since the days of Dana.

The introductory overview poignantly betrays a nagging fear that in the ten years that have since elapsed, the continent might have forgotten that European life existed west of la Royaume Uni. Watching the Ireland-by-numbers helicopter fly-pasts of forts and fields, the postcard snapshots of Guinness and Gaelic, I'm once again obliged to consider how stubbornly parochial Europe remained just a quarter of a century back.

By supplementing the usual French and English with Gaelic, the hostess imbues her opening pronouncements with the multi-lingual tedium of a flight-safety briefing aboard the *USS Enterprise*. It's a relief to find this sagging ordeal ended with the triumphant return of the pre-act postcards from abroad, those introductory vignettes of each nation's performers interacting with their host city's tourist infrastructure. First up are the Austrians, beaming at a waiter as he pours cream over the back of a spoon into their Irish coffees. Accessorised with legwarmers and American foot-ball helmets, their ensuing performance builds on this promising start: vintage, double-matured Eurovision cheese.

A Fawcett-flicked German (63 kilos, reports the voiceover, and a ping-pong enthusiast) coyly leading her beardy band-members around a war memorial, five Israelis feeding ducks in a park, two Danish couples meeting on a canal bridge: it's becoming more and more difficult to avoid the similarities between these films and the half-hearted scene-setting preambles to the era's contin-ental pornography. How thankful I am that this is not the case when the squatly hirsute Seid Memic-Vajta, 'winner of the pres-tigious Sarajevo festival', meets up with two leering associates and a frail ginger consumptive outside the National Gallery. At least until they start singing.

A number entitled *Layla* is followed by one called *Leila*: after half a dozen entries it's clear that it will take something special to stand out above or below the thick layer of gooey dross being slathered across the screen. Finland handsomely manage this with the accordion-driven reggae that follows.

In the thunderstruck aftermath of *Reggae OK*, the commentator's voice cracks and wavers like a bum-fluffed adolescent, and in sympathy I start to wonder if all this relentless abuse is permanently damaging my critical faculties. After another couple of finals, I think, I'll have undergone a full musical lobotomy, able only to process pop sounds of childish inanity, grunting my incoherent appreciation through sagging, moist lips, confused by and even sometimes afraid of more complex or challenging melodic forms. With mild horror I look down at my notes and see that next to *Humanahum*, sung by a Henri Leconte-alike and France's last entry before their monument-to-drivel boycott, I've put a double tick and the words 'best yet'. (That evening, my youngest daughter asks me what the tune is I've been humming since she came back from school. I don't know what she's talking about, I tell her; five minutes later she blurts, 'That! That one!' A snatch of chorus is lodged between my pursed lips, and in disbelief I let it escape: it's *Zoom*, by the Commodores.)

The Spaniards present what sounds like the theme to an unsuccessful daytime soap; the Dutch chug down Baileys throughout their introductory film before performing an entry that owes a great deal to *Chiquitita*. ABBA released what would be their final album in 1981, and rumours of a split had clearly encouraged the continent's performers to fantasise about plonking their satinette arses down on that vacant throne. For seven years the group had cast a mighty shadow over Eurovision, their astounding achievements eclipsing all subsequent winners. In 1981 that shadow loomed larger and darker than ever, as I discover when Cyprus split the chorus of *Monika*: 'Moni, Moni, Moni,' chant the members of Island, a little too pleadingly.

The Irish hosts perform with the volume blatantly cranked up, and then here's a sprightly young blond man in a fishing jumper, grinning shyly as he leads his backing vocalists (beards, blondes) along a windswept Dublin dockside. Though already thirty-four, he looks like a venture scout on a sponsored walk. *'Un artiste complet,'* trumpets the voiceover, before detailing Finn Kalvik's sole responsibility for writing, arranging and – conductor Sigurd Jansen's putting on his headphones, so here we go – performing *Aldri i Livet*.

The Melodi Grand Prix final, two months before, had been a coronation more than a contest. The cravat-wearing presenter, having stumblingly welcomed each preceding act with the help of a handful of prompt cards, dropped them in his lap while hailing, in tones of sombre unworthiness, the performer and composer of *Aldri i Livet*.

From the opening bars of that lovingly crafted keyboard intro, it was clear that we'd entered a different league: as if to prove the point, Finn performed at the MGP in what looked like a Coventry City shirt, along with complementary scarf. Once again, I didn't need to convince myself of its musical merits: sitting up in bed, I tapped my foot, nodded along and generally exhibited all principal symptoms of male-pattern musical appreciation. This, though, was more than Finn managed. Guitar round neck, mouth to mike, for three minutes he stood rooted to the spot. My thoughts, watching him bow and rise with a slight applause-acknowledging smile, were that for Dublin he'd need to work on his on-stage mobility, and perhaps think about a wardrobe change. Particularly when a tantalising freeze-frame suggested, if not quite conclusively, that his shirt was bearing an unhelpfully auspicious squad number. Having squinted at the fuzzy, over-coloured smudge for long minutes, I was obliged to conclude from the available evidence that Finn Kalvik had just performed his Eurovision entry wearing a huge number 0.

Perhaps concluding that having won him the national qualifier his performance wasn't broke, he doesn't fix it. He steps on to the Royal Dublin Society stage still wearing that white scarf and pale blue team shirt, and his hair remains coiffed in that wispy, extra-length David Soul cut. The one obvious departure is that instead of standing with his acoustic guitar, he's perched cross-legged on a tall white bar stool.

Next year the combo would work for Germany's Nicole: so huge seemed her guitar and so frail her physique that it would have been almost inhumane to force her to bear it aloft. But as a full-grown Norseman, whatever his hair might say, sitting down makes Finn look effete, inadequate and yet somehow unwisely smug. Get up, you big blond ponce, you want to shout, get up and let one of those singing girls behind you take the weight off their white-booted feet.

And being delivered from a chair makes his song seem somehow less consequential: its gentle plucking and background warbles grate and simper rather than soothe. I'm suddenly picking holes that went unpicked throughout the Melodi national final – Finn's irksome habit of singing out of one side of his rather small mouth, along with a certain overcrowded feel to the song's chorus. Nonetheless, as *Aldri i Livet* trills and plings towards its climax, it's hard to imagine 300 million Europeans gawping at their screens in harrowed silence as they did three years before when Jahn snapped those braces and launched himself off the stage. Friends of mine, friends with only a passing, culture-nostalgic interest in Eurovision, could all remember Jahn Teigen; Finn Kalvik meant nothing to them.

Almost immediately, here are Bucks Fizz on a cabin cruiser: being sandwiched between the hosts and the winners can't have helped Finn's case. Particularly as *Making Your Mind Up* highlighted his drably static performance with a vigorously physical routine incorporating much hand jiving, and of course that synchronised removal of the lower halves of the two girls' outfits. Just as Finn's stool cemented his pointlessness, so with that savage rip of Velcro Bucks Fizz earnt the votes that brought them victory: the ping-pong German wound up only four points adrift in second. It occurs to me that it's possible to spot a Eurovision loser – and perhaps even a winner – with the sound off.

From now on I'm just looking for sub-Finn performances. No shortage: straight up are a deranged Portuguese quintet, wearing pastel-coloured plastic boiler suits that suggest they're on a lunchbreak from the poultry abattoir. *Playback* seems to go on rather a long time – so long, indeed, that I do as they repeatedly order, this time with an eye on the DVD's time-elapsed counter. Well, look at that: 3.04, a full four seconds over the maximum permitted length. Consider yourself lucky, I think, at the same time forced to accept that I'm starting to know and care far too much about the minutiae of this whole idiotic business.

Belgium's *Samson*, the last dying embers of those Boney M-inspired disco eulogies to historical legends; a Greek duo with a rose on their piano and a performance so dreary that the Cypriots only give it six. A Swiss trio nudge their homeland into the style decade they haven't yet felt the need to leave; in gloves and tailcoats, the power-balladeering Swedes clumsily trample on ABBA's legacy. Then Björn Skifs takes his bow, and after six minutes of tin whistles and floaty dancing it's 'Good evening, Austria, could I have your votes please?'

After four rounds Finn still has company at the foot of the scoreboard, but then to lonely cheers Israel give two to Finland and five to Cyprus, and he's alone. There's a great Eurovision moment when the Yugoslavian jury forewoman is asked for her votes and screams back, 'I don't have it!', and another when Turkey's total is inadvertently downgraded to zero (the error is not corrected for three long rounds).

There's no green-room coverage to tell us how Finn is taking all this, but the French commentator seems aware that Eurovision history is tragically repeating itself: from the halfway point on he begins mumbling, in a sort of wan gloat, about the looming fate of 'la Norvège'. He snaps out of it, though, when the UK jury awards France a single point. 'Oh, la la,' he says, adding 'la la la la la' to emphasise his scorn and outrage as jeers ring out around the auditorium. (To explode the Eurovision conspiracist's most sacred cow – incoming udder shrapnel! – the French have proven far happier to vote for the British than we have for them.)

Bucks Fizz have to wait until the last round to sew up their victory, and as the beaming quartet trot back on-stage like over-eager children's TV presenters, they're joined by all the other acts to wave and smile and teach the world to sing. All the other acts but one – even on frame-by-frame slo-mo, there's no sign of a blond man in a football shirt. The credits roll across the irrefutable scoreboard evidence: nine points adrift from the penultimate pair of Turkey and Portugal, *Aldri i Livet* has by statistical inference just been voted – as indeed it remains – the worst Eurovision song of all time.

Naturally enough we land at Bangkok to discover the Koh Samui flight delayed. Down the quiet end of the transfer lounge, backpackers idly squish mosquitoes on each other's arms and necks; up at its breathlessly commercial hub, businessmen are slumped alarmingly over oxygen inhalers or prostrate on benches having their feet manipulated by surgical-masked masseurs. Each of the many retail outlets is manned by an idiotic surfeit of staff. How many Thais does it take to sell a pallid Westerner a bag of peanuts? Seven: one to take the cash, one to put them in a carrier, and five to clear up what happens after he discovers they're lobster and coconut flavour.

Refreshed by a nap and not yet familiar with Bangkok Airways' entry on www.airdisaster.com, I enjoy the quick hop to Koh Samui. Deep green, white-fringed and afloat in the softly glittering blue, the island announces itself from some distance as an unarguably wonderful place. Even the airport seems enticingly tropical, its single runway lined with bougainvillea and hibiscus, the largely unwalled arrival and departure halls sheltered by coconut-mat roofs. With a trip to Norway recently stuffed under my belt, and Finland next up, I step out into the blood-warm breeze feeling half in love with the man who has brought me here. Finn has even arranged a minibus pick-up for me, the splendid fellow, and as it crumps and clanks through the dusted shanties of the island's western coastline I again marvel at the triumphant non-nulness of his lifestyle. After twenty minutes we bump off the concrete-sectioned road and into the forecourt of an address I can read off the T-shirt my youngest daughter now wears as a night-dress: Big John Beach Resort, Tongyang Beach, Koh Samui.

A girlish young man identified by a badge on his chest as 'Gob' arrives with a glittering smile and a luridly orange welcome cocktail; as he hands it over I note the residents' blackboard on the wall behind him. Almost two-thirds of the thirty-odd slots are empty, making the two names near the top all the more conspicuous. 'P10 – Mr FINN. P11 – Mr TIM.'

A moment later I'm being shown into P11, a straw-roofed, marble-bathroomed hexagonal chalet twenty yards from Big John's compact stretch of beach. Stoutly eschewing the lure of a huge double bed – I've been in transit for eighteen hours – I change into my trunks and shuffle down to the sea. A dozen white plastic sun loungers are lined up under the palm trees on a slim arc of soft sand, but only one is occupied. Small mirrored shades, a magnificent head of burnished hair, a thin smile and a bead necklace that I recognise from his website photo. How very splendid to see you, Mr Kalvik.

The smile broadens; Finn pulls his trim and richly sun-seasoned body upright to greet me. 'Tim, yes?' he says, in the boyish, slightly tremulous tone familiar from our phone calls. 'We can talk right here.' And so begin the three days of my professional life that, until the memorable alarums of the third, I would have most trouble in describing as work.

Side by side on our loungers, Finn's bronzed, lithe feet form an uncomfortable contrast with mine, pallid and very quickly blotched with red from the shock of this sudden exposure to the sun mid-way through their under-sock hibernation. I can't help inaugurating our debut chat by paying homage to Finn's astounding physical condition: he could honestly pass for a man in his mid forties. 'I've only got one face,' he says, 'and I don't want to look like a wreck. I cycle 30km a day, I do a lot of sit-ups and push-ups . . . Right now I had five weeks without alcohol.' Though I'll witness him making up a little lost ground in that department, it's clear that for Finn this wholesome lifestyle is a professional prerequisite. 'Most of my earning is through concerts now, not so much records. I hope I don't sound big-headed, but if my gigs are mostly good ones, it's because I put all my energy into them, alone up there with a guitar on-stage for two hours. Norway is a country with only four and a half million people, and very often I play the same places over and over again . . . If you want to be asked to come back, you have to give your best.'

He hangs a leg off his lounger, tracing his toes idly through the warm sand. 'I work *really hard* for six or seven months, doing those gigs in Norway,' he says. 'So when I come out to here, or Fiji, or New Zealand, I feel I deserve to do nothing, just diving and stuff, for maybe two months. Then for three or four months I write songs, maybe I paint, constantly on the move to new islands, new places. I'm just going to get a beer.'

Beyond my feet, a tiny silver wave effortfully rises, furls and falls wearily on to the sand with a wet hush. Out in the smooth, shallow Gulf of Thailand, a Norwegian couple of Finn's acquaintance are spreadeagled face down on lilos, rotating gently in a light breeze. Further still, waveless gulf meets cloudless sky in a line interrupted by the hazy silhouettes of craggy, densely rainforested islands. We're at the centre of a bay that curves out towards the horizon in both directions; I look left, and spot a distant fisherman lazily hurling a net out into the shallows, and right, where two children are bent over the lapping wavelets, collecting washed-up coconuts. There is no one else in sight; it is a scene of gaudy perfection.

'This really is lovely,' I drawl, when Finn returns. There's a pause, during which he clicks open his beer and nods blankly at the distant islands.

'I don't dig small talk,' he says at last. Given the intimacy of our semi-naked beach-bound encounter, these words and their scowling tone are an unnerving jolt. 'People in Norway talk about the weather a lot, and I can't do that. I'm not a bullshitter, and that's why I have a lot of true friends. Most of my friends are people that are also very visible in the mass media in Norway, and I don't spend my time with small talkers.' I nod, wondering how big my future talk needs to be. Is it OK to ask where he got that beer? 'I've got a lot to give,' Finn says, sharply, 'so I like to spend my time with creative people who also have a lot to give.' That's a no, then.

The lilo-bearers walk up: I'm introduced to Bjørn and his wife Sissel, recently retired NRK news stalwarts of many years standing, her behind the camera and him in front of it. Hearing this, and keen to burst the small but swelling bubble of tension, I retrieve my camera and ask if she could photograph us together on the beach here, Mr Tim and Mr Finn. It works: as Sissel squints into the viewfinder, Finn suddenly becomes a star, cracking a brilliant smile and holding it as she snaps away. And, to my substantial relief, after she stops.

Our fraternity restored, we talk for another hour or so in the palm-filtered sun, watching two squat ferries lazily converge from the ends of that magnificent horizon. Finn tells me how he's rarely able to enjoy quiet holiday moments like this in Norway, and not just because of the obvious environmental differences: 'You understand,' he says, regretfully circling that big, coppery face with a manicured finger to signify the burden of celebrity. In haunted tones Finn describes the fan-disrupted Nordic camping trip that was his last. Padding back to chalet P11 through the chirruping, tropical dusk to change for dinner, it's not easy to mourn the loss.

Walking back down the beach between three Norwegians three hours later, replete with chargrilled sea bass and cold Heineken, my enthusiasm for Finn Kalvik's bachelor idyll has swollen into fearsome envy. 'You know,' says Bjørn, staring up at a black sky scatter-gunned with stars, 'even after paying for the air tickets and accommodation it's still possible to stay two months here and spend less than if you'd been in Oslo.' That's something to bear in mind, and I do so after returning to P11 to do jet-lagged battle with a temperamental satellite receiver and, rather more loudly, the three geckoes resident behind my water heater.

Still, I got to lead Finn's life for seventy-two hours, and how

I still treasure the sensuous, indulgent perfection of almost all of them. The sun would wake me at a forgiving hour, working through a small gap in the curtains, and after a breakfast that like almost everything in this part of the world blended the comfortingly familiar (bacon, eggs) with the lusciously exotic (jackfruit, sugar apple), I'd amble shirtless and barefoot past groups of underemployed straw-hatted gardeners to a palm-shaded sun lounger. After an hour or so of slack-limbed, book-over-face slumber I would be joined by Finn, and we'd talk through his life and pop Chang beers until the fat sun gilded his noble, Roman-nosed visage and was slowly swallowed by a sea of orange glass. If I'd gone home a day early there would be nothing but memories of uncomplicated good times.

The Finn Kalvik story, as I heard it from him and what subsequent sources I was able to muster, begins in 1947 in Fåvang, just north of Lillehammer, in the verdant heart of the famously panoramic Gudbrandsdalen. A realm of bracing valley vistas and medieval stave churches, it's a pastoral backdrop ill-suited to the rock 'n' roll soundtrack that ran through Jahn's young head as he sauntered past Tønsberg's oil refineries and shipyards. Finn's teenage influences were correspondingly acoustic rather than electric, British folk stars Roy Harper, John Renbourne and Ralph 'Streets of London' McTell. He first picked up a guitar at sixteen, and was soon sitting on hillsides plucking out his own compositions.

It sounds idyllic, though suggestions of a darker side emerged during an online chat session Finn held recently with his fans: asked by Tanja from Bergen whether his upbringing had spawned any psychological problems, he replied enigmatically, 'Yes, you could say that.' Certainly he brusquely deflects attempts on my part to delve into his family life at this time, or at any other; all I really find out is that his father was a telegraph operator. In late adolescence Finn and his family moved to one of Oslo's dreariest suburbs, an upheaval he has described as 'traumatic'; in 1983 he paid rather a lot of money for what he still describes as his favourite picture – a vibrant, muscular landscape that encapsulated his early childhood.

At the age of nineteen Finn was up on the stage of Oslo's newly opened Dolphin folk club, a baby-faced, beardless blond conspicuous amongst the tousled beatniks. It was through the Dolphin that in 1968, Finn met and befriended Ralph McTell, the latter selling him a 1936 Martin acoustic that he still owns. A year later Finn recorded a song he'd knocked together in twenty-five minutes in his parents' kitchen, and which was to define his early career.

Finne Meg Sjæl (*To Find Myself*), an almost painfully personal outpouring of folksy teen angst, brought Finn national recognition and an enduring reputation for frail earnestness. 'This song will be on my gravestone,' he laughs as we start on our first beer of a long day. '"Mr Kalvik – he's finally found himself." I wrote it when I was seventeen, I was just thinking about school, why did I have to go there every day, what am I going to do with my life . . . ? I was so young, but this song was the biggest thing for me ever.' He talks with great pride of the day his daughter told him her class had just been asked to discuss *Finne Meg Sjæl* as part of their literature syllabus: 'Just think, it's in every schoolbook in Norway . . . "Finn Kalvik – *To Find Myself*". I haven't had an interview for the past thirty-seven years when I wasn't asked, "So have you found yourself now, Finn?"'

Within a couple of years Finn was on the road, touring southern Norway in an old Volvo with a pair of fellow Dolphin regulars. In his songwriting he had now honed a lyrical line in big-picture philosophising, advising listeners not to measure time in inches and metres, and concluding that life was a glimpse between two eternities. Yet his first album, released in 1971, was a collaboration with lyrics by venerable poetess Inger Hagerup, then sixty-six, and a woman I warmed to on discovering her responsibility for this quote: 'The honest pessimist has always done more for humanity than any prophet of glad tidings.' *Tusenfryd og grå hverdag* (*Daisy And the Daily Grind*) went top-five and stayed in the charts for the best part of a year; only now did Finn cast aside his inbuilt Scandinavian caution and consider that performing music might constitute a proper career. But even then, every Norwegian musician knew that making real money meant looking beyond their country's famously lengthy borders.

'I watched Eurovision as a kid,' he tells me, 'oh yes, in black and white. My first memory was Nora Brockstedt, singing *Voi Voi*' – he breaks off to trill the chorus, which in copybook Song Contest fashion involves endless repetitions of the title – 'and I think that was doing quite well.' (Later I unpack my pared-down Eurovision travel library in P11, and find he's spot-on: *Voi Voi*, Norway's Eurovision debut, came fourth in 1960.)

Perhaps, I wonder to myself, Finn might have done better to recall the more representative performances that followed Nora, which in four years included three second-lasts and the nation's nul-points debut. Particularly when he takes off his shades, scrunches his eyes at a distant ferry and murmurs, 'You know, that was my dream, to actually represent Norway, that was a big dream.'

It was in 1972 that Finn first went to stay in Sweden, a country with more folk singers, and more people to spend more money listening to them. A particular attraction was the annual Västervik festival, the fjord fiesta where Finn established himself as a regular, and where, in 1977, he was to meet the man who would change his life for ever. Going east had given him larger live audiences to entertain, but by 1977 Finn's record sales were going south. The three albums he'd released since the first had all sold fewer; the most recent had peaked at thirteen in Norway, troubling the chart compilers for only five weeks. He needed to change tack, to try something different, and in Benny Andersson he met a former folk singer who had done just that to Eurovision-winning, globe-conquering effect.

It isn't hard to imagine what Finn saw in Benny, who arrived at the festival by Maserati and later that year would celebrate ABBA's fifteen millionth album sale. Rather more diverting is to speculate upon what Benny saw in Finn.

By 1977 the great man had steered ABBA masterfully through almost every variation on the pop theme; most enthusiasts, myself included, wouldn't find space for anything recorded after that date in their ABBA top ten (excepting the epic collision of soul-squeezing musical pathos and movingly stilted lyrical bathos that is *The Winner Takes It All*). Perhaps he just needed a fresh challenge. Perhaps in Finn – just a few months younger than him – Benny saw what he might have been in a Eurovision-free world. Perhaps it was an opportunity to give something back to the Scandinavian folk scene, to seek solace from the pressures of global celebrity in the comforting, home-spun world of fishing-jumpered guitar-pluckers.

Either way, despite having persistently turned down the music world's greatest names begging for his Midas touch in the studio, and despite a hectic and draining touring schedule (this was the year of the Australian tour that formed the basis of *ABBA: The Movie*), Benny Andersson somehow found time to invite Finn to ABBA's Polar recording headquarters. He stayed there for four years.

Finn was at Benny's studio when a journalist phoned to tell them that Elvis had died; he was with Benny in a cab when the news of John Lennon's murder came on the radio. He had his own key for Benny's house, and his own room there; sometimes Frida (Mrs Benny, otherwise known as the dark-haired one out of ABBA) would come and pick him up from Stockholm central station in the Maserati. 'Me and Benny were close,' says Finn, 'really close.'

In the studio Benny sprinkled his fairy-dust on Finn's gently impassioned croonings, sticking a keyboard hookline here, a solo there, bringing Agnetha and Frida in to sweeten and colour the backing harmonies, mixing together a pop-folk recipe that the Scandinavian public lapped up. The first of Finn's Benny-produced albums, 'Kom ut, Kom Fram' ('Come Out, Come Forward') was released in September 1979, and stayed in the Norwegian charts until the following July. The second, 'Natt og Dag' ('Night and Day'), hit the shops in March 1981. It had already toppled John Lennon's 'Double Fantasy' from the top spot by the time Finn triumphed later that month in the Melodi Grand Prix. He did so with a song taken from 'Night and Day', one that bore Benny's imprint less deeply than some, but unmistakably showcased the vocal talents of his wife and her blonde companion. *Aldri i Livet*, you may be astonished to learn, is the closest that a post-*Waterloo* audience has ever come to seeing ABBA back on a Eurovision stage.

'I don't have a bad word about Benny,' says Finn, before offloading a great many good ones. 'He is one of the few musical geniuses I have worked with, a really brilliant man, but he never speaks about his gift and I love that.' Smiling at the horizon, Finn tells me how the bearded maestro once anonymously composed a short jingle for an ice-hockey final, and how when it came over the Tannoy the stadium spontaneously rose to its feet as one, 'like it was the national song'.

With his album at number one and ABBA's gilded fingerprints all over it, Finn wasn't surprised to be asked to enter the Melodi Grand Prix, and barely more so to win it. He even had the foresight to record an English version, anticipating international chart success in the event of a triumph in Dublin. *Here in My Heart* was graced once more with ABBA's backing vocals, but Finn was never happy with the lyrics, provided by Ralph McTell in another unsuccessful attempt to escape from those *Streets of London*. 'Ralph's a really good friend and a great songwriter, but he told me the translation had been really difficult,' he explains. Nonetheless, as Finn will tell me more than once, just after the Eurovision final *Here in My Heart* won European Pop Jury, a pan-continental radio show in which teenagers from cities across Europe voted for their favourite single of the week.

So what were Finn's lyrics about? 'It started as an instrumental,' begins Finn, stroking a thumb across his thin, sun-blistered lower lip. 'And, well, I was married at that time.' A rare reference to the partner he had set up home with in the early seventies, his first and only wife and a woman whose identity I am not alone in failing to unearth. 'In the words, I'm saying I will never leave you in my life, and . . .' He snorts, and the snort becomes a chortle, and I watch with interest, and then some alarm, as Finn hurls back his head at the palm trees above and laughs and laughs and laughs. He hasn't laughed like this before, and in the two days ahead he won't again. 'I'm sorry,' he says, his voice still unsteady with merriment, 'but it's because for the whole of Europe I swore that I'm never going to leave you, baby, and here I am, having such a good time alone, and I haven't spoken to her for twenty-two years! That's *really funny*, you know! You swear to one billion people you're never going to leave your wife, and . . . I'm going to get another beer!'

While he's away I check the cans of Chang beer we've both just finished – 6.4 per cent, I note with a gawp, and pledge not to refresh myself further until the sun has settled into that big flat sea.

Finn returns, wiping his forehead with Chang-can condensation. 'Yeah, expectations in Norway were *really huge* for this song because of the ABBA connection, but . . .' A diffident wrinkle of that long nose. Surely, I say, winning the Melodi is a highlight of any Norwegian musician's career. 'Not mine!' he barks with feeling. 'No, no, no! I wasn't even sure I wanted to enter. I had a long discussion with Benny, and he said, well, it's up to you. He's a really great guy.' Having sold the thick end of 100,000 albums in Sweden, perhaps Finn wasn't possessed by the desperate urge to pursue Eurovision success as a means of breaking out of the Norwegian market. Or perhaps he's just forgotten that a couple of hours ago he was telling me how singing for Norway at the Eurovision was his greatest childhood dream.

'You know, I never really thought about what winning the Melodi meant. Then Ralph McTell said to me, "This is such a huge honour for you, representing your country like this."' His apparent reluctance melted further on the Monday after his Melodi triumph: on that day alone, 25,000 copies of *Aldri i Livet* were sold. 'It's funny,' he says, 'to think that this song was my biggest hit in Norway.' (It peaked at number three, defeated by the mighty axis of *Imagine* and *Shaddap You Face*.)

I'm beginning to suspect that Finn's reminiscences of his Eurovision experience are likely to be rather less fondly relayed than Jahn's. 'So,' I prompt, in a rather nervous whisper, 'you're, um, you're in Dublin, and, ah . . .' It's a profound relief to hear Finn's tone lighten. 'Yeah! It was funny – I was with my friend who was singing for Sweden [ah: Björn Skifs, the tail-coated rocker] and his band, and we had a police escort to our hotel. And then all this Irish coffee! It was eleven thirty in the morning, and people were drunk!'

The days up to the final were occupied with rehearsals and publicity commitments. 'All these big parties,' recalls Finn, 'with a lot of smoking around me.' Every other Eurovision artist I am to meet will inhale burning tobacco fumes with almost desperate efficiency; Finn, as he tells me proudly, has never once put a cigarette to his lips. 'I had some trouble with my larynx because of these parties, and there was a big panic in the newspapers at home: "Finn has lost his voice"!' He gathers himself with a throat-bobbing slug of Chang. 'But you know, it was in the air that we could do well, because I was working with ABBA and all that. Yes, it was in the air.' The tiny, rueful smile that now gently creases his big brown face is the last I'll see for some time.

I'd long been intrigued by Finn's stage outfit, in its way as controversial as that which had inspired the NRK's director to splutter threats in Jahn's face three years earlier. Braces aside, I know which one I'd rather have worn. But despite the conspicuously 'street' dimpled-rubber sandally-plimsoll things he wears to our evening beach dinners, Finn remains an anti-fashion folkist at heart. 'Oh, this shirt was one from my local ice-hockey team,' he sighs, without interest. 'And the scarf . . . I don't know. Benny and I wore scarves when we were hanging out in Stockholm nightclubs together.' Whatever other reasons he'll give for *Aldri i Livet*'s implosive failure, aesthetics won't be among them.

So there's Finn backstage in Dublin; Björn Skifs strides breathlessly in, perhaps pulling his sweaty lurex gloves off as he does so, and it's over to Vienna for the results of the Austrian jury. 'After six or seven countries have voted, I look at my chorus, my choir, and one of them looks back and says, "You have to hope now you don't get any points, Finn, it's better to get nothing than so small points." This was Anita Skorgan, who was with Jahn at the time.' A woman who knew the no-score.

I can feel our conversation slipping into a deep, black hole, but hearing these names animates my sombre, sympathetic visage into tickled delight. Anita! I'd thought there was something familiar about one of the girls leaning over the canal bridge in Norway's introductory filmette. What an astounding one-couple Eurovision industry those two were: together or separately, they represented Norway in all but one of the seven finals from 1977–84.

'I did not understand her position at all,' says Finn slowly, and thus chastened, I settle back into gentle, prompting nods. Admirable as Jahn's zero-hugging defiance surely is, most of us would surely empathise more with the weary, bitter scowl the man beside me now aims out to sea.

'It wasn't me up there on the scoreboard,' he mumbles. 'It wasn't "Finn Kalvik zero points", it was the country's name.' Did that help? I ask, wondering how it possibly could have. But Finn is now blankly surveying the tiny crabs that scuttle along the damp, dark sand at the sea's lapping edge. He's miles away, in time and space, back in the Royal Dublin Society's green room, twenty-four years ago. As I feared it might when we got to this point, the warm intimacy of those first hours is receding a lot faster than the tide.

'Actually you know there were three zeroes to look at,' he says, his sing-song Scandinavian delivery settling into a monotone. 'If you had 119 points it was 1,1,9 on the scoreboard, and we just had 0,0,0. One of my roadies said when he saw me, "Here he is – agent double-0 zero."' The battle to purge from my face the visible signs of amusement is short and inglorious. 'Yes, double-O zero, licensed to sing,' says Finn, casting a mirthless glance at me as the titters fade. 'I have myself made that joke.'

But your song wasn't the worst, I say after a recuperative pause, and, as I had with Jahn, do so with utter sincerity. 'Maybe. I have forgotten the others.' And indeed he has. He goes on to refer to the victors as 'Gin Fizz', and even after I gently correct him he thereafter opts – rather winningly – for 'The Fizz'. He thinks Johnny Logan was Ireland's entrant, when he wasn't. The only rival he can recall by name, or even by tune, is Björn Skifs.

Yet he has seen the contest on video since, and more than once. 'The first time I watch the tape, I hear the technician forgot to put on my guitar – on the first verse it's just me singing a cappella, *no guitar*!' He nods significantly before going on to dissect his performance in surprising detail: Finn's autopsy report is the most complete I will hear from any nul-pointer.

'My songs are the kind of songs that you have to listen to many times,' he says, 'and the more times you listen to them the more they grow.' This was certainly something I'd experienced – a month after first hearing it, *Aldri i Livet* was now a regular in my head, its melody emerging through pursed lips many times a day. Clearly, though, to embed a tune with delayed catchiness is to shut the Eurovision door long after the votes have bolted. You have three minutes to make an impression on eyes and ears, and Finn accepts he managed neither (though hearing him describe 1981 as 'the glitter time' I'm quite glad he didn't try too hard with the former). 'ABBA had these big shoes and Björn's guitar shaped like a star, it was very visual, that was the setting for Eurovision, but I was just sitting there in a chair with my guitar, like at my concerts . . .' On he goes, identifying and analysing in great technical detail the low-key aspects of the song and its rendition, eventually bringing these all together in a vocal parody that reduces *Aldri i Livet* to a funereal, Gregorian dirge.

I'd imagined that the problem would be getting Finn to start talking about that night in Dublin. For the moment I'm having trouble getting him to stop. 'When The Fizz were doing their winner song, I was standing behind this huge scene wall,' he continues, resolving the mystery of his whereabouts during the mass wave-to-the-camera reprise that brought every other performer back out on-stage. 'I never forgot this moment, I was alone there, and I guess I felt humiliated, really small . . . because of course I also had this dream, a dream about . . . about . . .'

Oh, Finn. I'd never imagined that a big Norwegian in mirrored shades lying on a beach with a beer in his hand could ever look vulnerable, but the cracked, fragile sigh he now releases isn't easy to endure. His doughty nonchalance is crumbling; that elephant in the room is now loose on our beach, and looking for a head to sit on.

'There was a party after, and I got a little drunk. A lot of people did. I thought Stig Anderson might come and pat me on the head and say never mind, but he took it real personal, he was really humiliated.' It's the first time he's mentioned ABBA's famously domineering manager, a svengali so ruthless that when he drank himself to death in 1997, Agnetha boycotted the funeral. 'Because, you know, a guy from out of the ABBA stable got zero points . . . he was *really angry* with me, shouting, "Why did you pick that song? It was too slow, I told you not to pick that song." There's a picture I've got at home of Stig standing with his fist in my stomach.'

Humiliation, assault – can it get any worse? Surveying the nul-points experience through the Teigen kaleidoscope, its sombre shadows diffracted into a whirl of colourful tomfoolery, I'd naively allowed myself to anticipate hearing many more tales of triumph over Eurovision adversity. But this was a trip to a majestically daft insitution's dark side.

Jahn afforded *Mil Etter Mil* a joyous and very public wake; registering the frail intensity of Finn's diction and bearing, I feel I'm intruding on private grief. If this was happening in Oslo, I'd probably have switched the recorder off by now, placed an understanding, apologetic hand on Finn's shoulder and gone home. But here I am, on a small island halfway round the world, with a very expensive plane ticket that tells me I'm not leaving for two more days. Another sympathetic nod will have to do.

'Afterwards I went to sleep OK. It only really hit me in the morning, when I saw all the voting charts in the papers. I must say that I didn't feel too well at the airport. I felt that everybody was looking at me, I felt like a loser. So on the plane from Dublin I got a little drunk again.'

Bjørn and Sissel wander up at this point, get the drift of what's being said and swiftly wander off again. With slight envy I watch as they shuffle around outside their bungalow, shaking sand out of sandals, hanging up towels, going about their slow-paced holiday pottering.

By opting to catch a flight to Stockholm rather than Oslo, Finn made what has to be considered a tactical error. Going straight back to Norway, Jahn did what every Eurovision watcher expected: we'd faced the music, and now it was his turn. He went home with his head held high, and his countrymen loved him for it. But Finn instead sought solace in the bosom of his homeland's neighbouring foe.

'The newspapers said I was hiding, that I didn't dare to come home. No one could get in touch with me. But it had been set for many months. I was there to rehearse with my new band – I was going on tour with a band for the first time, and I needed time to prepare. In fact, I was staying with Åse Kleveland's husband in his artist studio.' Once again I marvel at the tininess of Scandinavian society. But would he still have bought that ticket to Stockholm had he won? 'I was away like a week, two weeks . . .' He waves a dismissive hand about, then sits up suddenly on his sun lounger and turns to me, abruptly re-energised. 'You know, I talked to Benny about what happened, and he just laughed his head off! He's such a great guy – he arranged the song and all, but he could still have a big laugh about it!'

It's becoming difficult to avoid concluding that ABBA were Finn's family at this point, and Sweden his homeland: he's made no mention of how his wife, parents and countrymen in general reacted to his experience. 'I had letters from little girls in Norway, ten or eleven years,' is all he says when I tentatively broach this issue. 'They were saying they cried to see me get no points.'

In the light of Jahn's repeated outbursts about 'the bully big brother', an awkward question needs to be asked here, and figuring there isn't going to be a better time, I ask it. Didn't his countrymen hold it against him for living and working in the land of their natural enemy, for fraternising with them in international competition, and running into their arms for comfort afterwards? To Norwegians, he must have seemed like one of the 184 who 100 years before had voted against independence from Sweden.

'The brotherhood among Scandinavians is gone,' he concedes, with some reluctance; arresting words from a Swedish-based Norwegian named Finn. 'Even when I sort of rolled a six with Benny, and had great reviews and sales, I could never win any songwriting award in Norway because I was recording with Swedish musicians.' And indeed singing their language: in another of the online interrogations Finn regularly submits to, he was roundly castigated for abandoning his mother tongue in favour of Benny's during his years in the ABBA stable. His response is brusque. 'OK, but I never sing in English! At least, I never write in English. You know, in Dublin I was drowned in there, between the Irish song and The Fizz. The home country and the winner: both in English! My experience proved that the language had a lot to do with it. England was winning the whole time then, every second year.' There is no point, I'm learning, in trying to steer a Norwegian away from this grievously pejorative summation of the British Isles – all I can do is urge those planning to open their mouths never to visit Glasgow.

Finn is a patriot, he insists, but one of a very different breed to Jahn. For him it's more cultural, less visceral, the emphasis on art and landscape, not bloodshed and nose-thumbing regional rivalry. 'I am proud of my country, and my countryside, but come to Norway on 17 May, our national day, and you will understand that there is a lot of . . . *chauvinism*.' His weary tut suggests he's diplomatically foregone the *mot juste*. 'When I was a teenager I never felt comfortable on 17 May. These days I love to celebrate it, but then to make a sort of protest I used to go with a friend up to the forest with a case of beer. I get embarrassed to think of it now, but we would get drunk watching all these stupid people doing their parades.'

Yet, those Benny-led albums aside, Finn's most enduring works are the words of Norwegian poets put to his music. He stresses again that performers who ignore the whims of domestic culture do so at their peril. 'Some bands and singers have huge hits in Norwegian, and then they do something in English, and nothing happens with it. *Nothing*. Norway is such a small country . . . one should be aware of changing things like this. You could lose everybody.' There must have been times when Finn thought he had. Even today, most of the Finn-fan sites on the net are Swedish.

By the time he returned home from Sweden, 'Night and Day' was no longer number one, and within a month it had plummeted out of the top forty. For a record whose pre-Eurovision sales would make it the year's second highest-selling album (after Chris de Burgh's 'Eastern Wind'), such a precipitous slump was bewildering.

Finn returned to Polar Studios to record the follow up, but this time the twinkle-eyed beardy wasn't there behind the mixing desk. Despite his enduring loyalty to Benny, it's hard to imagine there was no connection between events in Dublin and the ABBA man's absence from the studio.

'It's weird that *Aldri i Livet* failed to achieve any points at all,' writes an online ABBA authority, 'but the weirdest thing is that this fact is completely ignored in any ABBA-book that relates to their outside productions for other Polar acts . . . I wonder if Benny himself was disappointed about this?' Splendid chap that Benny Andersson is widely acknowledged to be, he's also a hard-driven perfectionist. After six years of worldwide number ones, ABBA singles were now peaking lower and lower; if Benny had been worried that his touch was deserting him, the last person he'd have wanted in his studio was a card-carrying nul-pointer, the embodiment of his lowest ebb as a producer. Almost twenty years would pass before their professional paths crossed for a final time, when Benny allowed Finn to add vocals to an instrumental rather poignantly entitled *The Comfort Song*. Later, when I ask if the two are still in touch, Finn brightly replies, 'Well, I call him on the phone, and I always send him my new records.'

The album was, by common consent, a disaster. 'We worked really hard to make it sound like a Benny Andersson production, but of course we failed. It's the only record I have buried: I don't do one single song from this album live today.' It touched number thirteen, then disappeared. Finn was swiftly dropped by Polar; shunned by his adopted homeland, he found few friends waiting for him back in the old country. 'Some of my fans, who remembered me as a folk singer, were really giving me a hard time.' Few things in music are guaranteed to attract vitriol more magnetically than bad commercial pop-rock. Fiercely criticised for crass, desperate commercialism, he even found himself lampooned by newspaper cartoonists: Finn has been known to bracket himself with Bob Dylan, and there were at least faint parallels here with the 'Bob goes electric' furore of 1965.

'You know, I felt pretty bad about myself for a long time,' says Finn of this period. I have to remind myself he was thirty-four when he set off for Dublin, and had already endured and bounced back from career disappointments. But he doesn't seem to feel that age and experience softened the blow, instead pointing out that as his own composer, he bore a heavier burden than Jahn (and, as it transpires, every one of my other nul-pointers). The rest would always be able to point fingers, to share the blame; with history's most gifted pop maestro the only other name on *Aldri i Livet*'s label, this was never an option for Finn. 'The good part of this,' he says, bracingly, 'is that exactly because I was responsible for my own songs, it meant I could change my direction.'

The change was a U-turn. 'Working with Benny I was maybe thinking too much about refrains and catchy melodies.' After releasing a Benny-less album along these lines, Finn retreated to his folksome musical roots. 'Now I'm back to where I started. I'm a picker, a guitar picker. All the pop-rock songs I did with Benny that were hits, they're not what people want now. I'm famous for my picking tunes, my ballads. I'm a low-key guy.'

I will soon discover the dramatic extent to which this is not so. Certainly there's a jarring contrast between Finn's personal and professional lives at this time: in the studio he was putting nursery rhymes to music for an album entitled 'Little Parsley', then he'd step outside into a world of Gothic chaos. In April 1983, Finn's wife gave birth to their daughter, Malene; before she was walking her father had left. Twenty-two years on, she has yet to see her parents together in the same room. 'Divorce isn't a defeat,' he told an interviewer. 'It's an opportunity for freedom.'

Finn does not deny embracing this opportunity. 'There were a lot of women after that,' he says, a little smugly, 'and a lot of fast cars.' Though he'll complain bitterly at the financial cost of divorce, at this point there was still a lot of cash in the Kalvik bank from the 200,000 albums he'd sold during the Benny era. 'I lost my licence three times. Everything was a little wild.'

It was about now that Finn developed an extraordinary fixation with Ernest Hemingway (later, he spent a year or two modelling himself on Mel Gibson). 'I've read some of his books, but it's the way he lived that I love, travelling the world, doing adventures . . . you know, he would drink champagne at six in the morning and then write, and he did this for years! What a guy! Don't do it your way, do it the Hemingway!'

For a great many years Finn endeavoured to do just that. He started training with Norway's flyweight champion, and wound up sparring in his gym four times a week for seven years. He went out hunting. It's tempting – too tempting for me – to conclude that having killed off the music that brought about his downfall in Dublin, he now sought to kill off the high-voiced, slightly simpering fellow who'd sung it. But with tragic predictability, his experiment in macho pomposity ended with a bang, then a whimper: in Africa on a hunting safari, Finn's eardrums were blown out when the guy behind let loose an old Winchester. 'Now I have this tinnitus,' he says, tapping the side of his bleached and burnished head, 'like a Niagara Falls all the time.'

The horrors of this exasperating condition are brought to my attention that evening, as the four of us are rounding off another piquant, aromatic extravaganza under the stars. One of the young Germans dining at the next table wanders halfway to the sea, crouches down to wedge something in the sand, then pelts back as a pyrotechnic whoosh soars skyward.

'Ah, no, no!' cries Finn as the ensuing blast shatters the

bay's silence, clamping both hands to the sides of his head. An agonised wince annexes his features until we rise to leave; Finn doesn't speak during the short walk back to our chalets, and when I bid him goodnight from P11's mesh-doored threshold, all he can muster is a hoarse whisper.

As young Gob clears away the pawpaw skins and bacon rind of my penultimate Big John breakfast, I look down to the beach and see Finn prone on the now established interviewee's sun lounger. Walking down to join him, I slowly release a long sigh that attempts to bridge the widening void between the uncomplicated hedonism that should define Finn's life out here, and its flawed and troubled reality. 'I've always been working towards total freedom,' he'd said on our first afternoon. At the time, looking up and down the unpeopled, palm-fringed sand, I'd thought: Well, you're there, mate. But now I knew he wasn't.

It was in 1986 that, in his significant words, Finn 'started to run away from the country in the winter'. 'Every 20 December, the radio stations pay musicians for all the times they have played their songs that year, and I got this huge cheque, like an early Christmas present. I had no gigs in January, and only one in February, so I cancelled it and went to Lanzarote for the whole winter.'

While there he wrote *Malene*, a song dedicated to his three-year-old daughter, and which was to be his entry in the 1987 Melodi Grand Prix. (With multiple MGP entries almost compulsory for Norwegian artistes, Finn always knew he'd have to stick in another token effort sometime: 'I came fourth. Not first, not last – I was very happy.') 'I was getting on the aeroplane home every four or five weeks to see her. I think I've been a good father. Yes, I think so.'

As a divorced dad, Finn has generally managed to cultivate a guilt-free 'opportunity for freedom'. These days he dedicates *Aldri i Livet* to his daughter, and cites his favourite song as Don Henley's *The End of the Innocence*, helpfully encapsulated for me by an online authority as 'a first-person account of a young child watching his parents go through divorce'. 'When my daughter was twelve or thirteen, I was travelling all around Australia, and these islands' – Finn jabs a thumb at the hot sand beneath us – 'and so I bought a fax machine for her, so we could send each other drawings and stories. She loved that.' I nod, encouragingly.

All the time, though, his musical career was in steady decline. 'You always have a lot of ideas when you start as a songwriter, but then with one record after another you are running out and it's really hard work.' He sighs, heavy eyed, and of course he's hardly alone in discovering this uncomfortable truth. By 1987, after all, Finn had been recording for eighteen years, a shelf-life well beyond the sales span of most artists. Now forty, he took the path taken by many guitar-based songwriters desperate for an injection of creativity, and learnt to play the piano. When that didn't work, he bowed to the inevitable and released a greatest-hits album. This stayed three weeks in the top thirty compiled by Norway's largest newspaper, *VG*, two more than his studio follow-up managed in 1995. A lonely stump on their archived bar chart, it slipped in at number twenty-nine, then slipped straight out.

The year after, 'totally pissed off' with music, he took up painting. 'My career has been like my private life, filled with ups and downs. After my first single in 1969, nothing happened for a while; I was only twenty-two, and it looked like my career was finished, so I went to lessons to learn how to teach guitar. So when thirty years later I was fed up with music because I felt that I was just repeating myself artistically, it was easy to think: Now I need something different.' His father had been a keen amateur painter – 'I was brought up with the smell of turpentine,' he tells me – and in his early Oslo folk days, Finn had proved himself at the easel. 'I spent some time at art school, and I always liked artists – that guy in Sweden I stayed with after Dublin, he was like a father figure.' Asked by a Norwegian cultural publication to rate his interest in art, he replied: 'Eight out of ten – I love it!'

He says the intention was to paint for a living, though I'm not able to find out how many paintings he's sold, nor for how much. But over ten years he's certainly worked his way through an impressive range of topics and techniques, from an epic portrait of former Norwegian national football manager Egil 'Drillo' Olsen, depicted as a king on a hilltop, to a series of erotic paintings 'that I'm not so proud of now – I've hidden them away'. 'What I know about is music and women,' he told an Oslo journalist at the opening of his late-nineties exhibition, *Six Erotic Oils*. 'As a bachelor I have pictures in the bedroom that are not really pornographic, but definitely sexy.'

When I get home I uncover a gallery of Finn's art on his website. He's good: there's a technical proficiency that the cack-handed biro-doodlers amongst us can only dream of. Of the eighteen on display, most are oil on canvas; some have been created using his latest technique, painting with oils over a gel-treated photograph. But it's the subject matter that's most striking. Flesh-flaunting nudes aside, the two that catch the eye most compellingly lie side by side in the bottom row of thumbnails. One, entitled *The Nightwatchman*, shows a sour-faced woman in her underwear, toting a hefty rolling pin with accusatory menace. Next along, two hands extending from opposite ends of the canvas are joined at the wrist by police cuffs. One is delicately female, dangling lifelessly from its manacle. Its sinewed male counterpart is clasped tightly around a large revolver, finger on trigger, pointing straight down at whoever the other hand is attached to. The hammer is depressed; a small wisp of smoke rises from the tip of the barrel. This painting's title: *The Divorce Judgement*.

The late nineties might not have been the happiest time in Finn's troubled post-Eurovision life, but it was at least settled. By 1998 it had been three years since he swapped the recording studio for its paint-based cousin; what he produced there might not have been keeping him in the manner to which he had once been accustomed, but producing it endowed Finn a quiet professional satisfaction that he hadn't known for years. Then, walking home in Oslo one Saturday night, he found himself surrounded by a group of drunken youths. 'They asked if I was Finn Kalvik,' he tells me, slowly bunching a fist, 'and then they roar with laughter. Five, six, seven young people, drinking, and they all laugh in my face.' More so even than the childhood of the Baudelaire siblings, the story of Finn Kalvik's middle years is a series of unfortunate events. The latest, longest and most tragic chapter had just begun.

As I was aware from contact with the Melodi Grand Prix, it would be a challenge to categorise Norwegian state broadcasters NRK as reckless boundary-breakers. Nor, with apologies to Jahn and his surrealist collaborators, would one anticipate finding the nation's wellspring of humour dispensing a rancid tide of filth and controversy. Imagine a representative NRK comedy, then, and you might expect to watch a blond Mr Bean going about his gently hapless Nordic business, slipping headfirst into a vat of pickled seal flippers or knocking pigtailed milkmaids off their stools with his ladder-handling ineptitude.

For reasons that have yet to be satisfactorily explained to me, you would be terribly, terribly wrong. Here is a précis of comedian Otto Jespersen's monologue during a 2002 edition of NRK's weekly satire, *Torsdagsklubben*: 'Having ridiculed Prime Minister Bondevik at length, Jespersen finished off by encouraging "all good forces" to invite Christer Pettersson, a suspect in the murder of Swedish Prime Minister Olof Palme, to visit Oslo.' And here is an account of fellow NRK comedian Kristopher Schau's activities at an 'entertainment show' in Kristiansand in 2003: 'On Wednesday, Schau attached an outboard motor to a dead pig and used it as a boat. On Thursday he set light to the pig, and inflated rats and hamsters with helium to make "organic balloons", which ruptured above the audience. On Friday, a young couple he had invited on-stage pulled off their clothes and had full intercourse, as Schau unfurled a banner informing the audience that they were having sex to save the rainforest.'

Commissioned in 1998, the thrice-weekly NRK sketch show *Åpen Post* (*Open Mail*) was muted in comparison. Yes, there were complaints when one of the resident satirists dressed as a chicken to disrupt a rival channel's live report on a hospitalised politician's state of health. But Angry of Stavanger didn't pick up the phone when another comedian appeared in a jerry-built shrine manically decorated with photocopied images of a grinning, youthful folk singer, and in a wandering, loner-obsessive stutter delivered 'Finn Kalvik-nyhetene', the Finn Kalvik News.

'The joke they had is that there is no news about me,' says Finn, sounding at this stage only wearily offended, like a bald teacher finding his class giggling around an unkind exercise-book caricature. 'They have this brain-damaged guy talking about what was new in my life, but after a few seconds he would have a nosebleed, or faint, or maybe puke.' My sympathetic nod falters, then resumes with manic intensity. 'One of the guys who wrote it told me later they picked on me because of my up-and-down career. Because I was the perfect loser.'

Åpen Post's creators intended the Finn Kalvik News as a one-off, but, as the butt of its one joke informs me, 'people laughed so much they said they had to continue it'. The sketch became a regular highlight, a centrepiece of a show that swiftly graduated from cult hit to ratings smash. One critic called it 'the funniest TV programme in Norway for over two decades'; at the end of 1998 *Åpen Post* was voted comedy show of the year (the actor who accepted the prize dedicated it to Finn).

'Jesus! I mean, it was *so many years later*! A whole new generation were laughing at me – a generation who had no connection with my music at all,' says Finn, his voice now thickening in a manner that discourages flippant analysis of this latter statement. 'Three times every week for three months, and then after a few more months they reprised everything once again for another three months . . . And all these young drunk people laughing at me at bus stops. Sometimes twenty of them.' He pops open another Chang, and though it's a little early for me, and perhaps 28 degrees in the palm-tree shade, so do I. Something about the way this story is going, and in particular about the way Finn is telling it, persuades me that in the hours ahead I'll be needing as much 6.4 per cent alcohol as I can get down my hot neck.

I take a healthy slug when Finn tells me the show left him needing psychological help, and almost down the remains in one during the revelation that it drove him to contemplate suicide. 'These guys nearly killed me. They *nearly killed me*. It was so close you wouldn't believe it! One of the psychologists I was seeing gave me his home number, because I was so near the edge, and he said if you feel like jumping off the edge you have to call me. When somebody tries to take away something you have built for twenty-five years, and just for these idiots to have some fun on TV . . .'

My nodding winds down – I'll wake up the next day with a slight repetitive-strain ache in the neck – and I just sit there in cowed silence, tracing a finger blankly up and down the Chang-can condensation. Shielded by his reflective shades, Finn's gaze is angled right out at the horizon. 'Why do these things happen to me?' he says, tonelessly.

All Finn can suggest himself is that as a man and musician, he's just too honest, too earnest. 'I sing about emotion and feelings and loneliness,' he'll tell me later, 'and maybe those subjects are just too serious for some people.' There's certainly something in that. 'Anything I write about,' he told a fan online, 'I must have experienced myself.' Inevitable, then, that he just can't stop baring his soul and detailing the inner woes that Jahn so efficiently buried or glossed over.

'When you write a song from the bottom of your heart, you don't know what effect it's going to have on people when it gets out there,' he'd said on our first afternoon. Sometimes they will write to him in humbled gratitude – Finn recently received a letter 'from a lady in Trondheim who woke up one morning and was paralysed, then her husband left her, and she listened to my songs and it saved her life, got her back on her feet.' But sometimes they will stand around drunk at bus stops and laugh in his face. You can go to Eurovision and sing about love, or you can go to a folk festival and sing about life as a glimpse between two eternities. Trying to do both, it would seem, is a high-risk strategy. 'Thank you,' replied one online Finn-fan, 'particularly for your openness about the panic attacks you suffer.'

The calm heads around Finn offered wise counsel. 'I had

another really great psychologist, who died last year, and he said: the smartest thing is not to threaten, not to complain. So I never did those things.' In fact, in a pattern with which I was now becoming familiar, he proceeded to do them all. A moment later, describing his determination 'to fight back', he reveals how when *Åpen Post* was being prepared for a DVD release, he had his lawyers 'write a letter saying if they don't cut out the parts about me, we're going to sue them for many millions'. The anthology was duly released in an expurgated form, causing a DVD review site to protest that 'the only pity is to find the Finn Kalvik News taken away'.

As I discover later, throughout all this he was giving umpteen interviews to the national press, detailing his grievances in unwise detail. 'The joke is that I do nothing,' he told one journalist, 'but in fact I am very busy. I work ten to twelve hours a day!' 'These guys in *Åpen Post* bullied me,' he complained to *VG*. 'My songs are on the school syllabus, I get standing ovations at my concerts, and I sold 240,000 records from 1979 to 1981, so I know that people value what I do. These guys didn't accept what they were doing to my self-esteem, both as an artist and a human being. So I had a very difficult emotional struggle inside. It was difficult just to be me.' At the end of *Åpen Post*'s first series he told the papers he was planning to leave Norway, relocating to a country where 'artists were respected and valued'. When he lifts his shades to survey the maritime distance once more, I see in those sun-scrunched eyes the lonely glaze of a shipwrecked Crusoe.

From Finn's viewpoint, I can all too easily understand the difficulties of maintaining a dignified silence. After Dublin, there had been no one to fight back against, no redress procedure. But this time, the instigators of his humiliation were right there before him, re-humiliating him three times a week on national TV. What undermined Finn's spirited defence of himself, and rendered it in the truest sense pitiful, was the personal fragility that persistently fractured his defences. Sometimes his brave face would crumple in the course of a paragraph. 'It will take more than these two guys to sink me!' he'd bluster to an interviewer.

'I have balls of steel!' And then, in a protracted whimper about bus-stop sniggering, they'd soften into balls of porridge.

Of all the counter-measures Finn employed, none was bolder – or more foolhardy – than his demand for the right to reply. Duly paired with the show's co-creators, Harald Eia and Bård Tufte Johansen, on an NRK talk show, Finn presented the country with an agonising televisual ordeal. 'You have no idea how much I have wept because of you and your friends,' he told Johansen, after the comic had apologised 'for going too far' and offered a handshake. 'I told him people were laughing at me in the street, that I was suicidal,' he tells me, 'and he looked so shocked, completely wiped off the planet – these guys, I was their idol when they were twelve. I know they have my records at home.' I'm relieved to deduce, from their dates of birth and Finn's sales history, that this is at least statistically probable.

His retaliatory offensive reached an improbable zenith when Finn phoned the newspapers to announce that an Oslo gangland boss had offered to have the *Åpen Post* boys 'taken care of'. 'I had been singing in a lot of prisons,' he tells me, 'and one night I was in a nightclub, and this guy I recognised from prison came and said, "Fuck it, Finn, if you want, we can . . . *stop this.* You understand?" That's how pissed off my generation was with these guys. When I cracked that story it was on the front page. I only had to give the guy an OK, and those two comedians would end up in hospital with a lot of broken bones!' Finn lets out a bark of harsh, counterfeit laughter. 'But I said no. I'm a good guy,' he says, clanking the Kalvikworld emotional rollercoaster up to another summit. 'A good guy . . . *and a boxer with many years' experience.*' (Eia and Johansen later denied finding the threats anything other than hilarious.)

It's easy to criticise Finn's tactics from a PR viewpoint. He admits as much when confessing that as well as the wise psychiatrist, 'many, many friends told me to let the whole thing go'. Addressing Finn during an internet chat, a fan said 'maybe you should have tackled the *Åpen Post* situation differently, and taken it for what it was – an innocent joke!' And I sometimes find myself wondering about all those interviews he gave, all those calls to the papers about his Oslo underworld friends. Was there perhaps a part of him that revelled in the media coverage, that after years in the dark felt compelled to follow the spotlight, painfully glaring as it was?

Either way, it would take a far better man than I to turn the other cheek three times a week for six months. Particularly if he's seen the Finn Kalvik News, which I'm happy to describe, on the basis of a thirty-second clip that I didn't understand, as totally unfunny, largely due to its comic reliance on the presenter's cognitive handicaps.

What's more awkward is the revelation, or at least the consistent claim, that the *Åpen Post* producers sought and received Finn's prior approval for the Finn Kalvik News. They've also insisted that he appeared in one of the sketches voluntarily, and found it amusing. A media commentator presents a more credible analysis of events with his view that 'Kalvik certainly had no idea what he had agreed to'.

'That was the worst time for me, ever, but I got apologies and now I'm back on my feet.' I can see his well-defined jaw tighten. 'It's all over,' he says, in a slightly automatic tone that suggests a prescribed therapy mantra. 'It's all over.'

It is, I say quickly, of course it is, and rather clunkily fast-forward our reminiscences to what I know to be a happier present. After his four-year artistic interlude Finn returned to the recording studio, and plotting the chart-course of the albums released thereafter I'd been heartened to discover a renaissance. 'Three years ago I went to Prague, and recorded my greatest hits with the symphony orchestra there,' he says, instantly brightening. '"Klassisk Kalvik", we called it, and it went platinum – amazing! We're working on "Klassisk Kalvik 2" now. And my last album of new songs came out last year, and was in the chart for more than three months.' "Dagdrivernotater" (Daydrifter Notes) took Finn's career album sales past the million mark (and, as I calculate later, comfortably outperformed Jahn's most recent release).

Settling back into his lounger, Finn briefly describes a recent trip to the States, one that had incorporated a three-week

Harley-Davidson ride from California to Chicago. 'Anyway,' he says, 'at the airport in LA the customs guy is going through all my motorbike stuff and he asks what I'm doing, and when I tell him he says, "Mister, I wish I had your life."' I return his broad smile: after the drawn-out miseries of our *Åpen Post*-mortem, this is so much more fun to sit on a beach and listen to. 'But I never forget who gave me all this,' he says, his suddenly sombre, dignified expression suggesting I'm about to hear of an evangelical awakening on the I-80 out of Des Moines. 'I always thank my audience after my concerts for giving me such a good life, even for keeping me alive. Most artists don't do that. I'm very thankful, very grateful. You must remember this, always be humble.'

Afterwards I don't know whether to blame the heat, or the Chang, or both mixed up with those terrible spasms of jet lag that are still inciting acts of conspicuous physical and mental clumsiness. Whatever it is, over the course of the afternoon I somehow contrive to demolish the rapport I have painstakingly built up with this damaged, fragile fellow.

In a rambling and rhetorical exploration of Finn's recovery, I find myself exhuming the corpse of *Åpen Post*, declaiming the satisfaction he must feel that in the three years since the show went off the air, Finn Kalvik has just released his fourteenth, fifteenth and sixteenth albums. The joke may have been on him, I suggest, but he's still savouring the last laugh. Finn wearily extrudes a hollow chortle. 'Yeah, well, those guys are still all over TV.' (After I get home I look up Harald Eia's CV, and discover that he recently attracted attention when, during a sex-education parody on NRK, 'Eia discussed and physically explored the area of skin between his anus and scrotum'.) 'But why are we talking about this thing again?' Finn looks pained and confused. 'It's coming back, and I feel really shitty.' So of course do I, for jemmying open that well-stocked Pandora's box of buried memories and forcing his face inside.

Agonisingly, every time I try to lighten the tone, change the subject, move things along, something snags and we end up back in Dublin. I imagine he'll have been wryly amused by

Jahn's and Tor Endresen's decision to compete in the Melodi once again, but as his face screws up in confused disgust it's clear both that this news has not previously reached the Gulf of Thailand, and that Finn is anything but happy to hear it.

'Oh, if you've been really badly burnt, you don't try again! When I came fourth at the Melodi in 1987, I got rid of the zeroes and then I was finished with it, once and for all. I was asked this year to do a Eurosong for Sweden but I said no. I would *never, ever* do Melodi again! Never!'

Finn frets over the revelation of Jahn and Tor's Melodi return on and off for the next few hours, muttering about people who never learn, about the contest's decline in recent years. 'Last time I saw the Melodi there was a beautiful lady, very sexy, but she cannot sing in tune, not hitting one note . . . this competition is going to take her nowhere. And I don't watch Eurovision any more. The orchestra went, everybody is recorded, and then a lady from Russia runs out in a wolf skin and does a war dance. I say: "OK, this is the end for me!"'

Anyone familiar with the contest's burgeoning emphasis on glitzy showmanship in recent years is hardly about to disagree with this verdict, but Finn is no longer placated by my increasingly desperate nods and smiles of assent. 'And what does Europe mean? I'm a world citizen, not a European.' He's not sure he's ever even been to Germany, he says, and would certainly identify more with an American than a Spaniard. His words reedy and rapid, he recounts with great gusto the finer details of his Harley-Davidson odyssey.

I'm in the middle of articulating an impressed response when he's off again. 'I just can't understand why those two are doing it again! Anyway, I don't belong there, I don't believe in people voting for songs. I don't need these telephoning votes to prove to me how important my songs are. Not to be big-headed, but when you get letters from people saying you gave them the spirit to carry on, that's better proof for me!' The world citizen passes a proprietorial hand across his realm as it is laid out in soft white and sparkling blue before us. 'I have saved lives out there!'

Just after this memorable pronouncement, it happens. I

look down at my MP3-playing voice recorder, lying across the Finn-side arm of my white plastic sunlounger, and notice its little screen is unaccountably blank. I snatch it up, switch the battery, shake it, press buttons. Nothing. 'Just a minute,' I blurt, and race back to my chalet to discover, in ratcheting anguish, that random chunks of our day's conversation, perhaps totalling ninety minutes, have been lost for ever down some silicon vortex. Before the week is up this device will meet furious and repeated heel-shaped retribution on a cold London pavement, but spread-eagled on my bed with those crappy little headphones plugged into my hot ears, all I have the energy for is a long, low moan, as if I'm just waking up with an enormous hangover. Though when I listen through the stop-start recording again, and grasp that the bulk of the missing words cover Finn's account of a long-ago night in Dublin, I top that with a fairly impressive shriek.

'OK, let's just do it,' snaps Finn, cutting short my faltering, apologetic account of the technical fault which will necessitate a return to the events of 4 April 1981. In mind of those recent pronouncements on the inner shittiness engendered by my questioning, I'd expected a request to revisit his blackest day to be met with tears on the sand or a stonewall sulk. Uncomfortable as his brusque opprobrium is, I'm grateful to hear it. So grateful that I re-set the Dublin scene with indelicate haste and precision: 'Right . . . you've got your nul points, you're drunk, and Stig Anderson has just punched you in the stomach.'

In the pause before Finn starts talking, he turns to gaze steadily at me through his mirrored shades. Around those inscrutable lenses I can see his eye sockets narrow, the skin contracting. That hefty jaw juts further out, and I think: It's the boxer reflex. He's about to deck me with the old Fåvang one-two, the old elk stopper. Then he puffs out his cheeks, exhales slowly, and says, 'You know, there are worse things than getting no points in the Eurovision Song Contest.'

There's an ominous terminatory tang to this avowal, which I try to ignore even as I swiftly endorse it, emphasising that I've come all this way to interview its beach-burnished embodiment. 'I didn't worry about the zero points because *Aldri i Livet* was my best-selling single, from my best-selling album.' Listening to the recording on the flight home, the flat weariness of Finn's words has me sagging in aisle-sprawled empathy. He's running out of juice, drifting off like the computer at the end of *2001*.

'Yeah, maybe after that third record things were going slow . . . I don't know.' His answers become incoherent, his voice fuzzy and tranquillised. I remember the other Finn Kalvik I'd blundered across during my early research, a 'deceased ufologist who was a leading figure and magazine editor for Norsk UFO Center', and think: This is how he would have spoken. 'When you're used to living in one style and you have to take a few steps back, or you were playing in big halls and you have to play in smaller places . . . I've been through all that, I'm a survivor, I've balanced all my ups and downs . . . Time is running fast, but I'm not going to panic.' He girds himself with the dregs of his most recent Chang. 'I'm proud that I never gave up. And I'm proud because I always wanted to live like this, and here I am doing it.'

I've been to paradise, but I've never been to me. These heart-warming, Finn-affirming words prove to be the epitaph to our intercourse. Immediately afterwards, following a sort of snorted sigh that interrupts some fumbling enquiry of mine, he jumps abruptly to his feet and swiftly covers the short distance to his chalet. By the time he stamps out of it, an hour after sunset, he's tousled, red-faced and glowering, rasping bitter incoherences as he marches past the under-palm picnic table where Bjørn, Sissel and I are enjoying a brewed aperitif.

Dispatched at our usual place up the beach, at our usual table, my last supper offers a disjointed and grimly funereal contrast with its convivial, lavishly lagered predecessors. The four of us sip and chew in discomforting silence; at length, Bjørn diplomatically embarks on a round-up of his most memorable journalistic experiences, from being first at the grave of Nicolae Ceauşescu, to a four-week assignment in North Korea. Captivating as these reminiscences are, Finn's intimidating display of wordless, jaw-rippling rage restricts me to the odd dutiful nod or hum. Even the now traditional Teutonic pyrotechnics that rip through the night sky as the waiter clears away my unfinished red chicken curry fail to defuse the situation. When Finn presses a hand to his ear and winces, the many emotions tangled together in my head are confused further with a knot of sympathy.

The waters are not unmuddied during our Chang-fuelled after-dinner crisis summit, the two of us squatting side by side on logs in the tepid, breezy dark under Big John's beach-border palms. Popping open my second can, I rather rashly interrupt a prolonged tirade against media intrusion (and more specifically against me) to suggest that if he really hadn't wanted this meeting to happen, Finn could have saved us both a lot of heartache by saying so in the traditional manner: beforehand.

His protracted and vigorous response to this ensures that I don't say very much more. He punctuates his more heated and less intelligible pronouncements (the majority) by smacking the side of his log, and employs intemperate language. Flecks of Kalvik spittle spatter my bare thighs. The last outward ferry eases towards the unseen mainland, and as Finn rants beside me I track its steady progress in silence, wishing myself aboard, watching as its gay decklights merge into a frail glow. Long after it has vacated the horizon, its feeble wake washes up at our feet.

In the end, spent and disconsolate, I haul myself upright, heave out a kind of full-body shrug and leave him clenching his face muscles at the sea. It's in every schoolbook in Norway, I think, squinting through the P11 mosquito mesh as the light flicks on in P10: Finn Kalvik, go f . . . find yourself.

Finn's curtains are still drawn when I stumble out, ill-kempt and unrested, into another wincing-bright morning. With no appetite for an encounter and not much more for breakfast, I walk through the rush-roofed, hibiscus-walled breakfast hut and ask Gob to phone for a minibus. Half an hour later I'm stepping out into a thick, hot quayside miasma of dog and old prawns at Nathon, the port I'd been watching those rust-weeping mainland ferries steaming to and from across the Big

John horizon. For a moment I wonder why I thought coming here might cheer me up. Then I spot a stall flogging pirate DVDs for a quid a pop, and begin to remember.

Potholed, chaotic and malodorous, Nathon isn't easy to love, but in four hours I develop an affection for its energetic populace. For the delicate yet piquant chicken and coconut soup they serve me, for the tininess of the bill that follows it, for the Kalvik-banishing commercial distractions that crowd every one of the dusty, teeming streets.

I plug in my stupid, doomed MP3 player and allow *Mil Etter Mil* to accompany me through a sportswear bazaar luridly aglow with kaleidoscopic counterfeits, tawny curs yapping underfoot, tongues down, tails up, balls out. More of those winning confluences of east and west: seaweed and lobster flavoured Lays crisps, a hostel advertising 'continention breakfasts', a Rolling Stones hits album featuring *Get Off My Clown*. Desiccated corpse-husks of thumb-sized cockroaches crunching underfoot. A market alive with muscular aromas: roast chicken, alien fruit on the turn, sun-warmed seafood.

Aldri i Livet is next up on the chronological Eurovision playlist, but as Benny's keyboard intro plinks into my head I click back to Jahn with almost Pavlovian spontaneity. '*Krrrrrrrrroppp*!' he trills anew, as a phalanx of Honda C90s buzzes by, fags dangling from the mouths of the male pilots, wives and mothers – sometimes both – riding side-saddle behind. And not a helmet in sight: it wasn't difficult to accept Finn's revelation of the 300 road-deaths with which the country had recently marked New Year's Eve.

All around the locals are engaged in frenetic labour, their industry glaringly incompatible with the bone-wilting, back-dampening conditions: men lugging crated washing machines up a fire escape, tiny, flip-flopped women hauling trolleys of giant, stuffed Spidermen and Piglets twice their size. Above Jahn's approximate final warblings I find myself pondering the words of his one-time fellow punk Johnny Rotten: a cheap holiday in other people's misery. Sissel had discovered our evening beach waiter was on £25 for a ninety-six-hour week.

And he was one of the elite: what about those gardeners?

Thailand has enjoyed, and endured, long stints as the world's fastest-growing economy, and the frenzied commercial activity on display in these streets offered an unedifying contrast to the shambling nonchalance displayed by all foreign guests. Young travellers with the swirly tattoos and hoover-hairball dreadlocks of Lonely Planet long-termers shuffling listlessly in and out of the internet cafés; the elephant-centric souvenir emporia disgorging waddlesome Polo-shirted representatives of their parents' generation, here on day trips from the ritzy, gated holiday compounds that ring the Koh Samui coast. And me, now flumped down on an under-tree dockside bench, a sweaty sack of counterfeit merchandise in the lap of my damp shorts, an umpteenth palliative dose of Jahn in my ears. I'll keep this up for as long as it takes, I think, watching two floppy-hatted fishermen haul nets up on to the deck of their high-prowed little boat. For mile after mile after mile.

After spending much of the previous night failing to outflank a furious blond man guarding the Land of Nod, I hardly bother to resist as my chin sags down to my chest. What seems a moment later I'm violently roused by a horrid sensation below the shorts-line. One of the island's battered maroon and yellow cabs has bumped into a pothole behind my bench, and in doing so diverted much of the fetid fluid collected at its fundament to the back of my bare legs. Dopily exhaling an unintelligible flow of obscenities I realise something else: two floating female voices are serenading me. When a thin, clear masculine soprano joins them, using words that are familiar yet meaningless, I gather my full waking senses together and understand I'm listening to Mr F. Kalvik's ill-fated magnum opus. But this time I don't click it off. This time I listen, and keep listening until the three voices and their ringmaster's keyboard fade into silence.

'You know,' Finn had said almost exactly twenty-four hours before, '*Aldri i Livet* is now more popular than ever, for a whole new generation, because they just used it for the music on a big TV commercial in Norway.' Well, that's fantastic, I'd replied. What was the advertisement for? I remember thinking how snidely apposite it would be if he'd said 'cheese', until he actually did. 'It's one of the big highlights of my concerts, and when I play it at weddings the bride always cries. And it's twenty-three years old . . . amazing! This song has really . . . I am in lack of words – I don't know how you say this in English.'

'Stood the test of time?'

'That's it! It really has stood a test in time.' And he smiled as he said it, and remembering that so did I.

Aldri i Livet was such a sweet, simple, carefree composition, yet the fate brutally bestowed on it one distant night in Dublin had curdled those bright, pure notes into a discordant dirge that haunted its creator's life. The song's Eurovision meltdown had initiated the shockingly abrupt collapse of Finn Kalvik's burgeoning commercial success; no nul-pointer had further to fall. His wearying schizophrenic switches from braggadocio to conciliation, sometimes in the same sentence, mirrored the bewildering bipolarity of his biggest-selling single – *Aldri i Livet* was at once the triumphant zenith of his pop career and its kiss of death. That, as he himself accepted, was what had inspired the *Åpen Post* writers. As twelve year olds they'd cheered expectantly at the telly as Norway's hottest star sat on his stool in Dublin and waited for Sigurd Jansen to count him in. Yet by the time they were teenagers, he'd somehow disappeared off the face of the earth.

I flicked the player back, and gave myself another hit of Finn. The innocent sincerity of both song and singer had never struck me quite like this, as hard as a pissed-up Stig Anderson. It all suddenly seemed so random, so unfair. I remembered Finn's open and expectant demeanour as he'd walked across that windy Dublin dockside, hands in pockets, hope in heart. The boyish smile hadn't been wiped off his face so much as battered from it, with such ferocity that it was still too scared to return. *Aldri i Livet* hadn't deserved to get nothing, and nobody deserved the poisoned fallout that a quarter of a century later was still settling on its composer's bowed head.

With my gaze ranging blankly across Koh Samui's gently

steaming green hills, body brine blotting through my T-shirt, legs speckled with an unthinkable distillate of diesel and crab piss, I feel Finn's pain. If I'd spent two decades putting a demon to rest, you wouldn't have caught me chortling indulgently when two blokes started digging it up on national TV. Or when, a couple of years after that, I looked up from my sun lounger and saw a third walking up the sand towards me with it sitting on his shoulders.

Far from being the most enviable emblem of his triumph over nul-points adversity, Finn's beach-bum lifestyle was in fact the consequence of its stubbornly enduring curse. He lived for half a year in paradise, but not to escape his homeland's inclement weather so much as its inclement inhabitants. The face that sustained him throughout the bucolic summer festivals was a liability in Norway's urban winter, when those taunting drunks lay in wait at bus stops. It wasn't just lazy journalism that persuaded interviewers to keep on asking if Finn Kalvik had finally found himself: despite all the restless roaming, he patently hadn't.

An hour later I'm back for a farewell loll on the Big John beach, collating my pirate DVDs into their sleeves and cases by way of occupational therapy. Finn has flown: P10 is being serviced by an energetic surfeit of cleaners, and his sunbed has been conspicuously commandeered by a topless Russian grandmother. The palm trees are side-lit by another of those almost vulgar, Malibu-bottle sunsets, the garishly tiger-striped sky blotted by a smudge of barbecue smoke from somewhere down the beach. A fisherman poles his punt-like craft across the bay, off towards the port that now disgorges the last of the many, many ferries I have followed towards the unseen mainland in the past seventy-two hours.

Bjørn and Sissel amble up to say their goodbyes, and though none of us refers to the previous night's histrionics or their instigator, there's an odd, sombre fraternity to our conversation. It's as if we're at a wake, mourning a mutual friend who hadn't been easy to know. My phone warbles its need for a recharge, and when I check the screen I see the clock is still set to Oslo time. The nauseating jolt of jet lag this elicits is sharpened by another of misgiving and regret.

'I don't really need a watch here,' Bjørn smiles lazily, when I request a time-check. He inclines his red-brown head at the ferries converging distantly before us. 'They cross on the half hour.' What a wonderful insight into a protracted and definitively aimless holiday, I thought. Precisely the sort of holiday, indeed, that I hoped poor Finn might enjoy now I was leaving him in peace. For three days he'd never even seen those ferries, his mind's eye focused inwards, ranging restlessly over the rusty hulks of his past.

'You av chewdrer?'

The Big John receptionist is gamely bullying her delicate mouth into making Western noises, but so impenetrable is the Thai pattern of speech, its surprised, staccato yelps apparently forced from the stomach with a series of painful kicks, that it takes three repetitions and some jolly mimework before I realise she's asking if I have children. Three, I tell her, inducing a squeal that intriguingly blends fathomless admiration with coquettish sauce.

'Oh! Oh! You av *beeeeg power*!' she giggles, raising a hand to cover her mouth. I laugh, partly because I have rarely felt my internal batteries more completely drained, and I'm still smiling when the airport minibus arrives five minutes later. As we bump and slap our way up the concrete-sectioned road, I look out at the palm silhouettes and think: Yes, on the one hand I have just travelled half way round the world to make a grown man cry, at great cost to us both. But on the other, I have big power.

24 April 1982
Harrogate Conference Centre
Kojo
Finland
Nuku Pommiin

'Let me go check,' whispers the tentative transatlantic female. 'I think he might be asleep.'

It's midday, Finnish time: Jim Pembroke, musician, producer and songwriter of forty years standing, is clearly still keeping rock hours. Born in north London in 1946, Jim first went out to Helsinki in 1965 in pursuit of his girlfriend, a Finnish au pair; give or take the odd couple of months back in Finchley and a five-year nineties stint in Kansas, he's been there ever since.

Jim's modest experience in London pub bands sufficed to see him through the sixties in a procession of Helsinki-based beat and blues groups; in the decade after he took the Teigen-trodden path into Scandinavian prog rock. Wigwam enjoyed enduring success in their homeland – the band retains a healthy cult following – and after a UK tour supporting Gong came tantalisingly close to securing a big deal with Virgin Records. But 1977 wasn't the best time to be releasing an album entitled 'Daemon Duncetan's Request' (narrowly out-progging Jim's earlier solo offering, 'Corporal Cauliflower's Mental Function'), and adjudging the work 'too low-key and non-commercial', Branson's boys pulled out the Wigwam tentpegs.

After four years of dwindling success, Jim gulped down Virgin's bitter pill with a lunatic cackle of if-you-can't-beat-'em bravado. In the winter of 1980 he sat down and wrote what may be the only reggae number to feature an accordion solo, and entered it for the Eurovision Song Contest. Performed by the majestically mulleted Riki Sorsa, *Reggae OK* triumphed at the Finnish national qualifiers and, as I can hardly fail to forget, was prominent amongst *Aldri i Livet*'s rivals in Dublin. Despite the aesthetic disincentives of Riki's harlequin trousers and his backing band's walrus-themed face furniture, it earnt twenty-seven points from the international juries: sixteenth place was considered a solid result for a nation that had come home last the year before, and never finished higher than sixth.

Winning the Eurovision Artist Award Society's 'Originality Prize' was a bonus, and indeed a telling indicator of the contest's stifling artistic constraints, but no one was more surprised than Jim when over the following weeks *Reggae OK* hit the top ten in eleven central European countries, selling 100,000 copies. If he'd sold out, it had paid off. After years of poorly remunerated prog-rock toil, he'd made a stack of cash with the silliest song he'd ever written. Sod it, he thought, I'll have another go.

Perhaps inspired by that Originality Prize, for the 1982 qualifiers Jim decided to push the Eurovision envelope a little further. With cruise missiles at Greenham Common and Soviet SS-20s in silos all along the Iron Curtain, the threat of nuclear confrontation was the dominant issue of the day – this was the year of Nicole's success with *A Little Peace* – and nowhere was the threat more tangible than frontline Finland, a nation that shared a 1,200km border with the USSR. After all, wasn't Eurovision founded to stop another war? *Nuku Pommiin* (*Bomb Out*), Jim's follow-up, put a nation's fears into words, words that inevitably suffer rather in the translation mix:

If someone soon throws some nuclear poo here on our Europe
What will you say when we get all the filth on our faces?
If someone slings a bomb at your neck you probably won't even notice

Hardly typical fare to place before juries that the year before had given Jean Gabilou 125 points, and third place, for *Humanahum*. But then Jim was hardly a typical Eurovision songwriter.

The tune he set these words to was rather more straightforward: of all the Eurovision songs I would attempt to master, none proved less taxing. *Nuku Pommiin*'s four power-pop bar chords formed a simple framework for its furious lyrical polemic – this was about the message, not the medium.

Regrettably, the message was elucidated in Europe's most impenetrable tongue. From Portugal to Cyprus, Ireland to Yugoslavia, Eurovision watchers would gather merely that something had made these Finns pretty damn angry. What's up with this lot, eh? Elk crap in the sauna again?

''Ello?'

It's perhaps three minutes since his girlfriend went off to retrieve him, and Jim's wound-down Cockney is barely intelligible. I explain myself as best I can. 'Kojo?' For my benefit, he pronounces the name of *Nuku Pommiin*'s performer as a rhyme for 'mojo'. But in the course of the half-dozen conversations with venerable and/or retired Finnish music executives I've enjoyed to get me this far, I've been made aware that it's definitively Ko-yo. 'Yeah. Just . . . ah . . . yeah, um . . .'

In the background I think I can hear the growl-accompanied keyboard stylings of Tom Waits; maybe, I ponder while waiting for the man at the other end of the line to get his act together, this is the recorded sound of Jim Pembroke.

'Dubai!' Almost audibly, a penny has dropped in the Pembroke mind, and it's dropped into a slot it might have taken me months to guess at. 'Yeah – he's out there now.'

Dubai. *Dubai?* Hardly a destination you'd have thought likely to roll out the red carpet for impoverished losers. If only I hadn't just come home from Koh Samui, and discovered how nul-points trouble can thrive in paradise.

'Yeah, um . . . let me, ah, let me give you his cellphone number.' He does, and after appropriate thanks I let him mumble a farewell. It's already impossible not to picture his life in Helsinki as an enduring homage to that obscure celebration of Scandinavian groupiehood, *Norwegian Wood*. Every time I talk to Jim Pembroke thereafter, I imagine that following our goodbyes he'll crawl off to sleep in the bath.

Timo Kojo was twenty-nine in 1982. As a boy he'd been more interested in sport than music, displaying such natural aptitude for football and ice hockey that at youth level he represented his nation at both. For two years running he was Finland's technical football champion, the king of keepy-uppy; then, at seventeen, a series of injuries – a badly cut foot, a dislocated shoulder – cost him a year of training. To fill the void he began messing around in school bands, grabbing the mike to bellow out sixties soul covers. Encouraged by his violinist father, after graduation Timo dropped his first name and began to tour Finland with a band that majored in Wilson Pickett, with a sideline in transatlantic rock.

The Finnish music scene being as you'd expect, it wasn't long before Kojo met Jim Pembroke. They became friends; between gigs he began to roadie for Wigwam, and soon he was flatsharing with Jim in downtown Helsinki. When in 1979 Kojo finally made it into a studio, Jim went along to show him the ropes. The resultant English-language album, 'So Mean', was an immediate hit; it still shows up today in the my-favourite-records lists that are so unsurprisingly de rigueur amongst Finland's extensive online community. In 1980 he released a second album, and in 1981 a third: more of the same, though neither quite as successful as his debut. Pushing thirty, he must have started wondering whether that was it.

Finishing off his new Eurovision composition, it inevitably struck Jim that his flatmate's passion-cracked way with a tune made him an obvious choice to articulate the rhetoric of an impending apocalypse in a way that Riki Sorsa's harlequin trousers didn't. If Jim had asked him to perform *Reggae OK*, Kojo would have laughed the roof off the sauna, but as things stood both men understood he had little to lose. Make it to the Eurovision-selection finals in any Scandinavian country and the TV coverage guaranteed you at least a minor national hit. Make it to the contest proper, and, as Riki Sorsa had demonstrated, you didn't need to be ABBA to shift records across Europe.

Ten songs were performed at the 1982 Finnish final on 19 February, and a compact jury of music and media luminaries duly voted *Nuku Pommiin* the clear winner. In second place, thirteen points adrift, was Ami Aspelund's substantially more conventional Eurosong, *My Apple Tree*. In any other year, the jury would have played it safe. Indeed the next year they did, dispatching Ami and *Fantasiaa* off to the 1983 final in Germany. She came home with forty-one points, the best Finnish total since her sister Monica pulled in fifty six years before.

Wiltingly disheartened by The Kalvik Misfortune, I flick Andreas's disk of the 1982 final into my bedroom DVD player with diminished enthusiasm. I'd set off on this journey hoping to undo a great injustice, to restore the dignity and reputation of Eurovision's fallen warrior-minstrels, but after that harrowing night on the Big John beach I'd begun to wonder if I was trying to right one wrong with another. Jahn's what-the-bollocks exuberance when I'd met him had been followed by Finn's histrionic collapse; if there was any progression in these matters, my encounter with Timo Kojo could only end in the kind of Armageddon the man himself had prophesied in song. If nuclear poo was going to be thrown at anyone's neck, that neck would be mine.

Andreas's menu flicks up: five flags before the Finnish, five songs before I come face to long-ago face with my next nul-pointer. A vulnerable vocal tremor, a freeze-framed look of frail panic, the half-glimpsed hint of a backstage breakdown – any one of the above, Timo, and perhaps we should call the whole thing off.

1982 was a crisis year for Eurovision. The French drivel-boycott was supplemented by Italy's absence through sheer apathy, and the Greeks pulled out late after their new socialist government condemned the contest as a showcase for globalised commercialism. Rather more dramatically, the hosts Britain were involved in an apparently ridiculous colonial war that had already provoked many of the remaining countries. As the performers rehearsed, a naval task force was en route to the Falklands; exactly a week later, the *Belgrano* lay on the South Atlantic seabed.

Harrogate was the unlikely benefactor of Bucks Fizz's narrow triumph the year before. Boldly acknowledging its own obscurity, the 1982 transmission welcomes 300 million viewers with animated captions reading 'Where is Harrogate?' in every Eurovision language, soundtracked by the sort of jauntily pedestrian orchestrations that suggest a local Vauxhall dealership showcasing its facilities before the main feature to a very small afternoon cinema audience. I only remember I'd watched all this at the time when newsreader Jan Leeming steps out on to the stage, wearing one of those sparkly art deco headbands briefly popularised that year by Princess Diana. Ah, yes! I recall Jan and that outfit partly because my girlfriend's dad fancied her, but mainly because I did.

To my profound disappointment, if not the unflinchingly sombre Austrian commentator's, there is to be no filmed horseplay of Cypriots chasing each other round north Yorkshire's beauty spots. Instead, each competing nation prefaces its performance with an unapologetically blatant promotional film: 'Discover the miracle of the Mediterranean,' begins a typical caption, 'discover . . . *Israel.*'

As suggested by the Guinness-and-Joyce Irish broadcast the previous year, it's clear that just two decades back Europeans remained stubbornly ignorant of even their closest neighbours. We were consecutively urged to visit the realms of sand and horses (Portugal), then rain and viaducts (Luxembourg). Big Ben, alpine chalets, that weeing Belgian statue, windmills and tulips – it's all so dreadfully banal. And what a long twenty-three years it's been: the Spaniards didn't think twice about showcasing a bullfight in their slot, and the star dominating the Yugoslav flag stresses that though Marshal Tito has now been dead eighteen months, communist autocracy is alive and well.

In the trademark quaver I'd found so appealing as a youth, Jan introduces the show openers. Doce are four Portuguese girls dressed in highwayman homage to the year's most conspicuous pop success, Adam Ant; the caption that announces their entry's title remains the perfect encapsulation of Eurovision's improbable blend of the inane and the pedantic. 'Doce – *Bem Bom*' it reads, before seguing into the English translation demanded by tradition, and evidently settled upon only after lengthy committee debate.

'So unless anyone has anything else to add on *Jij En Ik*, we move to item 11a on your itineraries, *Bem Bom*. You will recall that in Gran Canaria last month we finally reached a consensus on Bom, which in line with the 1978 precedent of Denmark's *Boom Boom* we're opting to leave as is. It's the more complex issue of Bem that concerns us today. Yugoslavia?'

'Bem, Bem, Bem. We must all ask: what Bem it say to us? Maybe for you is more Bam, for you is more . . . Broom.'

'Yes . . . I'm not saying we should discount the likes of "Broom", but–'

'Bront!'

'Yes, Cyprus, or "Bront", but I think a degree of consistency is important. Adhering to the B-vowel-M format, we need something that captures the spirit of "Bem", but isn't "Bum".'

'Bum-bum!'

'Thank you, Turkey. The options, then, as I see them are fairly straightforward: Bam, Bom and Bim. A show of hands, please? Well, I think that's conclusive: the Bims have it.'

And there it is on the screen: *Bim Bom*. (The song was later released in Spain as *Bingo*.)

Another of Luxembourg's long line of Eurovision voice-for-hire mercenaries, the Franco-Russian Svetlana, comes and goes, followed by a brief film of a man handing his female companion a large salmon. Here, we sense, is a man apart from his fellow competitors, a man unwilling to kowtow to the convention that has persuaded other performers to do their patriotic duty beside an Edam. Here, once again, is the great Jahn Teigen.

How sad, though, to see him mumble through that linguistic professor's cravenly international reworking of *Adieu*, a thin and studiously uncontentious duet almost viciously shorn of novelty or character. No shades, no twangs, no leaps: in his V-neck and side parting, Jahn looks like Alan Partridge entertaining midweek diners at the Linton Travel Tavern. It's awful to see, like watching the lobotomised Jack Nicholson's vacant, wet-lipped smile spread across his face at the end of *One Flew Over the Cuckoo's Nest*. Jahn leans obediently against the grand piano as his wife delicately tinkles away, gazing into her eyes with almost parodic sincerity; only his hands, which on occasion shake with alarming violence, show what this neutered performance is costing him. I want the big Cuckoo chief to come out and smother Jahn, then hurl the piano through the backdrop and lead Eurovision's inmates to the freedom of a saner world outside.

Performers come and go, all struggling in vain to find a way around or over the mighty wall of cheese erected by Ronnie Hazelhurst's BBC orchestra. The Turks troop wanly off, wondering how their entry had been distilled to an imbecilic Co-Op jingle, and then here's a blond man in a Nik Kershaw jacket, mugging with studied insincerity before a banner that with commendable Ronsealed brevity reads FINLAND FOR HOLIDAYS. I rewind and watch it again: there's an unmistakable gleam of old-style Teigen-esque mischief in his eye, and for me that's a very good sign.

The film ends, we're back live at the Conference Centre, and with a carefully enunciated, BBC-researched warble of 'Ko-yo!' Jan introduces the same man, now clad from head to toe in screaming red leather, to 300 million Europeans.

Despite the distractions of his outfit and a lip curled in

comic disdain, it's difficult to imagine how he could look much more Finnish: he's one part Billy Idol to nine parts rally driver. In a ragged semi-circle behind him slouch an already smirking band of Blues Brothers, ties all at half mast, and lank Scandi-rock hair that's far too long for those trilbies. Ronnie H's arrangement launches the song with a fantastically inappropriate salesman-of-the-year fanfare, and *Nuku Pommiin* is in trouble before it's even started.

By the time the big chords give way to a strangely tinkling middle eight, jurors across the continent are already nipping out for a bratwurst or an ouzo. Kojo's triple-distilled rasp cracks and wanders; the percussionist batters a comically oversized marching-band bass drum with contrived imprecision. As the lead guitarist winds up a heartsinkingly insipid rent-a-solo, his red-suited leader does something I never thought to see on a Eurovision stage: he sweeps the mike stand up into his arms, and for ten fearful seconds strums it in energetic sympathy.

He's ticking every wrong box in the Eurovision catalogue. From the suit onwards there have already been more nul-points moments than I'd have imagined possible, and that's before Kojo succumbs to obscure temptation and smacks himself, really quite hard, on the side of the head, as if the bad thoughts were coming back. Apparently quite pleased with this action or its effects, he immediately does it again. By the time the song reaches its climax, a repeated refrain of '*Pom-miin*', he's slapping his temples with the frenzy of a bereaved Iranian. On sofas from Dublin to Dubrovnik, awestruck Europeans watch in frozen silence. But twenty-three years later, upright in a London bed, I'm making an awful lot of noise. Whatever else you can say about this performance, its magnificently wayward interpreter plainly doesn't give an elk's arse.

After a theatrical snore that no one outside Finland can know relates to *Nuku Pommiin*'s warning of an apathetic continent sleeping its way towards apocalypse, there's a giant, discordant orchestral crash. Probably intended to signify a nuclear explosion, it more convincingly suggests that the conductor has just substituted his baton for a skinned ferret. The great fear that reared up at me on a dark island beach – that I might never again find Eurovision funny – is loudly laid to rest.

A shellshocked Conference Centre audience stutters out a round of disjointed applause; the Austrian ORF commentator, after a long pause and in more than usually measured tones, can think of nothing to say beyond 'Finland. Kojo'. But I'm still whooping my ebullient relief when a Swiss girl bounds onscreen behind an enormous pantomime St Bernard.

A Cypriot girl in a toga; a trio of pastel-eyed Swedish housewives; three hefty, booming, Yugoslav women who look like the one from *The Golden Girls* we all thought was a man – a relentless procession of songs and performances that by most sensible artistic criteria, and all snidely aesthetic ones, deserve no more than *Nuku Pommiin*. But because their performers do not sneer, or smirk, or slap themselves about the face, they will go home with a respectable haul of points.

Not so the Danes, whose bravely synthesised offering is musically reminiscent of Orchestral Manoeuvres in the Dark, and whose Kojo-trumping outfits of banana and fuchsia lurex suggest wardrobe manoeuvres undertaken in similar conditions. Five points and second last in the bag: Eurovision has never responded well to contemporary trends in pop culture. There was a continent-wide intake of breath when a 1967 regulation decreed that half of all voting delegates should be under thirty; Sandie Shaw triumphed in what became known as 'the year of the young juries'.

The ORF announcer placed his finger firmly on the Eurovision pulse when he welcomed the glittery highwaywomen of Portugal on-stage with an apprehensive shiver: '*Ah – die punk ladies.*' Having sensibly tempered their apparently shocking appearance with the comforting banality of *Bem/Bim Bom*, they didn't do too badly. The only other song to score under ten didn't do so on account of its avant-garde alienation, or any recklessness on the part of its karate-suited Dutch performer. It was just shit. Have a good look at that monument to drivel, and you'll spot Bill van Dijke strung up from its lightning conductor.

And then, last up, here's eighteen-year-old Nicole, showing Finn Kalvik that to carry off the guitar/stool combo it helps if you're young and female. Romping to victory by a record sixty-one points, *Ein Bisschen Frieden* – as *A Little Peace* the last Eurovision winner to top the UK charts – ensured a final score-board bookended with pacifist anthems. It succeeded where *Nuku Pommiin* so spectacularly failed by obscuring its message in layers of anodyne schmaltz: *A little sunshine, a little gladness, to wash away all the tears of sadness* . . . none of your nuclear poo here. Nicole sang 'peace' fourteen times, 'love' three times and 'bird' twice, and she sang them all without slapping herself even once. With her big, white *Kumbaya*-ready acoustic, that pale face framed by great curtains of hair and a Pam Ayres dress, she was every jury member's perfect Euro-daughter, just as sneering, self-harming Kojo was their nightmare Euro-son.

When Nicole came out to reprise her triumph, she did so with verses sung in English, French, Italian and Dutch: thus ruthlessly promoted, *Ein Bisschen Frieden* went on to sell over a million worldwide. Predictably, the song's composer was a hard-bitten Eurovision pro whose 1979 German entry paid zesty tribute to feted pacifist Genghis Khan. On that occasion, Ralph Siegel backpedalled on the birds and sunshine in favour of such soothing lyrical sentiments as: *They carried fear and horror in every country, let's fetch vodka* and *he fathered seven children in one night*. (In a little-publicised case some years later, Ralph was accused of borrowing large parts of *Ein Bisschen Freiden* from a minor 1973 Julio Iglesias hit, *Alle Liebe dieser Erde*. The settlement was never announced, but it's interesting to see that a website devoted to cover versions brackets the two songs together.)

The Harrogate pre-vote show gave 300 million of us a good reason to put the kettle on. Ronnie's variations on *Scarborough Fair* and *The Grand Old Duke of York* play behind a tour of the region's stately homes; when Jahn briefly appears, being carried up the steps of Castle Howard in a sedan chair, his leer and the musical accompaniment's porn-muzak quality suggest scenes of vile decadence await him within.

'Here are the results of the Portuguese jury . . .' Another of those precise but oddly stilted disembodied voices booms out, unleashing a painful screech of feedback. How fond I'm becoming of the spy's English that once was every jury foreman's stock in trade: clipped and precise, yet fatally flawed by a tiny slip in enunciation – in this case, a tell-tale over-deliberation of the central syllable in 'Harrogate'.

In the second round of voting the perennial nul-pointers bag big votes off Luxembourg, prompting a tickled shriek of 'Norway – six points!' from our hostess and a lazy, ironic cheer from the audience. The awful, awful Dutch keep Kojo company at the wrong end of the scoreboard for eight rounds, before the treacherous Swedes – widowmakers once more – award *Jij En Ik* three points.

Once again a solitary Nordic male has been bent over and spanked with the big wooden spoon. Following Norway's brace of nul-pointers in 1978 and 1981, when Finland copped the big nix it seemed Scandinavia would be riding the Eurovision duck for ever more. What did they all do so wrong? Well, as thirty-ish Scandinavian males they certainly weren't about to pick up many sympathy points. Come on, the jurors are thinking, it's not as if that red-suited head-slapper is off back to a Portuguese barrel-repair sweatshop or the Zagreb hoof-glue rendering plant. Bollock it up at the Eurovision and a Scandinavian can go back home and fashion any number of lucrative new careers for himself: leather footstools don't just design themselves.

With Kojo now down and out on his own, an exceptional moment: perhaps because Nicole's runaway triumph means there's little drama at the top, perhaps in recognition of the host nation's distasteful fascination with the wrong end of the scoreboard, we are given a rare live shot of a nul point in the making.

In almost every other final I have watched or shall, the stricken are left to suffer in darkness and silence. But suddenly, here's the chap in red lounging flamboyantly in a green-room armchair, legs splayed over the arms, honing his Billy Idol lip curl. Their slouched deportment suggests that his surrounding Blues Brothers are long since past caring, but for their leader it goes beyond that: here is a man who never cared to begin with. Kojo clocks the camera, extrudes a lazy, lopsided smirk into its lens and raises his arms in mock triumph. As he does I know that I've seen this before, that taunting salute, that fuck-you-all sneer: with apologies to Jahn, here is Eurovision's one true punk moment. And that's enough to have me hauling the Fender from under the bed and banging out those bar chords.

'Some say architecture is frozen music,' drones the voiceover on the wonders-of-Finland film being played out on a ceiling-mounted screen in the arrivals hall. Well, if it's going to happen anywhere, I ponder dully, feeling like Jim Pembroke after three encores and a triathlon, it would be Helsinki. Late January; the fag end of Scandinavia's darkest, coldest month, in its darkest, coldest capital. Cold enough, even inside, to randomise my thoughts, to cause me to wonder what kind of architecture a frozen Eurovision might suggest, and to come up with the Pompidou Centre. And dark enough, even though it's pushing noon, to cast a forbidding shadow across the vast advertisement hoarding whose message causes trepidation to swell up in my guts as I wander towards the carousel.

'Facts about Finland,' it's headed innocuously. The second of the two lines of copy that follow – '2004: Finnet, first choice for mobile network in Finland' – is unremarkable but for its interaction with the first – '1962: best ever result in the Eurovision Song Contest, 7th'.

Five minutes in this country, and I'm already forced to confront Finland's unhealthy fixation with its appalling Eurovision history. As I had a day or so before, blundering across this study of comparative climatology on an Anglo-Finnish blog:

> *+5°C: Italian cars won't start; Finns are cruising in cabriolets.*

-10°C: Brits start their central heating; Finns start wearing long sleeves.
-300°C: hell freezes over, Finland wins ESC.

Reading that advert again, and again, my misgivings multiply. Seventh? That just doesn't sound right. By the time the more conspicuous of my two luggage items is parting the rubber-strip curtains, I've confirmed my doubts, courtesy of the Eurovision handbook delved from the first. April 7 1973, Nouveau Theatre, Luxembourg, Marion Rung, Finland, *Tom Tom Tom* (chorus: 'Tom tom tom tom tom tom, I hear the music, tom tom tom tom tom tom'). Yes, having finished last eight times, Finland could hardly claim to look back over a gilded Eurovision heritage. But *Tom Tom Tom*, with 93 points, came sixth. After forty-nine years of pain and disappointment, hope has curdled into a Finnish fatalism so bitter, they've airbrushed out the highlights. And here I am, picking up my Fender case, about to celebrate through public serenade the very lowest light of all.

Una Paloma Blanca trills simperingly from the taxi radio as we slap and slosh up the bus lanes, the pines and birches above bowed with fat new snow. There's a dour, ice-and-granite Soviet ambience to the streets; every passing face is hidden in a hood and angled down at the pavement. How could this place have produced the reckless free spirit who had smacked himself about in front of 300 million people, and whose eccentric chutzpah was still apparent in two-line emails sent twenty-three years later?

'Your idea sounds crazy but nice,' his first Dubai-dispatched reply had begun, 'and I'm always ready when it comes to having A LAUGH. I'm back in HELSINKI next week so LETS HAVE LUNCH.' The moment that landed in my inbox was the moment the post-Kalvik recovery process began in gleeful earnest.

We'd arranged to meet at Strindberg, which swiftly announces itself to me as an alarmingly upmarket restaurant clearly unaccustomed to serving foreigners in stupid and possibly offensive Cossack hats, and carrying slush-spattered guitar cases. I'm early, and though I've no idea what facial evolutions Kojo might have undergone since 1982, inspecting the incoming clientele – smooth executives shaking the weather off their overcoats and the odd lady-who-lunches doing the same to her hair – I figure he shouldn't be too hard to spot.

I sit down on a banquette near the maître d's lectern; a barman scuttles up. 'Beer?' he says, taking both nationality and alcoholic preference for granted. Moments later he returns with a frothing half-litre that's rather more than I'd wanted at this time of day. 'Not important to ask if you prefer a small one!' he chortles matily, winking at the Fender case. Here we go. At least there'd been no one at customs to feel me up for party-buttons.

I've taken three small sips when a proximate growl causes me to look up.

'Team?'

Above me stands a round-faced man in a docker's hat and a paunch-plumped fisherman's jumper, peering myopically through a pair of round, metal-framed spectacles.

'Koj . . . Koyo?'

I stand, we clasp hands, he snatches off his hat. Having done so he swiftly teases the gelled grey hairs that sparsely colonise his head into short, messy spikes; this act, and its concomitant exposure of a flamboyant ring similar to that worn by Ringo in *Help!*, at a stroke lays bare his CV. No less plainly, the enormous, messy smile that now fills half his face reassures me that here is a good, kind man of stoic temperament. Today, I think, standing to retrieve the Fender case from under the banquette, there will be no red-faced, wild-eyed finger-jabbing.

'You have a guitar?'

'Yes!' I blurt, driven by light-headed relief into an ecstatic statement of the bleeding obvious. 'I thought I'd surprise you.'

'How?' says Kojo, his waxy brow furrowing.

Two minutes in, and yet to be served with a writ or injured, I rashly overplay my hand. 'I thought we could play your song.'

'My song?'

'You know, um: *Nuku Pommiin.*' Its erstwhile performer shoots me a sharp look, more bemused than offended. 'I've learnt all the chords,' I continue, watching those jolly eyes narrow. 'We could do it . . . over there.' I point at a distant unoccupied sofa.

Kojo squints at the distant unoccupied sofa I'm pointing at. 'There? By the toilet?'

It's poor salesmanship, and we both know it. '*Nuku Pommiin*,' he echoes faintly, and a little coldly, as if greeting a girl who'd cruelly spurned his teenage advances, and was now here begging for an autograph. 'Ah, no.'

The game's up. Still, nothing left to lose now. 'Er . . . yes?'

After a pause just long enough to make me wonder if I'm shortly to find myself face down in the gutter slush with two halves of a Fender Bullet for company, he laughs. He laughs a lot, a drawn-out, tar-throated cackle that shows his nicotined teeth and stops all surrounding conversations. 'No,' he repeats, when at length he's able. Timo Kojo has just put the whole ill-conceived singalong scheme out of its misery, but the manner in which he's done so has simultaneously resurrected my enthusiasm for the quest ahead. As his laughter fades, mine picks up the slack.

Wiping our eyes, we follow the waitress to our seats; I'm interested to see Kojo exchanging smiles and nods with three or four tables, all occupied by well-groomed professionals and their elegant companions. We sit down, Kojo placing two packets of Marlboro Lights on his sideplate, and I ask who they are. 'Oh, you know. High-society people. See that woman? The richest in Finland. Her husband owns a lot of oil tankers. I mean *a lot*.'

Hardly the sort of company I expected an old nul-pointer to keep, but before I can think of a tactful means of saying so, Kojo offers an even unlikelier explanation. 'Most of these people I meet through my country club.'

I repeat these last two words, in incredulous italics; Kojo blithely sparks up a Marlboro and squints rheumily through the following exhalation. 'Yeah, for sure. For me it's a golf thing. This is why I was in Dubai, you know?'

I had assumed to the point of certainty that Kojo's time in the Emirates would have been occupied serenading Scandinavian guests in the sparsely peopled restaurant of a large, bronze-glassed hotel. 'I have a patent for a golf driving range system that you can build out on to the sea,' he says in a tone considerably more matter-of-fact than the words demand. 'In Dubai some hotels are interested.'

It's difficult to see how this extraordinary beginning to our conversation might be steered back towards the questions I need to ask: Kojo's got a meeting at three, which gives me two hours to get his whole story down. More fortunately than it would have appeared in most situations, a waitress chooses this moment to catch my guitar case with her right foot, causing her to drop a dish lavishly slathered in redcurrant sauce. Coldly muttering her way through the clean-up process, she leaves Kojo and me dabbing sticky spatters off our flesh and clothing. It's suddenly far easier to regroup the conversation. 'So,' I say, when we've finished, 'Harrogate.'

I'd already experienced the inflammatory dangers inherent in such a brusque opening gambit, but Kojo quickly reveals himself as a man at ease with his past, present and future. 'Eurovision was never my thing,' he drawls, with the mid-Atlantic, mid-Baltic intonation now familiar as the voice of middle-aged Scandi-rock. 'I was a rock musician, you know? I didn't get into music to sing la-la-la songs to Spanish grandmothers – I wanted to get girls!' Reaching round the table, he slaps my leg with blokeish fraternity; the waiter placing two plates of pasta and two glasses of wine before us widens his eyes. 'Or I should say *more* girls. We are in Finland: it's easy to find girls to have sex with!' If only the tourist board had stuck that on its Eurovision banner, I think. The faces now angling towards us from most surrounding tables demonstrated that in 2005 as in 1982, decorum is not a word to be found in the Timo Kojo lexicon.

'So I'm touring with this rock and soul band, and sharing a

flat in Helsinki with Tchim, sometimes being his roadie . . . we were really *not Eurovision*.' Well, Jim was, I say. At least a bit. Kojo's pained shrug is his first display of awkwardness; not bad going given what we're here to discuss. 'OK, I must say, I didn't like the song.' A sip of red wine; another Marlboro. 'The record company ask me to do it, and I told them straight.'

With the fag stuck in the corner of his mouth, he abruptly punches his hand. 'I said: the melody is awful, it's a nothing melody, you can't catch it. I'm sorry Tchim. The first version had a great middle eight, but then even this was taken out before Eurovision.' Kojo puffs his rosy, round cheeks out before expelling a long, lip-rumbling expression of pained disbelief. 'I hate the song, but I like the idea.' The idea? 'The no-war message in the lyric. It's very heavy for Finland with Russia right here. We really felt strong about what we were singing. There was a real understanding.'

But being in Finnish, this understanding did not travel far. If the rest of us gleaned from Kojo's performance that Finland was in mortal danger, we'd have assumed it derived from the populace slapping itself to death. I suggest to Kojo that Nicole's winning plea for peace, however cloying and vague, succeeded through being expressed with a simplicity that transcended the language barriers.

'Yes, but what is "a little bit peace"?' He snorts with grandiose derision, and I figure there won't be a better time to ask whether the man before me admits responsibility for one of Eurovision's most celebrated quotes. Asked the day after the final for his opinion on the winning entry, Kojo is said to have succinctly epitomised its singer as 'an ugly German virgin'.

'Yeah, why not? I can't remember saying it, but it sounds like me. I hate this taking the middle track, people who sing about big matters in this . . . blab-a-blab nothing way.' How joyously liberating to hear such words from a Eurovision performer's mouth; with the Kalvik blues now fading, it strikes me how lucky I am to be tracking down the entertaining misfits who wouldn't or couldn't play the Eurovision game, rather than its complacent, blanded-out winners. What's Nicole

Hohloch up to these days? Married to her childhood sweetheart, singing boompsadaisy schlager tunes and 'acting as an unofficial ambassador for her native Saarland', that's what.

Twenty-three years on, it's clear there was no false bravado in the smirk Kojo aimed at the cameras as the votes came in. 'Of course! For us this was a joke, this Eurovision thing. It's big for the record company guys, but bullshit for us. We went out to have some laughs, and we did.'

So what does a hard-bitten, road-wise rocker do for kicks with the Golden Girls and Jan Leeming for company, and Harrogate for a backdrop? The twinkle returns, with enhanced wattage. 'We had a couple of real good parties. These nice Portuguese ladies, we have a very good time with them.' The sequined Antpeople? 'They had black-and-white hats . . . I don't remember the song.' He's already confessed that not having once seen a recording of the final, he couldn't hum a single note of any rival entry bar Nicole's, or recall the name of any artist bar her. 'I forget a lot about Harrogate, but I remember a very nice Portuguese ass!' Ah, the *Bem Bom* bum. Here is one nul-pointer who didn't fail to score.

Perhaps inspired by this fond memory, or the interest its vocalisation has aroused at nearby tables, Kojo launches into further reminiscences of atypical Eurovision revelry. A big Man United fan, he bunked off a Eurovision press conference to inveigle himself into a session at the team's training ground, and so impressed the players with his keepy-uppy prowess that the gold record he subsequently dispatched at their request hung for many years on the changing-room wall.

Then, as glimpsed in the pre-vote interval film, there was that sedan-chair party thrown for the contestants at Castle Howard. 'I have to tell you,' Kojo says, with a wheezy chuckle, 'we had a little bet, maybe a dare. We all had a good smoke in that chair! You understand what I mean? I open the door to get out and all this smoke comes out with me and I have a *big smile . . .*'

He shows me that smile, and it's impossible not to return it. I'm seeing Kojo in the green room, what-the-fuck face, arms aloft; and I'm seeing him an hour earlier, delivering one of Eurovision's more conspicuous performances. It has to be done: with a prompting wink, I tap my temple. Kojo surveys me with a mixture of curiosity and concern; the latter becomes more prominent as once, twice, three times, I firmly strike my forehead with the palm of my right hand. Only as the fourth blow lands do his features relax in comprehension.

'This, yes, I don't know why,' he says, more soberly than my slap-happy performance demands. 'I didn't do it in rehearsal, you know: on-stage I do what I feel, I do my thing, and that night I guess that was my thing.' Like Jahn's splits, it was just one of those spur-of-the-moment expressions of on-stage *joie de vivre*, a helpless quirk. It might not have done either any favours in the voting, but at least they were allowed the freedom to leap and slap and dress up like berks ('Hey – I chose that suit myself!' cries Kojo in mock outrage when I later describe his red-leather two-piece in unflattering terms). How deflating to contemplate the ruthlessly choreographed modern contest's ratcheting intolerance of non-conformity: as Europe becomes ever more homogenous, its edges rubbed off, its national distinctions eroded, so Eurovision has evolved into a celebration of what makes us the same, as once it celebrated what made us different.

'So we have this all-or-nothing song,' says one of Eurovision's last true characters. 'We hear the others in rehearsal, and we are so different, we know we either win or lose. So when the Finnish newspapers are asking if we can win, I say – why not? I say it because I really don't care if we do.'

His protestations of nonchalance are more credible than Jahn Teigen's. But did he really feel no pain, sitting there with Finland stalled on the line as around them on the scoreboard the digits flashed into double, treble figures? His shrug is slightly less cocksure. 'I can be honest again, when the votes start, for sure that's exciting. That's what I liked about Eurovision as a kid. So when it starts . . . it's a crazy thing, but you think: Maybe.' Kojo forms his hands into a megaphone and launches into a Tannoyed announcement: 'Twelve points

Luxembourg, ten points blab-a-blab . . . Yes, we're excited backstage. It gets down to one point, the first voting, and we have nothing, but still, you know . . .'

But I don't, not yet, and I want to. 'After maybe six, seven country votes, at this time we're not excited, but we start to laugh. And our manager – a German guy – he bends down to me and says, "You know, we have to hope to get zero now. Zero is better than five, six. Zero is news."' He surveys a forkful of pasta. 'Although back in Finland, it was not the right kind of news.'

The moment I saw that baggage-hall billboard I knew we'd come to this point, and to Kojo's credit he doesn't choose to trail away into dot-dot-dots, to leave this dark corner of his story in the shade. He stubs out his cigarette, and for once doesn't light another. He shakes his head a little and those fleshy lips slide down at the sides and tauten. 'Here . . . well, here it was awful.' I didn't expect to hear of Jahn-style red-carpet motorcades, and I'm clearly not going to.

'In Finland Eurovision is very, *very* popular. You understand what I mean? I watched it as a kid, yeah, of course, in the sixties.' He wistfully hums the Eurovision fanfare. 'But in the seventies I stop watching. It becomes a joke for me, but not for Finland. I haven't seen it for many, many years.'

He's not joking: a moment later, when I mention my encounter with Jahn Teigen, he has no idea who I'm talking about. How could anyone – and a Scandinavian Eurovision performer of all people – not know Jahn Teigen? In deconstructing my shock on hearing this news I accept just how radical has been the restaffing of my internal rock hall of fame. In it, Jahn Teigen now stood proudly up near the front, perhaps obscuring half of Jon Entwistle's head and the Jam's rhythm section. And Kojo isn't doing badly, either: that performance in the Harrogate green room barged Martha and the Vandellas out of his way, and the revelations of the previous half hour have seen him leapfrog Ray Davies's brother and – do us a favour, Timo: turn round and punt him up the arse – Brian Ferry.

'Team,' he says, lowering his voice and leaning forward on table-planted elbows, 'what it is with Finnish people, they are so *serious*. And so *strange*.' In two words he encapsulates the enigma that is the Finnish race. I think of my recent trip to the Estonian capital Tallinn, watching golf-sweatered 'vodka tourists' from Helsinki downing breakfast beers with silent, grim determination as their children wanly sipped hot chocolate. And try as I might not to, I think of the shower heads that dangle beside every Finnish lavatory, public and private.

'Strange, serious . . . and *shy*. In everything! In politics, you know, to win an argument you have to use your elbows, but here they can't do that. They like to just sit behind the table.' The repeated us of 'they' to describe his countrymen is no longer a mystery. In the hour I have known him, Kojo has made it plain that he is neither serious nor, still less, shy. In a land of tight lips and held tongues he's a tub-thumping hold-forther, bearing personal responsibility for perhaps 70 per cent of all decibels being generated by the restaurant's several dozen diners. Consulting the menu he'd extracted and donned a pair of half-moon spectacles, without first troubling himself to remove his existing eyewear. Other than in his capacity for tobacco, and to a modest extent booze, Timo Kojo is not Finnish.

I suppose it was a bad combination. Scandinavians in general and Finns in particular are not bred to accept arrant failure – they're too efficient, too dependable, too doughty. You don't leave tips here: good service is guaranteed without the need for a grubby financial incentive. Mr Bean is a Nordic institution because he messes up with a consistency unimaginable to even the most gormlessly incompetent Scandinavian.

But though we in Britain might watch Eurovision for the same reason they watch Mr Bean, for them there's no silly side to the contest. The most recent UK winner, Katrina (of And The Waves renown), said that in a perfect Eurovision future, 'the Scandinavians would take it less seriously, and the Brits more so'. All Nordic competitors are weighed down with earnest national expectation, and none more so than Kojo in 1982.

Whatever Jahn Teigen might tell you, no Scandinavian nation has endured a more testing history than Finland. Many Swedes and Norwegians don't even consider Finns Scandinavian: ethnically and linguistically they're out on a cold limb, their historical and cultural origins utterly remote from their neighbours. As they remain, despite 600 years of Swedish rule. The ethnic Swedes who still form 6 per cent of Finland's population are an elite that enjoys enormously disproportionate economic and political clout: in Helsinki (bracketed even on the BBC website by its Swedish name, Helsingfors), most street signs are bilingual. Without wishing to call it an inferiority complex, there's certainly a sense of Finnish isolation.

When the Swedish empire began to retreat, the Russians moved in; Finland achieved independence only in 1917, and promptly lost it again to the Soviets in 1940 after a heartbreakingly heroic winter war. 'Since World War II, the Soviet Union's status as a superpower has meant that it could at any time end Finland's existence as a separate state,' states a startlingly matter-of-fact US Library of Congress report. 'Recognising this, the Finns have sought and achieved reconciliation with the Soviets, and have tenaciously pursued a policy of neutrality avoiding entanglement in superpower conflicts.' As the no man's land between NATO and the Warsaw Pact, for Finland the Cold War was always more about bombs and nuclear poo, not birds and love.

Eurovision had always offered Finns a chance to get one over on their fellow Scandinavians – and make a rare splash in Europe – but in 1982, it was more than that. Kojo's mission wasn't just to bring home the long overdue Eurobacon, but to use his elbows on their behalf to declaim the dangers of A-bomb apathy.

Yet as eagerly as he endorsed the nation's fears of nuclear conflict, Kojo's carefree conduct in the aftermath of Harrogate showed how completely he underestimated their parallel enthusiasm for Eurovision. He landed back at Helsinki oblivious of a bitter ongoing inquest: even before the final he'd been slated for bunking off that press conference, and after his green-room sneering, the whiff of blood was in the air. 'At the airport one guy came up and said real quietly, "Oh man, I'm sorry for you," and I see suddenly that this is worse for the Finnish people than it is for me.' Kojo shakes his head slightly. 'If I had apologised there to the country for letting them down, if I had looked sad, played the right game, I would have been forgiven.'

A tiny, snorted laugh suggests that though he's now glad he didn't do this, there have been times in the previous twenty-three years when he wished he had. 'But instead I stood with my arms up, a big smile you know, like hey: the King is Back!' With winning élan, he strikes the relevant pose. 'No humour, these Finns. I fought the papers, so they hit me back. The next day, all the front pages call me a country-cheater. What is it? A traitor.'

So began what he's reluctant to call the worst time his life, although it's hard to see how it wasn't. 'You know I'm big into ice hockey, so a couple of days after I get home I go to a game, and people around start dropping beer on my trousers. "Oh, *sorry*," they say, in this stupid voice. And sometimes in the street people were throwing Coke cans at me.' He laughed it off, and so did his friends: in truth, he says, most of them were still sniggering at the fantastic incongruity of their mate the scowling rocker doing Eurovision. But the histrionic hate campaign wasn't much fun for his parents. 'My mother had to listen to all this blab-a-blab at her working place, people saying this and that about me. It was hard for her.'

Kojo's eye-rolling indulgence devolved into shaken disbelief as the resentment lingered stubbornly on. 'Yes, I'm bred with it, the zero points. I'm famous for it. This was front-page news, and not just for one day. For two years I hear it all the time: "Oh yeah, you're the zero-points guy." And still sometimes now.' When was the last occasion? Idly rearranging his grey scalp-spikes, he considers briefly. 'I think last week. About once in a week, somebody, somewhere will talk to me about Eurovision.' It was a stand-off between him and the Finnish public: if he didn't apologise for Harrogate, or at least express regret, they wouldn't forgive him. Twenty-three years on, and neither party seems ready to back down. This, I'm thinking, could be the Kalvik Trigger. If it is, what he goes on to say snicks off the safety catch and begins to squeeze.

'You know a sports match that finishes with no goals? You know what they call such a match here?' I kind of have an idea, I think, without saying so. 'A "Kojo-Kojo".' He looks hard at me, successfully imparting a suggestion of what it is to live with this level of national ignominy, to be synonymous with worthless sterility across one of Europe's hugest lands. I'm now back on a beach in Koh Samui, watching a wild-haired, wild-eyed man stamping towards my sun lounger. 'Kojo-Kojo, zero-zero. This is what people say, even today, even twenty-some years after.'

It's difficult for me to conceive how two decades of that sort of business can affect a person, though not as difficult as it might have been a week earlier. I explain, as fully as I can bear to, my recent experiences in Thailand. 'Well,' I say when I'm done, 'you can understand that situation better than most.'

The expected curt nod of hard-bitten, martyrs-in-arms empathy is replaced by an extravagant curl of those substantial lips. 'No! I don't understand at all! For sure you want to win, but you have to be a realist. If the votes go bad, they go bad. Why should that be so shameful, so awful?'

I look at those lips, and wonder what their owner will do if I kiss them, hard and long. Thank you, Timo Kojo, thank you for not being embittered into twitching paranoia. I suppose the key distinction here is that Finn saw Eurovision as his gilded gateway to Abbadom; for Kojo, it was a chance to visit Man U's training ground and smoke pot in a sedan chair.

For two post-Harrogate years, Kojo found solace and employment in continental exile. 'Germany, Holland, Italy – a lot of peace gigs, many TV shows; I had a great reaction.' His manager at the time also represented Hanoi Rocks, huge-haired pioneers of Finn metal and often cited as a major influence on Guns N' Roses. What is it, I wonder, that unites these two apparently incompatible cultures: Eurovision was a joke to Kojo, but would he have laughed as loudly backstage at Yankovision? 'Finland has a funny thing for America, big cars and hard rock,' he says with a shrug. 'Too much corporate USA stuff, a lot of TV ads, like we are a little USA.'

Yet you don't need to look far, except geographically, to find the cultural influences that inspired Kojo's musical output in the pre-Eurovision era. His first four albums, all released or recorded before he put on that red suit of death, were heavily Americanised, English-language blues rock: 'So Mean', 'Lucky Street', 'Go All the Way', 'Hitparade'. 'OK, but I voted to join the EC!' he says, before embarking on a wandering diatribe against the euro. 'Five years ago it was one Finnish mark for a coffee, and now it's one euro – this is like six marks, it's really amazing how bad the prices have gone!'

For Kojo's recording career, Eurovision proved a watershed – a leaky one, with dead pigeons floating in it. 'Time Won't Wait', released in 1983, proved to be Kojo's final English-language recording; following an almost unnoticed Finnish album with Jim Pembroke, his studio output settled into the fitful release of singles. One in '89, two in 1990, then a gap of three years, followed by one of a full decade. (Nonetheless, with 159 studio tracks to his name, Timo Kojo has a back catalogue heftier than ABBA's.)

But touring was always his big thing: gigging all round Europe was just an extension of what he'd been doing all round Finland since the mid seventies. Through most of those early years Kojo shared a rowdy tour bus with Yankcentric rockers the Hurriganes, a band whose shifting line-up once inevitably incorporated Jim Pembroke on keyboards. 'Finland is a big country,' he says, 'and we spent a lot of time on that bus. I mean *a lot*. And so we spent a lot of time drinking.' Yet after all the gleeful tales of Portuguese girls and sedan-chair sensimilla at Eurovision, his reminiscences on those hard-boozing, hard-shagging times on the road seem oddly muted.

Only later do I understand why. Alongside him in the back row of the bus was Hurrigane's guitarist Albert Järvinen, a musician who had recorded with Motorhead's Lemmy and new-wave pioneer Nick Lowe, and who lent his evidently considerable talents to Kojo's first two albums. The pair shared some memorably drunken nights together on the road, until a stubborn adherence to the grimmest rock clichés assured Albert's graduation to less sociable narcotics. In March 1991, while playing a series of gigs in London, Albert overdosed in his hotel room. In his summing up, the coroner said that although just forty, Järvinen had the body of a seventy year old. Less than a year before, another of the original Hurriganes had drunk himself to death in Helsinki.

'It was very hard,' whispers Kojo, but he doesn't want to say more. In fact he doesn't even say half the above – the details of Albert's fast life and young death are gleaned from later research. It's clear that as well as mourning his lost friend, he's having a there-but-for-the-grace-of-God moment. Had Kojo carried on living as fast as he was in the early eighties, that could have been him. Finns drink, rockers do drugs. Try being both for more than a few years, and a premature demise from unnatural causes is almost guaranteed. In taking the wind out of his musical career, I suggest, nul points saved his life. 'Yeah,' he says, with a dry half-laugh, 'this and my wife.'

It's more than a mild surprise to learn that Kojo has been with the same woman for twenty-five years – they have three teenage sons. Clearly theirs is no conventional relationship: Kojo's tone while reminiscing on those Portuguese girls is very much that of a young rock-god about town, rather than a man well entrenched in a long-term relationship with the future mother of his children. 'Well, yes,' he says, analytically. 'You can call it an unusual situation. The mother [as he refers to her throughout] has needed a lot of nerve, dealing with all kinds of persons over twenty-five years. I mean *all kinds*!'

The mighty leap that propelled Kojo from the Finn-rock frying pan landed him in a distant fire. Leaving 'the mother' behind with three young children, in the mid nineties – for reasons he doesn't care to elucidate – Kojo relocated to Moscow. In his three years there, he did it all. 'I made a big-band record in Russian, and recorded with many big stars. You know Alla Pugacheva?'

I do: with 250 million record sales to her name, along with a stack of films, a self-edited eponymous magazine and a line of footwear, here is a woman who can rightfully claim to be Russia's greatest star. She inevitably counts a Eurovision appearance amongst her achievements: at Dublin in 1997, the stout and definitively feisty forty-eight year old silenced the audience by striding out in a pair of teetering (and self-designed) Pinball Wizard platform boots, before winning them round with a bellowed rendition of her anthemic (and self-penned) entry. In a year when Portugal and – yes – Norway went home pointless, Alla returned with a steady thirty-three.

Among Kojo's more unexpected Muscovite achievements were a series of prizewinning children's albums – 'soul and rock, played by real good players, but with lyrics for kids' – and an associated UNICEF concert in Red Square. 'Children singing about peace and love, live on TV in forty countries.' He sighs, his wistful tone explaining why I recall no such event. 'The Chechen war suddenly got real bad, and Coca-Cola and Heinz and all the big sponsors just disappeared. At the last minute it all went up in smoke. I lost a lot of money on that. Really, I lost it all. I was absolutely bankrupt.'

Worse, in fact. 'The big problem in Russia,' rasps Kojo half a Marlboro later, 'is you always have to pay behind the table to make any success.' With some reluctance he tells me about a call received weeks after he'd settled a $30,000 Moscow studio bill. 'This guy says, "Maybe you need to pay your studio bill now." I tell him I already paid, in cash, but when I call the studio, the engineer I gave it to has disappeared. I think: What the fuck? And then this man calls back. "Maybe it's a good time to pay – *now.*"'

Kojo bangs the table rather too hard; most of the coffee that's just been placed before me ends up in its saucer. 'I was afraid, really afraid. I know how bad the bad people can be in Russia, and these were very bad people. And I didn't have that money.' Just listening to him, seeing his confident, meaty hands starting to knot together, I'm feeling queases of empathy. With nothing more than eager charm and a way with a tune he'd earnt acceptance in a country not known for its willingness to welcome outsiders. But with his feet under the Moscow mixing desk, the happy-go-lucky naivety that defined much of Kojo's life almost had them shattered at the ankles.

Having somehow persuaded his music-biz contacts to resolve the situation, he returned home shaken and – once more – back to square one. But this is the man who laughs in the face of nul points, so I'm not surprised by his response when I ask if he wishes he'd never gone to Moscow. 'Why should I regret? I was hanging out with all these big Russian stars, all their bodyguards, a lot of beautiful girls. It's an exciting place, a big market . . . Most people were too scared to go, but I went and I almost made it. I can say at least I tried. What it is, Team, I love to hang around people, talking, dealing, bullshitting. It's easy for me, this kind of things. I love people. You understand?'

It's impossible not to admire the imperturbable, gung-ho optimism of this rock 'n' roll Mr Pickwick. The ever-spinning world of Timo Kojo has no predictable orbit, yet he's still enjoying the ride. 'Today? Well, you know, I need to earn a lot. I am bad with money, I have three boys, I like to eat good food, I like to travel. And I spend *a lot* on shoes.' (To Kojo's loud delight, I peer speculatively under the table just before realising this is a joke.)

His current musical undertakings range from corporate parties ('playing soul stuff, the way I started') to TV-ad jingle-writing ('good money, but I feel like a whore when I smile to these business guys'), but these days his is a portfolio career: of all the artists I'm to meet, Kojo is one of the very few not to press upon me a copy of his latest CD. It's no surprise to learn of those Marlboro-tinted fingers being wedged in a lot of very unusual pies. 'I'm doing a big promotion for a new champagne, Sibelius. We get it from a good-quality French producer, and we made a deal for the name with the Sibelius family, and a deal to give a per cent of the profit to new music in Finland.

We're going to sell it all around the world. The big year is 2007, fifty years after when he died.'

Then of course there's that country club, St Nicolaus, a half hour from Helsinki: 'the official golf club of Santa Claus', as Kojo calls it, and as it's billed on the rather ritzy website I later consult. 'Very high-society – these are my people now,' he says, with just the tiniest hint of self-mockery. 'I built up the club, found the money, hired these Canadian course architects . . . We play golf from May to October, and then have deer hunting there in the winter.' I shoot him a gawp: what does Santa Claus have to say about that? 'Not reindeer!' he blurts, reddening slightly. 'Just, you know, regular deer. Anyway I don't do guns. If I go to the club in the winter, it's for a drink and a sauna. Golf is my thing.'

And so we move to his most eye-catching professional venture. 'Team, I'm real excited with this ocean golf driving range. The beautiful part is that you need a lot of space for a driving range: land is expensive, but water is free!' The enthusiasm he's expressing is so heartfelt, that despite the project's apparent silliness I find I'm sharing it. 'Two guys and a diver can set the whole thing up in a day, jetty and everything. And then you can play all night! We use balls that float, and at the end of the day a guy goes out with a sea tractor to pick them up.'

Kojo looks at his watch, tuts in self-reproach at what he sees, then abruptly snatches up his phone and with a significant wink enters a number. 'Tchim? Yeah . . . I'm just back. Yeah, we played a few rounds out there . . . I birdied a hole where Tiger took a par! Yeah, see you tonight, Tchim, but first here's someone you need to talk to.'

As the tiny Nokia is pressed to my ear, I wonder if, despite all his cheery bluster, Kojo is now gently trying to remind me, and maybe himself, that Eurovision is a contest for songs, not singers. That it wasn't he who scored zero, but Tchim. A familiar estuary mumble emerges. 'Hi . . . Yeah, listen, I'm a bit tired. Haven't been sleeping too well . . .' It's now almost three o'clock.

Kojo rises and delivers a manly slap to my shoulder. 'I'm

having Tchim and a few people to my apartment tonight,' he says. 'You can come – why not?' Not an offer a man facing a night alone in an airport Holiday Inn is likely to turn down. 'OK, I write you my address.' Rather splendidly, remembering what this is requires three guesses, two pages of my notebook and a full minute. 'We've been in this apartment just a few months,' is Kojo's inadequate explanation, delivered as he trots away for a word with Finland's richest woman.

I'm left with an empty packet of Marlboro Lights and two inches of his wine for company, along with a glow of happy relief. Many surprises lay in wait at the bottom of the Eurovision barrel, but it was clear now that not all were moist and malodorous.

Outside it's already dark, a weak blizzard wafting around the narrow strip of bleak parkland opposite the restaurant, and into the big arched windows of the dour arcade alongside. But lugging that Fender case along the ice-varnished pavements I'm barely aware of the environmental discouragements: there's too much Timo in my head. How inspiring, how enviable to reach fifty-two and still lead a life so nomadically fluid, so unpredictable, that you can't even remember your own address. And how risibly feeble that my sole domestic relocation in thirty-eight years had seen me move eight stops down the 65 bus route.

Yet settling into an aimless, slush-scraping shamble, I begin to wonder what kept him on the move. Kojo-Kojo, I'm soon thinking, so bad they named him twice; the double-zero country-cheat pelted with cans by his strange and serious countrymen. When Kojo went to Moscow, he was running away just as fast as Finn Kalvik ran to Thailand – running from that lingering nul-points shadow, from a lifestyle that claimed so many of his contemporaries, and, maybe, from the overwhelming domestic responsibilities of trying to deal with three young kids after a rootless, self-contained life on the road. Ignominy and tragedy drove him away; perhaps he hadn't forgotten his address so much as displayed a fugitive's facility for blanking it out. Perhaps he was still on the run.

The streets fill as I wander about looking for somewhere to pass three hours. In doing so I at last find a use for this stupid, redundant and by now arm-stretchingly hefty guitar, hoisting it to deflect the arcs of bus-slush that slap heavily across the pavement every few steps. Its unavoidable presence also earns nods of long-suffering fraternity from buskers, and I'm soon enjoying what happens every time I put the thing down to rest my protesting biceps. Suddenly an exclusion zone opens up around me, those at its circumference aiming oh-no winces at their feet in preparation for whatever I was about to do that they would be asked to pay to witness: outside the central station, that's good for fifteen minutes of fun.

I spin a coffee out for an hour, vainly waiting for my brown-splattered trouser bottoms to dry, then repair to a state liquor store for a bottle of host-fuel. Neither commercial transaction proves as ruinous as Kojo had led me to expect: once sufficient to reduce foreign visitors to tears of confused rage, the price of alcohol in post-Euro Finland is now on rough parity with Britain's. And though the outlets that sell it are still starkly signed ALKO, the craven, substance-dependent shuffle once expected from clients is gone. So too the strip lights and white Formica that formed a wince-inducing preview of your looming hangover.

Additionally burdened, and rather lost, I blunder with hypothermic sloth and inefficiency into quieter, residential streets. Traversing a triangle of parkland, a frosted missile catches me square in the unscarfed throat; having so recently vacated a tropical beach – my nose is just starting to peel – there's a momentary concern that the violent, sub-zero impact might shatter my head, like a cook-chilled desert boulder. But how heartening that despite the tedious omnipresence of seasonal ammunition, the youth of Helsinki retains such enthusiasm for snowballing. Or so I think much, much later.

Kojo's flat, as I discover by some miracle of random navigation, is on the third floor of a block whose concertina-gated lift dates it to the early twentieth century. A door opens, and with a hug I'm welcomed into an expanse of new parquet, sparsely but expensively furnished. The duty-free fruits of Kojo's Dubai visit lie all around: a half unboxed home-cinema system, a swathe of paisley silk curtains draped over a huge sofa. 'The mother' is introduced to me – a woman whose gentle, tolerant features eloquently explain how she's endured twenty-five years of Portuguese girls and Muscovite escapes.

I'm handed a glass of red wine the size of a fishbowl on a stick and, with the unslakeable alcoholic thirst of a foreign stranger here to rake up his convivial host's most painful memories, dispatch it in minutes. As the members of Kojo's eclectic coterie arrive, so I'm introduced to every groomed, smoking one of them: an extravagantly cleavaged former model with her junior chaperone, a couple of music executives, a theatrical impresario, a model agent. Conspicuous in their absence are the mumbling misfits I'd previously imagined as a nul-pointer's default associates. Why didn't I know fascinating, glamorous people like these? And why, after many decades of grim evidence to the contrary, had I not yet learnt that drinking a great deal of wine very quickly didn't turn me into one of them?

The mother hovers about, topping up glasses, laying plates of smoked meat and cruton-topped salads on a vast dining table of curious construction. I lean down for a closer look: its sunken, glass-topped central section is filled with crushed ice, thereby chilling the cold buffet above. 'That is quite a thing,' I slur, nodding at the table as I'm joined by the only guest of humdrum demeanour, a chap in his fifties with John Kerry hair and a golf shirt.

'Thank you,' he replies graciously. 'It is my design. You can also put small candles in this to keep food hot.' I can say that I've never been so pleased to meet a quantity surveyor before. At least until he reveals that he never travels abroad without a set of bongos, 'you know – just on the off chance'.

Last to arrive, with a tiny woman in tow, is a pasty, slicked-back, Orbison-shaded man in a careworn black suit. When he sticks a finger under his sunglasses and rubs wearily at a wrinkle-lidded eye, I began to have an idea who it might be.

'Hoozat Fender in the hall?' he murmurs through barely parted lips, and all doubt is banished.

I'd wondered if Jim Pembroke's semi-comatose telephonic persona might conceal a table-stamping rock animal; it doesn't. He's almost sixty, after all. Yet in that shrugging, deadpan mumble, and in between drags, he seems happy to reminisce upon the fate of *Nuku Pommiin*. (He'd written the lyrics in English, he tells me – it's a tribute to the heroic impenetrability of the Finnish language that after forty years in Helsinki, Jim still generally avoids attempting to use it.) As its composer, he was there in Harrogate; his account of anarchic tomfoolery dovetails neatly with our host's. 'We had a game of dares going on, over the whole week . . . I think it was ten points for smoking in that sedan chair.'

We talk a little more, covering Wigwam's agonising near miss with Virgin, the curious online insistence that he was born and raised in Hull rather than Finchley, the sabbatical in the States during which he acquired the woman now nodding silently at his side – the same one, I now understand, whose voice first welcomed me into the story of *Nuku Pommiin*. This realisation, along with the shame inhibitor now swilling around my system, brings me back to the Fender, and the as-yet unrewarded pain it has brought me. 'Could I ask a favour?' I begin; the sentence that follows gets only as far as '*Nuku*' before Jim holds up a hand.

'Oh, come off it,' he drawls, as furiously offended as a man responsible for 'Corporal Cauliflower's Mental Function' is ever likely to be.

I find a space on a sofa, and sit in it with a big plateful of food in my lap. Finnish is happening all around me, a bewildering flow of senseless sound, like Japanese spoken by drugged Italians; in the hour that follows I understand only two words: 'IKEA' and 'perkele', a favoured oath amongst the Finnish seamen in Eric Newby's *The Last Grain Race* and, I learn, of Timo Kojo's. Still, having nodded and smiled my way through several hundred Icelandic gatherings, contact with sustained Nordic unintelligibility is these days a solace rather than a threat. And watching Kojo hold court is a great spectator sport: he's at the hub of it all, that hoarse, booming voice powering the proceedings, the definitive host with the most. The 'real good parties' that were his principal memories of Harrogate clearly wouldn't have been so good, or so real, without him. Having memorably failed to do so in Mr Kalvik's company, I was at last having fun with a Finn.

It's nearing 1 a.m.: I'm half into my coat and half through my unsteady farewells when a rangy, slightly whey-faced youth shuffles out of a bedroom. 'Eh! My youngest boy!' English is being spoken; I am therefore the intended audience; Kojo's son and I exchange slightly awkward nods. I gather that he's come to ask his dad for a little Friday-night funding – almost midnight it might be, but through long and bitter peaked-too-early experience, I'm all too aware that the Scandinavian weekend only really gets into gear during the early hours of Saturday.

'OK, son,' brays Kojo, handing over a crumple of notes that his boy surveys in a small, pale palm. We're in the hall when a disembodied yell booms out of the front room. 'That's for condoms!' Those young shoulders sag slightly, followed by a tiny sigh that suggests his father hasn't quite finished. Accurately so. As I hoist my guitar case, the boy snatches open the front door and bolts off down a dark stairwell, leaving me alone with the triumphant last words I will hear from Timo Kojo's mouth. 'Now go out there and fuck like hell!'

I'm in a taxi and halfway to the hotel before the echoing aftershocks of this spectacular utterance subside sufficiently to allow rival contemplations into my brain. They do so tentatively as we pass two lorries that an earthmover is slowly filling with kerbside snow. Surveying this thanklessly Sisyphean process, I accept that it's nonetheless consistent with those toilet-mounted bottom-showers and the men I'd seen steam-cleaning planes at Helsinki airport. Here was a country with an almost obsessive-compulsive sense of correctitude, of doing everything properly, efficiently, completely.

Precisely on cue, the driver leans his head slightly back to address me. 'Excuse me, but is it more accurate to say "a hotel *near* the airport" or "a hotel *by* the airport"?' His uncertain, nervous tone suggests that should my answer not tally with what he's been saying to English-speaking passengers, he'll pull over at the next safe opportunity and silently puncture his thigh with the ignition key. This much wine down the line, however, I'm well beyond semantic niceties.

'Um . . . I think either's kind of OK.'

His head bobs slowly. 'I see,' he murmurs, clearly disappointed. 'So you are not a native speaker of English.'

I say nothing, acknowledging only now just how awful life must have been here for Kojo after 24 April 1982. Finns were raised to do the right thing, precisely the right thing; in failing to do so, and then making a big joke out of it, he had soiled his homeland's defining ethos. How very splendid of him, then, to shoulder aside the crushing opprobrium of a nation, to emerge from his experience stronger, more stubborn, to walk on with a sod-you swagger. There was life after nul points, and for Kojo it was an indubitably good one.

Billboards and road signs alive with dotted vowels sweep past; the roads widen and empty as we broach the airport zone's warehoused hinterland. With a cushioned crunch the taxi pulls up at the Holiday Inn's empty, snow-drifted forecourt; I hand the driver his cash and clamber out, dragging the Fender off my lap, into the still, sodium-lit chill. As the yellow Mercedes pulls gingerly away my shudders of cold evolve into a quiver of relieved joy: the voyage that had scraped so painfully aground on the sands of Koh Samui was afloat once more. I watch those tail lights disappear behind a Saab dealership, then let my drunken delight out in a wild, primal bellow. 'Now go out there and fuck like hell!'

23 April 1983

Rudi Sedlmayer Halle, Munich

Çetin Alp	*Remedios Amaya*
Turkey	*Spain*
Opera	*¿Quien maneja mi barca?*

'Today we have to talk about a new died ESC-related person,' announced the news forum on www.eurovision-spain.com, 'as in this case the Turkish 1983 representative, Çetin Alp, who just had a heart crisis in his house.' Sitting down to check out the Eurovision latest on my fortieth birthday had initially seemed sad merely in the contemporary sense. Now I looked at the screen, with its associated thumbprint photograph of a rather tentative-looking fellow in glasses and a beige tuxedo, and felt my innards slowly bind themselves into a knot. Fourteen had just become thirteen; of all the nul-pointers who had died on-stage, Çetin Alp was the first to die off it. And that meant there would be no meeting with the man responsible for the most extraordinary of all the 943 songs performed since Jetty Paerl took to that Lugano stage in 1956.

I'd read a great deal about Çetin Alp and the Short Waves' performance at Munich in 1983, but it's not until six months after he was called to his eternal rest that Andreas's DVD anthology allows me to witness it with my own saucered eyes. The millions who beheld Çetin's three minutes are unlikely to forget them; but 1983 found me deep in the Eurovision void into which many fall between innocent childhood exuberance and pissed-up student irony. At nineteen, staying in on Saturday night to watch television was simply out of the question. (My vivid memories of Harrogate the year before remain an awkward enigma; it can only be assumed that what I recalled as a mild attraction to Jan Leeming was in fearful truth a desperate, slavish obsession.)

Introduced by an interminable wonders-of-Germany tourist-board promotion – it would be seven long minutes before Marlene Charell welcomed us to the Rudi Sedlmayer Halle – the 1983 final efficiently sets out its stall as the most lazily tedious production I have yet to experience. The cavernous auditorium bears down on an insultingly inadequate sliver of stage; Marlene, struggling with her tri-lingual introductory duties, commits so many stumbles, slips and floundering, blithering illogicalities that the online community later releases a final tally (twenty-seven, including thirteen in the voting session alone). If the French have been looking to justify their boycott the year before – and you can guarantee they have – here it is on 400 million screens.

Appropriately enough, Guy Bonnet marks his nation's return to the Eurovision fold with the evening's debut performance: who better to wipe the slate clean than the pianist veteran of two previous finals? Not so much playing his instrument as attempting to reanimate it with a weary facsimile of cardiac massage, Guy has the face and glasses of a student scientist, and the blue tuxedo of a diehard Europillock. (He's now a Christian rocker and an international-standard ocean fisherman.) This desperate start is swiftly redeemed by the now traditional appearance of a wonky-toothed Norwegian and his winsome missus. Finding no trace of the conductor's name on her cue card, Marlene boldly makes one up on the spot: 'Johannes Skorgan!' comes her cry, as we watch Sigurd Jansen fingering his baton in bemusement.

She has no trouble with Jahn Teigen, but I do. Despite the ludicrous nose-to-the-stage bow with which he introduces himself, this is not the Jahn of old. If anything, it's an even more dishearteningly castrated performance than that V-neck love-in the year before: he's wearing an if-you-can't-beat-'em white tuxedo, for pity's sake, and what's going on with these lyrics? I wasn't expecting much from a song called *Do-Re-Mi*, and I don't get it: each of the many choruses begins with the title, and ends in fa-so-la-ti-do. You shameless, cynical sell-out, I hear myself muttering. You're better than this. 'A performance that redefined unoriginality,' one of my Eurovision books had called it, and now I understand why.

At least until I rewind to savour Marlene's introduction afresh, and hear her name the lyricists as Jahn Teigen and Herodes Falsk. The old Prima Vera mischief makers . . . Sure enough, reviewing his performance in this light I can see that everything about it – that ridiculous dinner jacket, the childishly inane and contrivedly rootless lyrics and la-la-la melody, the way he spins round and plants a kiss on Anita's temple near the end – is a Euro-baiting spoof. The previous year Jahn's entry had been purged of alienating Nordic gutturalisms by that professor of linguistics; with Teigenesque bravado, he's now taken this initiative to its idiotic conclusion, ordering song and outfit off-the-peg from Eurovision Rentals. His smile is as overbearing and relentless as a Monty Python quiz-show host; the smile of a man having his cheesecake and eating it.

There are only three songs before Çetin, two of them performed by Sheena Eastons in bright yellow ra-ra skirts and matching calf-length boots; Sweet Dreams opt to sing on stools, thereby assuring the UK will not be adding to its tally of victories. 'The following entry is the Turkish!' beams Marlene, and as the conductor turns to face the orchestra, the German commentator describes *Opera* with something that sounds very like scorn. I've no idea what he's actually saying, of course, but his mastery of audible quotation marks for derisive ends would have earnt an approving nod from Terry Wogan in the booth next door. And then here is a bespectacled man in a tan tux with gold lapels, conspicuously lacking the Teigen grin such an outfit demands. With no extant recording of the following year's Balkan Song Festival, where Çetin was to win the Top Talent award, this is the only footage of him known to exist: he's part Borat, part Leslie Crowther. His glasses, horribly, are tinted yellow, casting a sickly, liverish shadow that seems to spread across much of his face.

But no one's really looking at him. Strung across the shallow stage behind Çetin are the Short Waves; no other backing band sounded more certain to bound on-stage in canary jumpsuits, yet the audience finds itself faced with a quintet of musketeers and Empress Josephines, a perplexing medley of brocade, towering wigs and Austin Powers velveteen ruff-frills. These, as the German commentator has doubtless just revealed, are the characters who will assist Çetin in performing a three-minute opera. When our man inaugurates this by raising his arms and turning to lead the Short Waves into an extraordinary, swelling yowl, a vocal homage to Sergeant Pepper's discordant orchestral climax, it's clear we are watching Eurovision history being made.

Çetin Alp's Eurovision career had begun in 1979, when at the age of thirty-one he was invited to enter Turkey's national pre-selection. Fifth out of eight wasn't a great result, but then it was pretty much a shambles all round: the winning song was disqualified when someone found a dusty recording of it in their singles collection, and the runner-up substitute was told to unpack his suitcase after neighbouring Arab nations began asking aloud if Turkey was absolutely sure it wanted to send a delegation to Jerusalem.

That lonely paragraph is the repository of public knowledge of Mr Alp's pre-Munich existence. In the many Turkish ESC forums I patronised, and the four obituaries I had translated, his entire professional career was condensed into three terse, almost brutal words: the *Opera* man. So conspicuous was this one song's Eurovision impact, and so predictable its shattering failure, that it came to eclipse all his other professional achievements. In life as in death, Çetin Alp was known only for the 'three-part song suite' composed for him by Bugra Ugur and Aysel Gürel.

An opera about opera, entitled *Opera*, their effort was one of the more desperate of that year's many attempts to circumnavigate the native-language rule, and in particular the subclause that states that 'short quotations from another language are allowed so long as they are no longer than one phrase'. (As well as Jahn's largely unilingual *Do-Re-Mi*, the Dutch pushed the regulatory envelope with *Sing Me a Song*, little more than an English-language list of musical genres from blues to 'ballad of folk'.) Along with twenty-four repetitions of its universally intelligible title, *Opera* also leavened its modest Turkish component with the names of five composers, along with half a dozen of their compositions (both repeated twice).

Opera, opera, opera, opera, opera
Opera, opera, opera, opera, Carmen, Aida
Opera, opera, bu gece operalarda
Tosca, Figaro, Fidelio var, coşkun aryalar

Long before we get to these opening couplets, though, it's clear that this song is going to do very, very badly – no other nul-pointer announces its intent with such efficiency. So convincingly does the spartan modesty of the performing area suggest a local variety show, when Çetin wanders near the side curtains I'm waiting for the old walking stick to shoot out and yank him neck-first offstage, followed by a muffled shout of 'Next!'

Within seconds of that introductory howl, Çetin's resonant baritone is roaming uneasily across a musical landscape whose jarring, rearing evolutions have been defying effective description for over twenty years. A wall of Chic-pattern disco guitars is demolished by a jauntily brassed-up mambo chorus, Çetin splays his arms and pulses out a long burst of deep vibrato, and I'm lost. So too the hapless Mr Alp, who unlike every nul-pointer I've encountered so far, seems certain of his fate from an early stage.

He's been shirking the camera's stare from the start, and as the central section's unhinged Latin oompah careers without warning into a crooned aria, Çetin suddenly seems to grasp the slavering, hundred-headed absurdity of what's going on up there. The thick lips tighten, the gaze shifts around behind those jaundice-shaded specs, the baritone begins to wander off its axis. Just before girding himself for the bellowed, Englebert Humperdinck finale, I see his face sag slightly, souring into a brief gurn of exasperation. I didn't write this daft rubbish, he's saying. Don't take it out on me.

I've seen *Opera* described as 'part ballad, part Dixieland rag'; as 'salsa squished into an aria sandwich'. *The Times*, in a recent Eurovision retrospective, called it 'Radiohead's *Paranoid Android* covered by the Divine Comedy'. For Allan Todd, an authority for the past thirty years who owns copies of every Eurovision recording ever released, it is simply 'the worst of all time'.

That it certainly is not: one man's meat, after all, is another man's cheese. Of the hundred-plus Eurovision songs I've already watched and heard, at least half I'd be happy never to experience again. But I defy anyone to listen to *Opera* only once. By any standards it is an extraordinary piece of music; put it on a Eurovision stage, and amongst the homogenous, formulaic ballads and pop froth it stands proud as a beacon of bold idiosyncrasy. In three mad minutes, it rewrote, defaced and ate the Eurovision rulebook.

This much was plain from the forum messages that trickled on to Eurovision sites in the days after Çetin's death. Scrolling through the tortuous efforts to instil respectful mourning with a sense of his uniquely esoteric contribution to the contest proved an oddly moving experience. 'Whenever I want to show "non-ESC-fanatic" friends something special and genuine,' wrote one, 'his entry is certainly among those.' 'Çetin left the world a remarkable performance, one of my first visual adventures and memories regarding Eurovision . . . *Opera* is a very special and funny song for me and will stay an evergreen for ever and ever . . . I always thought of it as being one of the strangest but very nice songs sent by Turkey.'

With a short wave and five Short Waves, Çetin departs the stage; it's a solace of sorts to see him superseded by the woman who will ensure that this night, his will be a pain shared. Barefoot, wrapped in a vortex-striped swathe of fabric that suggests a flag-sized air-stewardess neck scarf, Spain's Remedios Amaya knits those low, Latin brows beneath her thin headband and casts a deeply concerned gaze across the audience. Until three minutes before I'd never seen a Eurovision performer look so worried: perhaps she's still as thrown as the rest of us by what has just taken place on the stage. After all that noise and fancy-dress madness, she looks very, very alone.

Maria Dolores Amaya Vega (all flamenco artists seem to be given a nickname, though I never discovered what she did to deserve 'remedies') was born to humble parents of gypsy ancestry in Seville in 1962. By her teenage years she had already mastered the larynx-bobbing warble demanded by Spain's native vocal form, and her precocious performances in Seville's flamenco clubs swiftly earnt plaudits from Spain's greatest male exponent of the art, the late Jose Monje Cruz (nicknamed Camarón – 'The Shrimp' – 'on account of his wiry body and light-brown hair').

Curious impresarios followed in his wake: Remedios was young, swarthily attractive and vocally versatile – the perfect artist, thought producer Julio Palacios, to reverse the commercial decline flamenco had been suffering since the Beatles hit Spain, a trend accelerated by the pent-up pop-cultural creativity released after Franco's death in 1975.

The result was Remedios Amaya's eponymous debut, an album that fused traditional castanet-clicking stage-stampers with foreign-flavoured pop into a hybrid the critics called 'flamenco rock'. She was just sixteen when it came out, and eighteen when Julio produced a more blatantly commercial follow-up. Her first nationwide, big-label release came two years later, in early 1983, when the Julio-masterminded 'Luna Nueva' hit the shelves. The purists loathed what they called 'this techno-flamenco', bridling at its use of drums, keyboards and dance beats, but the album found favour with culturally influential modernisers associated with the newly installed socialist government, one keen to repackage Spain's cultural heritage for the post-Franco generation. So it was that despite the album's rather modest sales, its performer quickly found herself on a TV España Eurovision 'internal shortlist' that ran as follows: 1. Remedios Amaya's *¿Quien Maneja mi Barca?*; 2. *Como el Agua de la Fuente* by Remedios Amaya.

The executives plumped for the first, a sort of bold Arabian tango, its kasbah-thumping, slapped-bass beat overlaid with a strident mantra that was little more than the title's incorporated query – who's steering my boat? – repeated with ratcheting vehemence. The composers were two brothers, the hairier of whom was to double up as conductor on the night.

Remedios arrived in Munich two weeks before her twenty-first birthday. Few in Spain were aware that she had left behind a little boy not yet a year old: Luis, the product of her relationship with a chap from Madrid named Roman. In common with most of the younger nul-pointers I would later meet, Remedios went to Eurovision purely because she'd been asked to, because it would have been ungrateful, awkward and possibly traitorous to say no. A humble young mother more than satisfied with the modest local celebrity that had thus far been her reward, she came to the final unburdened by expectations of international stardom.

But this was Remedios's first trip outside Spain, and sweet-natured unworldliness would, in the days ahead, encourage her to read rather too much into workaday media attention. 'Everybody is asking me for interviews and photos,' she gabbled to a journalist from *El Periódico de Catalunya*. 'With the welcome I've had I'm really confident of winning!' She accepted an invitation to sing for Munich's extensive Spanish community, being received with an enthusiasm that did little to dampen her optimism. 'We're giving Eurovision something fresh and original,' she told the press. 'All the other performers tell me it's going to do really well.'

Back at home, though, her song's almost furtive selection was causing belated controversy. The more it was played, the more sharply it seemed to divide public opinion: one Spanish Eurovision nostalgic recalls 'a hard confrontation between her detractors and defenders, even on the streets'. There were suddenly a lot of cold feet under TVE desks: without warning, the Spanish viewing public discovered that coverage of the Eurovision final had been shunted off on to the state broadcaster's minority-interest channel, its place taken by the network premiere of *A Fistful of Dollars*.

Native Eurovision fanatics had yet to forgive TVE for a suspected act of sabotage four years earlier, wherein the Spanish, in the lead and voting last, oddly contrived to hand ten points, and victory, to Israel: TVE had earlier hinted at their reluctance to meet the financial and technical challenges involved in hosting the final, and though no conspiracy was ever proven, even the EBU's official history cheerfully outlines the rumours.

Lingering resentment was swiftly rekindled by Clint Eastwood's unscheduled appearance on the nation's screens, inciting Spanish Eurofans into a rage so bitter that over twenty years on the residual bile is still trickling out. Only the very drunkest gainsayer would find a good word for Remedios's outfit, but it's surely a little harsh to maintain – as the self-styled 'King of Love' did in an impassioned blog entry in 2004 – that by obliging her to wear it, 'TVE seeded hatred in juries'. 'This infamous blue-ray dress, the headband, her loose hair and a hideous excess of foundation and eye shadow – an unprecedented accumulation of nonsense.' These people: he even gives the name of the TVE make-up artist responsible.

What no one denies is that the hurried, shambolic process by which her song had been selected set a regrettable example for the B-team TVE delegation who accompanied her to Munich. The dress was almost randomly selected in last-minute desperation, and in failing to provide any complementary footwear the TVE stylists effectively obliged Remedios to go shoe-less ('It's more comfortable, anyway,' she said diplomatically). Rehearsals proved predictably disjointed; by the time she stood in the wings waiting for Çetin to finish, the girlish confidence of her press utterings had completely evaporated. 'She never talked back or argued,' a journalist remembered, 'and always did what the producers told her to.' But now the producers weren't telling Remedios what to do, mainly because they didn't know.

¿Quien Maneja mi Barca? has in recent years enjoyed a rehabilitation amongst the Eurovision community: in an online poll held to determine the nul-point song that least deserved its fate, it emerged as a runaway winner. In the memorable phrase of one happy voter, 'Long live the powerful, no-shoes woman!'

After the still-fresh alarums of Koh Samui, any good news for any nul-pointer – even when it arrives twenty years too late – is good news for me. 'Ole Remedios!' I cry aloud as Jose Miguel counts the orchestra in. How deflating to discover his co-composition more eager even than *Opera* to bemuse and alienate the watching millions. I don't know much about flamenco, but I know what I don't like. And I'm about to listen to it for three minutes.

Both songs are launched with a dramatically atonal symphonic crescendo, though this one sounds more like a prolonged orchestral sting in a horror film, as if Remedios is about to look down at her stripy dress and see a bloody metal fist punch its way out. That would at least warrant her increasingly visible fear: as she asks us, for the first of eighteen times, who is sailing her boat, it looks very much as if those brown eyes are about to start leaking.

Subsequent exposure to rival exponents of her art reveals the ululating, off-key caterwaul she then releases to be the authentic sound of flamenco. Imagine an emotional mourner being shaken violently by the shoulders and you're getting close. Easy listening it isn't: and this, remember, is flamenco lite, watered down for ABBA-land. After Çetin, it's almost too much. In the days since my return from Helsinki there have been moments when I've contemplated recommissioning my mothballed Fender duet scheme; from this point there will be no more.

In haunting empathy with her on-stage predecessor,

Remedios seems to sense the barren scoreboard harvest that looms. When the camera zooms in she quickly turns away, directing her incessant maritime enquiries at the floor, perhaps thinking: Sandie Shaw, me – it's one extreme or the other with this barefoot thing. But after a craven minute or so, something seems to snap. Her face hardens into a look of noble hauteur, then hardens further into angry defiance. Very quickly she's accompanying those quavery yowls with accusatory audience-directed finger-jabs, staring from face to unseen face in challenging rage. If someone doesn't identify this mystery navigator pretty soon, we're all going to suffer for it.

I still can't be having with the music, but her performance thereafter agreeably embodies the smouldering, frenzied essence of her national artistic form. Glowering imperiously Remedios twirls her skirt, showing a bare leg to go with the feet, covering the stage with as much haughty grace as that monstrous dress allows. She runs a hand through her thick dark hair, curls an arm aloft into a pose that cries out for a castanet, then shrieks out her song's final word, its forty-eighth 'who'.

'I didn't cry,' Remedios told *El Pais* the next morning, 'because all the other artists were so supportive, especially the Norwegian.' Good work, Jahn. 'And I know I sang well, because my friends told me. Nobody is to blame, not the song, not me, not anybody. It's just bad luck.'

It would be a while before Remedios came to understand that whatever you did to flamenco – spiced it up, slowed it down – the non-Hispanic world would never get it. 'I was very young,' she said in a TV interview ten years on, 'and I didn't yet realise that my sort of music doesn't please the juries.' Rare amongst her Eurovision rivals, Remedios's homeland was blessed, or cursed, with a native tradition of popular music that simply doesn't travel. Wincing through *¿Quien Maneja mi Barca?* a second time I find myself reminded of a Faeroe Isles restaurateur's response to the napkin-filling aftermath of my encounter with a platter of skate in tallow sauce: 'Perhaps for you it is a little . . . *particular*.'

Not that this would satisfy certain sections of the Spanish

press. One commentator, with snide reference to her gypsy roots, brutally dismissed Remedios as 'an illiterate peasant', and another suggested that to avoid such 'ridiculous performances' in the future, Spain should retire from the competition for good. The Association of Spanish Television Viewers demanded the dismissal of those responsible for selecting *¿Quien Maneja mi Barca?* and its singer, demands that were redoubled when the Director of Programming unwisely described the result as 'a glorious defeat – better than finishing seventh'. Several anonymous callers phoned TVE to mutter darkly that 'this would never have happened under Franco'. (In fact it had, twice: '62 and '65.)

Others spared Remedios, instead heaping scorn at the foot of that old monument to drivel. 'She endeavoured to act with dignity and professionalism,' said one paper, 'at this festival of maximum bad taste'; winner Corinne Hermès was pooh-poohed as 'a total medicority'. For some Remedios was even a martyr, 'laid down to the lions – a singing victim of political instrumentalisation'. More than one journalist earnestly portrayed her as an innocent patsy in a vile plot hatched by the militant socialists of TVE: Franco had milked much propaganda from the country's back-to-back victories in 1968/69, and here was the leftists' bid to undermine all that by making both Spain and Eurovision look really stupid.

Not to be outdone, certain elements of the socialist press outlined an even more ambitious conspiracy. 'They say that Eurovision is political,' claimed one editorial, 'and if it is thus, the new socialist Spain can hope for little in Germany, with its endemic xenophobia.' *La Vanguardia* went the extra mile, claiming that by singing 'gypsy music' Remedios had assured herself 'the same fate as those of that race persecuted so atrociously by the Nazis, whose repression was particularly brutal in the city of Munich'.

With this sort of stuff flying around, no one was surprised at Remedios's withdrawal from public life in the months that followed. After the release of an album recorded before her departure, and a brief appearance in a flamenco-based film, she retreated to Seville and little Luis. So profound was her disillusionment with music in general, and flamenco-rock in particular, that it would be an extraordinary thirteen years before her next professional appearance.

Over a decade and a half of confident democracy, Spanish pride in the nation's esoteric musical heritage had been restored. Traditional Shrimp-style flamenco was back in a big way, and Remedios Amaya's 1997 back-to-basics comeback album, 'Me Voy Contigo', introduced the public to a very different artist from the one they'd last seen roaring around the Munich stage in a horrible shower curtain. Gone was the bare-shouldered, wild-maned girl portrayed on her pre-Eurovision albums: the red-shawled Remedios that scowled out from this cover wore her hair in a painfully tight bun, sternly surveying the record-buying public with a look that said: 'Scrump for olives in *my* yard, would you?' No synthesisers, no drums, just her and a busy-fingered guitarist. And you know what? It went on to sell over 150,000 copies – comfortably the most successful solo release by any nul-point artist.

Her three subsequent albums haven't quite scaled those heights, but Remedios's lofty place in the pantheon of contemporary flamenco greats is assured. She's a regular at all the big festivals, from Nîmes to – it says here – Chicago, and a legend in her homeland who has even been honoured with a website devoted to rhyming eulogies in her name, though just after I came across it the iron blew up and fused the house, and since the subsequent reboot I've never been able to find it again. She still lives in Seville, the only nul-pointer who's now a grandparent.

'Your idea is funny. Different, is it?' So ran the reply to an email dispatched to Alicia of Montoya Musical, 'Sevilla's number-one flamenco agency', at onerous length identified to me by her record label as Remedios's management. As the agency's sole Anglophone, Alicia would be hearing a lot more from me in the months ahead, generally via email owing to the Montoya receptionist's lightning hang-up reflexes.

Alicia quickly proved herself prompt, courteous and informative. Of course a meeting could be set up; Remedios was away at the moment, but her friend would let us know as soon as she returned. Good news: she's back in Sevilla now . . . oh, but there's a flamenco feria on – best wait until that's over. It's over! Remedios is now happy to meet you. Is next week good? Excellent! Thursday would be fine. Listen, Remedios is a little concerned that she doesn't speak English, not a word, and nor does her friend. It isn't a problem? Even though you don't speak Spanish? OK, I'll tell her. Oh: I tried to tell her, but her phone was off. Maybe next week isn't so good now. And next week is the feria in Jerez.

By this stage Alicia's replies were no longer prompt; composed now exclusively of a brief flurry of shouty capitals, neither were they informative or courteous. I'M TRYING TO SPEAK TO REMEDIOS, BUT HER PHONE IS OFF AGAIN. WHEN I CAN SPEAK I'LL TELL YOU SOMETHING, OK?

After a silent fortnight, I began to recall my dealings with a Basque gentleman named Manuel Bazquez, two years previously. Manuel, I'd been told by a bilingual intermediary, owned many donkeys, and would be happy to sell me one for the trans-Hispanic pilgrimage I was then organising. Speaking through the middle man, Manuel confirmed his delight in offering me the pick of fourteen donkeys currently browsing his yard. That was on day one of our relationship. By day eight he had seven, by twelve, just one; as I was desperately organising a wire-transfer deposit and a flight to Bilbao, the despondent go-between phoned with inevitable news. Two days later, Manuel dispatched an emotional, self-flagellatory email *mea culpa* confessing that he hadn't in fact owned a donkey for two years. With this in mind, I sent Alicia a further email, asking for a straight answer on the Remedios issue. Was I wasting my time?

In failing to reply, she suggested I was. Yes, perhaps I could still cajole and coerce this reluctant and evidently reticent grandmother into recounting and reliving the betrayal, fear and humiliation that led her to lock herself away for a decade and a half. Or perhaps, in the cold, hard light of a post-Kalvik dawn, I could just leave her alone. When, after leaving it half-watched for long weeks, I resume my DVD journey through Munich '83 with a reprise of Remedios Amaya's enraged, audience-cowing finale, this seems by far the best approach for all concerned.

After the back-to-back tragedies of Çetin and Remedios in stage-slots six and seven, it's hard for me to concentrate on the acts that follow: it seems inappropriate, almost unseemly, like playing *Ding Dinge Dong* at a funeral. Out of respect I lower the volume, though five acts on I'm having to crank it back up to hear anything of the drearily muted Cypriot effort, performed by a pair of stool-bound strummers with such insipid torpor that even the Greeks slumped nose-first into their moussaka. On the eighteen occasions in Eurovision history that the two have appeared together, Greece has lavished maximum points on the divided island no fewer than twelve times. On every other the Cypriots have never failed to secure less than six from their mainland neighbours, or rather every other but one: in failing to coax even a single point from Greece, Stavros and Constantina managed what may forever remain a unique achievement in Cypriot Eurovision history.

Ah! But here's lovely Ofra Haza, Israeli wonder-voice and, it seems, another Eurovision discovery. *Alive* (*Israel Still Exists*) is a catchy and exuberant showcase for her astonishing vocal talent, and a boldly symbolic choice for a contest held in the city that, as anyone peering over a Spanish journalist's shoulder will be aware, gave Hitler his first break. Another class-of-'83 Eurovision tragedy, too: after finishing second and embarking on a highly successful international career, in 1997 Haza married a domineering and extravagantly dubious businessman, and abruptly contracted HIV. Apparently shamed by him into silence, she persistently refused medical attention, dying in 2000. Variously accused of deliberately infecting her, locking her in the bedroom for months and altering her will, her husband gave Israel's many conspiracy theorists almost too much to chew on when, a year later, he suffered a fatal heart attack while apparently doing crystal meth with two friends, who themselves promptly disappeared.

Belgium silence the audience with what sounds like a three-minute Gary Numan intro performed by trumpeting aerobic instructors, eventually vacating the stage for Corinne Hermès, French-born but Luxembourgeois for the night. Clasping her hands dramatically to her pink-clad chest and fixing the camera with a gaze of portentous defiance, Corinne powers her way through a torso-wracking turbo ballad that offers us a foretaste of the Céline Dion years ahead, but in most other ways her looming triumph marks the end of an era. French-language songs dominated the contest in the sixties and seventies, but only two have triumphed since 1983; Luxembourg hasn't bothered turning up since 1993, Monaco only returned in 2004 after a twenty-five-year absence, and the French themselves have now been waiting twenty-eight years for a Eurovision victory.

Snigger if you must, but to me these statistics are a poignantly eloquent reminder that Eurovision has failed in its proudest ambition. American Forces Radio might no longer present a threat to the European way of life, but only because the artistic values it espoused have already leached into almost everything we watch and listen to: in cultural terms the Atlantic gets narrower every year. How else to explain the ever-diminishing value of a Eurovision triumph? Corinne was to release only one post-Munich album, and these days earns her crust playing galas in Turkey.

No one who witnessed it is likely to forget Marlene's performance as hostess, but to ensure that even the deaf, sick or horribly drunk remember where they were on the night of 23 April 1983, in the pre-vote interval she does something no compere before or since has ever dared to. Tearing her Barbie ballgown off at the knee, Gin Fizz style, Marlene throws herself into the ongoing dance show, ending it held aloft by white-trousered young men, a picture of weary exultation. Panting heavily, she stumbles through the votes. Digits double, then treble; Çetin and Remedios are alone from a very early stage – the third round of voting – but at least they have each other, side by side.

In keeping with the front-of-house standards, the green room is a breeze-blocked, strip-lit cellar that would more happily host a junior netball squad's pre-match team talk. The competitors are squeezed together in tight rows of plastic chairs, their collective gaze raised at an overhead monitor. Corinne fixes it with almost furious intensity; Ofra and a couple of other front-runners with almost convincing ambivalence. As Marlene clumsily hauls the voting to a climax, we're only rarely shown any other backstage faces. Slowing the wide shots to frame-by-frame advance I spot Jahn's messy smile: he's loving it, messing about with his sunglasses, gurning, holding up notes to the camera that I can't read, even when I belatedly discover my DVD player's exciting zoom facility.

Employing this new tool with afternoon-devouring enthusiasm, I find no trace of Remedios and her conspicuous outfit. But it doesn't take too long to spot Çetin, half-hidden behind his backing group's wigs and tiaras, four rows behind a hooting Jahn. Perhaps aware that bewildered grief or thunder-faced embitterment is a tough one to carry off in fancy dress, the Short Waves opt for wry ruefulness. The one in the biggest wig idly fans herself, her small, lopsided smile carrying a hint of the I-told-you-so. The velveteen 'tache-twirler beside her is a half-slumped, half-smirking picture of uncrestfallen resignation.

But Çetin is not. At first I can only see his sickly yellow glasses and the Travoltine hair above, but when a foreground Belgian turns to her neighbour there's the whole north face of the Alp. I freeze it: a strange, lost look, scanning the monitor in mildly perturbed confusion, as if it's telling him that the 11.42 to Ankara is divided into two sections, with the rear four carriages terminating at Bodrum. On slow-forward, Jahn turns to the camera with a bestial roar that recalls the ephedrine-fuelled, lens-spittled mania with which Maradona celebrated his final goal for Argentina in the 1994 World Cup. Others smile, laugh, turn to each other, shrug. But Çetin sits utterly motionless, his expression unchanging. He looks at no one; no one looks at him. Then the last vote comes in, Corinne leaps to her feet, and in half a second Çetin and his Short Waves are brusquely barged aside by an engulfing tide of photographers.

'*Opera* was our first null in the Eurovision,' emailed Turkish ESC authority Olcay Tanberken when I requested his thoughts, 'so Çetin's career was affected by that. He was criticised a lot.' Reminiscences posted by Olcay's online chums coloured in the dark shadows. 'He took the zero points very hard because people always make fun of his song,' wrote one, 'and the whole media defined it as a shame for the Turkish nation.' The fat, black bottom line for Çetin was a nul-points afterlife that, in Olcay's words, produced 'nothing significant'.

Indeed so. There was that Balkan Song Festival award; someone recalled Çetin winning something similar in the US in 1990. But neither could be verified, and in the apparent absence of even a single post-1983 recording or live performance, I was obliged to accept the ruthlessly glib accounts that spoke of a shattered recluse, 'the lonely Çetin Alp', holed up for twenty years in his semi in the outskirts of Istanbul. Like Remedios, but without the happy ending.

In spurning the opportunity to rehabilitate a bullied victim, the newspaper obituaries were at least consistent with the front-page abuse that twenty-one years before had propelled Çetin Alp into early retirement. 'Died alone', reads the caption below an image of Çetin in his jowly, stubbled later days; a heartless depiction of his last, being lugged through the front door in a bright orange body bag, is labelled: 'Death of the artist who was remembered before every Eurovision song contest by his zero-score *Opera* in 1983.'

The odd comforting detail emerged. Çetin's son told the waiting press that his father had been due to sing at the Yenikapi Gar Casino that evening: evidently his professional purdah wasn't quite as grimly reclusive as I'd been led to believe. Quotes from 'Çetin Alp's driver' suggested a lifestyle inconsistent with the reports, as did the marble-floored threshold he was photographed crossing for the last time. Had it not been for the final paragraph of the final obituary, I might have been able to close Çetin's book with a tight smile.

Though conclusively attributed by most papers to a long-standing heart condition – the fifty-six year old had undergone cardiac surgery the year before – this one teasingly invited readers to speculate on a possible connection with a TV interview he had given the week before. I had to read that twice. What was Çetin Alp doing on TV?

The facts that emerged through deeper investigation of this event proved difficult to digest. Consequent to Turkey's deliriously celebrated debut triumph in the 2003 Eurovision, the 2004 final had taken place in Istanbul on 14 May. In a gesture of grand, almost imperial forgiveness, state broadcaster TRT invited each of the nation's twenty-five previous contestants, even the most perennially vilified, to a reception. It must have been a surprise when Çetin turned up, and an astonishment when he agreed to be interviewed – no one had seen him in this kind of company for years, and it was over two decades since he'd last answered a question that included the words 'Munich' or '*Opera*'. Who can say what coaxed him out of the house and into the studio; perhaps he felt that now Turkey had finally won the sodding thing, its journalistic representatives would at long last allow him to wipe the Euro-slate clean and move on.

Except they wouldn't. Faced with relentless probing into the events of 23 April 1983 and their grimly enduring legacy, Çetin eventually obliged his interviewer with a protracted mumble that veered from self-abasement to self-pity: he was sorry for what happened in Munich, for Turkey and for himself, but couldn't understand why people still blamed him personally; it had taken him years to regain his self-control, and he sometimes felt he would suffer for this one thing for the rest of his life.

All four days of it.

9 May 1987
Palais de Centenaire, Brussels
Seyyal Taner and Locomotif
Turkey
Şarkım Sevgi Üstüne

Perhaps shamed by that 1983 nul-point double – the first under the present voting system – for four years juries saw that no one went home empty-handed. *Diggi-Loo Diggi-Ley*, winner the following year, remains one of the ultimate Eurovision lyrics, and in 1985 Bobbysocks gave an ecstatic Norway its debut triumph. No one would call these years classics – Terry Wogan nominated the idiotic first as the worst in Eurovision history, and with only 56.9 per cent of the maximum votes, *La Det Swinge* was statistically the weakest winner to date.

Thirteen-year-old Sandra Kim's victory the year after made her the youngest ever winner, and brought the 1987 final to Brussels: with twenty-two acts this was the biggest Eurovision yet, which along with the ambitious laser show offered a foretaste of today's overstaffed spectaculars.

Another day in bed, another old Eurovision. We're halfway through the preludial overview of the majesty of Belgium's lace-making, sand dunes and clover-leaf motorway junctions when

Birna bustles in with a stack of ironing. 'A fine way for a grown man to spend his days,' she mutters, and I'm hardly about to argue. But like all the others who have come to mock, she soon finds herself lured in. 'This must be 1986 . . . no, '87,' she announces, standing right up to the telly, flat clothes clutched to her chest. As an Icelander she's a carrier of the virulent strain of *eurovisium scandinavius*, but I'm still impressed – certainly a lot more than I would have been six months ago.

'How do you remember?' I ask, rearranging my multi-pillow headrest. 'No one's even sung yet.'

'I've never seen this before in my life,' she replies briskly. 'It's her earrings – the compere's enormous earrings.'

Together we watch as the presenter in question, her extraordinary armpit-length pink gloves paying almost parodic homage to Madonna's recent *Material Girl* incarnation, bursts into song – English song, doubtless on the basis that it was safer to annoy the whole country rather than just one of the nation's Flemish- or French-speaking communities. Perhaps a variant of this garbled diplomacy is behind the popular Tim Moore range of Belgian casual wear (check out eBay.nl for some disappointingly dull examples). Perhaps another explains why our hostess for the evening has decided to call herself after the Czech resistance leader in *Casablanca*.

'Hello, I am Victor Laszlo,' she informs the bow-tied grandees assembled before her, and suddenly it's too much for my wife, who drops the ironing on the bed and trots out with a slightly unhinged cackle. After she's gone I fast-forward to the credits: no, no mistake, that's her name. Nice earrings, Vic. This is going to be a good year.

'Do you know how many of you are out there tonight?' asks our hostess. 'How many of you are going to meet twenty-two rising stars?' Twenty-one, I think, or I wouldn't be in bed watching this now, by Victor's ensuing estimate bumping the historically cumulative audience up to 500,000,001.

Despite the disturbing accuracy of my wife's accessory-based carbon dating, Eurovision is always a little slow out of the fashion blocks, and waited until 1987 before planting its many-starred flag atop Mount Eighties. Four years after Limahl had done his hair-based worst, he's paid fearsome tribute in female Norwegian form. Kojo's backing band had gone for the Blues Brothers look only a couple of years after the film's release, but here, a half-decade on, are two Israelis in black suits, thin ties and Ray-Bans. 'Hupa hule hule hule,' they sing, prancing about manically, 'hupa hupa hule hule.' *Shir Habatlanim*, translated by sundry Eurovision authorities as *Lazy Bums*, *We Two Bums* and *Bum-Song*, was almost martyred by a French-style, self-imposed drivel-monument boycott. 'This is not an appropriate example of Israeli popular music,' protested the nation's minister of culture, to (self-evidently) deaf ears.

Eurovision hasn't given Belgium much to smile about. Fud Leclerc, as we know, made an unwelcome name for himself and his country as the first-ever nul-pointer; no nation has finished last more often (OK – no nation except Norway), and Sandra Kim's 1986 victory remains their sole triumph in forty-nine attempts. To celebrate it, they entered a singer recently betrothed to the bereaved husband of a previous Belgian competitor who had died from cancer in 1984. Hooray!

Sweden's Lotta Engberg is the first act of the evening to celebrate Eurovision's oddly enduring fascination with the colour yellow. One of the Italians who follows her out raises another redoubtable conundrum: Umberto Tozzi wrote *Gloria* for Laura Brannigan, a song which I'll be uploading to my replacement iPod only should its disk capacity exceed 90 billion gigabytes, but which nonetheless stands head and shoulder-pads above the insipid ballad he and his mate Raf offer us here. What's happened to Eurovision songwriting? Without wanting to sound both dull and mad – but probably failing – where are the inheritors to *Puppet on a String, Waterloo, Poupée de Cire, Poupée de Son . . .* even *Making Your Mind Up*? It's a question that recurs to me later when Plastic Bertrand – how could I have forgotten? – strides on to the stage and grinningly lisps his way through a shockingly bland disco bopper. Viktor might have been over-egging her countryman's pop-punk 1978 hit *Ça Plane Pour Moi* in declaring it 'astounding', but after three minutes of utterly forgettable Euro-pap (and compellingly memorable camp prancing) I find myself in almost tearful, rose-tinted agreement. Naturally enough, this stalwart of the 'Name Ten Famous Belgians' parlour game is tonight flying the flag for Luxembourg.

Spain's Patricia Kraus comes out with Diana hair and Aladdin Sane make-up – no Patricia, not the stool! But it's too late – only ten points from Greece saves her from a fate that eighteen years later would have brought a slightly diffident Englishman and his unreliable voice recorder to her doorstep. Then she takes her bow, Victor shows us the gap in her front teeth and announces, 'An actress and singer, Seyyal Taner was born a star . . .'

That she was, and nul points or no, she'll die one too. One hapless Turkish journalist kicked off a recent interview by asking Seyyal Taner for her place of birth. The retort was as haughty as it was magnificent: 'Is there anybody who does not know?'

Tracking Seyyal down, and setting our meeting up, had proven consistently entertaining. I'd grabbed the first toothsome leads from Turkey's well-developed and rewardingly multi-lingual Eurovision community, buoyant after their nation's debut victory in the 2003 contest.

'Wow! Seyyal Taner was the only one with a personal light among those Doris Day types,' began one reply to my mass-mailed cry for help, concluding with the irresistible judgement that 'she was the best bad girl of the day!'

'She is a popular and successful singer,' wrote a more circumspect correspondent, 'and null points she got did not change this fact. Now she is a respected middle-aged lady.' A fuller biography advised me that she 'got sad for two years after her big fat 0, released three albums, moved to beach-town Bodrum, since did nothing, now suddenly she appear in a big soap opera we call *Istanbul is my Witness*'. Almost as an afterthought, this correspondent rounded off his reminiscences with Seyyal's mobile number: that afternoon began a brief but memorable series of telephonic exchanges with my first female nul-pointer.

Her call-answering salutation had been a huskily prolonged drawl of 'Seyyyyyal'; the words that follow this shortly after brusquely interrupt the mumbled explanatory introduction that in the pre-Kalvik era had been my quest's most dreaded component. 'I am in Istanbul traffic. It's crazy, you know. You can call Friday. Welcome-bye-bye.' So imperious was her tone – the perfect accompaniment to the almost aggressively sultry demeanour apparent from her publicity portfolio – that I listened to the line go dead with nothing more than meek resignation. I imagined Seyyal forcing her cabriolet through a logjam of knackered taxis with a volley of impatient expletives, huge shades propped on head, long scarf, cigarette holder. She sounded glamorous, a little louche and astonishingly self-confident. In short, she sounded famous.

I called her on Friday; she was at home. 'This is some job you have,' she teased mischievously after I'd explained myself, 'to travel all over meeting the zero people. Why don't you speak with Ahmed, the composer?' As she gave me his number I heard the now familiar sound of bucks being shifted: Eurovision judged songs, I was once more being indirectly reminded, not singers. I felt for her as I'd felt for the other nul-pointers, but it's a sad reality of human nature that the messenger always gets shot. If I reversed my Mondeo off a bridge, would anyone care how Ford took the news?

The next time I called, a timid, ancient factotum answered her phone. 'Seyyal Taner no Istanbul,' he eventually croaked. The time after that, she cut me short with a dramatic suggestion. 'I have a plan. You come to Istanbul next month, and then we go to bedroom together – is maybe more fun to talk there.' Maybe, I stuttered, realising just before the now traditional 'welcome-bye-bye' that she'd actually been inviting me to her maritime residence in Bodrum.

In the end, we didn't go to Bodrum together. Off-season there were no direct flights from Britain, and only one connection a day from Istanbul. If you were Seyyal Taner the latter logistical situation evidently wasn't a problem, but Turkish Airlines couldn't offer me a seat between the two cities for long weeks.

'It's OK,' yawned Seyyal when I passed this on. 'I meet you in Istanbul. We meet, we eat, we talk. Welcome-bye-bye.'

My taxi driver had heard of Seyyal Taner, but slaloming madly through the evening rush hour away from the airport, it was difficult to take our conversation beyond the non-committal nod her name elicited. Here I was in Europe, and I couldn't even say please or thank you, yes or no. With a nervous inward titter, I recalled the tribulations of Welsh striker Dean Saunders after a transfer to Istanbul's top club Galatasaray in the twilight of his career. Introducing his newly christened infant son Callum to the press, he was met with deafening roars of laughter: 'Mr Saunders,' spluttered a hack, wiping his eyes, 'you have called your boy Pencil.'

The closest I'd previously been to Turkey was while surveying its Eurovision-blighting Cypriot republic through a pair of holiday binoculars. This was a country twice the size of Germany, more populous than France, yet to me it remained an impenetrable enigma. With green eyes and blond hair, a surprising proportion of pedestrians we passed didn't look even slightly Turkish; the Arabic script I'd ignorantly imagined hampering my movements would be encountered only on the cover of a pirated *Aladdin* DVD.

Old men at a bus stop nasally relieving themselves in the gutter, minarets soaring from crumbling, corrugated slums, fearsome rust-streaked cargo hulks looming up out of the Marmara Sea. After a stopover in Zurich, it was like coming down with the cultural equivalent of the bends: I could only hope, for his sake, that I hadn't been followed here by the twitching obsessive-compulsive who a couple of hours earlier had loudly dry-retched watching me refill my water-bottle from an airport wash-basin. Following all those visits to the nul-pointers' moneyed, technocratic heartlands, and one to their Norwegian beachside consulate, here I was in Eurovision's wild east.

My homework had exposed the yawning socio-economic chasm that divided Turkey from the Brussels-based union its leaders were so desperate to join. Turkish men die younger than any other in Europe outside what we might tactfully call the continent's vodka belt, and only three-quarters of their women can read. Per capita GDP is half Portugal's, and hyper-inflation that hit 85 per cent in the late nineties endowed the banknotes in my pocket with more zeroes than a Eurovision reunion in Oslo.

But the closer we got to the centre, this harsh, stark picture blurred: huge plasma screens were hung up in squares, a mobile-phone advert filled one entire flank of an eight-storey office block. Istanbul was clearly going to be a City-of-Contrasts job. The commercial vigour was certainly compelling. We drove up a teeming boulevard lined almost exclusively with guitar retailers, then turned through the arches of a vast Roman aqueduct into another whose pavements were filled with gleaming ranks of new bicycles. My driver seemed at home in these streets. 'Shopping, very good,' he rasped, showing me his mummy-of-Rameses teeth in the rear-view mirror. A fast-food stall being wheeled out into the road gave them another outing. 'Turkish key-bap, very good.' I was looking forward to both, and told him so.

'Hotel, very good,' he announced soon after, although surveying the dusty edifice we'd pulled up in front of all I could coax out was a feeble hum. In a moment of disoriented weakness after our shopping/kebab bonding moment I had entrusted the driver to select my home for the night, and the wink he exchanged with the stubbled, smoking lord of the lobby emphasised what a shamingly inept piece of tourism this had been.

'Is new room for you,' said the receptionist as we creaked up the dark and ancient stairs. 'You pay sixty dollar, please?' We were outside the door now; a powerful, complex odour seeped out from the three-inch gap at its foot.

'Can I, um, see inside first?' The corridor light, activated by a ten-second timer switch, clicked off.

'Sixty dollar,' said the darkness.

Well, it was only one night. 'Fine,' I replied; the light clicked on, the door creaked ajar and a moment later I was alone inside.

Two walls were hospital-white, one pub-ceiling yellow, the

last a piebald blend of both; atop the lopsided wardrobe sat the lidless drum of emulsion required to finish the job. The lightly paint-speckled bed was of military aspect and cub-scout dimensions; the lavatory pan was home to three rusty nails and a frothy topping of decorator's relief. Even fully open the window had failed to clear the stench of economy brilliant white, nor that of its applicator's armpits. I peered out, striping a misplaced sleeve, and beheld a scene of decayed devastation, two blocks of half-demolished, half-abandoned shops and garages releasing thin spirals of orange dust into the evening sun. Beyond, Istanbul yawned away into hazy, ochred infinity, a mid-rise mess occasionally pierced by minarets and pylons. I was reminded of the first time my son played Sim City, and blew his entire civic maintenance budget on coal-fired power stations. Looking out there, and indeed in here, surveying the all-encompassing non-Oslo, un-Helsinki-ness of my surroundings, I grasped just how much Eurovision must mean to its Turkish hopefuls.

Their 1987 representative phoned my mobile as I was on my way out a second time, having popped over to the shops for a bottle of water a moment earlier (forget human rights and that wayward economy: the day a tourist willingly lowers his head to a Turkish tap is the day they'll have EU membership in the bag). I loitered by the reception desk as we firmed up our meeting plans; she seemed far less haughtily distant now that I was actually here.

'You have a nice hotel there?' It was central, I told her after a small pause. 'But you must ask me! I know all top-quality hotels!' The receptionist had been raising his eyebrows in a beckoning manner, and as I wandered towards the doors his entreaties became vocal.

'Just a minute,' I told Seyyal, lowering the phone from my ear and walking up to the desk.

'You lock room?' asked its proprietor, his high voice urgent. 'Last time I think no.'

The many concerns unleashed by this statement were at least shared. 'Who is that?' barked Seyyal, who had overheard it all. 'What is that hotel? Let me speak with this man!' Her outrage, and its concomitant concern, was touching. She was still at it two minutes later, as I re-emerged from my room, pockets abulge with the few remaining items of conceivable value I'd left there. 'I must speak with manager!' she boomed, imperiously.

'It's my fault,' I murmured, clomping back down the dark, unsteady staircase. And it was. In the course of my travels to date, I'd become lazy and a little spoiled, had it all too easy. Just ask the customs chaps at Oslo airport – I'd been the threat to their nation, not vice versa.

'Be careful,' cautioned the receptionist, now rather superfluously, as I walked past him towards the hotel exit, Istanbul's late-afternoon, late-winter sun betraying a coat of sandy dust that sheathed the glass doors. 'So many hungry people.'

With my excitement and curiosity now tempered by advanced paranoia, I walked the short distance to Taksim, the traffic ensnared square that was home to the sort of glitzy hotels Seyyal would no doubt have booked for me. No matter how un-Turkish some of the emerald-eyed daredevils jogging through the maze of log-jammed taxis might look, I looked a lot less. In a bid to win Seyyal over, I'd gone for a period hipster look that teamed a purple paisley shirt with a black velvet suit, a conspicuous wardrobe that my fellow pedestrians were appraising with the frank insolence it merited. 'Can I help you, my friend?' hissed a voice in my ear as I squinted at a street sign; without turning to encounter its owner I strode shakily away, my fear-ometer now cranked up past street crime to white-slave trade.

I'd wanted to walk to our meeting at Ortaköy ('means Widow Village', said a huskily tickled Seyyal), but unwilling to risk having a sack pulled over my velvet shoulders every time I stopped to look at the map I instead scrambled into a taxi. I was soon very glad I had. We bumped and hurtled up and down alleys, hit the road that ran along the Bosporus, and drove and drove and drove. Istanbul is vast, but because it's in Turkey no one is quite sure how vast: estimates of its population range from eight million to over fourteen.

As the old riverside palaces slid by, shielding the great waterway from view, I leant my head against the juddering window and wondered what my female nul-point debut would bring. It had been gradually suggesting itself since arrival that assumptions of her enduring fame were no more than conjecture, a rather silly extrapolation on my part from her all-star phone manner. Perhaps this taxi driver would be more help than my first – he'd already demonstrated a handy grasp of English during our football-heavy introductions.

'Do you know Seyyal Taner?' I asked, leaning forward to give my raised voice a chance against his ancient Fiat's orchestra of neglect and decay.

'Sure, I know.' That was something.

'Is she . . . you know, any good?'

His stripy, poly-cotton shoulders rose and fell. 'Maybe she . . . was.'

I shuffled through the cobbled streets of Ortaköy, a reassuringly twee realm of ethnic trinket marts and moderately bohemian tourist eateries, in the state of pensive trepidation that now coloured my pre-nul-points moments. If Seyyal's husky-voiced celebrity mannerisms were a sad façade, perhaps her deluded bluster concealed the tragic, forgotten life she now led. The online Eurovision community was always keen to protect its idols: maybe the soap-opera role they'd trumpeted was a walk-on cameo. It probably wasn't even a soap opera. *Istanbul is my Witness* sounded more like some kind of *Crimewatch*; maybe she'd played a corpse in a reconstruction. That glitzy seafront residence in Bodrum I'd pictured was a roach-scuttled flat above a kebab shop; her pampered existence there in fact a series of sparsely attended vocal engagements in its tawdrier bars. With my musical faculties abused and defaced by over-exposure to kitsch tat, it was far less surprising than it might have been a year before to find myself lost in the final verses of Barry Manilow's *Copacabana*. Now it's a disco, but not for Lola. Still in the dress she used to wear, faded feathers in her hair.

I was early, and for twenty minutes wandered amongst the

convivial early-evening loiterers outside our appointed river-front restaurant. As the seventeen-mile link between the Black Sea and the Med-connected Marmara, the Bosporus isn't really a river at all; but being almost a mile wide where I stood, it seemed a magnificent, muscular waterway. If the two seas it connects are the halves of an hourglass, the Bosporus is the stem between, subject to terrific currents that make for a stiff navigational challenge.

Neatly groomed young couples gazing at each other in moony silence, a benchful of chuckling, hunched old men, a scolding mother snatching her son's laser pointer. Svelte tabbies braided themselves between my velvet legs; high above, banking and swooping swallows celebrated twilight. It wasn't difficult to see what brought everyone here.

The grandly compelling prospect was dominated in the left-hand foreground by a marble mosque conceived on the scale of an opera house; this in turn was dwarfed by a suspension bridge that vaulted impressively across the darkening waters. In the gathering night and the challengingly nippy early spring breeze that accompanied it, a maritime procession struggled against or surfed atop the surface-billowing currents: shadowy bulk carriers, invitingly fairy-lit gin palaces. At the bridge's distant, tapering conclusion, the lights of Istanbul's other half dotted hillsides and clustered in beckoning profusion along the Bosporus. This, I grasped portentously, was Europe's final frontier. Cross the bridge and I'd be in Asia. In Kalvik country.

'Teeum?'

I look round, to be met with a happy-eyed woman in a black leather baker-boy hat, her olive face lightly freckled. She's much younger than I'd imagined, and significantly less regal. These disparities are explained when a companion – half a head smaller, discreetly voluptuous and wrapped from neck to ankles in a complicated swathe of red and purple silks – steps serenely from behind her and breathes, 'Seyyal Taner. Welcome to Istanbul.'

In fact there are three of them. The baker-boy hat sits atop Melis Sokman, who had sung at Eurovision alongside Seyyal, or more accurately slightly behind her. Her presence at least is consistent with the deflective tactical approach initiated by Seyyal when she tried to palm me off on the song's composer. A cock-up shared is a cock-up halved. More mysterious is the fourth member of our dining party, a rather younger woman who later dictates her name to me. Owing to the idiotic volume of spirits that our party had by then ingested, the best I can do now, looking at the relevant biro-smeared napkin, is N. Dogroll. By the same token, I can no longer be sure what Ms Dogroll was doing there, or indeed what she did elsewhere. At some point someone said something about selling clothes to gay club owners.

We cross the cobbles to the restaurant's well-attended outside dining area, and are with deference ushered to a prime river-view table. Calm, self-confident and almost carelessly glamorous, Seyyal has already suggested through her own actions that here is no soiled and lonely Lola, and now the actions of others prove as much. Three or four heads turn as we take our seats, snapping back to share their find with table-mates who in turn crane around for confirmation. When a waiter brings our menus, he is accompanied by a three-man welcoming delegation from the restaurant's management. Whatever the taxi driver had said, Seyyal Taner is not a was.

I sit next to her, and sneak an appraising glance as Melis and N. Dogroll inaugurate the nicotine festival that will be enthusiastically celebrated on their side of the table throughout our lengthy tenure ('I quit last year,' said Seyyal later – it was certainly no challenge to picture those thick red lips hosting a Marlboro). Slightly fuller of face than she had been in '87, on the wrong side of fifty she nonetheless still had it. There was the suggestion of a little 'work' around those round, brown eyes, which seemed slightly more startled than they had in Brussels eighteen years before, but the splendid mane of dark hair and boldly applied lipstick imparted the general impression of a sixties siren who had successfully spun out her prime.

A waiter arrives with a half-litre bottle of raki, the aniseed-derived native firewater. As yet unaware that the devil's own licorice is not here as an aperitif, but will be liberally served throughout the meal, I down a good throatful. One small choking fit later, I extract my (new) voice recorder and place it between me and the best bad girl of her day. 'So,' I gasp, my raki-ravaged voice already muffled by Melis and N. Dogroll's puffs and cackles and the dish-clinking arrival of the first wave of food, 'where and when were you born?'

'Is there anybody who does not know?' is the retort I'm hoping to coax out, but as the query hangs in the cooling night air, I'm left to contemplate its ghastly crassness. A woman of her age (and of course I already know her age), and of her era, would rather be asked where and when she would die. Short of a profound and echoing belch, it's difficult to imagine a more offensive introductory gambit.

My violent inward cringe necessitates a steadying draught of raki; the sudden awareness that almost all of the food before me contains aubergine in its horridest, soggiest forms means this and subsequent gulps of neat spirit shall slosh about my innards barely diluted.

Seyyal deals with my clumsy question by completely ignoring it. If she's affecting a front of blasé celebrity, she's doing a very good job: her demeanour throughout suggests that being interviewed by foreigners is a regularly enjoyed (and occasionally endured) professional obligation.

'So I'm a teenage girl in Istanbul, and I'm interested in acting, I had a talent and I knew I had a talent, nyeh?' This is the first outing for a favoured verbal tic, a 'no' that disconcertingly evolves into a 'yes', and can denote either. In this instance, however, it seems to mean: I'm in charge of this conversation, OK? It's left to my subsequent research, aided by several Turkish Eurovision fanatics and in particular a middle-aged structural engineer from Ankara who translated a great many profiles of and interviews with Seyyal for 2.5 cents a word, to fill in the hefty preceding gap.

So: Seyyal Taner was born in Sanliurfa, near the Syrian border and far closer to Baghdad than Istanbul, on 28 September 1952. Her family travelled to Istanbul – to Europe – 'during one harvest time', and never returned; clearly more prosperous than most, they enrolled their daughter at the city's American Girls' College. While there she did a little ballet, a little singing, and developed what was at the time an unusual fondness for Western rock and pop (Melis tells me how as late as the mid eighties, sourcing even mainstream Euro chart hits in Turkey meant a visit to a knock-three-times backstreet cassette pirate). Few of the big sixties groups, in consequence, troubled themselves with Turkey, but some time in 1967 Spanish-German beat stars Los Bravos, who the previous summer had gone top five on both sides of the Atlantic with the rather splendid *Black is Black*, came to play Istanbul. (Following consultation with my wife, it has become depressingly apparent that many people will be more familiar with this song in the Euro-disco incarnation released by La Belle Epoque in 1977.)

Seyyal has described herself at the time she attended this gig as 'wild, untidy and absolutely hyperactive'. What she doesn't say is that she was fifteen – in fact, by mathematical probability fourteen – when the Los Bravos bassist, driving out *Black is Black*'s epic riff, swapped winks with her. In the chortlesome words of one profile, 'The group realised Seyyal's interest and curiosity in music, and invited her back to Spain.' Within months she was shacked up in Madrid with German Harald. 'I met these big, worldwide musicians,' she tells me, 'Los Bravos, very famous. I met them here when I was a student [cough], and finished with my school [cough], and went with them to Spain when I was seventeen [sorry – I think I need a glass of water].'

How on earth can her family have reacted? Even today Turkish women are expected to be seen and not heard, and in fact ideally not to be seen that much either, and if possible kept away from books. It's difficult to imagine any girl of that age, then or now, being encouraged to accept such an invitation – particularly to Spain, where the age of consent was then twelve (responding to international outrage, the government recently raised it. To thirteen). And a girl from *Turkey* . . . 'I got in trouble with my family, nyeh, of course,' says Seyyal lightly, and for a moment I try to imagine the vortex of table-bashing, larynx-shredding, Harald-castrating rage unleashed by her actions. 'I say I would go for three months but I don't go home, and I don't contact home, I was scared, and my mother has to try with the consul to look for me. After one year she found me.'

By then, displaying a determination that matched her almost petrifying sense of adventure, she had made herself a star. When that summer Los Bravos began filming *Los Chicos Con Las Chicas*, a Beatlemania-inspired comedy musical, she inveigled herself into the cast (not a challenge given its plot, summated thus by an online Iberian enthusiast: 'In this film, the vacations of Los Bravos are in danger by the proximity of a feminine school.'). Though you'd be hard pressed to find a copy now, *Los Chicos* was a major hit in Spain when rushed out for release in early 1968. Amongst the 2.5 million who saw it were a group of Paramount executives, in the country to oversee filming of *Villa Rides*, a Sam Peckinpah-scripted bio-pic of Mexican rebel general Pancho Villa, who in 1916 staged what remains the most recent armed invasion of the continental United States.

'I was a young girl,' Seyyal tells me, for now but not for long excising adjectives relevant to her physical appeal, 'and the producers saw me, and they say my God, you must be in our film! And so I start to make movies with the worldwide stars.' A small, nonchalant smile. Yul Brynner (in a wig) was Pancho Villa, Charles Bronson his sadistic sidekick, Robert Mitchum an American pilot. At fifteen, Seyyal was already dining at celebrity's top table.

'A girl like me, that age, full energy, full dynamite, I couldn't stay quiet or still for one minute. I was a Mexican guerrilla girl in the film. A beautiful experience for me, to make this film in Spain with these world-stars . . . nyeh, it was big luck.' A waiter arrives: I hope he's going to lay some un-aubergined foods on our table, but instead – eeeek! – it's two bottles of red wine. Seyyal graciously nods for a glass, takes a sip, and after a slight grimace drops in a couple of cubes from our ice bucket. 'You know Yul Bri-ner? He give me my birthday cake on the set. He came, he kissed me, he said you are eighteen today, congratulations.' I ask whether he looked better with the wig. 'I think without.' I don't ask why she said she was eighteen, when in fact she turned sixteen during the Pancho Villa shoot. Seyyal Taner is one of the few showbiz performers who's been in the game long enough to have lied about her age in both directions.

Playing back this part of our conversation at home, I grasp the pertinence of a compelling phrase my structural engineer translator had supplied as the heading to one of the Turkish newspaper interviews with Seyyal: 'this woman makes rap while talking'. Her relish for these enthralling years is infectious, and her account of them relentless.

'At the same time, the owner of Paramount Pictures, he was, uh, fall in love with me.' The laugh she barks out here silences many tables; I can only assume Seyyal enjoys being encircled by eavesdroppers. 'He gave me a lot of opportunities to go to Hollywood, to be rich, to be famous, to be a *world-star*! Because, you know, I had a beautiful figure, nyeh. I was a girl who Hollywood really wanted, but I was too much for that man. *Too much!'* A marriage proposal was tearfully issued, and harshly rebuffed. 'I was in love with Harald, I was about to marry *him*. I said come on, you're my grandpa! So I fucked up with Paramount Pictures man. He was so sad. But he was more than fifty and I was eighteen [um . . . sixteen], it was just *unbelievable*.'

Very nearly. I really don't want to doubt any part of Seyyal's splendid saga, but trying to fill in the blanks later I find myself untangling a fist-sized granny knot of inconsistency. In 1967 Paramount was owned by an eccentric Austrian-born industrialist, Charles Bluhdorn, who had just turned forty, and was married (although one movie insider added a little grist to the Taner mill by claiming that 'Wall Street's mad Austrian' – who greeted difficult actors with the word 'fucking' inserted between fore and surname – 'bought Paramount as he figured it was an easy way to get laid'). I also find it impossible, after much

Jahn Teigen, Paris, 1978.

Above: Finn Kalvik, Dublin, 1981.

Left and below: Kojo, Harrogate, 1982.

Celia Lawson, Dublin, 1997.

Above: Thomas Forstner, Rome, 1991.

Below: Ovidijus Vyšniauskas, Dublin, 1994.

Above and left: Seyyal Taner, Brussels, 1987.

Below left: Wilfried, Dublin, 1988.

Below right: Daníel, Lausanne, 1989.

Munich, 1983.
Above: Çetin Alp.

Left: Remedios Amaya.

Above: Tor Endresen, Dublin, 1997.

Right: Gunvor Guggisberg, Birmingham, 1998.

Jemini, Riga, 2003.

detective work, to verify the details of her marriage to Harald, or its duration, or indeed Harald's very existence. All the Los Bravos line-ups in their swinging heyday feature Basque-born Miguel Vicents on bass, and while the band wouldn't have been the first to deceive their audience with a pretty-boy stand-in, it's odd that even the Los Bravos fan club is unable to confirm that any Germans other than lead singer Mike Kogel ever took to the stage in their name. 'You know, the only Spanish guy in the band was the piano guy, Hermanio,' Seyyal says at one point. Everywhere I look, the keyboardist is down as Manolo Fernandez (whose suicide in 1968, coupled with a barren chart run and Mike Kogel's departure, heralded the band's effective demise).

Well, so what? It was a confusing time for everyone, and for Seyyal in particular a time of dizzying upheaval. Furthermore, as she now announces in an airy drawl, 'You know, I always move with my feelings, I never like rules. I'm a . . . boheme. I do it all my own way.'

For the next five years she certainly did. Now married to Harald, or possibly not yet, or perhaps already divorced, in the late sixties and early seventies Seyyal travelled the world in textbook period fashion. 'I was sometimes in Africa, sometimes in India . . . I was interested in Buddismus, I went to Tibet at that time, I live there for three or four months.' Again I can't help asking how her family felt about their teenage daughter's eye-catching lifestyle. 'At first they was really angry with me, but after a year they understand that I am a girl who lives for art.' Melis overhears this, and I see a smirk spread across her freckled face. 'Flowers, films, mountains,' continues Seyyal, casting a careless arm aloft. 'Things catch me, I go for them.' She suddenly fixes her big eyes on me. 'Nyeh, I'm a real different person for Turkey for that time . . . I was anarchiste, a protestor girl in every way, always different, always against.' A single, significant nod. 'My mother understood it.'

At some point in this period she bore Harald a daughter, Melanie, leaving the child in Germany to live with her father. ('She studies computers in Hamburg, a very beautiful girl, plays nice piano,' says Seyyal later. 'But her voice . . . nyeh, not so good.') And throughout the early seventies she periodically returned to Turkey to make movies, playing the vamp in eight further films of gradually diminishing commercial import. Typical of her earlier output was 1972's *Vur*, described by an online fan as 'a cool violent western from Turkey, about two bounty hunters hired to clean up a gang of bandidos. One of them kills the boss, while the other one gets cozy with a sexy female gunslinger played by Seyyal Taner.' Those that followed earnt her an appearance on the cover of a recently published retrospective entitled *Turkish Erotic Movies*.

The films dried up, and by 1974 she was earning her crust from photo-love stories. Not the humiliation it might have been in other countries: these 'fotoromanlarda' were big business in Turkey's lingering pre-television age. Demis Roussos appeared in one as her love interest – insert wide-angle lens joke here – and Seyyal enterprisingly engineered an all-star cast for another by having herself photographed in poses of rapture or jealous fury alongside unwitting celebrities at the Cannes film festival.

The Turkish photographer who accompanied her to Cannes became her boyfriend, and it was he who first suggested a career in music. 'I did a little bit of singing at school, and I love music, but I never imagined it as a career.' Seyyal's first single disappeared without trace in the summer of 1975, but her pouting, bikini-clad form on its cover earnt a lucrative residency at a Black Sea casino.

Seyyal arrived for her debut wearing torn jeans and what my structural engineer calls 'a face full of nose rings'. The outraged casino manager immediately summoned one of Turkey's leading designers, who beheld Seyyal's 'magnificent body' and declared, 'I cannot dress this girl, I can only undress her.' So it was that she took to the stage wearing only a light pink piece of cloth, before announcing to the audience that she didn't know any Turkish songs. Her repertoire that night consisted of *Cabaret* and 'two or three German songs', but these were delivered with such sensual verve and energy that a bellowing audience demanded four repeats of each. 'This girl is an animal!' shouted the ecstatic manager.

'Seyyal Taner never waited to become a famous singer,' said a media commentator many years later. 'She went on-stage one night and became a star right at that moment.' The woman was a phenomenon. At fifteen she goes to a gig in Istanbul and within months is acting alongside the top film stars of the era; at twenty-three she steps on-stage with a repertoire of four songs and before she steps off Turkey has a new sensation.

No female singer in Turkey had ever previously dared to move on-stage; Seyyal, who had toured with Los Bravos and – one night in Germany – jammed with Tina Turner, didn't dare to stay still. 'We had nothing like that here,' she confirms stridently as the waiter tops us all up and finally delivers some food I can eat – grilled sea bream, straight from the Bosporus. It's full of bones but at that stage I don't care; even the head goes down the hatch almost whole. 'Nobody in Turkey can teach me or tell me any new stuff, no one. You have to find your own way at that time. I was the only person who can dance and sing and make her own costume, her own show, her own group.'

Norway and Turkey wouldn't appear to have much in common, but both are cultures where a little talent and a big fat sack of brazen self-confidence can take you anywhere. The cuttings describe her as 'the Turkish Cher': 'She did not have a great or unique voice,' wrote one profiler, 'but she was different, crazy in her clothes, rebellious, sexy, energetic . . .'

Seyyal later says she didn't want to be famous, that fame found her by chance, but if ever there was an example of someone making their own luck, it's right next to me now, knocking back the raki. Fortune favours the brave, and in showbiz they don't come much braver. In 1979, touring Anatolia at a time when nationwide political unrest had led to the imposition of martial law in the province, Seyyal found herself facing a huge and unruly crowd of right-wingers in the Black Sea resort of Sinop. Her carefully selected opening number, notoriously composed by a recently imprisoned local socialist, incited an instant hail of coins and missiles that forced her backing band off the stage; facing the barrage alone, Seyyal strode to the front of the stage and addressed the mob with deafeningly amplified righteousness. 'I am a woman,' she bellowed, 'but I am not afraid of you! I will not go! The man who wrote this song is one of the greatest writers in Turkey – we should all respect him! There can be no right and left in this business! Life is a cabaret, old chums!' Even shorn of that last fabricated exhortation, her words had an extraordinary effect. As Seyyal defiantly launched into an a cappella reprise of the inflammatory song, a deep silence fell over the audience; a moment later, in my engineer's words, 'the coins thrown on the stage are replaced by gillyflowers'. Her backing band sheepishly stepped back out from the wings, and in what has clearly been a career-defining tactic, Seyyal sang the song five times on the trot.

By then she was already a national pop legend. Her third single went to the top of the charts in 1976, and led to a huge-selling album. 'Suddenly I was *very famous*,' she announces, with an appealing absence of self-effacement. 'People are going crazy, following me everywhere. When I am walking right, they are walking right. I go left, they go left. You know what I'm saying, nyeh?' Extricating bream vertebrae from the back of my throat with raki-fuelled indifference, I nod.

Press profiles talk of this period as a golden era of Turkish girl-pop, with Seyyal as its queen of sass. Fan clubs mushroomed; in 1977 she was voted the sexiest woman in Turkey. 'You had no rivals,' simpered a recent interviewer, with reference to that time. 'You were loved and wondered at.' Her response: 'I still have no rivals.'

Yet it was the type of celebrity that rarely endures, and by the early eighties Seyyal was barely recording. As her career went off the boil, so Seyyal's personal life overheated. A tabloid exposé in November 1983 revealed a love between the 'brunette of the stages' and actor Halil Ergün; within months, she tells me, her moribund marriage to Harald was formally dissolved (though the Turkish media had been describing her as divorced for almost fifteen years). 'We are still friends,' she mutters, without conviction, when I probe deeper. 'But, you know, I was so young when I married him. And for a Turk and a German it was hard to meet in the middle.'

Harald aside she claims only four boyfriends, all of them long-term, most of them showbiz impresarios. 'They were charismatic, intellectual, Turkish in nationality but not like a Turkish man,' she told a female journalist recently, as they drank whisky aboard her current beau's yacht. 'And they balanced my personality – I am an ill-tempered woman!' This non-revelation was underlined in an accompanying account of the time she discovered photographs of another woman in her photographer boyfriend's desk: 'Everybody was in a panic. I broke the office to pieces, and then him.'

A scrawny stray cat scrabbles noisily up a tree beside us and begins mewing pitifully from a high branch; Melis leaps to her feet and dragoons passers-by and waiting staff into what swiftly becomes a complex and raucous rescue. 'And then in 1986 I make another boom record, nyeh,' drawls an oblivious Seyyal, leapfrogging the intervening years when – as I later confirm – little of professional import occurred. 'So once again I am very famous in Turkey.'

The blandness of her tone in declaring this repeated achievement is significant: in a pattern with which I was now familiar, conquest of the domestic market can often underwhelm. In Seyyal's case, the imperative for a career beyond the borders was made more urgent by her professional perfectionism and individual extravagance: 'While on tour,' wrote one media biographer, 'Taner wants to enjoy the same conditions as she has in Istanbul, and her new group Locomotif soon understand how she likes every detail correct on-stage. To achieve all this, she pays from her own pocket if required.'

This contemporary editorial view is succinctly encapsulated by Seyyal: 'Nyeh, it was hard work. And very expensive – I am getting one lira, and spending six lira . . .' Her red lips curl in weary scorn. 'Pah . . . this *mew-sick*, I pay too much: my money, my health, my brain – I paid a lot of things. What music gave to me, I gave two times music back.' A grimace evolves into a small snort of amusement. 'And then it's stupid, boring Eurovision.'

As soon as the E-word pops out, Melis enters the conversational fray with a vengeance: the four lightly bearded musicians who took to the stage as Locomotif, she swiftly emphasises, were originally her backing group. Nearly twenty years later, the 'Seyyal Taner and Locomotif' tag still rankles, a grievance that evidently outweighs any temptation to whistle nonchalantly away from the nul-points wreckage. Seyyal's CV is bulked out with conspicuous non-Eurovision achievements; for Melis, her career low-point has to double up as its highlight. 'All the stars go for Eurovision then,' she says; Seyyal indeed had tried the year before, falling just short in the national qualifier. 'If you are a big one, you go for it. It was such a big thing at that time.'

These last three words are becoming something of a catchphrase; it's as if we're recalling events from fifty years before, rather than just eighteen. 'But just think of this!' Melis blurts, hoarsely. 'Eurovision was in! It was *cool*!' As a bevy of waiters interrupt our debate, bustling around picking up plates and – inward sigh of fuzzy resignation – refilling glasses, I reflect that Turkey has packed three decades of pop-culture evolution into one and a half. They've been fast-tracked from solemn, Nordic-model Eurovision worship to jeering Brit-pattern scorn.

In 1987, though, the pressure was intense. 'It was *huge*, like a war!' Melis almost shrieks. 'Everybody watches it – we have only three TV stations at that time. Now it's maybe 400.' Indeed so: grisly and spartan as my room was, its incorporated satellite TV boasted more viewing options than the Big John beach bungalow and all my Scandinavian hotels combined. In a dedicated forty-five-minute quest for nipples and Al-Jazeera, I'd barely clicked through a quarter. 'So we felt absolutely that this was for the whole country, that we are promoting Turkey to 500 million Europe people.'

Across the Bosporus, all the lights in Asia abruptly flick off; my dining companions merely shrug when I point this out, and two minutes later they all flick back on. Sitting alone by the river, I'd been powerfully impressed by Turkey's strategic and mercantile importance: what a momentous coup to welcome into the EU a nation that straddled both the world's most densely populated continents. But now, reminded again of Turkey's shambolic infrastructure, I can't help asking my dining companions if this place is really ready to become the newest star on the Brussels flag.

'I hope it will be, that we are in Europe Union,' says Melis. 'Of course we want. The French are against, but everybody knows they are very selfish people. Maybe we must wait many years.' Ah: the true spirit of Europe. But perhaps it won't take them that long. After all, a mere twenty years bridge the pan-continental scorn heaped upon *Opera* with Turkey's first Eurovision victory.

'Stupid, boring Europe politic,' drawls Seyyal. A woman of deeds, not words – long decades before Turkey had even begun to ponder aligning itself with all those busy little countries to its west, she was over in Spain marrying a German. 'Turkey cares too much. About this and about Eurovision. At that time Turkey is always doing really so bad in this competition, but every year they expect more.' The record book, like everything else on the planet, isn't about to argue with her: Turkey first entered Eurovision in 1975, and in the pre-Seyyal era had only once broken into the top ten; after her it would take nine further attempts before they did so again. This mightn't be the most tactful moment to bring up Çetin Alp, but I do so anyway. Surely, I suggest, his pioneering zero made theirs a little easier to bear.

'Who?' asks Seyyal, genuinely clueless.

'You remember this super-weird song,' says Melis, and the tact issue evaporates. 'So difficult to listen to. In fact,' a guilty chortle, 'it was really the *worst song of Eurovision history*!'

Seyyal shrugs in continued ignorance, but accompanies her friend's burgeoning smoked cackle regardless. 'Why we have that song?' gasps Melis between helpless, cough-bridged guffaws. She's a great snorter, too, and in full comedic flow lets rip with a remarkable Woody Woodpecker machine-gun. 'For what?' At length she gathers herself, dabs her eyes and the end of that freckled nose, and after a final, rogue giggle, says, 'He died actually.'

A three-woman bray of explosive laughter; it's all getting a bit *Ab Fab*. 'We are good girls,' quavers Seyyal, 'but you have to be careful!'

For rather a long time they seem to forget I'm there, cackling, waving their arms about, babbling in Turkish – a surprisingly gentle, melodic language, with none of the phlegm-dislodging hacks I'd been expecting.

I sit back, fuzzily content, happy for a breather – in the post-Finn world, it's difficult to relax fully in a nul-pointer's conversational presence. I watch the ships pass under the bridge; I run my bleary eye across Asia; I down a litre of water in a rearguard assault on the rampaging axis of raki and red wine. Then, amidst the cross-table babel, the words 'Johnny Logan' snag in my ear, and I reluctantly stick an oar in.

It's a different Seyyal who talks me guardedly through the run-up to Brussels. 'Newspapers were saying that this time we must succeed in Eurovision,' she says, those soft features gradually hardening into an expression of wry, slightly bitter aloofness that will do her, give or take the occasional rant or cackle, for the next hour or so. 'TV company, music company, all my friends, all my producers, everybody say, "You can win it, with your style, your music, you're the person for European people." Hah!' How significant that for the Turks, the Scandinavians, for us, Europeans are someone else. Perhaps understandable from a woman born way east of Damascus, I think, but still: act like a gatecrasher, and you'll get treated like one.

'So in the end, I say, "Pah – why not?"' I suppose the money softened the blow, I suggest intemperately. 'Money? You make jokes?' A single bark of scorn.

'Maybe we make money if we *win*,' offers Melis, in a conciliatory tone; at twenty-three and with a significantly lower profile than Seyyal's, Eurovision success was inestimably more important to her. 'And maybe we think we *can* win: in the national competition here, you know, we were *by far* the first.' By now fully conversant with Eurovision's capacity to muddle memories, I don't point out that *Şarkım Sevgi Üstüne* in fact edged out runner-up *Günesli Bir Resim çiz Bana* by 142 points to 140.

Melis distractedly pops another cig in her mouth, hands one to N. Dogroll, and lights both. Glazing over, she sighs out a plume of smoke just above Seyyal's head, then pulls herself back into focus with a brisk shake of the head and a smile. 'But in Brussels it was *fun*! We were the party people, in every second! We were going about the city with Sandra Kim, doing photos in these ancient squares . . . One day, the King and Queen invite all the Eurovision singers to have champagne in the botanic gardens. At nine o'clock in the morning!'

Seyyal's furrowed look melts into a gentle beam of eager recollection. She clearly has no memory of Sandra Kim, whose 1986 victory had brought the contest to her Belgian homeland, but royalty . . . she's away. 'We are laughing with Queen and with King, and I was too laughing – my God! Like crazy! The Queen, she says, "Why are you laughing?" And nobody else is, all very serious. I say, "We are from Istanbul, we laugh always!"' No arguments there. 'We enjoy, we laugh, we dance – and we make beautiful joke with King and Queen!' I find I'm thinking of Jahn and Serge Gainsbourg in a Paris nightclub, of Kojo in his fume-filled sedan chair. And Rudyard Kipling: 'If you can meet with triumph and disaster, and treat those two impostors just the same.'

But as quickly as her mood has lightened, it darkens. For almost the entire meal Seyyal has been trying quite hard to steer us away from Brussels and its stupid, boring contest, but now she seems to sense there's no turning back. We've started, so we'll finish. And after that Bollinger with King Baudouin, it's going to be downhill all the way. 'Some things I didn't like so much,' she says, her voice lowered. 'This press conference. The people ask us just the *po-liti-cal* questions, because we are Turkish, about Cyprus, about Greece.' Her jaw clenches; she leans forward. 'We were so mad and sad and *angry*, and I start to shout and I gave them a beautiful big lesson, especially the Greek person, *nyah-nyah-nyah* – so *silly* and *stupid*. We are there for music, we are non-politics, why are you asking us this stupid, boring, politic questions? You have to *shut your mouth* and take care about us!'

She sits back and nods once, with fierce hauteur. It's a coins-to-gillyflowers performance: Eurovision's bitterest internal conflict, dismissed in a swift, majestic tirade. Melis rallies to the cause. 'This English guy who talks for the TV?' Her curled lip gives a clue: it's Terry again, more notorious across the sprawling Eurovision empire than I'd ever have believed. 'You know what he says? "Here are the ugly Turkish people."'

Not quite up to his normal repartee, I think. 'I'm sure he wouldn't have quite, um . . .' Sensing Seyyal's spine stiffen beside me, I tail off.

'We haven't forget what he says! People in Turkey, we were shocked by this!'

I nod, then mumble: 'Well, he's actually Irish.'

Seyyal bridles at this craven deflection; her nostrils flare. 'Nothing to do with Irish, England, Russia! It's in his brain, the problem!' She taps her head, then chinks a ring against her glass. 'There is good wine, bad wine, and good people, bad people. Who says those things is a bad person. Who give me no points – this is not bad people. This is just . . . bad music.'

Melis tilts her an aggrieved look. Thank Christ: for a fearful moment it looked as if they were all set to go Kalvik on my ass, make me suffer for the sins of the Wogan. Instead I can just sit back and watch them settle their artistic differences. On the recording, it now becomes difficult to tell who's who – they talk over each other, trying to get their point across first, and, failing that, loudest. In Turkey this doesn't qualify as an argument, but there's nonetheless a sense that the Locomotif power struggle is still being fought out.

Seyyal had been in showbiz since Melis had been on solids, but for a woman this was a weakness as well as a strength. Age hadn't been a problem for Jahn, Finn and Kojo, all in their thirties when the scoreboard let them down, but the harsh realities of the business meant that at thirty-five, Seyyal would have seen Melis – twelve years younger and six inches taller – as a threat. 'All women are rivals,' she told an interviewer recently. 'They smile to your face but one day they will stab you in the back. It's the reason why I have not been a good friend with women in any part of my life.'

Hearing *Şarkım Sevgi Üstüne* for the first time, Melis at least was modestly impressed. 'It was written by a Turkish guy, but sung in French at that time, a nice song. You know what is about?' My head, which appears to have doubled in weight since the arrival and dispatch of the most recent bottle of raki, manages a slow lateral movement. 'About love,' says Melis, 'but a *huge* love. Not for one person, but all people . . . friendship, peace . . .' She trails away, leaving Seyyal to smirk slightly at the humdrum hoariness of these Euro-themes.

Translated as *My Song is About Love, Şarkım Sevgi Üstüne* kicks off with a burst of quasi-kasbah ululating keyboard; I've downloaded it from Andreas's DVD on to my MP3 player, and I hand Melis the earphones. She plugs them in and her head jiggles in delight; soon she's mouthing along with some animation. 'Oh, it's a long time since I hear this in Eurovision version!' She giggles, handing the earphones over to Seyyal. 'But you know it's a lot on the radio now, at this moment. Yeah! One love!' And in the chorus, twenty-eight consecutive las – not a bad effort, but some way short of the Eurovision record of ninety-four set by Portugal in 1973.

They pass the earphones back and forth, Melis laughing, Seyyal rolling her brown eyes. I allow my lips to crease into a wistful smile: this is the closest I'll come to realising that regrettably abandoned intention to coax my nul-pointers into a singalong. After a couple of verses they take an earphone each, heads craned together across the table. Slowly, Seyyal's look of sullen indifference melts into resigned indulgence, and towards the end they briefly sing along together. For one night only, Seyyal Taner and Locomotif are reformed. And I'm back in my bedroom, two weeks before, watching Victor Laszlo cede the stage to seven white-clothed, dark-haired Turks.

If it had been just been Melis and Seyyal, *Şarkım Sevgi Üstüne* would have done just fine. Possibly even quite well. The mad-or-bad debate on the causes of Eurovision failure is irrelevant – *Opera* might have been both, but *Şarkim*, at least considered as a whole, was neither. Which isn't to say there's any difficulty in pinpointing its fatal flaw.

Two sparky young women in white gloves and fringed jackets, bouncing around in energetic formation: you want to look closer. But five blokes behind them, wearing and doing the same: you want to turn over. With her luxuriant Donna Summer hair, frilly tutu and microphone-stand-grabbing stage presence, Seyyal showcases the verve and allure that made her an instant star. Tonsorial history hasn't been quite so kind to Melis, but overlooking that stacked-up afro quiff, and in particular its bleached central stripe, it's no chore to watch her happily strut the stage. Both of them look like they're having the time of their lives.

The beat is relentless, driving things forward with a hyperactive sense of purpose that detracts at least a little from the cheesily ethnic keyboard fills. There's a very retro, rather commercial feel to all the breathless, shimmying vigour: you're almost expecting some period consumer product – a Hoovermatic twin-tub, perhaps, or the all-new Triumph Toledo – to be unveiled behind the band on a spotlit turntable. It's a shot in the arm after the shot-in-the-head, blandly plodding Euro-pap that's gone before and will come after. (The 1987 winner – and the only singer to take that big bouquet a second time – was the fearsomely insipid Johnny Logan. Despite this unparalleled success, or in fact because of it, the man christened Séan Sherrard has never managed to carve out any sort of extra-Eurovision career for himself.)

For a couple of jaunty verses it seems the disco-trousered buffoons behind Melis and Seyyal are merely there to pace about in flare-flapping unison and add a little musical authenticity: all have an instrument hung round their white-collared necks, even if this orchestra includes one of those irritating strap-on keyboards then so de rigueur. (You know what I mean:

think Herbie Hancock and – if you can bear to – Level 42.) And then it comes, the nul-points trigger. The background chap with the horridest haircut – half Manilow, half Melis – plucks the mike from Seyyal's stand and strides towards the nearest camera. From Reykjavik to Rome, you can almost hear the sound of jurors' pencils being dropped.

In a terrible, screen-filling moment we are made aware that there are to be none of the jaunty pop-smiles essayed by his female superiors. The head settles deep between the shoulders, the fists are clenched and gathered tight to the chest. A look of exasperated strain contorts the reddening features above: a compelling portrayal of advanced constipation, which when he begins to sing intensifies into one of mortal agony, as if he's just been shot in the back. In strangled distress he rasps his final words: 'My song is full of friendship, my road is the road to wisdom.' The Turkish entry is less than a minute old, but the points – all none of them – are already in the bag.

Melis plucks out the earphones and plonks them on the lavishly soiled linen with a small tut and a sigh. 'Pah,' she groans. 'That Garo Mafyan.'

'The Manilow guy, right?' I say, following up with an impression that may more convincingly suggest an energetic tortoise concluding the act of love. Wrong, say the concerned faces angled towards me. I catch N. Dogroll glancing significantly at my raki.

'He was conductor,' says Seyyal, slowly. 'And he destroy our song with his crazy, crazy speed.'

My ears have almost returned to their normal colour by the time I've had it all explained. The scurrying breathlessness of Locomotif's performance was not, I am made to understand, in any way intentional: old Garo, falling victim to what Melis calls 'Eurovision Stress Syndrome', whisked the orchestra to the song's conclusion fourteen seconds early. 'Maybe it don't seem much,' says Seyyal, a little shrilly, 'but fourteen seconds in three minute is like ten per cent!'

Of the nul-pointers I'd so far met, only Jahn admitted watching the relevant fateful performance more than once. But

Seyyal has clearly analysed her Eurovision demise with the scientific dedication of a forensic pathologist, going through the tape again and again to establish the precise cause of death.

'In the rehearsal, it was fantastic, beautiful singing, beautiful choreography,' she says, shaking her head. 'People *loved* it – the press say we were a favourite.' Indeed so: Martin Faulkner, a Eurovision authority who'd offered many helpful insights, told me he recalled more than one delegate tipping Turkey for a podium finish. 'But on that night . . . he start to go fast, we start to run, we start to shout, like fast-watch on a video. And nyeh: just like that it's finished!' A part of me wonders if she's clutching at straws, but watching the final again at home I concede her point. From the second verse on, they're gabbling to squeeze the words in; more than once, Seyyal shoots a look of concern in Garo's direction. And he paid the price. Brussels was Garo's third Eurovision, and his last. 'What is your limit in forgiving?' a journalist asked Seyyal some years later. It isn't difficult to picture Ms Taner's expression as she delivered her reply: 'I never forgive.'

'So: we were unlucky,' she says, pursing those enormous lips. 'You see: it was not my fault!' A nod of satisfied finality. 'End of story.' She shivers slightly, rubbing her silk-sheathed arms. Seconds later, an unbidden waiter glides up to wrap her shoulders in a fleece-lined cloak.

A rather sombre silence falls over the table. Seyyal shifts about and glances expectantly towards the maître d': we haven't even got to the voting and she's about to get the bill. 'No!' I yelp. 'Not end of story. Just . . . end of chapter. You went off stage, and . . .'

I'm counting on Melis, and she doesn't let me down. 'When the votes are coming through, we were just, pah! What? *What?* And it came to the final result and we were saying, "No, this is not us, this is not right."' She smiles helplessly. 'I called my parents, and they said, "Well, you weren't *that* bad." And Johnny Logan was so friendly, I love him, and the Israel guys, they were so nice, and sad, they cried with us.'

As she says all this, Seyyal leans forward and with an air of purpose slowly pours herself a tall raki. OK, she seems to be thinking, if you want to do this, let's do it. When Melis falls silent; she does it.

'We don't *cry*. We are angry! We are shocked: what, *zero*?' A look of pantomime disdain. '*Zero?* Is that what we deserve? Pah! Shit! You goddam liars European caaaarntries! You don't understand *nothing*!' I've come to imagine Seyyal's early film roles regularly requiring her to spit in a stubbled bandido's face, pulling the very face she now pulls. 'And then you know what I do?' Garrotte Garo? Torture Terry? Maim Melis? 'I dance! I dance like I am the winner!'

Everyone laughs, largely with relief. The fuck-you-all defiance of the bloodied-but-unbowed loser – this is why I'm here, talking turkey with Turkey's turkeys. I've come to taste the elixir of life after death: to a stage-phobic speaker-hider-behinder, there is no performer more awesomely heroic than the one who endures crippling, catastrophic indignity in the entertainment world's most powerful spotlight, then swats it away and moves on. As a devotee of *When Good Pets Go Bad*, I claim no immunity from the unwholesome impulse that draws crowds to the police tape, but there's no appeal in leering at the twisted nul-points metal unless I'm assured that the airbags and seatbelts have done their job, that the dashboard isn't spattered with ragged chunks of Kalvik.

'Nyeh, we party, we dance, and you want to know for why?' She's working us now: on cue, our laughter fades. 'Because there is something pure in a zero, it is a pure number.' She glances from face to expectant face, smiling inscrutably. 'The colours black and white, these are the strong, honest colours. Between them a thousand weak colours, with a little white in them, a little black . . .'

This is the sort of stuff she probably picked up in Tibet, I think, but without the inward sneer that would normally accompany such a conclusion. Drastically pissed as we all are – on my next visit to the facilities I'll sideswipe two ice buckets and wink at a passing waiter – Seyyal's poetic rationalisation has us in sober thrall. She's the maharashi, and we're the Beatles (sorry, N. Dogroll – you get to be Ringo). 'And in life everything turns always, so black turns to be white. Yin and yang. Life is short. Be happy.'

We all nod. Then Melis says, 'When I go home after Eurovision, this is what I hear at the airport: no problem, you are unlucky, it's all over.' She wrinkles her nose. 'But when I arrive at my apartment, there is written on the wall: "Locomotif woman – you are shit".' And we're back to the shrieks, the snorts, and a strafing burst of Woody Woodpecker.

Seyyal has been keeping her Eurovision cards close to her chest, but now they've been snatched from her hand, laid on the table. Suddenly, she seems more at ease: the cat is out of the nul-points bag, and there's nothing left to hide. 'Of course it is all psychology,' she says, in a new, confessional tone. 'People think you might win, and you do badly . . . maybe you think the same. It isn't easy. I laugh about this zero on that night, but after that I don't laugh so much. I stop making music for a long time.'

Ah, yes: 'Seyyal Taner got sad for two years after her big fat 0.' Defiant bravado is always a tough act to sustain. 'I go to your city, to London, trying to forget. There I cut my hair *real short* and have it with these funny, funny colours – in *red*, in *green*, in *peeeeeenk* – and come back to Istanbul.' Her lopsided half-smile says: I can laugh about it now. 'I had this emotional, depressive, crazy feeling, and all my days I am just running, running. Crazy hair, in sunglasses. No one notice who I am. One day I run along Bosporus, and I see some musician friends: I run past them maybe seven times and they don't see me.'

At this dramatic point, a dolorous tannoyed ululation falls down from on high – a muezzin up in the minaret of that marble mosque calling his congregation to evening prayer. No one else even notices, of course, but I can't help finding it a sombre counterpoint to Seyyal's darkest hour. 'I did nothing! In Istanbul and Bodrum, running, training, dancing, making bodybuilding, therapy, reading, watching, listening, but nothing else.'

The wailing intensifies, almost drowning her out; there's

something about a big composer persuading her to do an album – 'Come, Seyyal, I make a beautiful music for you' – and this selling fairly well, and getting her back on the summer-festival circuit. Then 'another two years of quietness', another album, another lull. It's a period neatly summated by my engineer: 'From 1989 to 1993 her good-quality albums made Seyyal Taner fans happy, although they did not attract attention as the ones in the past.' One harsher critic – and with her forthright character there can't have been a shortage – described thus her last original album, 'I am Coming': 'She is gone.'

'Seyyalname', the 2002 reworking of her greatest hits that she'll autograph for me later ('To Tim with love from ISTANBUL, Seyyal Taner') remains her most recent release. Eighties Turkish chart pop heavily seasoned with flavours of the month – a little pinch of Latin, a big dollop of techno – it wasn't a big seller. Sample review: 'An album that nobody is interested in, an artist that nobody yearns for, no concert offer and no extra job offer.'

She had failed to adapt, said the press: 'When her rivals switched to more arabesque music, she continued her line of pop.' Too Turkish for Eurovision, she was now too European for Turkey. She'd spent her formative years with Bronson and Brynner and Beatle-cut bassists; too late to change now. West is west and east is east, but Seyyal Taner was stranded in the cultural no man's land between. When back in 1975 that casino manager had beseeched her to sing something in Turkish, she'd shouted back, 'But I am a girl from Spain!'

Seyyal, of course, sees it all very differently. 'All Turkish pop music today is a continuation of my signature,' she told an interviewer. When challenged to justify this statement with reference to a certain popular female vocalist, Seyyal replied, 'Can we talk about good music instead? I only saw her once, shaking her ass and wearing something scaly, torturing a song. You see, I am still alone in my field, people still stand up and cheer for me. I am the only peerless artist.' Canvassing an opinion of Sertab Erener, who in 2003 won Turkey's first Eurovision title, I'm fixed with a look she might have kept reserved for a trouserless Terry Wogan. 'Oh, *come on*, I don't have any idea, I have *nothing* to say on this woman or her song.' When you're voted Turkey's sexiest woman at twenty-five, turning fifty can't be much fun.

That could have been it for Seyyal. Shortly after her 1993 album sank almost without trace, she moved in with the owner of the Dodo Beach Club in Bodrum, a millionaire yachting enthusiast who remains her consort. Life there sounds right up her street: in the online assessment of one visiting tourist, 'the sunbeds on the Dodo Beach pier and beach are very comfortable, however it is impossible to escape the loud music that plays all day long'. In twenty-five years, she'd made a dozen films, sixteen albums, played countless gigs and snogged Demis Roussos. More than enough to warrant early retirement for the best bad girl of her day, living out her days as the 'respected middle-aged lady' her countrymen had described.

But you only need to skim her CV to understand that Seyyal Taner did not get where she is by lying about on sunbeds, no matter how comfortable. In 2002, more than a quarter of a century since her previous thespian engagement, she successfully auditioned for a role in the distantly aforementioned soap opera, *Istanbul is my Witness*. For a woman of her character and background, it must have seemed a spiritual home: all soaps need a Joan Collins. I can just see her flirting and shouting and slapping her way through the plotlines. Infuriatingly, my sources let me down on the details of her part in *Istanbul is my Witness*, and Seyyal herself she isn't about to spill the chickpeas.

'I made a beautiful show for three years, but for the next series I am not in it,' she says, poker-faced. Her reluctance to refer to the programme by name suggests this departure might not have been her choice, but her stint there sufficed to rekindle Seyyal's celebrity: the neighbouring diner who at this point comes over to pay gracious homage is far too young to recall her musical prime. Bolstered by this, she perks up. 'And soon I am in a new show, very fun, very big, but I can't tell about this now.' A sweet, unusually prim smile. 'So one time again, acting is my life.'

With duty rather than enthusiasm she talks of another forthcoming greatest-hits compilation, 'from '76 to '81, my golden time'. She raises those neatly marshalled eyebrows at a waiter to summon the bill towards which she will refuse all contributions, and turns to me to deliver her summing-up. 'I am happy now. Maybe some time I like to do more concerts, in squares, for public, for no money. It's enough.' I think of the final question in her most recent press interview: 'What kind of a feeling is it, to not be able to say "Tomorrow is mine"?' Or more specifically, of her reply. 'Past, present, future: it all belongs to me!'

You just had to hand it to these nul-pointers, every one of them. I was utterly in awe of their reckless pursuit of fame and fun, the unquenchable spirit of adventure that had fuelled them since their teenage years. All had done what so few of us dare to do: they'd gone for it. Better still, all those I'd met thus far had got it. In their lives before nul points they'd shared Abbey Road with Beatles, been picked up at the station by an ABBA girl in a Maserati, represented their nation at two sporting disciplines, learnt English off Charles Bronson and Yul Brynner. Each and every one of them boasted a more eye-widening CV than all of your most fascinating, successful and dangerously eccentric acquaintances combined. Waiting while their lives flashed before their eyes, Death was going to need a good book, and maybe four cans of Stella.

Recall beyond this point is entirely dependent on the recording. All through the meal my hosts have been praising the purity and – ha! – smoothness of this particular raki, but 40 per cent alcohol is 40 per cent alcohol, no matter how you dribble it down your sagging chin and into your velvet lap. I'm as sure as I can be (which is to say not even remotely) that they've drunk more than I have, yet the bright intensity of my hosts' three-way chatter offers an unflattering contrast to my fuzzy, addled slur.

'Last chance for salad. No? You don't want? Ah: you need more ice in your red wine.' ('Thank you,' I croak feebly as the cubes clink in.) 'Can we ask you something . . . why you not trying to speak in our language? There are these little books, you learn one or two hours a day. Please, you be kind, buy a book, Turkish–English, and some time you read the pages. Please?'

'Thank you.'

Turkish nattering; a lull. Then: 'Teeum: you have been drinking raki and wine.' It's Seyyal's voice: you would never believe that its owner has matched the mumbling tramp beside her glass for evil glass.

'Thank you.'

'Teeum: I fly to Bodrum seven o'clock tomorrow, the morning. I must go now. Melis will take you to a taxi.'

'Thank you.'

Before she departs, and just before my recorder bleeps off, something worryingly odd happens: whispers, giggles, a cry of 'No, Teeum – shake, shake, shake, then put down fast!' It's a week, and five listenings, before I remember: one of the three was fortune-reading from the grinds in my coffee cup. I'm in no hurry to recall who it was or what she said.

A grubby hotel in Istanbul is no place to wake up after a night on distilled spirits. For an hour I lay slackly spread-eagled in the curtain-filtered sun, hands and feet hanging off the sides and end of my cub-scout bed, half-closed eyes on the half-painted ceiling as Joey and Chandler blabbered faintly at each other in high-pitched Arabic.

Hunched under the dwarf-dimensioned shower in a sort of skiing position, globules of recall bubbled to the surface in my slurried head, like corpses rising from a bog. Melis buying three roses from a distressingly soiled streetchild; N. Dogroll delivering a passionate eulogy to Jamie Cullum; one of the two summoning my taxi with an ear-bleeding whistle; me snatching Melis's roses as I tumbled into the back seat and – oh, foul and fiendish 40-per-cent curse of the Ottomans – handing one to the driver.

I found the second rose composted in my jacket pocket as I groaned and shuffled towards a breakfast buffet whose emphasis was rather more olive-centric than I'd have wished.

The troubling whereabouts of the third were revealed when I hoisted a pale and unsteady hand at the receptionist. The sickening wink that was his response meant an abrupt change of plan: instead of leaving my bag in his care while I touristed away the five hours before my plane left, I bundled it through the dirty glass doors and stamped raggedly away up the street.

The breathless, runaway energy of Locomotif's Eurovision performance was everywhere. There were too many people doing too many things, and doing them all far too fast: walking, talking, begging, eating, and most notably driving. It was as if Garo Mafyan, his musical career brusquely terminated, had wound up conducting Istanbul's traffic management. I imagined him alone in a smoky, screen-filled control room, eyes rheumily ablaze, empty raki bottle on desk, baton a blur in his flailing arms.

A bus bumped up on to the kerb at its stop, scattering the gathered queue; a police car in a state of alarming neglect reversed waywardly across a pedestrian plaza. Digital countdowns at the crossings heightened the sense of frenzied panic; every green light unleashed a slaloming stampede of battered yellow taxis, barrelling five or six abreast up three-lane potholed boulevards. Lugging my holdall around the kebab-shopped perimeter of Taksim Square, I wondered how I'd ever safely stop one: it was like trying to hitchhike at Le Mans. Then, recalling recent events, I stuck four fingers in my gob and delivered a shrill blast. A juddering shriek of rubbery protest, a flung-open door, and I was inside. 'Grand bazaar,' I said, feeling rather pleased with myself.

With sixty-five covered streets lined with 4,400 shops, the scale of the world's oldest shopping mall is unavoidably impressive, but two hours later I wandered out of its distant back end rather saddened. Yes, there'd been gold and slippers and carpets, but the vast bulk of the bazaar's 25,000 resident merchants had been energetically hawking precisely the same T-shirts and baseball caps that had filled every stall in Koh Samui. Nike, Ralph Lauren, Von Dutch – what brainless robo-consumers we've all become, what craven, biddable globo-dullards.

The lofty ideals that inspired Marcel and his mates in that Monaco hotel had seemed so sniggeringly twee, so unfashionably Eurocratic. A song contest organised by a committee of state-controlled broadcasters to foster European unity, a celebration of cultural diversity, a common front against the greedily creeping forces of transatlantic culture – oh, how quaint. Margaret Thatcher and her many pan-continental disciples had kicked that whole business hard up the arse. Market forces, small government, consumer choice. And now that we'd been given the choice, this was what we'd chosen: a world of sweatshopped, Yank-branded crap, piled high, sold cheap. You just can't trust consumers. As someone who walked out of that bazaar with seven pairs of Tommy Hilfiger socks, you can take it from me.

It was a lot better in the streets outside. Here the commercial variety was bracing: one shop selling nothing but mortarboards, another holsters, another ladders. And there was almost none of the wearily relentless tourist schmoozing that had quickened my stride along those covered streets: 'Please, sorry, new chemise for you, *mein herr*?'

With the 20,000,000 lira note in my pocket worth £8.20, or possibly 82p, I was having great difficulty recalibrating my bargainometer. And how do you decide what's cheap in a country where McDonald's do home deliveries and a qualified dentist earns less per hour than a London parking meter? Well, it was trial and error. And error, and error. When I finally got the hang of the exchange rate it became apparent that I'd already been shortchanged by a couple of million at a mineral water stall, and had blithely left a 200 per cent tip at the first of my many coffee stops. A minute later, though, I hammered out the deal of the century with a chap selling ten-colour biros by a bus-stop: a policeman uniquely committed to the eradication of unlicensed street vending leapt out of his car with a shout, sending my man pelting off down an alley and leaving me with three pens in one hand and the note I was about to hand him in the other.

As is often the way, my blearily unfocused wanderings somehow took me where I wanted to be. Tramping leadenly down a nondescript street of clothiers, I started hearing a lot of Polish being spoken. A vital discovery: no nation is blessed with such finely tuned budgetary radar. Anyone who travels around Europe with prudence aforethought will know what it is to turn up at the cheapest campsite or market or snack bar and find it overrun with pasty, smoking Stanislaws.

When two definitive examples slid out of a gentlemen's outfitters looking slyly content I therefore swiftly marched in, and after a busy minute swiftly secured an astounding deal on an unusually well-finished three-buttoned suit. I was loosening the required notes from my lira-wad when the dapper young salesman held up an apologetic hand and withdrew the calculator that had so efficiently facilitated our haggling. The agreed price, I grasped at tortuous and humiliating length, was the unit cost on a minimum wholesale order of 200 suits. It was only an hour later, waiting in line for a mid-morning kebab, that I began to wonder what on earth Eurovision was doing to me. As well cut and sharply styled as it may have been, the suit in question was also unavoidably, incontrovertibly and blindingly white.

What a splendid piece of work is the kebab. In its indigenous Euro-Asiatic incarnation at least: I exclude from this judgement those crusted cylinders of mixed quadruped that blight British high streets. The one assembled for me at that pavement stall, and dispatched between oil-faced mechanics on an adjacent bench, featured a dozen chunks of grilled lamb and half a mixed salad crammed into a sliced baguette hunk. All the major food groups present and correct for a little under 30p. If I could only eat one thing for the rest of my life, I thought, angling my lightly oiled chops up at the sun, this would be it. Though that's assuming I woke up every day with a fairly appalling hangover.

The taxis were so cheap, and the hailing process so entertaining, that after another heavily sedimented coffee I whistled one over and threw my bag in the back almost without thinking. 'Um . . . just drive about,' I said, with a vague circling motion of the right hand.

'No poblim,' smiled the driver, re-entering the vehicular fray with a manoeuvre that left a kerbside stallholder face down in his leather accessories. 'Music OK?' he called over his shoulder. 'Turrrrkish music?'

'No poblim,' I said, without thinking.

And so to the warbling accompaniment of Seyyal's successors we barrelled about for a happy half-hour, back and forth over the Bosporus, past mosques and under Roman arches, duking it out with all-comers, mirror-to-mirror. Throughout my driver delivered the now traditional commercially oriented commentary. 'Dis music city,' he'd call out as we bumped down a street full of bongos and organs. 'Dis book city . . . dis table city.' Occasionally his vocabulary wasn't up to it, and after a flurry of frustrated, impotent tuts and finger clicks we'd cruise wordlessly through laminate flooring city or reconditioned alternator city.

Old men fishing off the bridges, a central reservation carelessly stacked with Roman column tops, carved Byzantine slabs and other apparently unwanted remnants of old Constantinople. The usual cheap-laugh billboards and signposts: Titiz, Arcelik, the Grand Hilarium Hotel. And somewhere, on every street, further evidence of the hastening erosion of an extraordinary national identity. A chemists' window display dominated by pyramids of Viagra packets. A BMW dealer. A giant Tom Cruise failing yet again to look hard.

A droopy-eyed glance at my watch; best get cracking. 'Airport,' I called out, and my man nodded briskly. I'd more or less set up home in his back seat by now, but incredibly, the meter hadn't yet topped a fiver. I can't really complain at its subsequent quadrupling in the following fifteen minutes. Fall asleep in a taxi and you deserve all you get.

30 April 1988
Royal Dublin Society
Wilfried
Austria
Lisa, Mona Lisa

Two glaring misapprehensions had taken hold when first I clapped eyes on that list of post-'74 nul-pointers. It didn't take long to unearth the bikini-clad proof that Seyyal Taner wasn't a man, but it wasn't until I saw him next to Chris de Burgh at a 1988 Eurovision photocall that I discovered Wilfried Scheutz wasn't a woman.

I can't now begin to imagine how this dim delusion took hold – Wilma? Winifred? – but it was nonetheless a shock to have it so rudely shattered. Because Wilfried wasn't just a chap, he was a huge-faced, ham-handed hulk of a man, easily the most male of all the nul-pointers. Looming mightily over wee Chris, it was as if he'd just smelt the blood of an Englishman. In consequence, I wasn't as crestfallen as perhaps I should have been when it became apparent that my quest would have to be rerouted around the forbidding mass of Mount Scheutz.

'Hello, Mister Moore!' replied his wife Marina, minutes after I dispatched an explanatory email to the address given to me by Wilf's agent. 'Wilfried is in the moment on tour. He is back this weekend and is going to read your email. I hope, he will answer very quickly!' No other nul-point quest had got off to such a flying start; it was only after a fortnight that I began to harbour concerns. A couple of unanswered emails, an unreturned call to his agency, then a long, long letter sent to him care of the same, describing in frank detail my sympathetic understanding of Wilfried's predicament, and his associated reluctance to reply. On reflection, this made it easy for him to continue his stonewalling, and much harder for me to try another gambit. 'Dear Wilf – you know how in my last letter I said I quite understood why you might not want to meet me? Well, in fact I don't. I don't understand at all. Come out and stop hiding, you giant nance.'

But it's only when Andreas's DVDs arrive, bearing in their 1988 volume a Wilf-themed catalogue of ill omen and wrongness, that hope is laid to rest. I gulp in distress as the big feller rounds off his pre-act filmette, shot at a Dublin racetrack, by joyfully cracking open the bubbly to celebrate a win. I recoil as the camera pans back from the Royal Dublin Society's huge stage, allowing us to take in the box-shouldered, double-breasted bum-freezer that shrouds his vast torso, the creased matching strides, the great white barges anchored immovably to the performing surface. And then, after a faltering drum roll, I prepare myself for whatever sound this being is going to emit.

Lost in those mighty hands, the microphone seems like the mallet from a baby's xylophone, and holding it Wilf looks as comfortable as a shy veteran goalkeeper asked to say a few words at his testimonial dinner. The crow's-feet spread across his temples as he winces at the lights; he raises the mike to his lips. In conjunction with the visible signs of facial ageing, Wilf's earring and slightly bouffant hair accurately suggest that he's been in this business for longer than any of his Dublin rivals. His voice, however, does not.

In fairness to Wilf, *Lisa, Mona Lisa* is a musical nonentity: too many words, not enough tune. Not by accident did it come a comfortable last in an online 'best of the worst' nul-points poll, which attracted over 4,500 votes: here is Europe's wrongest song. With a little vocal finesse, it might just about have made a late-era T'Pau B-side. But Wilf doesn't do finesse. His lumbering, diesel-powered tones plough crudely into the opening verse, which diggiloo.net tells me is about a girl who paints fairy tales on her face. Beneath the wisps of that hair-sprayed fringe, Wilf's great tombstone brow furrows as he plod-dingly hunts for tune and meter, never too far off but never quite on. When his hefty female backing singer chimes melodically in at the first chorus, we all think: Why don't they swap places?

But strangely, even as it's all going so wrong, Wilf appears to grow in confidence. Even – eek! – in stature. He begins to hulk slowly around the stage, hand in suit-trouser pocket, smirking like some creepy motivational speaker. By the time the enigmatic object of his affections is tumbling through the glittering town, searching for someone who has a smile for her, Wilf looks as if he's determined to end that quest. And then, filling those cavernous lungs, he works up to the big finale. This is what he's been looking forward to, a chance to blast the audience flat with his maximum, unleashed throat-power.

What follows is transcribed by the compilers of diggiloo.net as a simple '*Woah . . .*' But the fateful exhortation that Wilf now releases shares little with a workaday vocal filler that has quietly serviced the music industry for many decades. Sustained and emphatic, it thunders raggedly from his gaping, tooth-crammed cavern of a gob like the final utterance of a man who's just seen the cable-car floor open up beneath him. Four letters, three dots, no points.

Just before that primal bellow finally empties his lungs, the orchestra crunches to a discordant halt, and for an awful second the audience sit in stunned silence. 'Ja,' murmurs the ORF commentator, above a smattering of bewildered applause. But here's the thing: Wilf is loving it. There's no relief in that face-filling grin, just triumphant delight. Having been selected without national qualification, this is the first time *Lisa, Mona Lisa* has been performed to a significant audience. A little concern at how it would go down was only natural, but that's all gone now. He scans the crowd eagerly, warmly, gratefully: Thank you, Dublin, thank you, everyone, you've been great. Take care now. Goodnight.

There is no televisual record of Wilf's brutal backstage reality check; the green-room coverage is devoted to the historic three points awarded by Turkey to Greece, and an unfolding battle for victory between Céline Dion and the UK's Scott Fitzgerald. Belgium also bears a blank by its name – no zeroes on the scoreboard this year, just a stark void – but two rounds from the end France give them five, and the ORF guy groans softly. No one else notices. Having been seventeen points behind halfway through the penultimate round of voting, to boundless audience excitement Céline somehow pips Scott by a single point. The Swiss delegation leaps to its feet as one: they haven't felt like this since the government doubled motorway tolls for foreign drivers.

Being thirty-eight, male and Austrian, the odds were stacked against the big man even before he opened his vast mouth. The demographic factors that doomed Wilf were those that had driven him to Eurovision in the first place: it was fifteen years since his biggest-selling Austrian single dropped out of the charts, and six since he'd had an album in the national top ten. On this basis, he didn't have much to lose. But he lost it anyway. Having peaked at number twenty-seven, *Lisa, Mona Lisa* remains Wilfried's most recent chart appearance.

As a price of his ongoing activities in the music industry, Wilf is occasionally obliged to give interviews. In consequence, and with additional thanks to Google language tools and the members of escforum.com, denial of personal access did not prevent me from conducting a patchily fruitful investigation into his life and times.

Wilfried Scheutz was born in 1950 at Bad Goisern, near Salzburg, and lived out a bucolic childhood he has described as 'not madly lucky', perhaps because it involved sharing a classroom with future fascist pin-up Jorg Haider. (To my great relief, Wilf has described Haider's waning political influence as 'something that makes me very happy'.) Let's then go straight to 1973, mainly because of the info-void that persists from his college days in Graz to the release of his first single. Wilf is twenty-three, and he's recorded a self-penned folk-rock number entitled *Mary, Oh Mary*, which immediately shoots up to number three in the national hit parade (in the all-time Austrian singles chart – what am I doing on these websites? – it's ranked at 698). Yet it's Wilf's next hit, 1974's *Ziwui Ziwui* that makes his reputation, despite making it only to number six. Hauntingly described as 'a half-roared, half-yodelled kick in the back of domestic popular music', *Ziwui Ziwui* establishes Wilfried as a founding father of the movement that would be known as 'Austro pop'.

Like Russian salad and British Leyland, this nation-noun combo should perhaps never have been allowed to get it together; left to breed they would eventually inflict Falco's *Rock Me Amadeus* on the world. But Wilf's 'malicious spin' on the genre is aimed squarely at the domestic audience: this is a country where a man with a BeeGees beard and a white jumpsuit undone to his hairy navel can have a big hit with a thumped-up cover of *Run Rabbit Run*. Churning out hard-rock near-parodies of Alpine folk songs, entitled things like *Bilberries* and *South Wind*, Wilf enjoys a steady stream of top-twenty singles – and a shallower trickle of top-twenty albums – that flows until the mid eighties. By then he's swapped the jumpsuit for leathers and a Harley, and is shacked up in the forest just outside Vienna with his Slovenian wife Marina and their young son, Hanibal. He's also retrospectively won me over by celebrating his thirty-first year with an album track entitled *Never Trust No-one Over 30*.

But popular music moves on, even in Austria, and Wilf's 1986 live album only just scrapes into the charts. Austro pop will not be declared officially dead until Falco meets an unhappy end in a 1998 car crash, but for Wilf it's already all over bar the roared yodelling. His 'musical monuments' have now all been erected, though they're still tall and shiny enough to attract the Eurovision spotters from ORF, who in early 1988 team Wilf up with a couple of veteran songwriters from Graz. *Lisa, Mona Lisa* is the consequence, a happy one only in that as Wilf's last chart single it creates a pleasing titular symmetry with his first, *Mary, Oh Mary*.

It's hard to imagine a performer nicknamed 'the hoarse bard' thinking much of the ploddingly feeble *Lisa, Mona Lisa*. Wilf has gone on record to describe leather trousers as 'the most beautiful article of clothing of the world'; how awful to picture him cravenly slipping into that polyester grey two-piece in a Dublin dressing room. So why his boundless on-stage delight? I can only assume that after a fallow five years he couldn't withhold his joy at being back in front of a huge, sell-out crowd. And perhaps, at thirty-eight, he was wise enough to know he might never get to experience that buzz again.

'After Wilfried's last place with the Eurovision Song Contest 1988,' wrote the compiler of one online biography, 'he is disappeared.' Well, not quite. Taking the holiday from music that is a traditional part of the post-nul-points recovery process, Wilf gamely essays a career in acting. In 1992 he bags a reasonably major role – a teacher named Walter – in a thirteen-part ORF drama 'set approximately around love, power, money and jealousy'. Though perhaps he doesn't do a great job of it, as his next (and final) screen appearance is a walk-on part in a 1996 TV crime caper.

By then Wilf's back in the studio, working on the first of the eight albums he's produced in the post-Eurovision era, none of which has yet found favour with a mainstream audience. Rather more productively, 1996 also sees Wilf founding 4Xang, an a cappella group that you'll no doubt be as happy as I was to see hailed as 'a genuine Austrian bomb'.

A middle-aged male four-piece, 4Xang (which I'm sure in German sounds a lot less like an offroad driving club) still tours the *Anschluss* lands with sufficient regularity – around ten gigs a month – for fifty-four-year-old Wilf to call it a full-time job. It's fair to say they have fun. A bald listing of their humdrum influences – jazz, blues, rock and classical – doesn't do justice to the silliness apparent in CDs entitled 'Alp Fiction' and 'Papa

Was a Yodelling Stone', or their fondness for pulling madcap faces and procuring percussive accompaniment from a big metal suitcase. In the words of kabarett-news.de: 'One power purely. Go! Shortly in Mainz and Nuernberg!'

So I guess it's all going OK for Wilf. It must be a little painful to see his 1997 best-of CD sitting there reviewless in the 'Schlager und Oldies' section of amazon.de, and having to deal with the occasional likes of me wanting to pick through his bins, but in general Herr Scheutz seems at ease with himself. He's succumbed to the temptation of old-rocker hair – shoulder length, and in his case dyed auburn – yet still cuts an unquestionably finer figure than the rep-suited Hagrid who lurched around the stage at Dublin. His wife – certainly ten years younger than Wilf – looks as bright and cheery as her email manner suggested, and their son Hanibal, now twenty-four, is a rock and jazz drummer who's up for the occasional father-and-son gig.

In his most recent interview, Wilf articulated an understandable disillusionment with the music industry – 'you could say it's almost eating itself' – and said that he was no longer concerned with traditional definitions of success: 'I'm primarily interested in mastering a task, for my own satisfaction.' In fact, other than Jorg Haider and his Freedom Party, there's only one thing that seems to really get under Wilf's tanned and leathery skin these days. 'Every year I think it can't get any more terrible, and every year I'm wrong.' Clue: it's on telly one Saturday every May, and isn't the FA Cup Final.

6 May 1989
Salle Lys Assia, Palais de Beaulieu, Lausanne
Daníel
Iceland
Það sem Enginn Sér

They were coming thick and fast now: 1989 was the third consecutive nul-point year. And the hat-trick performer – it had to happen sooner or later – was the first who had entered a world in which I was already included. Just nineteen when he stepped on to the stage at Lausanne – half Wilfried's age in Dublin – Iceland's Daníel Ágúst Haraldsson wasn't even born when Cliff Richard locked himself in the Albert Hall loos, and barely sentient when Agnetha clomped on to the Brighton stage in those towering silver platforms. All the other nul-pointers had already hit the professional heights when the big nix came to call; wee Dan hadn't even finished growing.

They'd won the right to host the final courtesy of a Canadian singer, a Turkish composer, and a one-point margin over Britain's Scott Fitzgerald, but none of that was about to stop Switzerland claiming the Eurovision bragging rights. Céline Dion had given them their first victory since Lys Assia back in that inaugural 1956 contest, and by naming the Lausanne auditorium after the singer of *Refrain* they reminded us all that Eurovision had come home. They also reminded us what a very strange country they lived in, courtesy of an introductory film in which a violin-toting child of indeterminate sex was driven around his or her homeland in his or her daddy's gigantic Mercedes, sombrely waving at armoured military vehicles. The 1987 contest had been a strident celebration of European fraternity – at one point in the pre-voting film break, we'd seen a mountaineer planting an EU flag on a mountain top – but the message here couldn't have been more twitchingly isolationist. We're loaded we are . . . but don't even *think* about it. Switzerland: look, but don't touch. When at the film's climax the child steps out of the Merc to be greeted by the over-toothed reigning Eurovision champion, you're expecting him (or her) to demand to see Céline's papers. And wouldn't that have been awkward.

Céline sings – twice – and then there's a record five-language introduction, comprising the usual suspects, plus Italian (spoken by around 10 per cent of the Swiss population) and Romansch (tongue of choice for fewer than one in a hundred natives, but the language selected for that year's Swiss entry). Young as he was, Daníel is far from the night's youngest singer: filling what one of my Eurovision guides calls 'the graveyard second spot' is a twelve-year-old Israeli boy in chinos. He's a steady quarter-tone off-key, with a toothily persistent smile that must have clenched jaws across the continent. But thank Christ somebody loved Gili Natanel enough to hand over a few votes: hard to imagine knocking on his door, nul-points questionnaire in hand, and finding myself welcomed inside by an untroubled twenty-eight year old.

As you'd expect from the hosts, everything's well organised but dreadfully predictable. The pre-song films all require the relevant artists to interact as best they can with lazily selected national props: a train, a cow, a music box. After the *Te Deum*, the tedium. The Brits finish second (for the twelfth time), the Turks try and squeeze 400,000 syllables into their song and wind up with five points, those in between have once more trawled their sartorial inspiration from a pop galaxy far, far away (in this case Madonna's 1984 lace gloves and ra-ra skirt phase). Though that's not nearly far enough for Denmark: they give us a stoutly venerable soap-opera barmaid backed by a couple of grey-haired Dick van Dykes, clicking their digits through a number that owes a lot to Max Bygraves' 1954 rendition of *Gilly Gilly Ossenfeffer Katzenellen Bogen by the Sea*. But this is Eurovision. They come third.

Following the tradition that gave us Riki Sorsa's pre-Kojo Finnish reggae, we have Finnish flamenco: it's beginning to look as if they're scared to show us their own musical culture in all its blank-faced, alien weirdness. Another titch: France's eleven-year-old Nathalie Paque, a sort of Mini Pops Kate Bush. (The Israeli child appears to have disappeared, but I swiftly tracked Nathalie down: she's currently spa manager at the Bangkok Marriott. Slip her 2,500 baht and she'll fix you up a ginger foot scrub.)

A Spanish girl with Brian May hair scrunches her eyes closed so tight that she might be enduring an ice-cube enema (probably not on Nathalie's treatment card, but you can only ask); perhaps inspired by this, few of the following acts trouble to stock up many visual memories of their time on-stage.

And then the hosts – Benny Hill's straight man and a woman with the dress of Queen Isabella I and the face of Victor Laszlo II – gather to introduce the twentieth of the evening's twenty-two songs, *Það sem Enginn Sér*. 'Each of us has a dream that no one else can imagine,' intones the male half of the partnership, only in French. 'This is the theme of the very mysterious Icelandic entry, *That Which No One Knows*. Young Daníel asks the moon to show him the way to find his dream, and swears that he will not share this secret with another soul.'

Well, that sounds all right, even if it does take me fourteen rewinds to translate. The portentous poetry is rather compromised, however, by the ensuing film, in which Dan and his compatriots arse about in a cobbled village, snatching children's hats and mobbing an old chap with a vast wheel of Gruyere balanced on his head. Such is the gleeful nonchalance of Eurovision artists unburdened by national expectation: first invited to the finals in 1986, in that year and for each of the next two Iceland had finished a lowly but consistent sixteenth.

But standing out on that big stage beside the grand piano manned by *Það sem Enginn Sér*'s composer, Valgeir Guðjónsson, Daníel doesn't seem quite so lackadaisical. He's undoubtedly a good-looking young chap, in an orphaned, androgynous sort of way, but those pallid, delicate features and cropped hair impart a look of consumptive desperation; one might almost imagine him auditioning for the workhouse choir. Carefully described by one critic as 'the most interesting of the night', Dan's outfit is one of unparalleled bagginess: billowing white shirt buttoned to the neck, windsock-wide grey trousers yanked up closer to the nipples than even Simon Cowell would dare. On anyone else, such generous tailoring would impart an expansive swagger, but poor, wan Daníel looks like a remorseful urchin turning up at court in his fat uncle's wedding suit.

Let's get the good news out of the way first. There are two important factors in Daníel's favour: despite a marginally dodgy high note, he has a fine and surprisingly powerful voice. Second: it's a decent song. Far too gentle to ever win Eurovision, and with a rather jarringly jaunty chorus, but a spirited effort nonetheless. Though there's no longer any practical purpose in doing so, that evening I get out my guitar and falteringly decipher its chords. Months later, *Það sem Enginn Sér* is still well up in my hum-along-a-Eurovision top ten. Sadly, as I'm now well aware, singing a good song well has never been at the top of a jury's checklist. Eurovision success – and more particularly failure – is decided by eyes, not ears.

Awkward and immobile, Daníel clutches the microphone in one knuckled hand while the other, held stiffly to his hip, fidgets itself into a knot. When the music kicks in he goes dutifully through the motions, raising his hand to that moon of his, lightly jiggling his legs. But his heart's just not in it. Whenever he tries to smile, it comes out somewhere between a shuddersome corpse-grin and the vicious leer perfected by

Malcolm McDowell during the first half of *A Clockwork Orange*.

Every time the camera zooms up to his face Daníel blinks first, turning away to survey Valgeir, his backing singers, the ceiling. The only time he doesn't, he tilts his head back, treating the watching millions to an unfortunate approximation of casual disdain. Like the man said, this is between me and the moon: you lot keep your fat noses out of it. If Dan has a nul-points moment, this is it.

As the song nears its conclusion he begins to seem marginally more at ease, though the kiss Dan plants on the crucifix round his neck after the final, muted chord is one of brittle relief. He almost grimly acknowledges the applause: I did it, *I did it*, and my trousers didn't fall down or catch fire and I wasn't sick on the piano and I didn't say poo instead of moon or *anything*. I've rarely seen a Eurovision performer depart the stage so swiftly.

Two songs later the final act, Yugoslavia's Riva, emerge from the wings, a five-piece symphony of period hues: black and white and red all over. A flavourless wodge of bubblegum rock 'n' roll, *Rock Me* also bends the native-language rule so far you can almost hear it yelp in protest. Its composer, the ambitiously self-styled 'Quincy Jones of the Adriatic', might have utilised only three words of English in compiling his lyric, but each (the title inevitably appended with 'baby') is repeated eighteen times.

The pre-vote interval show represents a memorable departure from the drab efficiency of the production to date. That slavish adherence to national stereotypes inspires an unlikely tribute to William Tell, in which a happy chap with a crossbow bounds on to the stage in an outfit that explores the overlap between jumpsuit and lederhosen. The trickshot preamble of burst balloons and decapitated carnations gives way to an enduring drum roll: here come's the inevitable Bramley-on-bonce finale. The drums fade to silence, he chews his moustachioed lip in theatrical trepidation, and then – thwack! The bolt slams into the board he's standing against, a clear two inches or so left of the intended fructiferous target. To uncertain applause he desperately frees the missile, clumsily wedges it into the apple and in shifty triumph holds the impaled fruit aloft. Then, adding insult to averted injury, we're shown a slo-mo replay, patently filmed during some more successful rehearsal, in which the fruit is pierced right through its pips. Bloody Swiss, I'm afraid I think. And that's before the Sony logo ghosts up on the screen: for the first time, a Eurovision final has been brought to us in association with a corporate sponsor.

There's very little green-room coverage in the voting, and none of it features Daníel. We have to imagine his tribulations as he watches Luxembourg and Turkey, who have kept Iceland company for round after pointless round, belatedly pick up votes. Yet there's obviously a new interest in the race for the wooden spoon: when *Bana Bana* and *Monsieur* break their ducks, the hosts want us to know it. 'Ooh! Premiers points pour Turquie!' they pipe up, to lonely cheers. 'Premiers points pour Luxembourg!'

It might be sympathy, it might be *schadenfreude*, but in all likelihood this unusual focus on the scoreboard stragglers is down to the slightly unfortunate result unfolding at the front of the field. *Rock Me* was hardly an obvious winner – UK runners-up Live Report publicly berated its blandness and Terry called it 'Eurovision's death knell' – and the crushing enormity of its subsequent commercial failure cemented the contest's evaporating influence on Europe's record-buying public. It was recorded in French and English ('It happened once upon a time, the son of a mayor invited me to listen to a great piano player'), but failed to chart anywhere outside the Balkans; such was their humiliated embitterment that the following May Riva became the first winners not to show up at the contest they had brought home.

It's tempting to think of Yugoslavia's debut victory as Eurovision granting communism a sort of lifetime achievement award, now that it was a harmless, wheezing invalid about to peg out. The prospect of going to Zagreb for the final wasn't nearly as scary as it would have been three years before.

Or indeed as it would be three years after: the revised Eurovision annals now discreetly credit Riva's victory to Croatia.

With 293,000 inhabitants, Iceland is comfortably the least populous Eurovision nation. There are more Maltese than Icelanders, and almost twice as many Luxembourgeois. Twin this demographic with my wife's nationality, and you'll understand why I didn't anticipate much difficulty in tracking Dan down. When I mentioned his name she chewed her lip a little, then said, 'I'm pretty sure my mum knows his girlfriend's dad.'

Busying myself with the more obvious looming obscurities of Lithuania's 1994 unfortunate, I stuck Dan on the back burner. There he simmered away happily, my pet nul-pointer, just waiting for the call. Or rather the email: some cursory Googling swiftly revealed the existence of a 'contact me' button at danielagust.com.

Visiting this site, however, offered pause for thought. Birna had some idea that Daníel's post-Eurovision career had seen him embark on a very different cultural journey – 'indie stuff' was the phrase used – but by taking the form of a scribbled, bearded and violently flatulent spider, his homepage's menu screen told of a man who was not as other nul-pointers.

Accessing the clickable links on this creature's scrawled legs did not undermine that hypothesis. One section displayed photographs: of barbed wire, of bottles hung in trees, of the hollow-cheeked, hollow-eyed man himself in poses glaringly beyond the norms of Eurovision's artistic expectations. Dan outside a mosque in a woollen cape, Dan in a knackered felt trilby with 'Beauty' written on it in four different languages, Dan sticking his pale, bearded face and one hand out of a dense bush.

The videos revealed by clicking the next leg along were no easier to square with the timid young man who had taken to the Lausanne stage after Marianna Efstratiou. He's tying strings to his bare toes, he's tying these strings to a tree, and it's getting darker, and darker, and, oh, bugger it, there's something really odd happening but it's now too dark for my ancient monitor to deal with. Next up: an old Saab crunches to a halt on a stately, gravelled drive, Daníel runs out, mummifies himself from the knees down in packing tape, sprays his feet gold and flailingly breakdances with practised incompetence to the point of exhausted collapse.

The soundtrack to these diverting events is an ethereal symphony of strings and synths; the lyrics, all in English, tell of stars being swallowed and stingrays lying in silt. One couplet rhymes 'soft moss' with 'amorphous'. It was going to be very hard, I understood, not to describe the artist responsible for all this as The Male Björk.

Given what I've just witnessed it's hardly a surprise to find that the biography accessed via leg three finds no place for the most conspicuous aberration of his musical youth. The compact resumé confirms what I've already learnt from my nul-pointers: that a career in entertainment is blighted more drastically by Eurovision triumph than scoreboard-propping ignominy. Win and you're forever shackled to whatever it was you sang, which by well-worn precedent is unlikely to age well. Lose, and you can reinvent yourself. Dan's CV reads, in full: 'Was in an icelandic pop/rock band which had six gold records and topped the Iceland charts on numerous occasions. Did some theatre work in Iceland singing and dancing and acting (*West Side Story*, *Jesus Christ Superstar* and more). Done some film and documentary soundtracks in Iceland as well as some music for dance theatre. Was the lead singer in GusGus. Made a solo album which will be released by One Little Indian in 2005.'

GusGus? That would be the indie stuff Birna had mentioned. Even I'd heard of them, though without actually hearing them. An electro-dance collective with a shifting and usually extensive line-up, they'd broken out of Iceland in the late nineties and – it says here – sold 250,000 albums in Britain and the US. The band's biggest hit, *Ladyshave*, was a salute to depilated masturbation. If my visit to Turkey had taken me to the dark side of planet Eurovision, Daníel Ágúst had long since relocated himself to its most distantly orbiting moon.

I fired off an email through his website and waited. For three days, a week, two weeks. Figuring he might be on tour or in the studio or tying string to his toes, I approached the press office at One Little Indian records (also Björk's label): a friendly young woman there supplied me with a mobile number. There was no answer; I left a message. I did so again perhaps five further times in the following week, without effect. There was only one thing for it. With time running short and the Daníel trail as cold as a silted stingray, I let Birna loose on to the densely tendrilled Icelandic grapevine.

It took a little longer than I'd thought. Icelanders are as Eurovision-fixated as the next man (assuming he's Norwegian); no other televised event empties the streets of Reykjavik more effectively, and the expatriate community in London organises a well-attended big-screen bacchanal on that special Saturday in May. Yet when Birna spoke to friends and family, she found herself fighting through a thick fog of collective amnesia. 'Daníel Ágúst?' they'd repeat, incredulously. 'But I thought you said this book was about the zero-point people.' Even when she persevered, citing the year, they still wouldn't have it. 'But I remember 1989! I watched it at Siggi's house. You remember Siggi – tall, glasses, went out with your dentist's first wife's cousin . . . Look, I know we've never won it, Birna, but I think I *just might* remember getting nothing at all. It's your husband again, isn't it? He's put you up to this. Filthy little cod-thief.' Well, that was one way of dealing with it. Some nul-point nations took it out on others, some on their own, but when that Lausanne scoreboard got too much for the Icelanders to bear, they simply stuck their fingers in their ears and went la-la-la-la. For sixteen years.

Birna was putting out Dan-feelers all over Reykjavik by now. She had a cousin on the case who knew a bloke who knew him, a TV journalist. An old schoolfriend weighed in with his girlfriend's number, but again it went stubbornly unanswered. A couple of days later Birna got the TV bloke's number off her cousin, and that night gave him a ring. I listened in growing trepidation as her cheery Icelandic salutations subsided into sympathetic clucks and hums and a muted farewell. 'It isn't looking great,' she said, clicking the phone off. 'Apparently Daníel never wanted to do Eurovision at all. He was sort of bullied into it and found the whole thing a complete embarrassment.' She let out a small, defeated sigh. 'He hasn't talked about it for years and his mate doesn't think he's about to start now.'

Oh, Björn and Benny's bared bottoms. I had never for a moment imagined that the land of my in-laws would let me down. But what could I say? After Koh Samui I wasn't about to twist any arms: if Danny didn't want to talk, I wasn't going to force him. How could I, in any case? Those I'd met up until now had to varying degrees seen our encounters as a chance to put the record straight, point the finger, share the blame; in general, to make it plain that they hadn't deserved their nul points. But Daníel's stigma, it seemed, was harder to shift. The shame he was still trying to live down wasn't that he'd come home from Eurovision without a vote to his name. It was that he'd gone there in the first place.

An hour and two bitterly ingested stiff drinks later, the phone rang. It was the TV guy, who tonelessly dictated to Birna a strangely prefixed number where he said Daníel was now awaiting my call. '0032?' I mumbled, jabbing the relevant numbers into the keypad. 'That's not the code for Iceland.'

An insubstantial voice answered after half a dozen rings. 'Is that Daníel?' I said, a little tensely.

'Yeah,' came the whispered reply, 'it is.'

Icelandic has a soft, almost lisping intonation, and here was a definitive example. Trying not to sound desperate, I began to outline my project. Almost instantly I was politely interrupted. 'Yeah, I know what it's about. You've been sending all these emails and leaving messages.'

'Oh . . . OK,' I said. 'So you got them, and, um . . .'

'I got them and I didn't reply. But, you know, in the end I had to admire your, ah . . . determination.' An expression of reluctant, wry amusement, more nasal than oral. 'I'm living in Brussels. Come over here any time and we can talk.'

With as much decorum as a man hoisting a clenched fist in

triumph can manage, I wound down the conversation. 'Dan!' I yelled, not yet aware that in doing so I'd woken up two-thirds of our offspring, and in fact hardly caring even when the blearily alarmed evidence tottered downstairs. 'You the man!'

Slumped against the Eurostar window I watched the relentlessly arable flatlands of northern France spool by. The bare trees flicking past, the pylons that marched in columns across bald, brown fields: it was a skeletal, colourless landscape, half-viewed through eyes that hadn't yet come to terms with our 6.26 a.m. departure. All the business about soft moss suggested that Daníel took a lot of his lyrical inspiration from the Icelandic landscape, and I could only hope for the sake of his creative wellbeing that he wasn't trying to coax poetry from this sort of prospect. There isn't much mileage in sileage.

The next time I creaked open an eye we were in Brussels, the derivatives traders and grey-haired daytrippers who'd shared my carriage rummaging about for bags and briefcases. As arranged I phoned Daníel, who'd kindly agreed to pick me up. 'I'm just outside,' he murmured. 'In a white Saab.'

'The one from your video?'

'Yeah – same one.'

I can't tell you how cheered I was by the bonding chuckle this exchange engendered. In all our communications to date Dan had exuded the sombre resignation of a dutiful but squeamish child who knows it's his turn to clean out the guinea-pig hutch. The email he'd sent to confirm the date of our meeting read, in entirety, 'Tim. Thursday 10th is fine. Daníel.'

With the keen eye of a moto-dullard I spotted the Saab from a great distance, pulled up in a taxi rank. Propped against it, conspicuous against the white paintwork, was a slight, bearded figure in a black velour tracksuit. Had it not been for my familiarity with the fuzz-faced bush-emerger pictured on his website, I'd never have recognised him.

'Tim, right?' And the pale lips visible through his Edwardian face hair twisted into a shy, slightly ironic smile.

Daníel drove us smoothly away from the modestly bustling

centre ville and into the low-octane, mid-rise suburbs of Eurovision's spiritual home. I could sense we were heading north-west, edging ever closer to the Grand Palais, where two years before Dan's lunar serenade, Locomotif had gone off the rails. Then we turned into an unremarkable sidestreet, passing a sign that identified it as a cul de sac. Oh dear, I thought, glancing left and right at the drab and rather forlorn retail premises to which it was home. From a quarter-million album sales to a flat above a shop.

The Saab slowed, but didn't stop. At the end of the road stood a pair of lofty, wrought-iron gates, the apparent entrance to a small park. We bumped across the dividing threshold, from tarmac to gravel, and there before us, hemmed in on all sides by the massed flanks of sixties apartment blocks, was a moated castle. Feeling my jaws part company, I turned in dumbfounded awe to Daníel. A half smile, raised eyebrows, enigmatic silence.

Daníel swung the Saab round on the wide bridge that crossed the moat and crunched to a halt before the overwhelming edifice. I got out and craned up at its hefty central section, a stolid and plainly medieval block of pale stone topped by an extraordinary, bulbous-tipped spire, like a Leonardo-designed space rocket. The rather fancier wings attached to each side were brick built and slate roofed, added at a time when gracious living had replaced the foiling of murderous enemies as the castle's chief purpose. And this was no windowless ruin: squinting through the expanses of leaded glass I caught a twinkle of chandelier.

Daníel eschewed the imperious arched entrance, and I followed him under a small side doorway. We passed through a workshop, a dim studio filled with hessian-clad dummies and into a small, comfortably domesticised kitchen. A young blonde woman was in there, stocking the fridge from the supermarket carrier bags piled about her feet. Who's a naughty Dan, I thought: she had to be many years his junior. Then she looked up, with a brilliant, expectant and suddenly very familiar smile. Ten years was a long time, but she hadn't changed much. It was Kristin-Maria, our first au-pair girl.

Daníel oversaw our happy greetings with a knowing smirk. 'I talked to Kristin about this English Tim guy who was coming here,' he said, once I had finished expressing my many-sided astonishment with clucks, chuckles and a tumbling stream of befuddled light profanity. 'She worked out pretty quickly it was you, but we thought it would be funny to make it a surprise.'

We picked apart its sister surprise, their occupation of Chateau Rivierin, over a light lunch on the moat-side terrace. (It had by now been established, to my paternal relief, that I wouldn't be souring our encounter by taking Daníel aside for a stern lecture: the girl I had last known as a wide-eyed seventeen-year-old was here not as his bit of skirt, but as his artist wife Gabriela's studio assistant.) One of Iceland's growing army of adventurous millionaires had acquired the chateau after a business associate put it up as collateral on a loan he was then unable to repay; for the last three years, while half-heartedly trying to flog the place, he'd allowed it to be used as an absurdly grand workspace for his artistic compatriots (also resident here, over in the east wing, was an Icelandic architect).

'We've had quite a time here for the last two years,' sighed Daníel, as at my feet a carp broached the moat's surface with its gaping, alien gob. 'Last spring we drove down to Bourgogne and came back with 160 litres of wine. We had a couple of parties here, and the whole lot was finished before the end of summer.' He shook his head, mulling over those memories of untrammelled debauchery, but sadly opting not to share them. And now the party was almost over. In the last few weeks an offer (of €2.5 million) had been accepted; they'd have to be out in two months.

Daníel ruefully scanned the grounds, and following his gaze I found my eye snagged by the props and backdrops of his more recent artistic endeavours. There was the bench he'd sat on while spraying his bandaged feet gold, there was the bush he'd stuck his hairy head out of. At some point, I supposed, a nul-pointer would politely welcome me into the comfortable, modest family home that befitted their stolid, uncomplicated post-Eurovision existence. But it didn't look like happening soon.

He showed me around after lunch. It was almost too much. The palatial halls of the ground level were weighed down with ornate plasterwork; a shed-sized, crest-topped Gothic fireplace presided over each. We took the lift – the lift! – up to the top floor, where Daníel opened a trap door that granted access, via a stepladder, to the interior of that peculiar spire. A tiny window set into this allowed confirmation that we had reached vertical parity with the spectacularly incongruous apartment blocks around. 'See here?' said Daníel, indicating a graffito carved into the window's wooden frame. '1915 – Guerre!' it read.

We clomped back down the ladder. 'That's it, really,' said Daníel, although the lift buttons had told me that at least two floors remained unexplored between the ground and the top. 'Maybe we can talk where I work. Up here, in the back.' I followed him along a route I could not have retraced unaided. Up a small section of spiral staircase, across a panelled hallway, round a few more twists and turns and into a dimly yawning attic, a beamed roofspace of ecclesiastical enormity inadequately illuminated by a trio of small dormer windows. At one distant, lonely end, emerging from a jumble of upended microphone stands, cables and keyboards, stood a monitor-topped desk. We walked up to it, our footsteps filling the dark eaves with echoing creaks. 'I've been up here eight hours a day for the past two years,' he announced, easing himself into a leather executive chair. I actually gulp: forty-five minutes up here on my own and I'd never blink again. Dan leans over to extract a typist's stool from under two guitar cases, and pushes it over to me. 'So,' he murmured, smoothing his moustache with thumb and forefinger, 'what do you want to know?'

For three or four hours we're up in that dark, churchy roof, our conversation kicking off with Dan the boy and progressing, via Eurovision, to Dan the man. He tells me his parents separated when he was two – Icelanders are generally pretty good at divorce, and theirs seems to have been amicable – and he lived thereafter with his mum in Reykjavik, humming along with her 'great vinyl': Nina Simone, the Beatles, Elton John, 'and Bach, which I loved'. His father sang in a dance band 'crooning tunes, you know, like *Danny Boy*,' he says, a self-referential smirk bending his beard, and later became an actor. Yet despite the encouraging genetics, he insists that as a child he had no musical ambitions, indeed no ambitions of any sort, his financial and vocational needs satisfied by a weekend job in a bike shop. Until he was thirteen, when a school band asked if he wanted to front them at a concert they'd been asked to do. For a 'youth celebration at a sports hall', which in fact ended up with Daníel giving his first public performance at Iceland's national stadium, singing for an audience of 5,000.

Icelanders are splendid like that. An astonishing number make a living through some sort of artistic endeavour: both because they're disproportionately talented, and because of their less gifted compatriots' almost overbearingly enthusiastic support. Reykjavik, a city the size of Southend-on-Sea, somehow manages to sustain nine theatres and an opera house; at the last count (my wife's), it hosted twenty-eight live-music venues. In short, it's the sort of place where the first time you step out on to a public stage, you shouldn't be surprised to find a significant percentage of the national population gathered expectantly at your feet.

'You know, it was quite a trip,' says Dan, smiling into his clasped hands as he recalls this youthful deflowering. 'I wasn't really interested in making a future out of being a pop musician, but even at thirteen I found I loved being on-stage, I really loved it.'

None of my nul-pointers had enjoyed as auspicious a professional debut, but for Dan it proved something of a false dawn. It was only after four years of vocal inactivity that a former bandmate approached him at their high school, and suggested resurrecting the partnership. The consequence was Ný Dönsk (meaning New Danish, and culled from a newsagent's foreign-magazine section: 'to be honest I never liked the name'), a Dan-fronted 'pop-rock' six-piece. By the spring of 1989 they were recording their first album, which was to feature Daníel's songwriting debut: with slightly more relish than embarrassment he describes this as 'a completely silly and absurd story about a turtle who escapes the pet store'. That's excellent, I tell him. Anything that differentiates a nul-pointer from Finn Kalvik is these days gratefully seized upon, and here is the polar opposite of the brittle soul-search described in *To Find Myself*.

Daníel is also unique as a nul-pointer in declaring almost complete ignorance of the Eurovision phenomenon. Iceland was invited for the first time only in 1986, he reminds me, and he doesn't recall it being broadcast before that. Yet it's huge there now, I say, picturing the shiny-eyed enthralment that the *Te Deum* fanfare inspired in all but a glum couple of the dozen Icelandic au pairs we've had since Kristin-Maria. Dan fiddles with his mobile and shrugs. 'I really know nothing about Eurovision,' he mutters guardedly.

His mild reluctance to discuss the contest's domestic significance is understandable. A sense of Nordic isolation encouraged the Finns and Norwegians to elevate Eurovision from a singing competition to a poll of their homeland's international worth, a rare opportunity to stand up and be counted, side by side with the Euro big boys. For Iceland, a remote enigma even to its fellow Scandinavian nations, all this was powerfully magnified. When Hofi Karlsdóttir brought home the Miss World crown in 1985, all the well-developed moral objections were swept joyously aside: she'd put Iceland on the map, and that was all that mattered. It was the same in 1984 when Jón Páll Sigmarsson triumphed as the world's strongest man, and would be even after his sadly premature death was linked to steroid abuse. When it comes to raising the national profile, there's no such thing as bad PR. In the thirty-three years since Bobby Fischer defeated Boris Spassky to become America's first chess world champion he has blotted his copybook so fulsomely you can barely read it, yet the swivel-eyed anti-Semitism that made Fischer a passport-less pariah was no barrier to Iceland recently granting him residency and a hero's welcome. The Spassky match, you see, had been played out in Reykjavik.

I say as much to Daníel, who nods non-committally until I describe Eurovision as a musical beauty contest. 'There's nothing musical about it,' he interrupts, a little sharply. 'I admire ABBA, but that's it. This contest means nothing, in terms of music, in terms of artistry, it's just a silly competition. Sometimes it's funny to watch, but it's really sad too, because the music, you know, it's lousy.' The intensity of this outburst seems to shock Dan as much as me. Funny to watch? Lousy music? Well, you know, that goes without saying. Except that he's just said it, and I'm not programmed to cope with hearing this sort of stuff from a contest veteran. Over previous months my Eurovision compass has been drastically reset, from magnetic scorn to due respect. I've been compelled by the force of Teigen to grasp the geopolitical, EU-defining clout Eurovision can still wield, and been brought face to Finn-face with its full destructive power. And now here's some whippersnapper dissing it. There's a slightly uncomfortable silence before he speaks again, this time in a conciliatory whisper. 'That's at least to my taste.'

I cough, and riffle distractedly through my notebook. The jollities of our castle/Kristin introduction have allowed me to forget Dan's initial reluctance to meet me; our conversation, I now remind myself, is unlikely to be completed without awkwardness. 'So,' I say, as bracing and businesslike as I'm able, 'how do you get from escaping turtles to Eurovision?'

Smiling again, just about, he tells me of Ný Dönsk's late-eighties pop-rock adventures, the college gigs, the body painting, the 'strange costumes'. 'But it wasn't a full-time job, still more like a time-consuming hobby. I did other stuff when I could.' Indeed: although I maddeningly don't find out about this until months after our meeting, Daníel's extra-musical career encompassed an endeavour that would enliven any CV – when the state broadcaster set about dubbing several series of *Top Cat* into Icelandic, they hired him to do the voice of Benny.

He was still living with his mum, and in Christmas 1988 met the girl who would become his wife. Shortly after, coming off stage at a Ný Dönsk gig in a Reykjavik café, he was approached by Valgeir Guðjónsson, a songwriting stalwart who had entered two of the three Icelandic Eurovision qualifiers to date, and already triumphed once. 'He said he liked my performance, and then asked me to do it with him.' Only an awareness of Daníel's already obvious distaste for the word 'Eurovision' – he often simply refers to it as 'the gig in Lausanne' – prevents me chiming in with a ribald snigger. 'Of course I wasn't too keen on these types of songs, but I really respected him as a musician and I wanted to work with him, to see how it was working with a professional. I'd only just started doing this band, you know, for a year and a half.' Dan nods firmly, as if he's only just understood the forces that drove him, against his better youthful judgement, on to that stage in Lausanne. 'For the experience – that was the reason why I decided to take it on.' Though I suspect he must also have been flattered by the approach. And as a stage-struck nineteen year old, the prospect of getting in front of a national TV audience, and then 500 million Europeans, would surely have been an enticing one.

Apparently not. Daníel says he can't really remember too much about the national qualifier, though it was his first time on TV (unusually so: in a pithy encapsulation of the country's media-density/population ratio, the average Icelander has appeared on television four times). He recalls nothing of his four rivals, not even the two he only narrowly squeezed out. He's blanked it all out, and he's done so because for this very unusual nul-pointer, the most painful memories are of victory rather than abject defeat. For Daníel Ágúst, winning the qualifier was a far more appalling tragedy than losing the final.

'Yeah, I hoped I wouldn't win,' he says, redirecting his visual attention from his fingernails to my face, as if to emphasise the sincerity of this arresting statement. 'It was my last year in college, and the final exams were coming up in May and I wanted to do well in those. This contest was at the worst time, you know, and I thought it would ruin four years of hard work.' He checks himself slightly. 'I didn't want to run away from the contest or anything, I really wanted to do the job properly, sing as well as I could. But all the time I was hoping, please don't let me win this. My exams, the band's first album . . . I have other things to do.'

He means it, absolutely no doubt. While his more senior co-competitors still dreamt the Eurovision dream, Daníel had woken up and smelt the café. An uncomfortable truth had been working its way to the surface ever since *Waterloo*: Eurovision had stopped making stars. After their victory in 1976, Brotherhood of Man topped the chart in thirty-three countries, selling six million copies of *Save All Your Kisses For Me* – I can't help thinking the word 'somehow' is missing from that statement – and Nicole's *A Little Peace* shifted a million in the UK alone. These days, such feats are unimaginable: Céline Dion's portentous 1988 success was, in hindsight, the exception that proved a rule.

Even if you wanted to fashion a glittering career from belting out Eurosongs, which Dan emphatically didn't, a Eurovision stage was no longer the place to fashion it. Too green to recall the contest's glory years but smart enough to know they were long gone, for Daníel a Saturday night spent revising irregular verbs was more valuable than one frittered away serenading half a billion Europeans. He was the first performer I'd met not raised to respect Eurovision. Perhaps that was the secret Dan wanted to share with the moon: tell you what, crater-face, this whole thing is shite. Listening to him I can sense the holy grail of Abbadom being tarnished – it's as if Jahn and Finn and all the rest have died in vain, inspired by some defunct, discredited ideal to chase an impossible dream.

Daníel diplomatically stresses how much he learnt from working with Valgeir Guðjónsson – 'it gave me a lot, especially in terms of how to interpret lyrics, how to use my vocal cords, and I'm ever grateful for that' – but struggles not to bear him a grudge for writing the winner. Did he like the song? 'Hmmmmm,' he says at length, a noise that can be effectively translated as 'Look – Iceland is a small place, and I'm a nice guy, so please don't ask me questions like that.' But it was a decent tune, I suggest, and the lyrics were pleasingly offbeat. 'Yeah,' he says, with a dry, low-watt chuckle. 'I always wondered what the moon found out.'

Cheering up my nul-pointers by mulling ruminatively over the happy memories of their victorious qualification has become such an ingrained interview gambit that I find myself banging on and on about it, even as Daníel's voice fades to a glum whisper. 'No matter what I thought, everybody seemed, well, to like the song, and the group performance, so I just had to go with it,' he mumbles, addressing himself to a biro. I can't catch some of his words, and this isn't the time to shove the recorder right under that beard or snap at him to speak up. Dan sniffs and surveys the ceiling. 'But, you know, I guess that when you are a participant in a competition, you should always be prepared for the chance of winning.' It's extraordinary – a perfect inversion of the heart-punching anticipation with which all my other nul-pointers had contemplated the possibility of final victory.

Daníel's prize for winning the nationals was – in a neat twist on the poisioned-chalice theme – a cactus. 'I took it with me to the gig in Lausanne for good luck,' he says, that bitter grin softening into something more playful. 'Don't win! Don't win! Don't win!' His gleeful chants fill the dark eaves with more happy noise than they know what to do with: the echoes bounce around us for some time. 'It worked perfectly,' he smiles, when they've stopped. Again I'm bewildered by this upside-down conversation.

With the agony of success now behind us, Daníel eases back in his leather chair and prepares to savour defeat. 'When they heard I was going to Lausanne, my family and friends, and the band, they all just thought it was really funny,' he says, legs stretched out, hands behind his head. 'And actually it was. The whole trip to Switzerland was fantastic, so much fun. The people I was with, we laughed our heads off.'

What with backing singers and technicians there were ten in the Icelandic gang, and Daníel reminisces fondly on their rapport, with particular reference to the Gruyere-based tomfoolery depicted in that introductory filmette. I ask how their famously sensible hosts reacted to this flippancy and its associated shortfall in respect, and Daníel shrugs slightly and says, 'We were just amusing ourselves. We weren't rude to anyone.' Was there a what-the-hell thing going on, given the diminished expectations derived from the unshakeable mediocrity of previous Icelandic performances? 'We never talked about things like that. We never talked about the competition, we were just having fun.'

The fun wound down, though, as the contest proper approached. Daníel was never comfortable with his meet-and-greet commitments – 'I'm shy, I don't like shaking hands, all the smiling stuff' – and with Iceland still a Eurovision parvenu, and its teenage representative a fish out of indie waters, there was little mingling with fellow contestants. 'We were told to mix, but I just felt silly. It was like some kind of gala, pfffff, I don't know.' He thoughtfully twists a small tuft of beard. 'Although some Maltese guy did send me a postcard afterwards.' Not sure how that happened: Malta weren't even competing.

Dan freely admits that a lot of what occurred in the day or so before the final 'didn't get put in a safe compartment in my memory'. 'I remember Céline Dion, of course, and the guy from Modern Talking who I think wrote the Austrian song – it was really something to see him, in his big blond hair and his huge suntan.' Daníel nobly sustains his interest, and a sardonic smile, as I detail the notable career achievements of Dieter Bohlen, who that year made Eurovision history by writing two entries (German and Austrian), and whose contributions as performer, producer and composer have put his name on 290 million record covers. 'Well, I haven't forgotten his leather trousers,' is the considered response.

Ah: trousers. I tactfully suggest that Daníel's own legwear that night, those pleated, billowing mainsails, might establish him as pot to Dieter's kettle. A fair-cop nod. 'Well, yes, but they weren't my choice.' Not for him a Teigen-esque sartorial showdown with the authorities. 'Someone told me to wear these trousers, so I did. I just accepted it as another part of my role, another part of the task I had to finish.' So there's Dan, out on a stage he doesn't want to be on, wearing strides he doesn't want to wear, about to sing a song he doesn't want to sing. The grim fatalism is coming back.

'Yup, I was nervous,' he murmurs, narrowing those slightly sunken eyes. 'If you listen back to the performance, I was quite shaky on the first line.' I have, I say, and yes – you were, a little. He's not offended. 'So it was not a good start. I went off on the wrong foot, if you want. But I think I finished it, the rest of the song, quite well. So I don't know if my singing affected it, that we got zero points . . .' Not at all, I say, wondering how I can explain that the reason they did wasn't the song, or his voice, but the expression on his face. An expression that I now see wasn't a sneer, or a throwaway smirk, but the pained, whey-faced grimace of a timid young man doing something against his will. To look at, but not only to look at, he was a pale but stout-hearted conscript heading out alone across no man's land. Try to tell a three-minute joke the next time you're in the throes of chronic indigestion and you'll know how Daníel felt. Do it with a starched tarpaulin tied round each leg and you'll know how he looked, too.

Other than commending the professionalism that coaxed a solid vocal performance from Eurovision's most reluctant competitor, I don't know what else to say about his time onstage. Except that bit at the end, when . . . 'Oh, I know what you're going to say.' With a self-mocking, self-conscious and rather girlish giggle, Daníel grabs a handful of black velour from his tracksuit's chest and presses it to his puckered lips.

'I don't know why I did that kissing thing,' he says, 'it's so *silly.* Guess I must still have been nervous.' Has he always worn a crucifix? A look of bemused merriment. 'You look at your DVD again. It's a pagan symbol – the hammer of Thor.'

Daníel was third last on the stage, but doesn't recall any of the acts that went before other than his immediate predecessor. 'That Greek woman – she was pretty good.' And after? 'Well, I'm sure you know that the guys who won were last out,' he says, sticking his tongue very hard into a bearded cheek and raising a sardonic eyebrow. '*Rock Me,* baby. A *lovely* song, oh yes.' His cheek tents out further. 'I was really glad to end up last when I learnt that this song got the first place. Then it all seemed quite logical to me.' We share a rather fatuous chortle.

Daníel's green-room memories aren't so much patchy as threadbare. He doesn't remember any ratcheting sense of gloom as the juries came and went without saying 'Islande', nor whether there was any sympathetic camaraderie from fellow competitors after the voting finished. He's watched the 1989 contest since on video, 'once, about ten years ago', but even that failed to defibrillate his flat-lined powers of recall. He just shrugs helplessly as I try to get him going, and in the end I find I'm going through the usual nul-points debrief on autopilot. All the succour and balm I'm accustomed to dispensing at this point splurges uselessly out over a wound that has never existed. His song wasn't the worst at all, I drone, and single men never get any sympathy votes, and as for the Dick van Danes making the podium, well – those 1989 juries weren't just out of touch, but half blind and stone deaf. And then I'm chuntering on through stage two of my spiel, saying how it's better to get zero than three, before winding up with the usual *schadenfreude* finale, contrasting Riva's post-Eurovision career implosion with his quarter-million album sales. Throughout it all Daníel smiles gently, as if he's doing the humouring.

'One hundred points, ten points, three . . . it was all irrelevant to my state of mind,' he announces, expansively. 'Some of the other Icelanders with me . . . well, there were different takes on it. One of them . . .' He checks himself again, as the diplomatic vigilance required to ensure an easy life in the small world that is the Reykjavik music scene kicks in: it's difficult not to recall at this point that Valgeir Guðjónsson, the song's composer, was in Lausanne as Daníel's pianist. 'Maybe I shouldn't go into that. It was obvious that one of them didn't like it, that we didn't get any points, but the rest of us really didn't talk about it. OK, that was that, finished.'

Still, it was Saturday night, and as a teenage Icelander Daníel knew what he had to do. 'We got drunk and sang and told stories, the usual Icelandic-having-fun stuff,' he says, with a laugh. 'It wasn't quite a celebration, but our posse went out into Lausanne and had a great time.' An achievement in itself, I suggest, and Daníel coaxes out a polite smile.

So the next day you all flew home, and – 'I don't remember,' he interrupts, and I think: *You don't remember?* You've just performed for a live TV audience almost 2,000 times huger than your national population, and it's gone as wrong as it could go, and *you don't remember* whether the next day you flew home to face the funereal music or, I dunno, stayed behind to explore the 500 different hardware models on display at the Swiss Federal Institute of Technology's Computer Museum? 'I was quite unconscious of everything, as I said, I was young and I wasn't paying too much attention to the details of what was going on, or my surroundings.'

Feeling impotent and slightly exasperated, I say that, well, anyway, at some point you came home, and there would surely have been a fairly major reaction, from the media and on the streets of Reykjavik, and how was all that? He gently touches his head with one hand and shrugs helplessly: sorry, it's all gone. The virulent collective amnesia that wiped the 1989 result from the nation's memories has clearly not spared their 1989 entrant. A couple of weeks later Birna helpfully recalls the Icelandic Monday-morning front pages: Dan and the gang grinning rather manically and holding both hands aloft, each with a linked thumb and forefinger. It's zero, but we're a-OK.

Time to move on. I ask Dan whether he got anything positive out of the experience, and sensing that the Eurovision end is nigh, he instantly brightens. 'All I really regret now is the first line of my performance,' he says. 'But it was a fantastic experience, singing in front of 500 million. I value that, it's quite a gift to someone who's starting his career.' Somewhere in the unseen sky the clouds part, and an oblique shaft of dust-particled sunlight bursts through the small window behind me.

'No one in Iceland gave me a hard time about the gig in Lausanne, or if they did I didn't notice. There was no blame, no pointed fingers. I didn't have to ask for forgiveness. And the zero-factor . . . well, it meant I could start over and learn new things.'

A heaven-sent teacher's strike allowed Dan to pass his exams without taking them, and for a while he considered studying sociology at university. His girlfriend discovered she was pregnant – I later calculate that the baby was conceived just prior to Daníel's Lausanne trip – and though they hadn't planned a family, when the daughter who remains their only child was born in December 'we just embraced the situation'. Ný Dönsk's debut album was completed and released just before Christmas and swiftly went gold, thereby shelving that planned future in social science. 'You could say 1989 was a big year,' he concludes, drily, 'and that this gig in Lausanne wasn't at all the biggest thing.'

In the five years afterwards Daníel recorded many further gold-selling albums with Ný Dönsk – 'maybe five, maybe seven', he says, with that now-traditional mastery of detail. His songwriting contribution swelled with each album, until he was responsible for 'at least half': 'I was writing about society, anger, death, myself, friendship,' he says, and I shed an inner tear for the reptilian pet-shop breakout described in his first lyrical foray.

Stricken by artistic ennui – 'I just got tired of making music the same way, over and over' – Daníel left Ný Dönsk in 1994; the band continued in his absence, and he's joined them for a couple of reunion gigs. Newly fascinated with the musical possibilities presented by technology, Dan bought a computer and taught himself the arcane art of sampling and sequencing. In Iceland's fertile creative community it didn't take long to find a group of likeminded collaborators, and in 1997 GusGus, a sometimes seven-piece, sometimes ten-piece group whose name in print generally appears after the words 'seminal electronica collective', released their debut, 'Polydistortion'.

The album's instant success meant tours of Europe and the US: eight years have passed since 'that gig in Lausanne', and here he is living the rock dream. But Daníel is not a man for whooping self-congratulation. He might have been GusGus's chief vocalist, and its most prolific songwriter, but even as 'Polydistortion' nosed up the US and UK indie charts – and spawned three Icelandic number-one singles – he remained studiously underwhelmed. 'I like being on-stage in front of a crowd, but all the stuff around it . . .' He sighs. 'Touring I never liked, that whole rootless feeling.' How great, though, I suggest, to have gone from nul points to that level of jaded stardom: oh no, not *another* coast-to-coast tour of the States. The pause that follows allows Daníel to crack a thin smile. 'Yeah, I guess as a Viking I should have loved all that stuff, going off around the world, conquering new territory.'

His arch, slightly robotic tone suggests he's encountered this sort of trite cobblers in many a GusGus profile. Yet how extraordinary that this should be so, that in eight short years Iceland should have progressed from a mysterious, jury-alienating cultural enigma to the land of a thousand music-page clichés. Daníel's own post-Eurovision reinvention was impressively radical, but it surely couldn't have happened without his homeland's abrupt and bewildering emergence as a major exporter of offbeat international hits. It's a telling indicator of the speed and extent of this metamorphosis that not one of the many foreign journalists who interviewed GusGus was ever aware of their lead singer's Eurovision past. For an achingly hip electro-dance outfit, that was a brontosaurus-sized skeleton to keep wedged in the closet. Yet no one even tried the door.

For some time, as that dusty shaft of sun moves slowly across the dark planks, we debate how Iceland's unlikely musical revolution came to pass. Most conversational roads lead us to the Sugarcubes, the influential but bonkers punkish mavericks whose late-eighties line-up famously incorporated Björk. 'They definitely encouraged people like me,' says Dan, 'but only because there's something in the Icelandic character that makes us more confident in our own abilities, prepared to try different things, artistically.' The seamless flow of his words, and their earnest clarity, suggests this is something he's pondered at length. 'When you live on an island, in a harsh weather environment where you can almost hibernate for six months of the year, in total darkness, you have to keep yourself busy with something creative or you just wither away,' he says, which as the veteran of many Icelandic Christmases I'm not about to dispute: my preferred seasonal creative outlet involves Photoshopping mythical beasts into those round-the-tree family line-ups. 'Plus to make a living here you have to be multi-talented, prepared to take on many different jobs, to be adaptive. And everyone in Iceland wants to be their own boss.'

GusGus appears to have been the unstable essence of this national ethos. 'We did bits of everything: some experimental tracks, some chart-topping stuff . . . We'd work in groups of three or four, then try to pool our ideas. It was kind of a humanised factory.' Hardly a sustainable creative process, you'd think, particularly with the own-boss gene thrown in the mix; after a slightly less successful second album, Dan once again succumbed to the five-year-itch that drove him away from Ný Dönsk. And so, albeit with significantly less brazen chutzpah than I'm accustomed to, our conversation reaches the stage when a nul-pointer hands me a copy of their Latest Solo Offering.

The usual response is to thank them and politely stick the CD in my bag, but I'm frankly curious to hear what Daníel has been doing up here, alone in the beamed and vaulted gloom, eight hours a day for two years. 'Sit here, between the speakers,' he says, inching my wheeled chair towards his with an outstretched foot until it's optimally placed for full stereo reception.

There's more than a little of *The Shining* about this attic: as he clicks play and rotates the volume, I wonder if I'm about to hear, loudly and incessantly, that all work and no play makes Dan a dull boy. And though I don't, 'I Swallowed a Star' proves a consistently eerie work, with mournful strings underscored by Dan's breathy, sinister musings on overwhelming darkness and other forms of void. Sometimes he's a mid-pubescent Tom

Waits; at others, and he's going to hate me for saying this, he's Björk played at 12 rpm. It's difficult to square this funereal paranoia with the soft-voiced, slight young chap nodding gently along beside me, even if he is wearing nothing but black and sitting up here alone in a castle attic. Even the moss-and-stingray stuff sounds inestimably more haunting than I remember, like incidental music for a slow panning shot of the Somme's dawn aftermath. I think: You've been up here too long, mate.

After three tracks Dan abruptly leans forward and, wincing slightly, hits eject. I wonder if I've allowed my harrowed inner shudderings to manifest themselves, particularly when he roots through a pile of hand-labelled CDs and sticks one in, saying, 'Here's a song I've been working on more recently – more kind of . . . *up*.' It's called *OK*, and – merciful Saint Jahn – it's a veritable finger-clicker after the unsettling dirges, music that's life affirming rather than life ending. As its pulsing beat fades, the room already seems brighter: if Daníel was in a dark place, he's come out of it.

'Well,' he says, rising from his chair, and walking slowly across to the window behind me. Dan looks out, scanning the squat, glowering apartment blocks that he's evocatively described as 'tenement fortifications', then peering down his nose at the distant moat. 'See here,' he says, beckoning me with a soft chuckle. I press my face to the ancient, mottled pane: staggering back from the trees behind the moat with a vast bundle of fir branches clutched to her chest is Kristin-Maria. 'Bit early for a fire, isn't it?'

'Ah, no,' says Dan. 'That's for Gabriela, my wife. She needs them for her work.' As we stand there by the window he talks me with quiet pride through Gabriela's burgeoning artistic successes: the ongoing studio endeavours relate to her pavilion at the forthcoming Venice Biennale, the contemporary art world's most prestigious exhibition. Daníel cheerfully announces that in the post-GusGus era she's the big breadwinner, and that he now spends a lot of his attic hours editing the video works that are a major part of her artistic output. 'I've got a few on my

Mac here if you'd like to see,' he says, and we clomp back to his desk over the bare boards.

I spend the next ten minutes wishing I was more aesthetically aware, more critically articulate, and much, much less childish. The first video, one Gabriela recently directed for her close friend Björk, opens with the dependably unconventional songstress emerging from a hayrick, almost unrecognisable beneath a Sumo-sized cladding of sandbags. As she squats down to spawn a lard-smeared dancer, I sneak a nervous sideways glance at Daníel: his otherwise inscrutable features show the barest hint of amusement, which is good enough for me. 'That must have been fun to do,' I say, to excuse the preceding giggle.

'A lot of mess,' he says, with a half smile.

The second, featuring Dan in a cameo as a medieval vagrant, is dominated by a hessian-skinned, bulbous-headed monster. At its climax, this unsettling, faceless being is laid down in a white room and cut open, bleeding a thick black fluid that Daníel quietly identifies as 'the bile of melancholy'. A woman – 'that's Gabriela', says Dan, and it's the only time I'll see her – bestrides the leaking entity, dips a sackcloth tail in the grim ooze and energetically spatters her surroundings, hula-hoop style. Her Venice installation was to win much acclaim, which as a Dan-clan well-wisher and the father of three half-Vikings gave me great pleasure. But as a creatively stunted philistine, when I get home I'm quietly reassured to find a Biennale press release that describes Gabriela's work as 'bizarre'. Not a word bandied lightly about at Venice, where a child with Down's Syndrome was once put on display with a placard reading 'Second Solution to Immortality' hung around his neck.

When it's over I issue a complicated, upwardly inflected hum, which in the absence of an appropriate artistic vocabulary is intended to express my approval. Daníel nods forgivingly, and we troop out of the attic. A moment later Kristin-Maria is snapping our farewell pictures in the early-evening sun, Dan and I leaning against the Saab, looking over the moat bridge, beaming foolishly into the lens from close range, all with that perpetually remarkable edifice towering up behind us.

He graciously offers me a lift to the station; getting into the Saab I spot a pair of filthy football boots in the rear footwell. Daníel confirms that they're his, which I find more surprising than I probably should: anyone familiar with European club football will be aware that this is just another field of human endeavour in which his homeland has achieved a success wildly disproportionate to its population. And then we're scrunching up the gravel, over the moat, and I look over my shoulder to exchange waves with Kristin-Maria and pay final homage to the Chateau Rivierin and its resident bohemians. A collision of the antique and the avant-garde, a beacon of shrieking incongruity in the definitively dull suburbs of a city that is Google's top match for 'most boring European capital'.

As we coast up the darkening boulevards I ask Dan where he'll go when the chateau's new owners turn up in two months. 'Back to Iceland, I guess,' he murmurs, non-committally. Dan and Gaby's daughter, now fifteen, is about to go to college in Reykjavik, and they'd like to be there with her. 'But it's hard to say,' he murmurs, bumping over a tramline. 'I never really know what I'm going to do next until I do it.'

He pulls up alongside the station taxi rank; I turn to face him, we shake hands over the gearstick and I thank him for an extraordinary day. Another nul-pointer I was very glad to have met, another happy stride away from the fading miseries of Kalvikland. Walking up to the quiet, rather gloomy concourse, I turn round for a final wave and a last glimpse of Daníel's gentle, beard-shrouded smile. The nul-pointer who never was, or never should have been; a laconic, understated anti-star, almost dismissive of his undoubted talents. And I'm not just saying that because he voted for my mother-in-law when she ran for his homeland's presidency.

4 May 1991
Cinecittà Studio 15, Rome
Thomas Forstner
Austria
Venedig im Regen

Born just a few months after Daníel Haraldsson, Thomas Forstner was working in an antique shop when he entered an Austrian national talent show entitled 'Newcomer of 1988'. An angel-voiced, angel-faced Vienna Boys' chorister, young Tom had been winning such contests since the age of three; perhaps at eighteen he may have worried that his career had nosed over its Aled Jonesian peak. His triumph as Newcomer of 1988, secured with a ballad pertinently entitled *Still Hoping*, proved it hadn't.

Part of the prize was a studio session with permatanned hitmeister Dieter Bohlen, who in a couple of months knocked out *Nur ein Lied* (*Only a Song*) for his latest protégé, and produced the resultant single. 'Meeting up with Dieter Bohlen is a fantasy come true for Thomas,' was the rather overwrought judgement of whoever wrote the 1989 Eurovision final programme notes. Austria's state broadcaster ORF was no less excited, failing to heed the Wilfried lesson by selecting *Nur ein Lied* as its Eurovision entry without recourse to a national qualifier.

Daníel didn't want to go to Lausanne, but for Thomas it was the stuff of dreams. You can see it in his eyes in the short film that preceded his performance, cheerily tilting a glass of Switzerland's apparently famous wine at a bucolic fraulein. Mainly, though, you can see it in his hair. If Dan's chemotherapy crop was an act of alienated Eurovision rebellion, then what of Tom's stupendous mane, a bouffant, Farrah-Fawcetted flick-fest that was the contest's follicular essence? And few Eurovision historians discuss the 1989 final without reference to Thomas 'The Hair' Forstner's outfit, a satin-lapelled lilac bolero jacket with matching voluminous trousers. With a fringe and a heart-shaped beauty spot, he could have been Adam Ant's valet.

Part Richard Clayderman, part Jason Donovan, fine-featured Tom was the full Eurovision package; what with that and a powerful Bohlen ballad to belt out, he couldn't fail. And didn't. 'Bravo, Thomas, bravo, Thomas Forstner!' cheered the ORF commentator as their man took his bow – I've been listening to him since 1981, and that was the first time he'd raised his voice. After two rounds of voting, *Nur ein Lied* was actually in the lead, and despite fading came home a solid fifth: the best Austrian result since 1976 (as indeed it remains), a track record that helps explain the state-funeral tone now familiar to me from many hours exposure to the ORF booth's output. Coming the year after the Wilfried debacle, this was heady stuff for Austria, not so much Eurovision's bridesmaid as its confetti-eating tramp.

Nur ein Lied was already a hit when Thomas came home, charting in Switzerland and Germany and staying top of the Austrian pops for ten weeks. He was, quite suddenly, a huge star, that big-haired choirboy look irresistible to pre-teen Austro-screamers and their mothers alike. Forstnermania gripped the country, and held it tight throughout the summer of 1989. There were TV shows, public appearances and sell-out stadium gigs, all conducted in an atmosphere characterised by this contemporary joke: What's 25m long, screams and has no pubic hair? The first row at a Thomas Forstner concert.

As a teen idol, Thomas might have been fleetingly concerned by the approach of his twentieth birthday. Particularly after the Dieter-composed Christmas follow-up to *Nur ein Lied*, released just two days before Tom bid farewell to his teenage years, peaked at number thirteen. Dieter gave him one more roll of the chart dice, but after the English-language *Miles Away* failed to break the top ten in June 1990, Tom was left to fend for himself. Herr Bohlen didn't earn $250 million by throwing good studio money after bad. In the following year, Tom released two further singles, each on different minor labels and co-written with composers of proven obscurity. Neither charted. Before he'd even had the chance to release an album, his career seemed over. Until March 1991, when ORF came knocking at Tom's once fan-thronged front door.

They did so in the aftermath of an unusually eventful but typically inglorious 1990 Eurovision campaign. The female half of pre-qualification favourites Duett fainted live on-stage, but swept to victory after being allowed a second chance; the day after, a viewer phoned up ORF to comment that the winning song, *Das Beste*, seemed uncannily familiar to a song of the same name, sung by a band called Duett at the 1988 German qualifiers.

None of Eurovision's many statutes is more fiercely enforced than the 'original song' rule, which has been behind half a dozen disqualifications since 1968, when Norway's Odd Borre (that's right) accepted that with Cliff Richard due to follow him on to the Albert Hall stage, it might be an idea to come up with something that sounded a little less precisely like *Summer Holiday*. (Rather more in the spirit of that revolutionary year, Juan Manuel Serrat refused to make the trip to Britain when the Spanish authorities forbade him from singing their entry in Catalan, though being entitled *La La La* it's unlikely that even Franco himself would have noticed. Juan's last-minute replacement went on to pip *Congratulations* by a single point, and Cliff ended the evening – I just can't say this often enough – locked in the gents.)

With *Das Beste* disqualified, Austria was obliged to make do with the 1990 qualifier's runner-up, *Das Second Beste*, or rather *Keine Mauern Mehr*, which limped home from Zagreb with a double-figure finish. Despite Tom's Icarus-like career path, the national broadcaster figured he was worth another go. As his presence in these pages will suggest, he wasn't.

Surely aware that at the 1991 final in Rome he'd be singing in the last-chance saloon, Tom pulled out all the stops. His was a three-pronged assault on Eurovision glory: a host-flattering musical tribute (*Venedig im Regen*, or *Venice in the Rain*), a sparkly outfit, and his hugest-ever hair. Each in their way contributed to his looming notoriety as the only Eurovision veteran to score nul points. Though puffed and preened into an astounding beehived mullet, his hair is already thinning: poor Tom's not yet twenty-one, but there's a lot of scalp on show beneath the blowdried teasing. Plus he's finally succumbed to a Teutonic tonsorial urge and had it cut behind his ears, leaving a bouffant beaver's tail to flap against the collar spangles. Nein, nein, nein!

His outfit is that of a Torvill and Dean-era figure skater, a spandex jumpsuit teamed with a close-fitting, heavily sequinned waistcoat, and – oh, my – matching cuffs. 'A game lad in an après-ski jumpsuit,' was Terry Wogan's verdict. As Thomas turns to face the camera he looks a little startled, and so do we: Eurovision fashion is typically a solid four years behind the times, but he's just been shaken awake after nodding off with his finger on the sartorial rewind.

The song Tom now performs is consistent with his appearance. A study in cheesy bombast, *Venedig im Regen* is infused with the inane sentimentality of the Germanic musical phenomenon schlager, if not its uptempo, boompsadaisy beat. It's a song written for a big voice, an Engelbert or a Tom Jones, and no matter how he strains, our ex-choirboy finds himself more than a few watts short. Thomas seems to know he's already blown it: his expression throughout the performance never progresses beyond desperate, counterfeit enthusiasm. It hardly matters that he has one trick up his spandex sleeve that his compatriot Wilfried so conspicuously lacked – he can hold a tune.

The show is compered by Italy's two previous Eurovision winners – conqueror of Zagreb Toto Cutugno, and Gigliola Cinquetti, whose 1964 victory as the sixteen-year-old singer of *I'm Not Old Enough to Love You* was oddly unaccompanied by controversy (wisely retitled *This is My Prayer*, the song was later covered by a fifty-year-old Vera Lynn). If I may once more succumb to the lure of crass generalisation, the voting is a predictable shambles. 'Helsinki, no Belgium,' splutters Toto, 'no . . . Istanbul!' Throughout the procedure he and Gigliola squint sceptically at the TV monitor beside their podium, as if it's transmitting an impenetrable Magic Eye image. When their knockabout incompetence is compounded with technical problems, stalwart EBU scrutineer Franck Naef briefly takes charge. All in all, it isn't a good year to yield the most controversial result in Eurovision history.

After the last vote comes in, Sweden and France are tied with 146 points. 'Mr Naef! Mr Naef!' yelps Toto, and Franck wearily pronounces his verdict: though the two countries have the same total, and the same haul of maximum points, in accordance with the subclause introduced two years previously Sweden win by virtue of scoring five second places to France's two. (His underwhelmed tone is explained by a muttered aside picked up by a nearby microphone and transmitted to the gleeful millions: 'And that means the little witch has won!')

Jeers and whistles ring out around the Cinecittà auditorium; even the implacable ORF guy uses the word 'chaos'. But by then, of course, he's in a sulk. And by then, Thomas Forstner appears to have left the building: in the extensive green-room coverage that heralds the contest's denouement, there's not a sign of that inflated mane and its owner's equally conspicuous outfit. For the second time in three years, it's goodnight Vienna. And goodnight Tom. That's it: without fuss or flouncing or a histrionic press conference, he simply checks out of public life.

To say the Thomas trail has gone cold is to pay inadequate tribute to the months I spend hacking away at the internet permafrost. There are vague suggestions that he emerged in 1995 to release a schlager single with the incongruously dramatic title *If the Sky Burns*, but finding no concrete evidence of any additions to the Forstner back catalogue more recent than *Venedig im Regen*, I email his last known record company. The reply is instant: 'I'm very sorry, but I can't help you to get in contact with Thomas Forstner. He was formerly a Warner Music Austria Artist but I think he has no record deal at the moment.' A tip from an ESC forum suggests a connection with a children's charity, and I find a site connected with a 2002 'Light in the Darkness' benefit gig whose line-up incorporates his name. I email every associated address, but cast no light on Tom's post-Eurovision darkness. 'I know about Mr Thomas Forstner,' writes the sole respondent, 'but I have absolutely no personal contact to him. I'm working in a bank office!'

The only promising lead is a chap called Gunter, a fellow Vienna Boys' Choir alumnus who has left a post on a choral message board seeking information on his old chum Thomas's whereabouts. I email him and a day later receive a reply whose introduction elicits a gasp of joyful disbelief: '*Lieber Tim, hier ist die Adresse von Thomas Forstner.*' Expectation management is efficiently delivered by the sentence that follows the suburban Viennese domicile thereafter supplied. 'I wrote to him there,' reads my Google translation of Gunter's farewell, 'but he did not announce himself. Harm!!!'

A couple of weeks later, with two letters to the stated address both apparently given the Gunter-predicted brush-off, I cast my Tom net wider. Very occasionally, with a whoop of glee I'll unearth a single Google-translated piece of jigsaw: in an Austrian list headed '100 important facts', there between 'In Germany, was a sausage with three ends developed' and 'Inspector Columbo a Peugeot Cabrio 403 drives' is 'Thomas Forstner as a computer programmer works now'. Following a rather brilliant piece of detection that ought to have bagged me a Peugeot Cabrio of my own, I find Tom on a (presumably obsolete) list of famous Austrians' birthdays, Google in the date and his name and discover, on an arcane genealogy site, that Thomas Forstner was married – can't pretend that's not rather a turn-up – to a woman called Vanessa in Klagenfurt on 14 October 1991.

Less useful, but perhaps more fascinating, are the snippets mined through a long trawl of chat rooms and message boards. Erotikforum.at proves alarmingly productive: I learn of Tom's hair transplant, and that the young Herr Forstner managed only six days of military service before succumbing to the 'heavy fear and panic reactions' that earnt him a reprieve. Elsewhere, former fans reminisce upon Forstner gigs and autograph chases, and grieve the moment 'when he sang *Venice in the Rain* in such a wrong way'. For every fond musing, though, there is a snide riposte. 'Our Eurovision performance is like our football team, a national joke! Wilfried, Thomas Forstner, Faeroe Isles 1 Austria 0 – do we like pain?' (Very possibly – just ask Graz-born literary deviant Leopold von Sacher-Masoch. Harm!!!)

Tom crops up in an interview with Austria's 2002 entrant, who rather unnecessarily calls him 'a Song Contest prostitute who failed because he tried too much', and brackets my man with Tony Wegas, who took up Austria's Eurovision reins after Thomas, and in 1997 spent two years in jail for mugging old women to support his class-A drug habit.

So be it. Resigning myself to a process of elimination, I set about contacting all the Thomas Forstners I can find. Some I filter out before that stage: the local footballer, the geology student and the tree surgeon, all of whose photographic depictions could only be consistent with my Tom had that hair transplant proved merely the tip of a huge and horrible iceberg. Though there's no photo of him, I also elect to dismiss the historian Thomas Forstner, whose name crops up with unsettling consistency in reviews of works such as *Grüss Gott und Heil Hitler!* and *Der Vatikan und die Entstehung des modernen Antisemitismus*.

But there are plenty of others. Every day yields another Forstner harvest; I find one email address and Google unearths three more. 'Sorry for contacting you out of the blue (and in English),' begins my standard email. 'This is probably going to sound really stupid, but are you the Thomas Forstner who sang for Austria in the 1989 and 1991 Eurovision Grand Prix?' Slowly the replies come in: 'I am not this Thomas Forstner'; 'Sorry! Good luck from a different Thomas Forstner'. It isn't thomas-forstner@gmx.de and it isn't thomas.forstner@students.jku.at. Most dishearteningly, it isn't the only likely Thomas Forstner I'd found, a jazz trumpeter: 'I don't think it's the same guy,' replies the bandleader. 'In the years you are talking about he is playing trumpet with the Bamberg symphony orchestra.'

I'm noticing that none of my respondents ever comments wearily that this is by no means the first time they have been taken for *that* Thomas Forstner. Initially I assume this is down to the unenduring celebrity garnered by my Tom in his one-year micro-career, but the sheer numbers of namesakes I'm encountering suggests that it's also a question of statistics. When a Google search for plain 'Forstner' yields 445,000 hits, I give up.

Not quite knowing what else to do, I put out a calling-all-Austrians alert to friends and family. So it is that a week later I'm on the phone to Wolfgang, a banker who lives next door to my friends Adam and Eleanor, and has done for long enough to attain an astonishing command of English. 'Yes, I remember Thomas Forstner – that blond, short guy. Catered for the mature ladies, an ideal-son-in-law type.' There are probably ways of bringing Tom's teenybopper audience to Wolfgang's attention that don't involve telling the pubic-hair joke, but regrettably I can't think of any. 'Well,' says Wolfgang, rather quietly, when I'm done, 'you seem to have followed his career more closely than I have.'

Wolfgang wasn't born when Austria won its first and only Eurovision title in 1966, but he namechecks Udo Jurgens with some pride and a familiarity that suggests the contest has a more durable popularity in his homeland than some compatriots had led me to believe. 'Until the nineties, you know, the state had a broadcasting monopoly, and Eurovision was kind of pushed down our throats,' he says. 'It was all over the TV and radio for many days. Do you remember this guy Wilfried?' That's funny, I say – I was just about to ask you that. 'Well, he was quite a big deal – one of the first actual Austrians to make our charts. Before it was just Queen and ABBA, and many German bands. But his Eurosong . . .' A small sigh. 'Nobody forced him to do Eurovision, but I guess it was near the end of his Austro-pop career, so maybe he needed to try anything. Everyone in Austria knew it was a crap song, but we still kind of liked it.' Wolfgang laughs, a little helplessly. 'It was a schizophrenic situation. We knew he would fail, but maybe we didn't care so much any more. We were accustomed to a bad result, to nobody understanding our taste in music. Then came Thomas Forstner, and then we had commercial radio and TV and Eurovision was not so big. Now it's like a schlager contest, I guess, and for most people, young people, it's just not cool.'

I'm not sure why it takes me so long to remember that a near-Austrian has been an important if indirect part of my life for the previous six months. Andreas replies to my email with the promptitude I've come to expect from his neighbouring nation's non-Wilfriedian community. His opening paragraph echoes Wolfgang's account of Eurovision's declining popularity in Austria, whilst emphasising its apparently contradictory power to supply the *coup de grâce* to an ailing musical career: 'The ESC isn't really big in the German-speaking countries . . . I mean, some people watch it to make fun of it but no one really takes it seriously. So if you score badly at an ESC – or even 0! – it's definitely the end for you!' But Eurovision didn't kill Tom's career, I think: it was already dead. Five singles, four labels, two years: 1989–1991, RIP.

The second half of Andreas's brief email is more arrestingly pertinent. 'As for Thomas Forstner, I remember that he was interviewed in the Austrian national final of 2002 (or was it 2003?) – so maybe someone at ORF could help you.' I dispatch an email to the contact he then supplies, and within fifteen minutes this lands in my inbox: '*Hallo! Hier Thomas Forstner's Emailadresse.*'

And there it is. Just like that. I was never convinced that the address his old choirmate had given me was anything other than a childhood residence, but here I have a Tom contact known to be recently active. It's a eureka moment, but determined to avoid a repeat of the Wilfrieds, I take a deep, calming breath and settle down to compose a missive as diplomatic as is reasonably possible in the circumstances. It isn't easy – I can beat about the bush as much as I like, but in the end my thrashing is going to dislodge the word 'zero', and that alone might well be enough to consign me to Tom's desktop dustbin.

And perhaps it is, because he never replies. As the days evolve into weeks, elation congeals into dismay, then hardens into resignation. What are the options? I could go over to Austria and roam the Viennese suburbs, or the comely lakesides and market places apparent in Klagenfurt's civic homepage. I imagine myself leaning out of witch-hat towers and tram windows, beckoning my elusive quarry with coaxing calls: 'Tommy, oh Tommy, pray where are you now?' Or I could just move on.

Because perhaps it wasn't desperation I saw in those big round eyes on the Rome stage; perhaps it was no more than brittle fatigue. Thomas had won his first talent show at the age of three, and ever since had been persuaded to do things – by his parents, by Dieter Bohlen, by ORF – that he may not have wanted to do. Perhaps he'd just had enough, and now wished only to be left alone with Vanessa, programming computers and having plugs of thigh-hair embedded in his scalp.

30 April 1994
The Point, Dublin
Ovidijus Vyšniauskas
Lithuania
Lopišine Mylimai

The modern Eurovision Song Contest was born in Dublin on the last day of April 1994. The year before had witnessed the debuts of most bits of the now bloodily fragmented Eurovision stalwart Yugoslavia; a couple of months after the 1993 final, the EBU merged with its ex-Soviet counterpart the OIRT. The Irish, in consequence, found themselves addressing invites to nations whose presence would until very recently have been utterly unthinkable.

There are some funny new flags on Andreas's DVD menu screen: when the scoreboard flashed up Russia, Romania, Estonia, Lithuania, Hungary, Poland and Slovakia, the watching West grasped for the first time the heady, mind-spinning realities of post-Cold War Europe. It was a moment that once again showcased Eurovision's unlikely but enduring willingness to shoulder a burden of historical enormity: in an only slightly silly way, seeing Estonia's Silvi Vrait take to the Dublin stage as Switzerland's Duilio walked off it seemed more tangibly significant than the signing of any treaty.

Back in their mid-seventies pomp, the Soviets had boldly launched a socialist alternative to the EBU's western spectacular, broadcast by the OIRT from Sopot in Poland. It should have been a winner: with its tarty make-up, fixed grins and general air of ersatz, wobbly set ineptitude, there had always been something slightly Warsaw Pact about Eurovision. No recordings survive, but the Intervision Song Contest's artistic standards are apparent in its 1980 winner: Finland's Marion Rung, a representative of the OIRT's sole non-Soviet member nation, and a woman who had twice sung at Eurovision with her homeland's traditional lack of success. Her victory was Intervision's swansong. The year after, the signs went up outside Sopot's Opera Lesna: 'Song contest cancelled due to imposition of martial law'.

Yet the Marlboro-smoking, Wrigley-chewing, Benny-strength Eurovision proper had for years been finding its way through a chink in the iron curtain. With a big aerial, a little technical adventurousness and a devotion to Lulu more powerful than the fear of summary arrest and voltage-based re-education, plucky Estonians could pick up the contest's Finnish transmission. 'For us, it wasn't only a chance to hear Western pop,' said a now elderly Estonian whose underground Eurovision club met in the capital Tallinn for thirty-five of those special Saturdays. 'We could also see how people interacted and dressed.' Poor chap. At this very moment he's probably battling through the Baltic wind in a pair of madly flapping Dan-pants.

Estonia's long-standing exposure to Eurovision may have contributed to its 2001 victory, the first former Soviet state to win the contest. Though it conspicuously wasn't much help at the nation's 1994 debut, when Silvi Vrait returned from Dublin with two points, her countrymen cheered only by the fate of their rival Balts from Lithuania, who managed two less.

The Irish had won in 1992 and '93, and perhaps having exhausted every national cliché, opened the show with a parade of huge-headed papier-mâché mannequins tottering alongside the Liffey (only through internet assistance would I be able to identify these as caricatures of leading Irish musicians, including Bono and Sinead O'Connor). It's all rather foolish, but recalling the desperately isolated 'visit Ireland – PLEASE' tone of the 1981 final, I can only conclude that all their Eurovision success has helped bolster Ireland's self-confidence as an international player, just as Norway's failures encouraged the bitter battening down of cultural and political hatches.

Sweden is first out, with a duo who set the tone for the contest, and indeed most subsequent finals. All creative energy has been expended on entertaining our eyes, leaving little for our ears to latch on to: one's wearing a bowler hat and a ball-gown, and the other's a native American with a pink cactus flower sprouting from his bald head, but the tune leaking fitfully from their garishly painted gobs is a worn retread of *Love Lift Us Up Where We Belong*. Finland in corsets and nighties, Russia in a bride-of-Frankenstein cowled red robe, a Dutchwoman with an owl, all trotting out faux-emotional mid-Atlantic inanities. Musically, it's the dullest Eurovision yet by a vast margin, a dismally determined assault on the lowest common denominator: in terms of artistic influences, Bananarama and Bon Jovi are about as extreme as it gets. Even those dependably entertaining loose cannons Malta and Cyprus have dutifully nailed their artillery to the decks with a pair of ponderous plod-alongs; when a Greek bounds on with a bouzouki and yells '*Diri, diri, diri, diri!*' I almost whimper in grateful relief.

The debutant nations, perhaps playing it safe in a bid for mid-table respectability, are a particular disappointment. The Bosnians get a hero's welcome, but their offering proves only that they've given up guns and put their faith in the ballad-box. Nothing, though, plumbs the dreary depths with quite as long a line as the duo who, in an act of almost perverse defiance, turn up in outfits as bland as their song. Being Irish, they win.

Two blokes in jeans and rolled-up shirtsleeves droning turgidly on about their very distant youth weren't expected to do well, and the suspicion has been widely voiced that Paul Harrington and Charlie McGettigan had been put out there to take a dive. Hosting Eurovision was a ruinously dear undertaking, and with three victories in the last seven years there wasn't much promotional value to extract that the Irish hadn't already extracted. Plodding and drab, *Rock 'n' Roll Kids* was Ireland's *Springtime for Hitler* – a copper-bottomed, sure-fire loser. And one that somehow ended up romping home with the highest winning total to date.

Perhaps with all those disturbing outfits and the unsettling presence of so many ex-Commies, a dose of unchallenging nostalgia offered the stuffy west-of-the-Wall Eurovision juries a port in the storm. 'It was '62, I was sixteen and so were you,' drawled Paul and Charlie, and the leathery electorate looked up from their voting charts and thought: Ah yes, happy days. Why didn't we bomb the Cubans again? *Rock 'n' Roll Kids'* runaway victory sounded the death knell for the jury system. When the contest next returned to Dublin – to the twitching disbelief of the state broadcaster, just three years later – telephone voting had made kingmakers of the European public.

Coming on-stage after an Estonian who might have spent the afternoon ladelling dumplings into dinner trays, Lithuania's Eurovision debutant is a chunky, stubbled, rather careworn skinhead of middle years, wearing PVC trousers and a suit jacket whose straining chest is severally accessorised with diagonal zips. It's difficult to believe that Ovidijus Vyšniauskas, who in the brief film beforehand sat laughing behind a piano in a shapeless fisherman's jumper, has chosen this outfit for himself. Moonfaced and tight-lipped, he looks like Phil Mitchell forced on to a catwalk at the point of a broken bottle.

Lopišine Mylimai begins with a wailing snatch of guitar that gives an utterly misleading impression of what is to come, except in suggesting it won't be at all good. Seeing Ovidijus in his jumper I'd been looking forward to some offbeat Slavic folk, but no: it's another rent-a-ballad, sullied by a dismaying axe solo, and delivered with as much emotional sincerity as that conspicuously ill-chosen wardrobe will allow, which is very, very little. 'The smell of your lips is like rain,' runs a translation of its first line that I discover later.

Ovidijus – the 'j', if the Eurovision comperes are to be trusted, is pronounced as a 'y' – looks unhappy with his lot. His unlubricated Meatloaf rasp cracks in places it shouldn't, the microphone is visibly shaking in his hand, and towards the end that large face crumples slightly. We're watching a man die alone, far from home and dear ones. Yet though a decade later that online poll will declare *Lopišine Mylimai* the second-worst Eurosong of all time, it isn't easy to see how it ended up 226 points shy of *Rock 'n' Roll Kids*. In a year of soul-siphoning musical tedium, the song also known as *Sweethearts' Lullaby* was just another drop of cheese in the fondue, no better than a dozen or more rivals but certainly no worse. I can only assume it's his age, his sex and those trousers.

The interval act introduces what will become known as the most lucrative Eurovision-launched phenomenon since ABBA. All I can really bring myself to say about it is this: it's Riverdance. And then, for the first time ever, we're introduced to the jury spokespeople by live video link-up, rather than just encountering their propaganda-broadcast voices. The Swedish telematron, the Hungarian granddad with a tumbler of whisky on his desk: with faces put to votes, Paul and Charlie's rapidly inevitable victory seems immediately less mysterious. For ten rounds of voting Ovidijus has nine performers keeping him company, before his own countrywoman, with a strident bark of 'Norway – wan pant!' begins the process that will leave him conspicuously alone. There are no backstage shots to see how he's taking it, but with 226 points for the winner, that 0 has never looked smaller. After the most humiliating debut in Eurovision history, it would be five years before Lithuania dared return.

Hampered by a certain inconsistency in official renditions of his name and its incorporated accents, tracking down Ovidijus isn't quite as simple as I'd hoped after my 'world of Forstner' hunt through the cyber haystack. After a long afternoon I home in on two Ovidijus Vyšniauskases – a weightlifter, and a performer listed as having appeared on Lithuanian Television's 2002 New Year's Eve bash. More realistically than Thomas Forstner the mulleted teen idol and Thomas Forstner the Nazi academic, they could be one and the same. But the LTV listing mentions a live-music venue in the capital Vilnius that appears to have welcomed their Ovidijus in the past, and within four hours of emailing the Kolonada Club I have his mobile number in my inbox.

What follows is the most unnerving telephonic interchange of my adult life. After a dozen rings, my ear is assaulted by a damply breathless, basso profundo growl, as if I've caught Chewbacca at a bad moment. It's two in the afternoon, Lithuanian time. 'Um . . . is that Ovidijus?' I've had a stab at the j/y substitution, but the following silence encourages me to volunteer a few alternatives, the unhappiest of which comes out as 'Overjuice'. Silence, then another snorting snuffle, like a bear waking up after winter.

'Do you . . . speak English?'

The response is contradictory but final. 'No!' snarls the bear, and the line goes dead. That night I dream I'm sleeping in a field in the back seat of an abandoned car. A rustle wakes me, and there, looming over the headrests, is the massive, grinning head of Ovidijus Vyšniauskas.

Already aware that I will never dial that number again, in the morning I track down – via the ever-helpful Kolonada – a man called Valdas who claims to be Ovidijus's agent. He's almost too helpful: after a quickfire exchange of explanatory emails, his office posts me a message reading thus, 'Mr Tim Moore. The Ovidijus will meet with you at 9th of March in town of Kaunas as we told. As you know the Ovidijus don't speak good English.'

It's less than a week away. Can he really have agreed to a meeting so swiftly? Without any confidence that I'll ever use them, I book flights and a hotel room in Kaunas, coughing up an immoderate sum for a chauffeur transfer from Vilnius airport. With two days to go I phone Valdas's office. 'I give you number for him,' says the woman who answers, 'but as you know the Valdas don't speak good English.' Ah: it's the voice of the emails. I was rather hoping Valdas would be in Kaunas to translate for us, I explain. 'OK.' Not quite, I say: as you know, he don't speak good English. 'No problem.' Well, it kind of is. Will anyone else be there to translate? A shuffle of papers; a pause. Then: 'As you know, I don't speak good English.'

A little under forty-eight hours later, I'm stepping off the Gatwick Express with dark thoughts inveigling themselves into my ponderings. Is all this business down to innocent incompetence, or is something more sinister at work here? And why were they so apparently eager to invite me over? Either Valdas is planning a huge global relaunch for The Ovidijus, or the whole thing is a trap to chasten – no, punish – the mockers.

All in all, it isn't a great time to settle down with the reams of Lithuania facts I've printed off from the internet. Waiting at the Baltic Air gate, I swiftly learn that the waxy-skinned beanpoles around me have been killing each other with an efficiency bested only by Colombians and South Africans, and killing themselves more readily than the nationals of any other country on earth. (The prominent appearance of Austria in this latter chart siphons away any lingering temptation to doorstep Wilfried and Thomas.)

And though few nations in the region can look back over a glowing history of ethnic tolerance, it's still a shock to discover the appalling tradition of pro-active anti-Semitism in the city I'm about to visit. In June 1941, with the advancing Nazis not yet on the horizon, the townsfolk of Kaunas embarked on a frenzied massacre that claimed the lives of 3,500 local Jews. When the SS arrived, even they were taken aback; the supply of enthusiastic volunteers was to make the city a centre for the imprisonment and extermination of Jews from as far away as Marseilles.

What kind of holidaymaker does this troubled land attract? The virtualtourist.com message board has the answer: 'You guessed it right – I am going to Vilnius come May, because I have never eaten bear, and I would certainly like to try it before EU rules prohibit selling their meat. I know that in the Baltics in general, the hunt for bears is legal. So, rather then eating smoked pig ears, could someone recommend me a restaurant where bear is served (and where, if needed, I could make a reservation by mail)?'

By the time we troop aboard, I'm already up to speed with the potato-centric diet and basketball prowess that are cause and consequence of my lofty, pallid fellow passengers' twin distinguishing characteristics. I'm also conversant with Lithuania's pride in its lingering pagan tradition (it was the last European kingdom to accept Christianity, and pagan temples were well attended until 1790), and aware, thanks to the captain's welcoming announcement, that the temperature at Vilnius airport is currently -18°C. In seven Icelandic Christmases and an ascent of Kilimanjaro, I've never faced anything quite that extreme. And night is only just falling: the mercury's hardly about to head north.

Baltic Air's inflight reading material provides further indigestible food for thought. I learn that my arrival overlaps with the nation's pagan-flavoured Lenten fast, which culminates in the 'burning of an effigy of our archetypal scapegoat figure, The More'. Naturally I have to read that last word twice, and even when satisfied there's just the one 'o' I can't stop gagging slightly on a mistimed swig of the Lithuanian lager I've just bought off the stewardess for a quid. I'm the archetypal scapegoat, and he's the pagan pyromaniac. It would certainly explain the indecent haste with which I've been summoned here, and the nonchalance regarding the whole interview business. Of course no English will be spoken. The Ovidijus will address The Moore in the international language of petrol and matches.

We cruise over Germany in silence: a quiet lot, these suicidal murderers. Glancing across at the cropped head pressed glumly to the window opposite me, I despair of the enigmatic melancholy that is my lazy, default perception of East Europeans. For almost a year now, the three Baltic states have been EU members – all this lot are bona fide economic migrants, electricians and bricklayers heading back home for a quick visit; I look at my sallow neighbour and see paint spattered on his hands. Yet still I know so little about them. All of them: I've been able to find out almost nothing about The Ovidijus – must remember to cut that out when I meet him – beyond a translation of his entry's lyrics and the official 1994 Eurovision biography. For the third time since morning, as we touch down at Vilnius I get it out and go through it again:

'Ovidijus Vyšniauskas was born in 1957 in the small Lithuanian town of Marijampole, and after singing in the church choir went on to to study cello and percussion as well as choral conducting. Later he took up synthesiser and sang and played in several groups before devoting himself full time to composing and singing. He writes and arranges his own songs, working closely with his friend Gintaras Zdebskis on the lyrics. Ovidijus is a frequent television and radio guest and has represented Lithuania at many international festivals including the Cavan Song Contest, and has been a frequent prizewinner.'

There's only one guy toting a name card in the arrivals lounge, a chilly, strip-lit lobby that feels more like a provincial railway terminus. 'Mrs Noone', it reads, which means I'm compelled to withdraw 200 Litas from a cashpoint, visit the gents (oh dear: lit by ultra-violet to deter those intravenous drug users who haven't yet learnt to pre-mark their veins in biro) and pace loudly about stamping life back into my underclad feet, all whilst waiting to satisfy myself of her non-existence. When the last Baltic Air passenger shuffles out into the fearsome cold, I approach the – yes – waxy young beanpole holding the sign aloft. 'I think that might be me,' I say.

'OK,' he replies, looking down with a cheerful shrug.

Our people carrier rumbles out through broad, moribund streets, the haggard Soviet apartments interspersed with garishly lit chrome-and-glass car showrooms. 'So,' I say, once my chauffeur has told me in the most proficient English I've yet heard from Lithuanian lips that it's going to be a ninety-minute drive, 'what do you think about Ovidijus Vyšniauskas?'

I'm heartened that he understands me first time, but not by his reply. 'A singer, yes?' And that's all he has to say. Zero points? News to him. He didn't even know Ovidijus had been to Eurovision. When I prompt him with the year, he emits a small titter. 'But in this time I was nine year old.' Once again I'm forced to accept the epic scale I'm working on: for some people, 1994 was a very long time ago. The break-up of the former Soviet empire seems recent history to me, but this chap – a proper grown-up who's already shown me his public-service-vehicle licence – would barely have a sentient memory of life in pre-independence Lithuania.

Not that this has precluded him from nurturing an impressive hatred for his nation's former overlords. Russia, he wastes little time in telling me, used Lithuania as a dumping ground for its hoodlums and undesirables, whose burgeoning influence in the post-Soviet years lies behind that extraordinary murder rate (and I'm guessing the ultra-violet lights in the airport loos). 'Many Russians are still here, but they are not speaking Lithuanian, so for them is not any good career. Ha! My father must learn Russian in school, but why he must speak it with them today? If they are not mafia, they are cleaning the road, with . . . like this [he mimes the act of sweeping with an enthusiasm that makes me glad we haven't seen an oncoming vehicle for fifteen minutes] in one hand, and in other hand vodka bottle.'

He mellows into silence as we leave the streetlights of Vilnius behind, spearing through conifer forests and vast agrarian swathes of flat blackness. But as Kaunas takes illuminated shape ahead of us, he begins to extol its virtues with ratcheting emotion. 'This city is true capital of my country,' he says, his quavering intensity enhanced by the many tram-tracks the road now traverses. 'No Russians here!'

The hotel he drops me outside is spanking new, well appointed and almost painstakingly pruned of character. Its restaurant is already closed; having clad myself to the point of limb inarticulation with almost the entire contents of my suitcase, I head outside.

It's heart-attack cold: my innards clench in shock as a frigid gust blasts straight through five layers of textile protection. Browned heaps of snowplough dung are piled up around lampposts and tree trunks, with the bits they've missed hardened to a lethal, translucent crust. Every drainpipe disgorges a fat gout of glassy lava, caught in suspended animation. And where is everyone? It's only just 11 p.m., yet the streets are eerily unpeopled, Chernobyl-empty. They can't *all* be at home assembling me-shaped wicker men.

On the corner of what looks like the main drag I find a twenty-four-hour café, and heave open the door to join the two policemen who are my sole fellow customers. They're wearing hats and coats, and so is the waitress who takes my order. Wisps of exhaled condensation accompany her response, which being a serviceable 'Just one moment please' encourages me to ask for her thoughts on the big O and his big O. 'Ovidijus lives here in Kaunas,' she says, encouragingly, 'but his music . . . I don't know. It's maybe for older people?' Soon after she appears with a beer that's too cold to drink and a kebab too enormous to complete. The bill is 10 litas; offloading the other 190 is clearly going to take some work. As I glean next morning from the *Lithuanian Business Review* in my bathroom, I'm now in Europe's cheapest country.

I've emailed the details of my hotel to Valdas, and received a reply promising that The Ovidijus will meet me in the bar there at 10 a.m., translator in tow. I yawn and count cars as I wait: 100 Audis and Hondas go by before the first Lada. In material terms at least, they've come such a long way in such a short time. The Scandinavian plumbing in my hotel room would have been beyond the reach of even the most energetically corrupt party official, and prone in its splendid incorporated bath I'd read *Lithuanian Business Review*'s account of a chap who'd spent the 1980s making TV aerials out of the runners from old kids' sledges, and was now the millionaire boss of the country's largest firm of satellite installers. My breakfast buffet could have been laid out in Zurich without adverse comment, yet between the wars Lithuanians found themselves obliged to casserole crows.

At ten past, a tiny young russet-haired woman with something of the Lulu about her pushes open the bar's door with a

Christ-it's-bitter-out-there shuddering huff, and before it closes a grizzled, rheumy hulk of a man in a vast overcoat squeezes in behind. A decade on he's almost hairless, but there's no doubt who that is, hanging his coat up and acknowledging my silly little wave with an uncertain nod. And the good news is he doesn't appear to be armed, or gripped by any emotion more threatening than gruff bemusement.

We shake hands and order hot drinks – coffees for me and the translator, a disarming green tea for the man I've now internally abbreviated as the Ov – all in an atmosphere of slightly circumspect affability. They don't really seem to know what they're doing here, and when the translator introduces herself as 'woman of music office', I know just how they feel.

In inevitable consequence, the ensuing two hours cast only random patches of half light around the pitch-black, dripping-echo cavern that is the Ov's fact warehouse. I learn of a small-town childhood spent mastering judo (eek!) and half an orchestra – guitar, saxophone, drums, piano, double bass – but nothing of the years between school and his mid twenties, when Ovidijus plumped for a full-time career in music. His influences, I'm told, range from late-fifties' Italian infant soprano Robertino, to 'romance melody rock – Deep Purple, by example'; his nearest West European equivalent would be 'maybe Joe Cocker'. But I never really get a handle on the man and his music, his level of fame and success, the highs to balance that obvious low.

Many of the questions I fire at Lulu ricochet waywardly on their way to the Ov, with the returning answers shooting back miles over my head. I ask how Ovidijus's feelings for his country are expressed in his music, and after a prolonged and intensive conference between the pair, receive the confident response: 'Twelve.'

Sometimes, though, there's a suspicion of deliberate deflection. I'm particularly eager to hear of his experiences as a Soviet-era rocker – he was thirty-four when the tanks went back to Moscow – but even my most assiduously simplistic probings into this arena are ignored, rebuffed or clumsily brushed aside. Did the Soviets make it difficult to play music or write songs? 'For him, in personally? No. Everything was fine.' What about for others? Were lyrics censored? 'Oh, some say this, but the Ovidijus he don't know.' How did he feel when he saw the demonstration at the Vilnius TV station in 1991, when the Russians killed eighteen people? 'Uh-ha.' When the anti-Soviet movements really got going across the Baltic states, all the music and ballads involved earnt them the nickname 'The Singing Revolution' – was Ovidijus involved in this? 'Robert Plant.'

I can only assume that old habits die hard: excluding a twenty-two-year hiatus between the wars, Lithuania was under Russian control from 1795 to 1991. Shoot your mouth off to a nosy Englishman in the Iron Curtain days, and the next time you belted out *Smoke on the Water*, Alexander Solzhenitsyn would start banging on the cell wall.

He's been glowering throughout my investigations into life under the Soviet yoke, but when we get towards Eurovision, the Ov settles into a pudgy, rueful smile, like a retired heavyweight asked to recall a mildly humiliating knockout. I'm belatedly struck by his resemblance to Kojo; though four years younger, he looks at least a decade older.

The Ov, naturally, never watched Eurovision as a child. 'He knew that it happened,' says Lulu, 'but the first year it is in TV here, 1994, is same year he is singing. So he never see it before he is in it.' Like Daníel, but for very different reasons, the Ov had no understanding of the contest's magnitude, and seemingly as little respect for its heritage. When I ask whether being selected to represent his country in the Eurovision was the most exciting moment of his musical career, he listens to the translation unfold with a wondering frown. 'The Ovidijus say he has been competing in many international contests, and he has been winning ten of these, so just one more did not seem so important.' Where were these? All I've been able to discover about the Cavan Song Contest, as namechecked in his Eurovision CV, is that Cavan is in Ireland. 'All countries, as in Bulgaria, Romania.' I try to look impressed, but apparently fail.

After further mutterings, the interpreter diplomatically announces that of course Eurovision was very interesting to the Ovidijus, and that he was very responsible to sing for Lithuania in the final.

Lopišine Mylimai, he says, came to him in a single afternoon. Lithuania's admission to the final had been only belatedly confirmed; one afternoon he was rung up out of the blue by 'director of concert halls and everything' and asked to deliver a song, pronto. With no time to organise a national qualifier, selection was a shambles that year. As indeed it remains: in the spring of 2004, a bored Lithuanian prankster who had submitted a cassette recording of Michael Jackson's *Ben* was astounded to receive an invitation to perform in the televised semi-finals.

Then living in Vilnius, the Ov sat down in his apartment, banged out a tune 'in three minutes', then rang up his long-term collaborator Gintaras Zdebskis and put in an order for lyrics. I've developed quite a fascination for the words he quickly supplied. 'You are untouched by me, my dream is pouring you its wine in that night of ours': there's a poetic mystery not often encountered in Euroland, along with a noble chasteness we haven't experienced since Gigliola Cinquetti's spirited defence of her virginity back in 1964. Is it about any woman in particular?

The Ov curls a fleshy lip and – it's only been a matter of time – pulls out a packet of fags. Speaking now like a solicitor defending a sulky criminal client, the translator says, 'He tell me it is not about any person – only about love.' Muttering darkly to himself, he pops a thin, dark cigarette in his mouth and sparks it up. I look down at the stretched red packet: the Ovidijus has just set light to The More. Something has upset him, and I'm not sure I want to know what.

'What he says,' I'm told in this new bureaucratic monotone, 'is for Lithuania was first time in Eurovision, and nobody understands here what is the game, how to do what kind of music, what kind of text. Everything was done quick, too quick to make it better.' Another whispered confab. 'Also in Dublin, the music arrangement is bad. The Ovidijus was not satisfied about the pianoforte player, who was a woman.' She purses her lips; to pursue the legal analogy, she's now informing the desk sergeant of her client's improbable and morally odious alibi. 'He says as we all know women do not understand what real love is, so he would prefer men to play his pianoforte.'

With that off his meaty chest, the Ov cheers up: a moment later he's even happily confessing that the guitar solo – which in the certainty of its addition by some bored Irish session musician I've just described as 'terrible' – was his idea. There's much laughter as we discuss his wardrobe, the work of a Lithuanian designer chosen without consultation 'by some family friends'. 'All so fast, no time to change nothing.' Dublin incorporated 'many good times and warm people', though he found certain of his rivals a little remote: 'some are looking at him like he was from, you know, not Lithuania, that he was Russian'.

He got on famously, though, with 'the two brothers from England, who win the competition'. When I put him right on both these scores, he shrugs amiably. 'But one thing bad: they tell the Ovidijus their song is fourteen years old. This is unlegal, yes?' If true, certainly, I say. 'It is true.' Not knowing how to respond, I find myself relating Paul and Charlie's post-Eurovision careers, how *Rock 'n' Roll Kids* didn't even make number one in Ireland, and how after a solitary album the pair split, with Paul now presenting *Music from the Movies* every Monday night on Dublin's Lite FM, and Charlie playing pubs. It's at this points that the Ov, eyes alight, blurts his English-language debut. 'Pubs!'

Even having watched the video that Gintaras recorded for him, he recalls few of his fellow Dublin competitors and their musical endeavours. He's been particularly diligent in erasing the deux-points Estonian effort from his memory, explaining that Lithuania has a good friendship with Latvia, but with Estonia there is no connection in music, in language, in politic. Once more I'm reminded that in Eurovision, you make those lazy assumptions of cross-border fraternity at your peril. The

Ov's strongest memory of the evening is one of general awe at the contest's pomp and scale, 'the scenes, the light, so much cameras and professional work'. It hadn't been like this at Bucharest or County Cavan.

If that was a surprise, the result as it unfolded backstage was not. 'Maybe he hoped it will not end for him like that, but it wasn't nothing like a shock.' He thinks he may have attended an after-show party of some sort, and certainly remembers shunning the commiserations offered by some fellow competitors. 'The Ovidijus don't like it for people to come and say sorry, he like it to survive everything alone. And when he come back to Lithuania, it's good, because then he learns who are not his true friends.' The Ov juts out a stubbled jaw; its jowly appendages tauten in manly defiance. Before me is the hardbitten son of a crow eater.

The national nul-points hangover was more pained and enduring than I'd been led to believe. 'The magazines are writing a lot about it, more than if he would have won. He said that in other contests, when he won the first stage or the second stage, in the magazines, there was only a small little place, but when he lost all the magazines were full with it. So it seems we are living where good news is not good news.' And indeed where 400 million viewers across Europe are not four dozen Bulgarians in a field.

'Some are saying that he is the wrong singer for Eurovision, some are saying that he is just a too bad singer. For about maybe one year, he feels he has done something wrong for Lithuania.' The Ov narrows his pouchy eyes and chuckles in quiet disbelief: the combined effect suggests he can't believe he allowed himself to care that badly. 'But then he understand that when someone says something bad about you, you can learn from this.'

At thirty-seven, the Ov might have felt like a senior canine signing up for a course of new tricks, but if so he passed with distinction. 'He was sad, the Gintaras was sad, but they print a new song together and it become very popular, a big hit.' By way of emphasis, the translator delivers an enthusiastic round of applause. 'And it is a song about Lithuania, about our beautiful islands in Baltic.' The first half of the title she then gives is concealed by a strident parp of sax in the bar's grisly muzak, and the second by a rumble of heavy Ov laughter. 'He tells that if they enter this song at Eurovision,' chortles the translator a moment later, 'it would be worse than last!'

Whatever it's called, that song remains a highlight of the gigs that along with 'expensive parties' are now his professional mainstay – it's two years since the release of the Ov's last album, another of the greatest-hits anthologies that my nul-pointers have been releasing in such profusion. He reckons to do one live show a month around Lithuania, and every summer goes off on tours that have to date encompassed Russia, the US and almost everywhere in Europe. 'His wife is not so happy about it!' trills the translator to their amusement if not mine: how could I have neglected to establish his family circumstances? Such is my flustered embarrassment that when he fills me in – the eldest of his three children is a twenty-seven-year-old daughter based in Norway, the youngest a boy of four who lives with him here in Kaunas – I merely nod and smile without considering the implications of those chasms in age and geography.

Other than that he fishes, keeps terrapins and goes hunting. It isn't a challenge to picture him engaged in two of these three hobbies, but at the risk of diluting Lithuania's appeal to the world's most appalling tourist, he's never even seen a bear, let alone killed and eaten one. He clearly loves life here in Kaunas, saying what a shame I couldn't see the city in summer, and urging me to check out the river Neman, a durable inspiration to him. 'Is most proud, most Lithuanian city,' says the translator, 'not like Vilnius, with so much Polish and Russian.' I'm beginning to get a feeling that the Ov understands a lot more than he's making out; certainly, this latter pronouncement causes his eyes to bulge in paranoid alarm.

With slight reluctance he reveals he was amongst the 91 per cent of Lithuanians who voted to join the EU – the highest proportion of any new member state – and feels it was a big step for the nation, if only because 'before not anybody can find our country in a map'. But when I ask whether he feels European, whether he'd feel closer to a Swede than a Russian, he considers his answer for some time. 'The Ovidijus say if someone ask what is your nationality, he would say "musician".' It's the old keep-your-nose-clean KGB-era self-preservation again.

He talks tactfully of the importance of preserving 'all small cultures in this EU big culture', and to that end extols Eurovision as 'a popular way to have all countries together to show their cultures'. Even if they're all now singing in English: 'OK, but it's good they do this, better than for him when no one can understand what he is singing.' So how did he feel about Lithuania's five-year post-Ov Eurovision absence? 'This is just a law of the competition.' I'm not going to tell them it isn't: relegation of the bottom-placed nation was indeed a new addition to the Eurovision rulebook, but this merely precluded Lithuania from entering the 1995 contest. Instead I ask if he'd consider entering again, and after a dutiful address on allowing opportunities for younger musicians, and perhaps mentoring them through the process of artistic competition, he lets out a lip-wobbling, tongueless raspberry and turns those hang-dog eyes on me in weary exasperation. A long mutter in the translator's ear. 'You know,' she smiles, 'he says if you are not coming here to talk, he will have forgotten about Eurovision. When it's good fishing, he doesn't even watch it.' A lugubrious laugh from him, a shriller one from her; no choice but to join in with a simpering, apologetic chortle.

We wind things up with a round-up of his future ambitions – he still dreams of making a record with 'someone world-known, a legend' – and a swift retrospective of his career to date. 'The Ovidijus says he is proud and lucky to have job that brings joy to people,' says the translator, looking a little misty-eyed. Yet what strikes me isn't the good fortune of all the veteran performers I've encountered, but their astounding resilience, still getting up on-stage and baring their souls, strutting their stuff, after twenty, thirty, forty years.

The Ov rustles out his greatest-hits CD and insists on penning his own touching dedication: 'From Ovidijus to Tim, thank you for nice meeting.' No, thank *you*, I say, and after checking my watch ask if I can buy them lunch, somewhere more . . . Lithuanian.

'Ah, I must return to office,' says the translator, wrinkling her nose in apology, 'and the Ovidijus has practice for concert on Friday. But you have many people to meet also?' Um . . . I do? 'Aiste, Skamp, Aivaras – other Lithuania performer, from other Eurovision year?'

The sensation that now annexes my internal organs is interestingly akin to that experienced stepping out of the hotel doors the night before. Somewhere along the rusty, fractured chain of communication that put me in a room with the big man before me, my mission was never properly explained to him. That I'm not talking to every Eurovision performer, nor even to every Eurovision loser, but solely to the tits-up, egg-faced, losers' losers, the non-starters amongst the also-rans. 'That's right,' I mumble, avoiding both sets of eyes as we shake hands.

Sagging under the twin burdens of shame and remorse, I shamble round-shouldered up to my room. I'd hoped to spend the bulk of my remaining twenty-eight hours in Lithuania with the Ov, being taken round the deep-frozen delights of Kaunas, bonding over a fireside bottle of plum brandy. Now what? I stick his CD in the player under my telly, and listen as the music overpowers the grating swish of nail-studded winter tyres coming up from the street. I desperately want this to be the most rewarding auditory experience of my life, but of course it isn't. Even to ears that have heard it all in the last few months it's a challenge, an ill-fated marriage of east and west. Mildly anthemic MOR and snatches of slap-funk bass are interspersed with mournful solos on a sort of synthesised balalaika; one track suggests *Those Were the Days* covered by Doctor Hook. Ten minutes later, fuelled by penitence and boredom, I'm down in the street buying a massive pair of checked old-lady mittens from a tiny woman manning an outside stall.

And after another five I've finally managed to stretch, yank and bully them over the two pairs of gloves I'm already wearing.

Contact with his fellow citizens and the monstrous environment they are currently enduring makes it easier to understand the Ov's hard-bitten, I-will-survive take on his Eurovision disaster. The lowest temperature recorded in Kaunas in 2004 was -19.1°C, and the highest 33.2°C; unflappability in the face of extremes is the entry-level requirement for residence. Stamping woodenly up Freedom Avenue with my features in frigid spasm, I'm surrounded by people who've grown up knowing how to take the rough with the rougher: a gloveless old woman reading the paper on a bench; a quartet of kneeling, headscarved beggars; a drunk in a wheelchair, slurring abuse at a local TV crew.

The collision between east and west apparent in the Ov's music is no less messy on the streets of his home town. A basement supermarket in which I seek climatic refuge is teeming with schizoid shoppers, excitedly appraising the camembert and balsamic vinegar before filling their trolleys with great drums of sauerkraut and tins labelled only with the smiling head of the animal puréed within. There's a preserved-meat aisle to die for – cannonball salamis, a whole cured ham for a fiver – and a fresh-produce aisle to die at: box after malodorous box containing the ineptly mummified victims of a terrible avalanche on the lonely eastern face of the EU's fruit and vegetable mountain.

Back outside, the quest for generated warmth propels me at ever greater speed along ice-glazed pavements thinly populated with housewives dressed and made-up to appeal to ABBA-era kerbcrawlers. A street vendor sits hunched before a towering rack of CDs and cassettes, which I scan for as long as I can bear to stand still: some Sting, a lot of Bon Jovi, entire columns of poodle-haired Lithuanians. But no Ov.

The buildings recede, pavement gives way to frost-scrunched grass, and there I am in the spindle-treed emptiness that looks out over the confluence of the two mighty rivers that converge at Kaunas. To my left the Neman, the Ov's muse, and to my right the majestic Neris, lazily relentless conveyor of plucky swans and knobbled hunks of ice. At 5 p.m. it seems like 5 a.m., the park around me an unpeopled wintry wasteland, the low, pink sunlight more dawn than dusk. I turn to inspect the factory chimneys smudging the rosy sky with carcinogens, and when I turn back the rivers have turned to gold, their ice hunks to black, the combined effect suggesting the clinker-topped outflows from some alchemist's foundry. It isn't hard to understand what draws the Ov here.

'Well, you know after Eurovision it was real difficult for him.' The young taxi driver ferrying me back to the hotel is responding to my hypothermic mutterings, using English diligently acquired during engagements as a Bristol-based strawberry picker and carpenter. 'His career . . .' Tutting in empathy, he jabs down at his dashboard with outstretched fingers as we pull up. 'But my parents like him still. He does charity TV shows, and I hear a pretty song he is singing with a nice lady.'

Four hours later I'm prostrate in my room, innards aglow with a local aperitif memorably described in the hotel bar's menu as 'bread-smelt alcohol made with old technology'. On a room-service tray beside me lies the plate I've just managed to clear: three cheers for sour cream, guaranteed to enliven even the chewiest crowburger. 'Next up,' drawls the over-excited ESPN announcer, 'big guys throwing beer kegs over a high wall!' With a bloated, intemperate grunt I fumble for the remote, flicking through until I hit something black and white. Snow, newsreel music, a caption: '1960 Winter Olympics, Squaw Valley, California.' I can't imagine who's broadcasting this, or why I spend the next forty-five minutes watching square-jawed skiers acknowledging cheers from the podium. But I'm glad I do.

For an event staged forty-five years ago it's extraordinarily slick, the smooth camera work almost contemporary, the crowds enthusiastic but well drilled. No confusion, no petulance, no sequinned salopettes and certainly no Eddie the Eagles. It's a masterclass in how to organise a major international event. Halfway through the Nordic Combined, I roll over and lethargically retrieve my travelling Eurovision library, creasing open an illustrated anthology at pages relevant to the 1960 Eurovision Song Contest, broadcast live from London's Royal Festival Hall three weeks after Squaw Valley's polished and professional closing ceremony. I admire Nora Brockstedt's fur-trimmed folk outfit, thrill to the presence of Fud Leclerc, beam broadly at the judicial dithering that saw the French belatedly docked two points, and the consequent audience rowdiness that hostess Katie Boyle struggled to quell. And, finally, I raise a bedside toothmug in honour of the winner: Jacqueline Boyer of France, with her musical tale of a fellow who owns two castles, one in Scotland, one in Montenegro, and goes by the name of Tom Pillibi. Before Georg Thoma crosses the line for Nordic Combined gold, I've fallen in love with the Eurovision Song Contest all over again.

3 May 1997
The Point, Dublin
Tor Endresen
Norway
San Francisco

If the 1994 final had set the modern contest's overall tone, by 1997 the last details of today's Eurovision were being coloured in (notable exception: the native-language rule, abolished in 1999). The 1996 victory of Irishwoman Eimear Quinn's *The Voice*, the floaty, folky antithesis of pop, had again besmirched Eurovision's once-proud reputation as a hit-maker of commercial finger-clickers: Australia-born UK entrant Gina G's chart-friendly *Ooh Aah . . . Just a Little Bit* signally failed to impress the juries that year, yet went on to sell a million copies worldwide.

If Eurovision was going to once more reflect public musical opinion, something had to be done. Astoundingly, the EBU did it. Out went the arcane restrictions on backing tracks – in two years' time the orchestra, with its tiered ranks of sombre hornblowers and fiddlers, had gone for good – and in came phone voting. In what was to be a successful trial, the public of five nations – the UK, plus the techno-axis of Sweden and all the German speakers – would take responsibility for points distribution, with the obvious proviso that one's own country was excluded from the process. (Successful at least in technical terms: the results were skewed both by a potent blend of expat loyalties and drunkenness. Britain, home to half as many Cypriots as Cyprus and half as many Irishmen as Ireland, would give both islands seventeen points to share – along with a what-the-bollocks six for Iceland, a third of that nation's total, by simple virtue of penultimate performer Páll Oscar bagging votes from those who had blundered home from the pub to catch Katrina, the night's final entrant.)

The almost desperate pandering to populism expresses itself within the 1997 final's opening seconds. Isn't that Ronan Keating walking out to assume compere responsibilities? Well, yes it is. And in place of the dickie-bowed grandees who have stocked the auditoria of yesteryear, here's a reasonable approximation of a mosh pit, an unruly sea of noise, heads and banners. And flags, amongst them a lot of blue-and-white crosses on a red background, proud standard of a nation in the Euro-form of its life.

In four contests after 1992, Norway had come in no lower than sixth, with *Nocturne*'s victory in 1995 interrupting a record-breaking run of Irish wins. When the Eurovision came to Oslo in 1996, the home nation finished second; by 1997, Norway found itself in the extraordinary position of taking a strong showing for granted.

They're third out, after Cyprus and Turkey have showcased Eurovision's new allegiance to contemporary trends, leading the way with a pair of lively ethno-dance numbers. It's immediately clear that Norway has no intention of following them. As the camera pans away from the drunk-looking audience and back to the stage, the ORF commentator delivers a précis of the lyrical themes about to be explored: 'Woodstock, Jimi Hendrix, make love not war, und flower power,' he intones, without enthusiasm. 'Tor Endresen, Norvegen, *San Francisco*.'

Halfway through the long zooming shot that will eventually fill our screens with his big, happy face, it's plain that Tor, a sprightly man of early middle years, has gone for a look even more retro than his lyrics. The guitar he's energetically strumming is a rockabilly semi-acoustic as old as Eurovision itself; the early days of rock 'n' roll have also donated the Elvis-twitch that has annexed Tor's right leg, and his canary-yellow jacket with its embroidered lapels. The music he then eagerly launches into is consistent in taking its cue from a genre that predates the thirty-year-old events he's singing about by a good decade. It's nice-boy, side-parting rock 'n' roll, jollied along with plenty of snare drum and the Little Richard falsetto 'Woooooh!' that Tor gamely throws in after an off-key adventure in the opening couplet.

He's clearly a seasoned performer is Tor, grinning into the camera, belabouring his guitar with assured showmanship, letting out dextrous, powerful vocal flourishes and even essaying a small kick, a kind of demi-Teigen, which he just about pulls off with dignity intact. Perhaps he's doing all he can to distract us from the inanities escaping his mouth: *San Francisco* quickly proves itself an even lazier parade of period catchphrases than the ORF guy has led me to believe. Slapping the language rule in the face until it begs for mercy, the song incorporates such popular Norwegian expressions as 'man on the moon', 'blowin' in the wind' and 'California dreamin''.

Only as Tor winds up to his big, air-punching 'Woah yeah!' finale do I understand what he's trying to do. Just three years before, on this very stage, Charlie McGettigan and Paul Harrington had served up a crusted dollop of nostalgia and won. If *Rock 'n' Roll Kids* had bagged a Eurovision points record with the torpid, no-tune namechecking of Elvis, Jerry Lee and blue suede shoes, what might Tor achieve by rocking up the beat and really cramming in those period references? The two Norsemen frenziedly flapping the 'VICTORY FOR NORWAY' banner seem to have a pretty good idea. Who can blame them? I know which one I'd rather hear again. As indeed I do, often, between the moment I watch Tor walk off for what will be an uncomfortable backstage vigil, to the moment he opens the door to room 312 at the Hotel Bristol in Oslo.

'Tor Endresen tried lots of times to enter Eurovision,' emailed Andreas as I began the process that would take me back to the land that had last welcomed me with a compulsory round of cell-based nude bouncing. 'Still making music, but has pretty often changed record companies.' While awaiting a response from the most recent of those revealed in the discography I consulted as the 14,312th visitor to his official website, I did a little online probing.

From the modest English section in his own site I learnt of Tor's astounding persistence in the Melodi qualifiers: in the decade that separated his 1987 debut from the triumph of *San Francisco*, he'd entered no fewer than eight times, finishing runner-up on three occasions and third on two. I was made aware of his year of birth (1959), his home town (Bergen) and his recent sell-out Christmas tour, in which Tor had travelled the monstrous length and modest breadth of his homeland while playing forty-one churches in twenty-six days. If that offered a literal suggestion of life after nul-points death, there was more tangible evidence in the form of a quoted result for Norwegian Artist of the Year, 2000. OK, so Tor didn't win, but he beat A-ha into fourth place.

Elsewhere the pickings for Tor's non-Norwegian fans were slim indeed: the sole English-language sighting unrelated to his whereabouts on 3 May 1997 named him as one of the 255 artists, along with Gerry and the Pacemakers (and indeed Helge Schneider and the Firefuckers), to have recorded a cover of *A Whiter Shade of Pale*. I'd been reduced to fumbling through a list of foreign-language versions of *Rockin' Around the Christmas Tree* when an email from BareBra Musikk (calm down: it translates as 'Only Good') pinged into my inbox. In it was Tor's mobile number.

In recent years, Norway has devoted a hefty slice of its oil billions to establishing itself as the nation with more miles of subterranean road and rail per capita than any other. In conjunction with his clearly active touring schedule, this was to cast rather a blight over my initial communications with Tor Endresen. 'Oh, hi – yeah, my record company told me you . . .' was the extent of his contribution to our debut conversation; 'I think we're . . .' and 'Ja?' perhaps definitive later examples. Only once did he manage to squeeze in the word 'tunnel' before our traditional crackle-beep sign off, but by then I had already begun to suspect advantage was being taken. Yes, Norway has the world's longest road tunnel, but unless Tor was passing through it by drunk elk that couldn't explain why five hours later his phone was still dead. In the end I got Birna to call him. And it worked a treat, the filthy old goat.

'Had a real nice talk with your wife,' he said when I phoned him the next morning, his notably more relaxed voice settling into the mildly Yank-tainted English that is the nul-pointer's lingua franca. 'A lovely lady you have there.' The small pause here allowed us both to reflect on my comparative unloveliness, condensed as this was in his next sentence. 'She tells me you're writing about all us poor no-point guys, right?'

My faltering efforts to cast the endeavour in a gentler light were swiftly cut short by a gotcha snigger. 'Ah, it's OK. I'll meet you. Just first I need to get the go-ahead from my agent – he's in Thailand just now.' Thailand?

'It's not Finn Kalvik, is it?' I blurted.

Well, you should have heard him laugh. 'Ha ha ha!' he went. '*Ha ha ha ha ha!*' Then, after another half-dozen or so: 'No! Finn Kalvik is *not my agent*!'

So there I am again, striding guitarlessly through the Oslo airport customs just past dawn, jogging on to the train, catching a distant glimpse of the world's most majestic scenery as we slam through the awakening suburbs, hopping out at the central station to discover – ooooh *Christ* – that it's spring on the calendar, but not in the air.

Tor is in Oslo to film a TV show, and he's staying at the plushly venerable Hotel Bristol. I've got a couple of hours to kill, and opt to suffocate them slowly over a pair of coffees in a slippery Chesterfield armchair near the back of the Bristol's dimly panelled bar. The bill is enough to reduce a Lithuanian to tears, and perhaps prostitution.

While I'm there I call Sissel – not the Koh Samui Sissel, but an old Norwegian friend of mine. As a resident of Bergen and reliable purveyor of lurid gossip, I figure she might have the low-down on Tor (who I will have to remember to call 'Toor'). 'Endresen? He's pretty popular still in Bergen, in all Norway,' she says, in a slightly flat tone that implies a life of disappointing non-controversy. 'But you have met Teigen and Finn Kalvik also, yes?' Her trademark phlegmy cackle erupts into my ear. 'Ah, Teigen! He was playing here last year at a festival. Looks quite old now, but he's still a great performer. We love Teigen!' And Finn? Hearing her delight subside, I instantly wish I hadn't asked. 'Well, I hear him a lot on the radio, like he refuses to be forgotten, fighting on the edge. And there are jokes in radio and TV: you understand, he was the joke.' I understand, I say. 'He took that very bad, he was really insulted.' I'm about to wind things up when that cackle abruptly bursts forth anew. 'Oh, yes! I know a girl who was in bed with Finn Kalvik! He's had a lot of women!' This cheers me up more than perhaps it should, and fifteen minutes later I'm knocking on a third-floor door with a smile on my face.

Two things strike me about the open-shirted, open-faced man who welcomes me in to his surprisingly compact temporary home. One is that he's still wearing his orange-hued TV make-up, and the other is that despite this – and the inevitable Marlboro Light in his hand – he looks significantly younger than forty-six. With his dark semi-quiff and a family-friendly twinkle in his eye, he's the Shakin' Stevens to Jahn's Iggy Pop.

'Do you mind if we stay here?' Not at all, I say, as he clears a space on the bed, hanging his dark-grey stage jacket on the back of the room's only chair and carefully relocating a guitar case to the floor. 'You know, we have this law against smoking in bars, so . . .' With a wry shake of the head Tor stubs out the Marlboro; within a minute he's got another on the go, along with a minibar brandy.

'We're here filming a kind of high-school reunion thing, back to 1960 – we did a lot of Everly Brothers, *Bye Bye Love* and *Wake Up Little Susie*. Yes, it's a busy time for me.' Before I can stop Tor he's off, pulling us as far away from 1997 as he can with a rundown of his recent and forthcoming engagements on-stage and in the studio. The 30,000 tickets sold for that Christmas church tour (in the company of Anita Skorgan, amongst others), the session to over-dub songs for the Norwegian release of *Tarzan 2*, and the rapidly approaching release of his latest album: 'My favourite ballads of the eighties, recorded with the Estonian Symphony Orchestra.' There is no time to take on board the full scale of this project's post-Eurovision majesty. 'And then this summer I'm doing *Chess*, you know, the Björn and Benny musical. I'm the Russian.' It's the most relentless I'm-still-standing sales pitch I've yet been treated to.

He sits in the chair, I sit two feet away on the bed and in this oddly intimate setting we go back to Tor's childhood in sixties Bergen. 'In the east of Norway the radio and all the local bands played Swedish pop, but in Bergen it was all about Radio Luxembourg. Actually I wrote a song about it.' What, Bergen? He smiles, wrinkling his tangerine foundation. 'No, Radio Luxembourg. It was in fact one of my Melodi songs: came second, I think in 1992. So that was a shame, but at the end of that year, when Radio Luxembourg closed down, mine was the last song they played.'

The last song ever played on Radio Luxembourg? I'm impressed to the point of awe. 'That's fantastic!' I say, though listening back to the recording it's more of a squeak. All nul-pointers have a claim to infamy, but I'd been concerned that Tor might be the first not to offset this with a claim to fame. Instead, he's just trumped everyone. It's dubbing the little fat blue one in *Top Cat* into Icelandic, and driving about in a Maserati with ABBA's beardy genius all rolled into one: a Benny sandwich.

'So we had all this rock and roll, and the big ships and all – it felt like Bergen was a twin city with Liverpool. Of course I loved the Beatles. When I was four or five I had a big thing for their version of Chuck Berry's *Rock 'n' Roll Music* – I used to spend a long time in front of the mirror, singing with a brush.' When his teenage peers were into Led Zep and Bad

Company, Tor was learning to love Elvis. 'People laughed at him then, but I always liked the real showmen. And I liked to copy them. I'm a very good impersonator, yes I am.' By way of intended demonstration, Tor raises his brandy miniature with a wink, and launches into wheedling, nasal semi-Cockney. 'Have a swig of that, me old china, that'll blow the back of your shirt up!' He raises his eyebrows promptingly; all I can manage is a soft, uncertain chortle. 'Oh, come on. How about this: What are you *doing*, Miss Jones?' Well, it's a better Leonard Rossiter than I'd have managed.

Happily, Tor's gift for mimicry is expressed more effectively, and more lucratively, in his chosen field of professional endeavour. 'I got an award from Disney, for my Norwegian over-dub of the songs Phil Collins sang in the first *Tarzan* movie. Elvis, of course – I've done him *a lot*. Tom Jones: he's my kind of guy. In concert I do *The Green Green Grass of Home* and *Kiss*. And then the Beatles.' Tor clearly knows how to push my buttons – most of which are labelled 1966 – and astounds me afresh with the aftermath of a Beatles medley he performed in Bergen a few years before. 'Yoko and Sean Lennon were there, and Cynthia. She wrote to me afterwards saying, "That was the greatest post-Beatles Beatles experience ever".' But instead of leaving that sublime revelation hanging in the air, Tor brusquely yanks it down. 'Then one time I worked with Pat Boone, and he asked me to tour with him. I asked him why, and he said, "Son, you do the best Speedy Gonzalez mouse I've ever heard."'

Arriba, arriba, Tor. Let's not run away with ourselves. First band? 'I was seventeen, messing about with guitar in the school gym, when this guy in my class, Are, heard me and asked me to join his band. White Rock, a kind of a dance band. It was fun, but that ended with national service. But you know the nice story, about my new Melodi song?' Remembering my encounter with Jahn, I tell him a little bird (or rather a fifty-six-year-old blond crow) had mentioned it. 'Yes, and it's in a duet with Are. It's been really good to work with him again.'

Once again I'm cheered by the tight-knit happy family that

is the non-Kalvik Norwegian music community. Did White Rock make any records? 'No, my first single wasn't until 1983, with this other dance band called Salex.' (I look it up later: with *Window Cleaner* on the B-side, I wish I'd enquired deeper.) You'd have been twenty-four by then, I say. What paid the bills? 'I was playing a lot in bars around Bergen, doing my Beatles and Elvis stuff. But it was tough – I was already married, and with a kid. And then in 1985 I got one more child – you know, I have *five* now – so I decided to cut down on music.'

To do what? Apparently reluctant to declare any income not earnt through showbusiness, he ignores this enquiry. 'I just cut down, I didn't stop. I was still playing every Wednesday in this bar, and one time a producer came in and asked me to do an audition, and then I found I had my first real record deal.' The producer was a chap called Pal Thowsen, and it was as vocalist for his eponymous band that Tor released his first albums, their content rather grimly described on a Swedish fansite as 'eighties uptempo classic AOR rock'. A departure too drastic for most, you'd suspect, but as a father in his late twenties Tor couldn't afford to be precious. 'If someone asks me to sing, and they're paying,' he tells me later, 'I sing.' You suspect this practised musical chameleon would rather describe himself as an artisan than an artist.

'We did an album in '86 and then one in '88 – it was a bit rock, a bit pop-fusion, maybe like Al Jarreau. And there was a hit single, *Black Rain*, a big radio hit.' Elsewhere I encounter a claim that this was narrowly pipped by A-ha as the title soundtrack for the James Bond outing *The Living Daylights*: a lofty ambition for a single conspicuous by its absence from the *VG* chart archive. Ditto the two albums Tor's mentioned, which may explain his delight when a chap at NRK – another admirer of those Wednesday gigs – rang Tor out of the blue and booked him for a four-part show of musical nostalgia. 'It was called *Lollipop*, and I played this kind of singing waiter, in humoristic form. In those days there was only one TV channel, so this was a big, big break.'

Bigger than he could have imagined: uncomplicated retrospection has always played well in Norway – how else to explain their enduring love for Jahn Teigen? – and Tor played it better than most. 'Yeah, that was my breakthrough as a solo artist. But it worked because we did it properly, with passion. Everything had to be just right – we even got the correct old microphones from the NRK museum.' Those four programmes eventually swelled into sixty, spawning albums (one sold 120,000 copies) and an ongoing national roadshow. Almost twenty years on, the Norwegian public are still sucking hard on Tor's *Lollipop*.

With his foot in the NRK door, the Melodi Grand Prix was the next step. After Tor's first effort limped home ninth in 1987, his appearances became almost traditional. And tantalisingly well received: after finishing fourth in 1988, he was never out of the top three thereafter. His eventual triumph was accompanied by an almost audible sense of national relief. 'You know, in 1997, I was thirty-eight, so it came along at a late time,' says Tor, sinking back into his chair and flicking another Marlboro out of the packet beside him. Late indeed. Six months older than the Ov in his annus horribilis, Tor is the most senior performer to have suffered light entertainment's ultimate indignity.

He sighs a plume of smoke up at the ceiling, and when his eyes drop back down to meet mine they're lightly glazed. 'One of my first musical memories, you know, was *Poupée de Cire, Poupée de Son*.' As he gently hums a brief snatch of Serge Gainsbourg's 1965 winner, I imagine a little six year old jiggling about in front of a black-and-white telly, brush-microphone held to mouth, in a spotless, neatly trinketed Bergen sitting room. Taking the first tentative steps of a journey that will come to such a brutal conclusion thirty-two years later.

For some time he circles around the wreckage, talking at great length and in utterly confusing detail about the Eurosong that had been his intended entry, apparently rejected by NRK for a refrain that they felt owed too great a debt to *Give Peace a Chance*. At any rate, he seems keen to emphasise that *San Francisco* – co-written with Arne Myskall, a friend and collaborator since the Salex days – was very much a second choice. 'We would never have done a retro song,' he says, 'if we knew then what we know now.' Hoping not to appear impertinent, I ask Tor what he does know now. 'With the juries!' he half shouts, sounding both aggrieved and astounded that I don't appear to know what he's talking about. 'This year, '97, to try and turn the Eurosong to a younger audience, all juries had to be under thirty!' His tone leaves no room for dispute, although I know for a fact, albeit a shamefully dull fact, that by unusually long-standing EBU decree, each eight-strong national jury incorporates four members over thirty and four under. By the same token, this doesn't seem a good time to call Tor's attention to the introduction of jury-circumventing televotes that year.

'So we had this old-fashioned song – the only one in the whole show – and then I was told I had to use the orchestra. More bad information: I think I was the only performer who did! The sound was terrible! I had mail, even from Sweden, telling me to protest! And everybody knows it's harder for a guy on his own – the girls get a few votes just for turning up.' A look of embittered helplessness clouds Tor's friendly features; a swig of brandy, a deep drag and it passes. 'I'm not looking for excuses. It's over, history. And you know, they still ask for that song at my concerts.'

The smile that accompanies these last words is a little on the sardonic side, but it's something to build on. Disregarding the final hours there, I suggest, being in Dublin must have been quite an adventure. 'Oh, we had a *hell* of a week! Really, it was special. Of course I know a lot of the NRK guys there well. Maybe the nicest thing was to meet Ronan Keating and play ghee-tar with him backstage.' Not for Tor the stand-up rows with producers that had characterised Jahn's kick-against-the-pricks nul-points preamble, or indeed any Kojo-esque post-mortem tirades against ugly German virgins. 'Every night we had a little Eurosong party in our hotel bar. One time I was playing the Nicole peace song, a beautiful song, and a German TV guy comes up and says, "Oh, that's so nice, that's better than the original!"'

Still, it's not a surprise to find his memories of the night itself rather less complete, and rather more dark. When I ask him what he thought of his rivals that night, he lavishes semi-coherent praise on the interval act, then abruptly fixes me with a look of frail, shellshocked panic. 'Who the fuck won? I can't remember who won.' His smile, when I enlighten him, is rueful rather than relieved. 'Yes, yes, oh dear. In fact I met this Katherina one time afterwards, and she told me it hadn't gone too well after her Eurosong success.' There is no malicious revelry in his tone, nor in my off-topic research notes detailing Katrina Leskanich's post-Eurovision fate.

Having clung together doggedly through the twelve lean years that followed the global success of *Walking on Sunshine*, Katrina and the Waves swiftly fell victim to the curse of Euro-triumph. They would split before their Eurovision cash-in album hit the shops, leaving the band as a two-hit wonder and the headline to a dozen off-colour post-New Orleans hurricane headlines. Katrina herself waited five years before releasing a solo album (poignantly – or perhaps snidely – entitled 'Turn the Tide'), and these days supports Spandau Ballet's Tony Hadley in his travelling eighties roadshow. There can have been few more heart-rending studio sessions than that which spawned Katrina's most recent single: the 2004 release of *Walking on Sunshine*, in Flemish.

Ronan has clapped the last act off stage, the interval show is on and the juries are out. We're into the valley of death, and Tor's hotel room seems to be getting smaller all the time. 'The only thing is,' he says, coughing and letting his syntax wander, 'when the scores, you know, start to come in, we are just watching there this TV monitor . . .' A long pause, a longer drag, a girding slap on his thigh. 'What happened, you know, *it wasn't fun.* This is big-time television in Norway – every-body sees it. My country had been thrilled when I won the Melodi because I had been trying so many times, and then . . . I disappointed them.' He breaks off, scratches his head, stands up and covers the tiny distance to his minibar. 'I'm taking one more of these,' he murmurs, taking out a brandy. 'Please – you take something. It's on NRK.' I return his tired smile and say if it's all right I wouldn't mind a beer, thinking I wouldn't mind eight beers and a promise signed in Tor's blood that he isn't about to go Kalvik. In a room this size, that could make a fearsome mess.

'Until that moment I hadn't thought about Norway. Because nobody, *nobody* had considered it was possible to get zero for this. Yes, I can say it was a shock.' On the early evening of 3 May 1997, Norwegians turned on their tellies with a sense of genuine expectation. By the time they turned them off, their country stood, as still it stands, alone at the head of the nul-points table.

Tor raises the miniature to his lips; it's almost empty when he puts it down. 'I'm the kind of guy who doesn't let these things . . . but, you know, there were photographers there, and I'm trying to smile all the time, but of course they get one picture where I'm looking kind of gloomy, and then that is in all the papers: CRUSHED!' Spitting the words out, he traces an imaginary headline between thumb and crooked forefinger. '*Crushed.*' In silence Tor drains his Remy Martin; I tilt back my Tuborg.

'Well,' he says, at length, drawing the back of a hand across his lips and looking me right between the eyes for the first time in a while, 'this is a special story. You know it's the first time anybody asked me about it?' In what I hope is a steady voice I tell him I had absolutely no idea. He smiles, but in a way that says, 'I expect you're wondering why you've been brought here, Mr Bond'. 'Ja, but it's OK, it's OK. One consolation is that your slaughterer man in England – Terry Vaughan?' I correct him. 'Yes, him, he says – well, somebody told me he said this anyway – "OK, I'm not sure about his song, but what a performer!"' I can't thank Terry enough for those wise words.

'So, when it's over, my producer calls and says, "Remember: it's just a silly little song. *A silly little song.*" And at the end of the daaaay, as your cab drivers say, at the end of the daaaay, me and Jahn [Teigen] and Bobby Sox [Norway's 1985 Eurovision winners], we never have such a happy audience as when we come together to do those Eurosongs. It's the happiest audience in the world!' The words of a man who in May 2001 was the star of a three-day 'Euro Song Cruise' from Oslo to Copenhagen and back.

The absence of one notable Norwegian from this rundown of fellow Euro veterans becomes more conspicuous shortly afterwards. 'But you know, some people take it too seriously. This guy, I won't say his name, he's been in Eurosong a couple of times, and he took it *so badly*. I was back home in Bergen having a beer, I was almost over the whole thing, and this guy called me and he almost starts crying. Him! I had to give him, what you say, consolation. Because he was so crushed about this, it was everybody's fault, not him. But I guess he meant well.' There's nothing to say. *Finn Kalvik: A Warning from History*.

Three Norwegians; three very different approaches to shattering humiliation. If Jahn embraced failure and Finn ran halfway round the world to escape it, then Tor took the sensible and very human middle way, being really, really pissed off for a while, and then getting over it. When I ask if he'd rather have got zero points than three, Tor deflects the question: clearly, like most of us, he wouldn't. 'If you're in love with music, and I can't live without it, you just have new ideas and move on. After a couple of days the bad feeling was gone. You're going to ask if I got lesser gigs?' I shrug sheepishly. 'I didn't. In fact when I come back home after Dublin, the next weekend I have two gigs and they are totally packed. Before I go on-stage I think, Ah: maybe everybody wants to see this . . . special animal, this big loser. But at the gig I see they just wanted to support me.'

And with that Tor's off on another whistle-stop PR tour, highlighting the cabaret show he's about to take on the road with his *Lollipop* co-creator, detailing the extent of his even more demanding two-church-a-day Christmas 2005 tour and sundry other engagements: 'all things I could never do if I won in 1997, because if you win Eurosong you can't choose what you do'. I almost don't want to check up the *VG* chart archives, but when I do a sad truth makes itself plain: the last of Tor's four albums to break the Norwegian top forty dropped out the week after Dublin.

Whatever the long-term fall-out, back in the summer of 1997 he was touched by the public's supportive response, give or take the odd bus-stop baiter ('Eh! Eh! Zero-points man!'). 'Most people are so sweet, they tell me to forget it. And a couple of years later, when I went in again to Melodi Eurosong, everybody says, "Yeah! That's the way to do it, you show them motherfuckers!"' He nearly did. *Lover* came in third.

That was in 1999, the year the language rule was finally abolished: every one of the ten Melodi finalists performed in English. Clicking through Tor's post-Eurovision discography, it had swiftly become apparent that *San Francisco* remains his most recent Norwegian-language recording. Coincidence? Tor says it was never a conscious decision, just a product of having grown up listening to English-singing groups. We end up talking a little about Norway's cultural identity, and then Europe's, and Tor latches eagerly on to Jahn's suggestion that the country's record non-haul of Eurovision points may have helped swing people away from the EU. 'Everything has an impact. Sure, I voted No – I was so pissed that politicians from other countries couldn't take the trouble to come to Norway to talk about the EU. My mother says, "You see – Germany won in the end."' As soon as he says this, he seems to regret it. As an entertainer Tor is the type who might on occasion rock the house, but never the boat. 'But I'm European, for sure. My new record was done in Tallinn.'

Yet alone amongst his compatriot nul-pointers, Tor has never pined for success beyond the continent's longest frontiers. He's recording in Estonia not because he's a proud Europhile, but because it's cheap. As a realist and a true professional, he knows which side of the Norwegian border his bread is buttered. 'I've sold 600,000 albums here in Norway,' he says, 'and I've done that by knowing who are my audience, and by having a sense of music history. Eurosong is not maybe a hip thing to be in these days, but why should everything be for young people?'

As a serial Melodi-enterer, all he's ever sought from the

competition was the domestic exposure, not a hiding-to-nothing shot at international glory. 'I never wanted to win Melodi,' he says, and I'm inclined to believe him. 'My big hits came from the songs that came second or third. That's what I hope for this time.'

Chewing his lip, he leans forward and settles into a previously unessayed intense whisper. 'You know why I'm in it again? Because I'm a stubborn son of a bitch, and because I'm Gemini.' You're . . . Jemini? 'Yeah, and us Geminis like things to be . . . *correct*. If the pictures are hanging a bit wrong, all that . . . And I *don't like odd numbers*! I had one album with eleven songs – it *really* upsets me still. And before this year I have nine Melodi entries . . . *so I had to do it again*!' In one way I'm heartened by this belated display of the nul-points nuttiness I've come to expect, almost to treasure. But only in one way. This space is far too small to be shared with a suddenly wild-eyed obsessive-compulsive in orange make-up.

Quietly, I suggest that in numerophobic terms he'd better leave it at ten. He sighs, then smiles. 'For sure. This is it, the last time. Our song is kind of an anthem, inspired a little by my Christmas concerts. Hey – I'm just playing with the text, if you wouldn't mind to see?' Well, isn't this something? My second contribution as a lyrical consultant; I'm really putting my stamp on Eurovision 2005! Only I'm not, because after a fruitless search for the relevant notebook, Tor starts looking at his watch. (In the event, *Can You Hear Me?* fails to make the Melodi's final four, with Jahn's *My Heart is my Home* winding up last of those who do.)

Before I go there's the traditional presentation – not Tor's latest CD, with its Balto-symphonic arrangements of *Broken Wings* and *How Deep is Your Love?*, but 1999's 'Blue'. 'Yeah,' he says, acknowledging my thanks with a smirk, 'it's the one with eleven songs.' Though if he's looking to explain its modest commercial impact, I'd direct attention away from the Gemini-alienating track listing on the back, and towards the photograph on the front. Tor from the waist up, eyes closed, lips parted, black raincoat held slightly open, looking for all the world as if he's being orally pleasured by a kneeling person or persons unseen.

'Oh, one thing,' says Tor, after we've shaken hands. 'You have Jahn's phone number with you? I think I may have a gig for him in Spain.' I do have it, and reading it out from my mobile's address book fancy myself being cosily inducted into the nul-points brotherhood. 'He's really a genius,' says Tor fondly. 'So . . . *verbal.* Like Frank Zappa or someone.'

Padding down the thickly carpeted corridor, I recall Jahn describing himself as 'not a typical Norwegian musician'. And that's exactly what Tor is: a family entertainer, a straightforward, down-the-line pro with a wife and five kids back in Bergen. No shifty hangers-on or microbreweries, no underage elopements, no paintings of handcuffs and guns, no electro-dance paeans to female masturbation. Frankly it's about time.

3 May 1997
The Point, Dublin
Celia Lawson
Portugal
Antes do Adeus

I'm looking through the *VG* website's Eurovision archive, and there it is: '1997: *San Francisco*, Tor Endresen, 24 av 25.' He didn't come last after all! I feel like calling him up with the good news. Tor's hung up on numbers, but it's letters that have spared him: by opting to rank equal-scoring countries in alphabetical order, the Norwegian press have (in an act of childish desperation) leapfrogged their man above his fellow '97 nul-pointer.

When Eurovision underachievers moan about politics, they're usually popping open an umbrella term for points lost to petty cross-border enmities. For Portugal's contestants, though, that noun has always been uttered with a little more resonance. Unusually long sections of the Portuguese Eurovision agenda have been composed with the sombre profundity of a constitution. Few native singers would bracket their efforts with Tor's self-proclaimed silly little song; there are no Wogans in Lisbon.

Ever since Spain's debut in 1961 there had been disquiet at the musical soapbox being offered to a fascist dictatorship – only by inviting Yugoslavia as a counterbalance was a crisis avoided – and when Antonio Salazar's Portugal applied for entry three years later, the grumbles swelled into angry calls for a boycott. After these came to nothing, unknown activists phoned in a bomb threat that led to a high-security cordon being thrown around Copenhagen's Tivoli Concert Hall, and the juries went on to mete out justice in the only way they knew: Antonio Calvario came home without a point to his name.

This painful baptism was to have a profound effect on his nation's songwriters. Whilst the rest of us settled into the drooling imbecilities of the *Boom-Bang-A-Bang* era, Portugal's thriving community of lyrical subversives stealthily hijacked the contest as an outlet for impassioned (if necessarily well camouflaged) political protest. In 1967, Angolan singer Eduardo Nascimento – pipped a year earlier as the contest's debut black contestant by Holland's Milly Scott – delivered an allegorical diatribe against his colonial overlord Salazar's regime, entitled *The Wind Has Changed*.

Perhaps irritated at failing to decode Eduardo's mournful paean to democracy, the Portuguese authorities took a rather sterner line against José Carlos Ary dos Santos, who supplied the words to the country's 1973 entry. 'We're going to grab the world by the horns of misfortune,' ran the penultimate verse of the extraordinary *Tourada*, 'and make fun of sadness.' Probably nonplussed rather than outraged, the secret police opted to err on the side of caution, declaring the song a vile catalogue of anti-materialist sedition and throwing José in jail. Though not for long: he was out in time to see Fernando Tordo come home from Luxembourg with eighty points and tenth place.

But it was Portugal's 1974 entry that bequeathed Eurovision an unlikely assist in what remains Western Europe's most recent revolution. Just after noon on 25 April that year, the national radio broadcast Paulo de Carvalho's *E Depois Do*

Adeus, the cue arranged by pro-democracy rebels in the military to take to the streets. 'In your body, my love, I fell asleep,' sang Paulo, as soldiers marched from their barracks with carnations in their rifles, 'I died in it and after dying I was reborn.' Not troubling themselves with this unsettling image – I'm thinking *Alien* chest-bursters here – the soldiers were cheered through the streets of Lisbon; by the end of the day, and with the loss of just four lives, democracy had been restored to a land enslaved by dictatorship for over forty years. Some consolation for Paulo, who nineteen days earlier had followed ABBA out onto the stage at The Dome in Brighton, made a frightful mess of his middle eight and wound up joint last.

The hated regime was no more, but Portugal's unshackled songwriters didn't want anyone to forget how hated it had been. 'I'm singing the praises of a land that is reborn,' sang former army lieutenant Duarte Mendes in 1975, 'for there can't be enough songs like this.' So indeed it proved. The year after, the two socialist MPs handed the lyrical responsibilities kicked off with, 'I could call you my homeland, and give you the most beautiful Portuguese name.' In 1977, Os Amigos managed to condense forty years of pain and injustice into the most unforgettable opening stanza in Eurovision history: 'Portugal was the reason why one day my brother died.'

Perhaps satisfied at having produced the honed antithesis of the contest's lyrical dementia, or perhaps belatedly recognising that this sort of stuff wasn't doing them any favours with the juries, Portugal abruptly changed tack. In 1978 they trotted out *Dai-Li-Dou*, and within five years we were deep into *Bem Bom* territory. Securing EU membership provoked a melancholic last hurrah in 1987 ('In my country, sadness is called loneliness'), but otherwise Portugal settled into a run of unchallenging ballads remarkable only for the consistency with which they finished eighteenth. Until 1996, when Lucia Moniz secured sixth place – the nation's best result – after revealing that her heart had no colour. (Seven years later she re-emerged as Colin Firth's non-Anglophone girlfriend in *Love Actually*.)

Consciously or otherwise, Portugal's 1997 entry, *Antes do*

Adeus (Before Goodbye) echoed Paulo de Cavalho's portentous *E Depois Do Adeus (After Goodbye)*. Probably otherwise: it's difficult to peel away too many allegorical layers in the former's bitter-sweet recounting of a failed love affair, though being a Portuguese love affair that didn't preclude a namecheck for Communist poet Jose Saramago. The vocal messenger was a young woman dressed in black who stepped rather uncertainly out on to the Dublin stage twelve acts after Tor Endresen. By name, Celia Lawson hardly sounded Portuguese, but her dark hair and brown eyes ensured she certainly looked it.

I watch Celia's performance more times than most, convincing myself I'm doing so in order to pick up clues as to the stubbornly mysterious fate bestowed upon her song, rather than because she's comfortably the cutest nul-pointer to date. *Antesh do Adeush*, as it emerges from her lips, is an understated cocktail-bar smoocher, well suited to the unexpected huskiness of Celia's voice. If you're desperate to pick holes in it – and after the fifth hearing I am – you could argue the song's a little on the torpid side for Eurovision. And that abrupt, slightly atonal ending wasn't a good idea, catching the audience offguard and so tainting their applause with a fitful uncertainty that could have influenced any vacillating juries. But the bottom line is that in the online poll of which nul-point offering least deserved its fate, *Antes do Adeus* came home a comfortable second (to Remedios Amaya's full-on flamenco shriekathon).

It's not the song, and it's not the singer. On the third run through, now as brutally critical as a *Pop Idol* hatchet-man, it occurs to me that Celia is possibly a little overdeveloped in the jaw area, and on the fourth that her leather-look bodice top might be a tad tight in places it shouldn't. But in essence, being young and female, she's the physical inversion of the nul-point stereotype.

Her backing singers are a slight liability – a vaguely slappable assortment of suited, sunglassed *Matrix* agents – and, oh, I dunno, maybe all the juries are holding their fire for overwhelming favourite Katrina, who's up second last. But in general, I'm clueless. If her performance begins a little tentatively, it's in a way that invites sympathy rather than scorn. 'The girls get a few votes just for turning up,' Tor had complained, and I can't begin to understand how this girl hadn't.

There's no sign of Tor and his canary-yellow jacket in the green room: he's either run back to his hotel for some minibar solace or is down in the backstage toilets doing a great big Cliff-sulk. But there's plenty of Celia, looking small, lost and very, very young at the far end of a *Matrix*-agented sofa, glancing about the room with a rather helpless smile that seems more connected to awe at her surroundings than her unfolding fate. As Ronan leads the victorious Katrina and her Waves back out towards the stage, there's Celia in the hailing throng, clapping heartily, looking genuinely pleased for them. I've seen nul-point backstage faces hardened with bitterness, sagging in confused dejection, pulled madly about by sod-it-all hysteria, but I've never seen this.

'Celia Lawson released an album just before the ESC 1997,' emails Andreas a couple of weeks later, failing to buck a well-established trend by ending this sentence with the words 'before disappearing'. Though, again as ever, that isn't quite the case. She has her own website, for a start, even if it doesn't appear to have been updated for some years. But there's a little biography, which kicks off with a deeply touching black-and-white snap of an infant Celia standing on a chair with a toy Fender round her neck, and ends with a brief personal message that includes an email contact and the site's only words in English: 'So long suckers of Rock&Roll!!'

One, two, three emails are fired off to the specified address, without reply. Feeding the biography into Google translator I find mention of sundry record labels and music publishers, and after a little telephonic foolishness get through to one who speaks English. 'Yes, I have a number for Celia,' says the polite young chap at LX Publishing, 'but it's a long time since we speak to her. At this time she is sometimes singing on the cruises, on Italian boats.'

I'm thinking what fun that would be when, at the end of a week spent acquiring familiarity with the Portuguese for 'if you would like to leave a message', Birna answers the phone as we're sitting down to supper. After conveying her quizzical uncertainty through a series of wondering hums, she hands me the receiver. 'I almost put the phone down,' she whispers. 'Sounds just like one of those foreign telesales people.'

In a sleepy, hoarse voice apparently assembled from elements of Russian, Thai and Spanish, Celia Lawson introduces herself, then, as fulsomely as her slightly medicated delivery permits, expresses an enthusiasm to meet me. 'Oh, it will be funny to talk about Eurovision once more. I am with holiday here in Lisboa, sometimes in Sintra. You come, why not?'

In the event, it's Sintra, the palace-strewn World Heritage hill town 30km west of Lisbon that I'd last passed through as a student, with a consequent memory bias towards holiday economics. (So cheap were the taxis that I recall taking one to the supermarket.) A family week in the Algarve excepted, that was also my most recent trip to Portugal; standing outside Lisbon arrivals I'm glad to be back. For a start, this is my first gloveless nul-points pilgrimage since Thailand. The condensation-bottled beer ads on the airport billboards are perhaps a touch ambitious this early in spring, but with a coat on I'm overdressed. And when the bus into town arrives, the driver cuts short my Euro-fumbling with a dismissive wave: last time transport was cheap, but now it's actually *free*.

Well, almost. But even when I do have to stump up for the next leg of my journey, the forty-minute ride to Sintra is a snip at €1.30 – a lot less than half the price of a short-hop central-zone ticket on the London tube. This disparity aside, bumping along through the suburbs in a carriage full of lunch-break students and office workers, I find I'm feeling at home. Portugal, famously, is Britain's oldest ally: through thick, thin and Fascist dictatorship we've been an item, and no couple stays together for 600 years without sharing an outlook on life. There are lemon trees between the dusty pink apartment blocks, and birdcages on the balconies, but most are familiarly girdled with graffiti. And my fellow passengers are straight out of a London-model, post-colonial melting pot, a testament to globe-spanning ethnic harmony.

More to the point, there's none of the shouty Latin histrionics that should by latitudinal logic colour the journey. Everyone is either gazing dully out of the window, reading the overhead adverts or muttering almost inaudibly into mobiles. And they're all a bit of a mess: crumpled jackets, cheap shoes, none of the preening haughtiness you'd expect in most European capitals. I look around warmly: these are my people.

I phone up Celia when we're halfway, to confirm my safe arrival. 'Oh, I'm so pleased!' she laughs. 'It's really *so beautiful* here. You will love this town!' It's a delight to hear her sounding so much brighter, more alert. I don't even mind when she goes on to explain that she's going to be a little late, owing to a rescheduled dental appointment she's currently en route to. In benign content I listen to her bounteous apologies, just happy to listen to Celia discussing her everyday business, like the down-to-earth, gyroscopically well-balanced young woman she is. Or so I've been hoping since my previous conversation with her, two evenings earlier. 'I'm sad, very sad,' she'd mumbled, sounding more melancholically Russian than before. 'Just walking about Sintra, in this rain, feeling sad.' An hour later I'd gone back to her website and found a new pop-up advert: 'Find Christian singles in your area!' It was a bad night all round.

But that was then. It isn't dark, it isn't raining, and when I get off at Sintra into a steeply pitched, multi-coloured realm of Moorish turrets and tiles, it's impossible to imagine anyone who lives here feeling bad about life for too long.

It's about a mile into the old town, around a road that clings to the rippling valley slope. The air is deliciously tainted with woodsmoke and lavender; whistling along the sinuous pavement I suck in great draughts, gazing up at the castle that crowns the highest hill and the streaky, ochred palaces and villas stacked up beneath it, tutting at the ale-centred philistinism that blotted all this out to me twenty years before.

Celia has arranged to meet me on the steps of the Palacio Nacional, the sturdy white edifice whose Klansman-hat kitchen chimneys dominate the old town. I sit down to wait, idly ticking off further evidence of cross-cultural London–Lisbon fertilisation: their old numberplates are just like our old ones, and imagine if that postbox wasn't blue, or that phonebox wasn't white. Isn't that beer truck a Bedford? It is. *Ay caramba*, mate: I didn't even have to change my watch.

A lazy peloton of club cyclists eases up the steep, tight road ahead and swishes past out of town; an old man in a big beret tilts back his head as he passes a restaurant, savouring a whiff of lunchtime garlic. OK, the presence of a cheesy accordionist and one of those foolish road-bound sightseeing trains suggests this place might get a bit much in the summer, but for now, as a nul-point venue, it certainly knocks room 312 at Oslo's Hotel Bristol into a cocked hat. A cocked hat containing squashed up bits of a half-painted bathroom in Istanbul.

Celia's late; later than she'd said. A school next door to the palace disgorges a flock of teenagers, who mill about in front of me and provide the first solid evidence that Celia's manner of speech is down to geography, rather than methadone. The air is filled with lispy 'ssshhs' and drawled 'owws'; everyone sounds slightly drunk. Then I look round and spot a slight figure, the front half of her head cowled in a pair of black-lensed Yoko face-hiders, pacing slowly across the square before me.

I stand up, bully my features into an I-come-in-peace face and raise a hand. A smile underscores Celia's huge shades, followed by a wince and two fingers pressed lightly against a swollen right cheek. 'Tih? So-ee, I a lidl bi lay,' she says, apparently by way of explanation. 'Too mush anasedic in here, you unnerstah?' I follow her across the flagstones, thinking: Well, this is going to be interesting.

We go straight to a dark, half-empty little restaurant on the other side of the square, patrolled by a hungover waiter whose chair-scraping, plate-slamming inartistry dominates much of my recorded conversation with Celia. In conjunction with her post-dental incoherence, it makes the transcription process a laborious challenge. Even there and then, with Celia separated from me only by two feet of knackered mahogany, it's difficult to decode her statements with total confidence until the mouth-slackening medication has worn off, roughly around the time our coffees are blearily crashed down in front of us.

Celia takes off her welding-grade sunglasses to reveal a pair of bright brown eyes, underhung with pouches of fatigue and lightly ringed with grey. Her hair, faintly streaked with lines of blonde, hangs across her face. The artfully grunged-up effect works a lot better than its description suggests – when the waiter isn't punishing crockery he's gazing moonily at Celia from behind his bar-mounted coffee machine – but mentally downloading the image of her fresh-faced twenty-two-year-old Dublin self, I can't help thinking that the last eight years haven't been too easy.

With her orally forgiving bowl of pasta ordered, we make a start on Celia's family background. It takes some time, this epic tale of colony-hopping wanderlust: her Indian paternal grandmother was a Portuguese army nurse who 'married in Bangalore this Lawson guy, originally from Bolton' (she still has relations in Lincolnshire: Celia's half-British mother was born a Morgan); after being separated from her husband in the war, she pitched up in Bombay, and then Goa, where Celia's parents met and married. It's a microcosm of Portugal's convoluted multi-culturalism.

As a colonial administrator, Senhor Lawson was obliged to decamp and retreat along with Portugal's crumbling empire. From Goa the family moved first to Timor, and then in the early sixties to Angola, where Celia was born two months after the Eurovision-catalysed carnation revolution. A year later, in 1975, the outbreak of a vicious civil war in the African colony forced the Lawsons back to Lisbon (in Celia's early teenage years, the family moved to Sintra). 'And that's all I know,' she says, blinking those tired eyes.

It was her dad who first got Celia into music, who bought her that toy guitar, who took the soul-squeezing photo of her hanging it round her infant neck. 'He was a singer, he played guitar. For fun, you know, a hobby. In Angola he played with an army band, they win talent shows on radio, they were quite known.' But when, as a fourteen year old, Celia applied herself to learning the guitar, she did so without paternal instruction or encouragement. 'It was like a revenge on other girls,' she says, working up to a winning snigger. 'My teeth were all out of place – yes, still then! – and boys didn't pay me attention. So I teach myself the guitar, and carry it into school, and in one week I have boys talking to me!' An invigorating tale of one girl's unorthodox triumph over orthodontic disadvantage: our laughter ricochets off the panelled walls and low ceiling. 'Oh,' says Celia at chortlesome length, 'do you mind if I smoke a cigar?' I'm hardly surprised when my assent leads to a packet of Marlboro Lights being plopped on to the table.

Evidently impressed by the perks of rock-chickery, Celia applied herself to developing the relevant talents with great enthusiasm, and almost instant success. 'I like to imitate people, behind their backs,' she says, with a mock-evil narrowing of the eyes, 'so is why I speak all these languages, and sing like all these singers.' And so, at the age of fifteen, she found herself fronting a multi-lingual covers band called Summertime, playing bars, clubs and – within a couple of years – some of the biggest hotels in Lisbon. 'One moment,' she says, hoisting out a laptop from her shoulder bag and powering it up beside her pasta. A minute later I'm looking at a photo of the 1989 Summertime line-up: four arms-folded blokes in jeans and trainers, and beside them a hunched, timid girl in sunglasses, two-thirds their height and half their age.

Her parents are slipping off our conversational radar, and when I ask how they felt about their fifteen-year-old daughter's conspicuous lifestyle, Celia's response is a blithe shrug. 'But already I'm going alone to England, to see my aunties in Peterborough. And you know I was making some big money – only real rich kids have attitudes that I have at that time. I have all the records I like, all the clothes. In Carnaby Street I'm buying my leather jacket, oh yes, with these big metal, how you call, pins.' Studs, I say, and she repeats this word with a savouring, nostalgic grin.

I'm looking at the jacket a minute later, as the waiter slams two glasses of wine down perilously close to Celia's laptop. 'That was us,' she says, clicking up a picture of Mital, the all-girl hard-rock ensemble she joined at the age of eighteen. Though once again the baby of the line-up, this time she's the wised-up, cocksure one with her arms crossed. One of the others appears to be wearing a Pringle jumper under her leather. 'Rock, heavy metal – it's my first love.' She smiles. 'For this band I did my first songwriting, kind of Iron Maiden style.'

At this point, to Celia's babbling excitement, I announce that my son shares his classroom with the Iron Maiden lead guitarist's daughter. When I go on to reveal that the band's lead singer and creative genius (oh, how my typing fingers twitch over the inverted commas) drinks at my local, her eyes almost treble in size. 'Bruce!' she squeals. 'Uncle Bruce!' It's a long minute before I can coax her back to our timeline.

It didn't take long for Celia to outgrow the Pringle-rock of Mital, and before her eighteenth year was out she'd accepted an invitation to join established Lisbon-based headbangers V12, playing the capital's big venues and a lot of festivals in the south of the country. The relevant photo shows a performer homing in on the big time: the previous shots have both been grubby snaps taken outside backstreet bars, but here's Celia on a serious stage, knee-deep in dry ice, bent backwards, aiming an eyes-closed AC-DC rock shriek at the overhead spotlights. I've said it before, to Jahn, to Kojo, to Daníel, and here I am saying it again. Eurovision and you: why?

'Oh, but I was always quite a fan,' she says, inscrutably. 'As a child I was watching many, many Eurovisions. My first one I watched is 1974, I remember that one so well.' Ah yes: Paulo de Carvalho's dissolver of fascism. We share a happy sigh, and then I think: Hang on. That was a month before you were born.

'Um . . .' I say, before mumbling out the chronology. Celia cuts me short with a hold-it-right-there raised palm.

'There's one thing you must know about this,' she says, low, sombre, leaning slowly towards me on her table-planted elbows. 'I'm lying to you.'

I do my best to match the explosive laughter she now releases, but it's not that easy. Here I am about to steer our conversation into the Bermuda Triangle of Dublin 1997, and my co-pilot has just leant across and yanked the control stick clean out of its socket with a crazed whoop.

Let's go back a bit, I suggest, seeking refuge in dates and facts. We're in '94, right? 'Well, and that year actually was my first involvement with the Festival of Song [Portuguese state broadcaster RTP's Eurovision qualifier]. I was in the backing group, the choir, for one of the songs.' (I check it out later: sixth out of ten in the first semi-final.) From this followed other TV appearances, singing Elton John covers on RTP's big Sunday-night light-entertainment show, and getting to the final of the native *Stars in Their Eyes* with her self-evidently uncanny Oleta Adams. As 1996 came to a close she was recording her first album, and had just been contracted to write songs for an expensively promoted new boy band. Still just twenty-one, it was all happening for Celia Lawson.

The way things were going, it can hardly have been a surprise when at the start of 1997 she was approached by veteran composer Thilo Krassman, who had conducted Portuguese entrants at five Eurovision finals. On 7 March, Celia went out on to the stage at Lisbon's Coliseu dos Recreios, and delivered a rendition of Thilo's composition that convincingly saw off nine Festival of Song rivals. 'That day was a new page in my life history,' she says, puncturing the portent of these words by numbing her tender mouth with a noisy and protracted cheek-to-cheek wine sloosh. 'I had been with my boyfriend for four years, a long and complicated relationship, almost a marriage, and that morning we split up, completely.' The morning of the contest? The morning before she went out on live telly and sang 'Before goodbye, your dreams were mine; paradise, you were by my side'?

'That's right,' she says, nodding slowly, 'that's right.' Her eyes are fixed on mine; those puffy mouth pouches on the affected side of her face lend a Godfather-ish menace to this utterance. 'We said goodbye, and I go to the festival, and then I win: it's like a new life.'

The professional exposure Celia had already enjoyed did not in any way prepare her for what happened in the two months between that day and Dublin. 'I was making videos, making TV, newspaper interviews, all the time, *all the time*, three, four a day.' Just thinking about it seems to plump up those eye-bags. 'Then some doctor gives me pills to keep me up.' What a touching gesture, I think; how thoughtful, how responsible. 'At first it was exciting, all this tasting success . . . Just my father, he was the only one who tried to calm it down. He was very, very serious: go slow, tomorrow is another day, take it easy. You know.' A crooked smile.

Celia's little-girl-lost performance in the Dublin green room was the culmination of three days of overwhelmed awe. 'I was like the youngest performer, like a kid with all these big international singers. I went around getting albums from everyone; it was really fun.' She considers this latter statement while laboriously dispatching one of the half dozen mouthfuls of pasta that are all she'll manage. 'Fun, but . . . I remember I was in this VIP room with Thilo and his wife, and his wife's friend, and they're all so jetsetters, and I was not comfortable. Those parts, really I *detested* them.' Her wince of oral pain makes the small evolution into a gurn of disgust. 'Really bad. Yeah, I was happy to have my mum and dad there.' Having spent her mid-teens jetting off to England alone, perhaps the stresses of Dublin dredged up a belated bout of adolescent insecurity.

Celia shoots me a sudden look of urgent befuddlement. 'Your name! I forget your name!' Failing to purge my voice of a slight quaver, I remind her. 'OK, Tim. OK. There's something I wanted to tell you, Tim, and that's about the hotel.' She goes on to talk for some time, and with taut intensity, about the daft extent of the official entourage that filled a whole floor of her hotel. 'Even we have two doctors . . . One of the backing guys, he has his grandmother! Like maybe thirty people total! To me it didn't seem like Portuguese Eurovision committee – it was like a holiday camp!'

Her point isn't quite clear, but I gather from this tirade's pasta-muddled denouement that as well as the obvious distractions of an anarchic and unwieldy delegation, there was an economic grievance: Celia was personally made to foot the bill for some or all of the excess beds in her room, and some or all of the excess nights she was obliged to book. The bottom line is that she was narked then, and she's narked now. 'I can't eat no more,' she drawls, pushing her pasta away. 'Just cigar now.'

Very warily, watching for any sign of Lawsonian instability, I move us from the hotel to The Point in Dublin. We talk about her dress – she mentions a large embroidered gold galleon that I'd somehow missed in the course of all those viewings. We talk about the preceding acts (affectionately discussing her rivals in some detail, Celia proves that she's forgotten less about '97 than Tor remembers. 'Oh, this Norway guy!' she exclaims, when I mention him, clapping her hands. 'I was so sorry I never speak with him afterwards! I try to find him, but he's gone.' Tor, I recall, never mentioned Celia). And then, prefacing it with a throatful of vinho and a *cri de cœur* on the injustice of her looming fate, I move us on to her three minutes on the Dublin stage.

'You know, it wasn't three minutes,' murmurs Celia, looking a little mischievous. 'You saw my big mistake?' My eyes widen. 'Oh, come on! We're live, direct, and I jump off, forget some verse, go right forward to the last chorus . . . it was *fantastic*!' She's laughing again, anyway. 'The orchestra, my singers, they did such a good job to cover it . . . but what a mistake!'

I manage some sort of indulgent chortle, convinced that it's another of her fanciful creations. But when I get home and compare the lyrics of *Antes do Adeus* with her Eurovision rendition, there it is: she misses out a whole verse, and is therefore obliged to repeat the last. Four hundred million of us were never told of tears heard in all the street, or that in the other face of the moon your dreams were mine.

Celia smiles benignly throughout my potted account of her green-room performance, chipping in with a laugh when I mention her animated round of applause for the triumphant Katrina, who in besting Celia's total by 227 points has just inflicted on her the worst defeat in Eurovision history (Tor of course being alphabetically spared this ignominy). 'Of course, I was happy for her,' she says simply, pausing to sing a husky snatch of *Love Shine a Light*. 'Who wouldn't be?'

Nevertheless, when her fellow competitors began to trickle away to the after-show party, Celia found herself succumbing to a powerful desire to be back with Mummy and Daddy in her hotel room. As soon as she got there, though, Thilo came knocking, and with a brusqueness perhaps borne of her lyrical mess-up, insisted that she come down and do her duty. 'So I go to this party for maybe fifteen minutes, do what I must do, go back to my room. When I wake up in the morning, I make some phone calls, I don't know . . .'

She trails off into a disjointed mumble – something about her mum and dad going to India, about newspapers, about a border (or possibly boredom). Somehow I can't bring myself to demand, Thilo-like, that she amplifies and repeats it all. Instead I wheel out the Teigen/Taner hypothesis, suggesting that her countrymen might have pinned the blame on Europe. 'No,' she says, rousing herself to coherence. 'People here were divided. Some didn't like the song, and some didn't like me.' The disarming candour of this bleak assessment suggest that my deliberations on continental fraternity will not thrive in Lawson-land's stony soil, but I sow the seeds anyway.

Severally prompted, Celia mutters something about Portugal being perceived as more backward than its EU brethren, and asserts that she only feels Portuguese when she's outside Portugal. Would she feel more American than, I don't know, Norwegian? The question brings her to life. 'Can I say something first? This Katrina, you know she was American?' I do, I say. 'OK, and after she wins, she says: "Once more the British have to get help from Americans."' Celia looks at me searchingly, as if I'm now expected to snort or curl my lip or – this is a Latin country – spit furiously on the floor. Because I don't, she carries on herself. 'Well, I'm sorry, but I don't think she is a lady to say this.' She settles back, haughtily; only after two forkfuls of risotto do I feel ready to return to my original query. 'Oh, America, not Norway,' she says, carelessly. More clinking of forks and glasses. 'Actually I'm just saying that because I don't really care where Norway is.'

The fatuous manner with which she announces this rallies me to the Nordic cause. For a minute or more I deliver a heartfelt but stupidly pompous valediction to Norway's plucky nul-points martyrs; when I'm done, Celia looks modestly chastened. 'I guess for some of these guys,' she says, 'their whole life is to compete in Eurovision. And that wasn't such a situation for me.'

No regrets, then, I suggest. She recoils theatrically. 'Regrets? Of course! Oh, God! I regret completely that I go to Eurovision! I wish I had stayed in the bath!' There is indeed no mention of the contest in her website biography. So not even the thinnest silver lining? 'The positive,' she replies, quickfire, 'is that because I did Eurovision, now I can go on TV any time I want. Maybe I can't sell records or make shows, but TV is always there, until the end of my life.' She sits back and folds her arms, challengingly, but I'm not about to argue. Maybe there's an Icelandic small-world telly-thing going on here. '*Until the end of my life.* But I don't go on, because I don't want.' A defiant, last-laugh grin.

'And of course I get some money from the song, in time of Eurovision it is played on the radio. A few years ago it was on many times, almost every day. You know: here is the failure song, everybody.' Gauging the resilience of the so-what face Celia's pulling, I ask how she feels when she hears it now. She seems to shrink a little. 'It's difficult,' she almost whispers, lightly scratching at a flake of table-top varnish. 'It's difficult because the lyrics talk about a . . . painful situation in my love history.' I'm trying to work up a look of therapeutic sympathy when Celia's body almost bursts in a sudden but prolonged release of savage comedic expression. The twenty-eight recorded seconds that follow are distorted to speaker-buzzing incoherence. It's good to hear her laugh, but that's at least twenty-three seconds too much of it.

Celia had all but completed her debut album when she went off to Dublin, and a couple of months after she came home to Sintra, 'First' was almost apologetically released. So profound and instantaneous was its commercial failure that by autumn Celia had stopped describing herself as a performer. 'A career is being born, and then straight away it dies.' She looks resigned rather than dismayed. 'It was born in March at the Festival of Song, and a few months after, there it is, a small, dead thing . . . I have had my drink of fame, and I know I will never have another. That's it, finished.'

As the more enduringly contented of my nul-pointers had demonstrated, it helps to have another iron in the fire when 400 million people take turns to piss on the hottest. Celia, already blessed with a portfolio CV at the age of twenty-two, insulated herself from 'all the shit about Eurovision' by getting stuck into songwriting. And with almost instant reward: Excesso, Portugal's first home-grown boy band, had by Christmas shifted 120,000 copies of an album she'd co-composed. There were nominations for song of the year and other awards; the Celia-penned title track is still available as a ringtone.

That's great, I suggest, but in fact it wasn't. 'No one in Portugal knows it is me writing this! Even my agency doesn't want to put my name on the record, because of what had happened to me. So no one called, no more work like that.' Well, that's really shit, I say, and Celia nods stoically. 'But one funny thing is that one of these boys in the band falls in love with me. Deeply-deeply! But I have to tell him: sorry, I'm into heavy metal.'

This time the chortling is shortlived. 'Then I have enough of all this,' says Celia, flatly. 'I had pride as an artist, from fifteen to twenty-two it was all I had done, but then I have to walk away. My father has a contact with TAP, national airline, and I go there for a job.' So here's Portugal's 1997 Eurovision performer, telling me how just six months after representing her nation in front of the entire continent, she's pacing down the aisle of an Airbus, returning seat backs to the upright position.

'The passengers were not easy,' she murmurs, heavy eyed. 'Here is a person who was on their TV just before, and now she is like their servant, working for them.' Though that wasn't the reason she didn't last long. 'I'm made of too special material to be sad about that, but I don't like cleaning up vomit. And then there was this boy I had to look after.' On a flight to Angola, it fell to Celia to chaperone a profoundly disabled child; describing his condition, she wells up. 'Irons in arms and legs, he couldn't talk, he was deaf. He had only his eyes . . . I was crying all the time.' There's a short break while Celia endures a reprise. 'Day after, that was my last day.'

With a painful gulp, Celia swallowed her pride and went back to the music business. It was like starting all over again: she found herself singing in hotels and recording local-radio idents. But within a year she was writing modest hits for the latest wave of boy bands, and within two she was back on telly, providing backing vocals on variety shows. By 2000 she had secured a lucrative residency at the Estoril Casino – Portugal's most lavish – and was working up nice sidelines as a karaoke-tape artist and a prolific composer of advert jingles (researching this later, I make the happy discovery that Coca-Cola translates from Portuguese as 'cocaine glue'). Finally, five years after Dublin, she felt ready to stick her head above the chart parapet again.

'Faith' was the title of Celia's second album; it's fair to say it didn't muster a challenge to the George Michael release of that name. Of all the post-Eurovision recordings released by my nul-pointers, none made as modest a commercial impression: entered together in Google, album and artist procure three matches, two of which link to Celia's own website. 'I am certain,' she writes in the relevant cyber section, 'that I have created an album with ten original rhythms, that in my opinion bring something new, something of the discotheque, to Portuguese Rock!' The entry, dated 2002, is the last she'll make.

'There was a cabal against me with this album,' she says, simply. 'I came back alone with a thing of my own, that I produced myself, and everyone was . . . woah, no! What's she doing back here?' She chooses this auspicious moment to re-don her hulking celeb shades. 'They all thought I was dead.'

For the next three years, Celia Lawson, singer, songwriter, performer, set about killing herself off. The Estoril residency gave way to occasional stints on cruise ships, and she stopped returning calls from ad agencies and TV stations. In 2003 she sent a song off to the RTP Eurovision-qualifying committee, under a different name: 'I didn't even get a call about it,' she slurs, her after-laugh tinged with weary mania.

Her most recent Googled whereabouts were at Lisbon's Tivoli Theatre, where in November 2004 she appeared in a musical comedy entitled *Kiss Kiss*. I'm keen to untangle a related anomaly: on one site she's down as scheduled performer for the show's whole four-month run, on another she's right at the end of the cast list with an asterisk by her name, and a third contains no trace of a Lawson, Celia. 'I quit,' she says simply, as the waiter shakily scoops up my saucer full of euros, tinkling half on to the floor with a muttered imprecation.

We step out into an overcast, blowy afternoon, the wind chasing litter across the palace's deserted forecourt. I comment again on Sintra's charm, in slight defiance of the now imposingly desolate scene before us, and Celia enthusiastically concurs, outlining her plans to buy a place here instead of renting. 'It's expensive, but I don't care,' she announces, expansively. We shuffle about for a bit, then Celia asks if I'm in a hurry; when I tell her I'm not she suggests we take a short cut back to the station. A minute later we're scrabbling down a near-vertical hillside, trying to follow a path that generally doesn't exist. At length the undergrowth recedes and we're in a lavishly fly-tipped car park near the valley bottom. Celia sits down on a low wall: it's cigar time.

The two hours I spend in that car park form the most poignant, most affecting of all the many encounters my quest has or shall involve me in. With a Marlboro up and running

Celia begins to discuss her Eurovision experience in a very different manner, one that finds room for a great many previously unexplored theories. In a furtive, significant murmur she tells of conversations overheard in the Dublin hotel, conversations about money, 'the money you have to pay if you want to win'. There's a lot of stuff about Expo '98, held in Portugal the year after Eurovision, and how in some way – jealousy, unpaid kickbacks, she's not quite certain – this deprived her of many votes, particularly from the French. On she goes, speaking faster and faster until I'm catching only half-snatches: '. . . and the third rumour – no, the *fourth* rumour . . .'; '. . . we all know about the Balkan countries . . .'; '. . . some day I will make a data research of this . . .'

Pausing only to light another Marlboro, Celia moves on to the events that led to her departure from *Kiss Kiss*, in a new and careless tone that contrasts with the tale's comprehensively unnerving content. Her troubles began with a dispute between Celia and the show's hair stylist, a row 'about some fucking extensions' that somehow escalated into a feud. And then escalated again, to a point where Celia succumbed to a conviction that the stylist wished her harm. Harm of the fatal variety.

Too scared to sleep she began wandering the streets at night, occasionally pursued by another man, 'a guy with a tired arm', and regularly confronted by a group of five children who would stop in front of her and stare.

'In the middle of the night?' I hear myself enquire, faintly.

'That's right,' she says, pushing up her shades and giving me that Robert de Niro look again. But I'm not scared; just very sad. Feeling I ought to say something, I raise the possibility that these children, and the man with the tired arm, simply recognised her; she's earlier said it still happens. She narrows her eyes, then her features mellow with happy enlightenment. 'Yes,' she says, nodding rapidly. 'Yes, yes, yes. I *like* this theory.' Oh, Celia. It's becoming increasingly difficult to convince myself, as I've so far just about been able to, that this conversation is for her a beneficially cathartic experience.

Her family stepped in. Having left the show, she was invited to stay with one of her Peterborough cousins, a publican who bought Celia a big PA amp and allowed her to scream out rock anthems after hours, alone in a back room. Returning to Portugal, she went up to her uncle's house in the rural north, and spent some months there 'like a hermit, just watching animal documentaries on TV'. From there she made two visits to nearby Santiago de Compostela, which allows me to discuss my own pilgrimage to the city a couple of years previously. That I undertook this in the company of a donkey should by rights have lightened the mood, but Celia just nods distantly as I falter through a repertoire of set-piece twit-v-ass anecdotes. 'I have to beg to God there,' she says when I give up, 'because I had been a pagan, oh yes, solstice, moons. I did one love ritual, and then bad things happen. So after Santiago I was for many months going to church every day.'

She forgets my name again; again I remind her. 'Tim,' she says, gently, 'you think about people the same as me?' I mercifully can't recall the non-committal blatherings that now escape my lips, except in so far as they procure from Celia a single, disappointed nod. 'Well, Tim, it's all a lie,' she sighs, shades back on, unseen gaze fixed at the dimming heavens. 'You think I live rock 'n' roll? I don't. Christ Jesus, I was an *air hostess*.'

As darkness falls Celia retracts her affection for the town above us. 'I have nothing here,' she mutters bleakly. 'Well, I have a boyfriend, but he won't speak with me. I don't know the, huh, arrangements with him. And except him – *nothing*.' Thereafter she holds waywardly forth on anarchy, on Margaret Thatcher ('she was a good one, no?'), on a friend lost to drugs. This last reminiscence catalyses another of her wide-eyed epiphanies. 'So many bad things happen to me,' she says, in slow, dawning wonderment, 'and yes: *they all began with Eurovision*.'

It's a horrible moment: I want to sever the connection, tell her not to take on so. But because she's right, I can't. Instead I just sit there, watching the streetlights flick on in the hillside above, contemplating the pustular underbelly that heaves unseen beneath that fluffy, frothy fiesta of silly little songs.

Without warning, Celia leans slightly back and fills the dim old valley with a throat-shredding burst of high-pitched girl rock. The short silence that follows is ended by a distant bark that swiftly multiplies into a twilight canine chorus. 'My first song,' she breathes. 'I wrote it right here.' And with that, and a carefree little hum, she jumps to her feet. 'Come,' she says, lightly, 'next train to Lisbon in ten minutes.' I hadn't anticipated going back to Lisbon until the morning, nor travelling there in Celia's company, but I scamper up the hill after her just the same. It seems the least I can do.

Just outside the station Celia jabs a finger at a little Peugeot parked outside a bar. 'Was my car,' she calls out over her shoulder. 'I sell it before I went to the US.' On the platform, and afterwards in an empty strip-lit carriage, she expands on this revelation. For the last three years she's been putting together a new album, and now that 'On the Road to the Unknown' is finished she's been travelling to Britain and the States, recruiting a band to gig the material. 'I am the band, in reality,' she says, as we creak and squeak out of Sintra. 'But it is not Celia Lawson. It is Ira, I-R-A.' We chortlingly agree that she might wish to adapt that for certain European markets. 'It means "anger" in Portuguese. It's back to my first love. You like metal?'

If it's good, I lie, and out come the laptop and earphones. The gap between my desperation for a nul-pointer's new material to impress me, and the expectation of it being able to do so, has never been more yawningly cavernous. There are no limits to the musical possibilities of what I am about to behold: it could be a sobbing child banging a saucepan, ten minutes of hissy silence, a backwards remix of *Antes do Adeus*. 'Here we go then,' I say, plugged in and palpitating as Celia, Mac in lap, clicks up the opening track. Please, I pray silently, please let this be at least 400 times better than I think it's going to be.

Ten seconds into *Nights in Baghdad* it is wondrously,

gloriously apparent that through the dark, swirling chaos that shrouds planet Celia, the beacon of her musical talent shines as bright as ever. The grinding, distorted power chords that blast in after a haunting Arabian intro give no doubt that her studio alchemy has produced some especially heavy metal, but of twenty-four-carat quality. From shrieking rage to whispered entreaty, Celia's voice is an extraordinary instrument, far too potent and adventurous to be kept on a tight Eurovision leash. The production is slick and distinctly more imaginative than is typical of the genre – bongos, a bit of flamenco guitar, multi-tracked fado-esque Celia harmonies.

Seeing my head bob, but hopefully not the nascent tears of relief threatening to spill down its sides, Celia pulls out my right ear phone. 'Lyric and melody,' she half-shouts, 'all mine.' I bob, smile, hold up a thumb. A mighty chord rounds the track off; I pull out the phones.

'That's great,' I say, 'that's really, really good.'

Celia seems shyly delighted. 'And it's the first time an English guy will understand my words!' she says with a beam, before launching into a track-by-track account of the album's lyrical themes. By focusing on sin, religion and 'a capital message of anger', this proves to be a backward step, a step that becomes a flying leap when Celia describes one song thus: 'This is about how I come back from the *dead people*, and I make the *sushi*! Ha ha ha!'

When she reveals that the title track is subtitled *I've Killed the Monsters Under My Bed*, I interrupt with a blurted enquiry into the album's release date. The bottom line is that there isn't one, or possibly even an interested label, though this doesn't appear to concern her too much. 'All the money I save, from advertising songs, karaoke, from Estoril casino – all has been spent on this,' she says, but with pride rather than regret. She shows me a promotional photo she's had done: Celia standing before a floodlit castle, looking like a demonic flamenco dancer in a Shakespear's Sister video – great, flouncy dress, back-combed, hip-length mane.

'Is that hair all yours?' I ask, then wish I hadn't.

'My family goes to India often, and every time I make them carry home for me much, much human hair.'

We creak slowly through the streetlit suburbs, talking about her plans for Ira. She's hoping to go to Seattle soon – 'the world's loudest city, wooh!' – in search of suitably hardcore musicians and gigs, plus maybe back to England. 'I was there in fact a few months ago, for work,' she reveals. Music work? Another of those reckless smiles; there's nothing to hide now. 'Hotel work. As a maid! But I didn't have the right papers.'

The train sighs into Entrecampos station, and off we get. A forest of roof-top neon has alerted me to a nearby plethora of hotels, but the niggling mystery of Celia's continued presence – it's nearly 10 p.m. – has yet to be resolved. 'Um . . . I'm just off to that Ibis up there,' I tell her, and Celia shrugs and says she'll walk with me, mumbling something about meeting a friend later.

Our conversation falters into a rather stilted discourse on flight times and bus numbers on the chilly, uphill walk. But as I reach towards the handle on the Ibis's glass door, Celia says, 'So – that was my life, what you see.'

I turn and thank her, for inviting me to her country, for showing me her beautiful home town, for sharing so much of her time with me. And then, because that all sounded rather crap, I tell her that her new album is fantastic, and that she's due a break, and that in spite of all her setbacks she's still doing things that everyone around – which sadly means me and the tramp zipping himself back up across the road – could only dream of, and if that's her life, then it can't be bad.

'No, not bad,' says Celia, quietly. 'More and more I try to enjoy it every day.' And with a sideways smile and a wink, she turns back down the hill.

9 May 1998
National Indoor Arena, Birmingham
Gunvor Guggisberg
Switzerland
Lass' Ihn

I sift through silver disks and pull another bonus offering from the bottom of the Andreas stack: the 1998 Swiss Eurovision qualifier. Can I face it? That I find I can is down to the heart-warming spectacle of catching a nul-pointer in happier times, on the verge of rousing victory rather than dreadful, barren defeat. Not that it's much fun to witness reigning champ Katrina Leskanich step out on-stage as the pre-vote interval act, bravely working through a rendition of – oh, have a heart – *Ding Dinge Dong*. Seven months on and for her it's come to this already.

The handsomely deserved winner, bagging a runaway 400,000 votes, is a tall, slender, corkscrew-haired brunette with beady green eyes and a shy yet minxish grin, now reprising with leather-trousered gusto the violin-accompanied torch song she's co-written with Switzerland's 1990 contestant. Gunvor Guggisberg is twenty-three, but when the result comes in she looks half that age, literally jumping up and down in unrestrained glee. It's the tenth anniversary of Céline Dion's victory; the host, a former Swiss representative herself, invokes the Wailing One's name by way of evidently favourable vocal comparison.

But of course Gunvor spectacularly fails to emulate her Canadian forebear, and six years, eight months and twenty-four days after failing to do so she sends me this electronic message:

> Hi Tim
> Thank you for your several email and your letter offer. But I don't wanna talk to you about my experiences at the Eurovision Song Contest. Hope that you understand.
> Regards,
> Gunvor

My initial response to this inbox arrival is a loud and prolonged denigration of Mittel Europa's humourless pomposity, its unappealingly stubborn reluctance to accept failure, and, while I'm about it, its stupid, mulleted popular music. After Tommy and Wilf, it's a nein-danke hat trick. What's up with these people?

I'm still not sure to this day, but by the end of that one I know precisely what's up with Gunvor Guggisberg. No Forstner cold trail for her, no sparsely fact-speckled Scheutzian wilderness. Acquiring Gunvor's postal address has involved painstaking detective work with IP address registers, but a cursory glance at the bounteous online biographies archived under her name makes it abundantly apparent that I will be making no additional efforts to track her down. A barely credible catalogue of scandal, betrayal and relentless humiliation, the Guggisberg tragedy makes Celia Lawson's seem like a skip-along nursery rhyme. Gunvor: I do understand. Regards, Tim.

Gunvor's name derives from a Scandinavian heritage: her Swedish great-great grandfather is proudly feted as the composer of that country's national anthem. Raised in Bern's mid-rise suburbs, the curly-haired toddler quickly demonstrated the genetic endurance of this musical ancestry, encouraged by her parents, both office clerks. By the age of five Gunvor was singing in school and church choirs ('from that moment I always wished to be on a stage', she said later), and soon after began to improvise precociously on the family piano. But it was as a tap dancer that she would enjoy her first taste of performing glory. Coached by mother May Gun, a frustrated ballerina, at the age of thirteen Gunvor won the Swiss championships, the first of seven national titles she would secure in this demanding yet inarguably peculiar discipline.

Her parents split when Gunvor was sixteen; she would reveal that the trauma endowed her with 'an unhealthy father complex'. Sharing a two-room apartment with her mother and younger sister, the teenage Gunvor nobly endeavoured to fill the paternal void. 'She shouldered all our problems on herself and took responsibility for the household,' May Gun recalled. 'It was too much. Really she missed out on adolescence.' The *Guardian* would later deride Gunvor as 'a middle-class tap-dancing champion', but it's clear that her journey to the stage of Birmingham's National Indoor Arena was a genuine up-by-the-boot-straps job, and not just by Swiss standards.

Supporting the family meant taking a secretarial position as soon as she left school, and by the age of twenty Gunvor was supplementing the meagre Guggisberg coffers with cocktail-bar engagements that exploited her personable charm and blossoming vocal versatility. In 1997, while working in the Air Force ministry's personnel department, she idly put her name down for Switzerland's two biggest talent shows, and rose to abrupt prominence by winning both. 'A voice such as Céline's!' trilled an excited media, not for the last time. 'Gunvor sings as a world star!'

The defence minister invited his talented employee to his office in the Upper House, serving coffee in return for a song; after Gunvor was dutifully selected for the forthcoming 1998 national Eurovision qualifier, he issued a public statement affectionately wishing her well and pledging telephone votes from every extension in the ministry.

So far, so Celia. Just two months separate the pair; Gunvor's youth is arrestingly underlined in an interview during which she names her childhood Eurovision hero as Johnny Logan. Like Celia she entered the contest without a professional recording to her name, and like her was chaperoned through the procedure by an elder Eurovision statesman: electro-fiddle under his chin, Switzerland's 1990 entrant Egon Egemann would stand beside Gunvor on the Birmingham stage as she sang the song they'd written together. Music by Egon, words by Gunvor: her lyric to *Lass' Ihn* (*Leave It*, in the *Sweeney*-esque Google translation) was a pack-your-bags ultimatum to a recidivist philanderer.

Perhaps by coincidence, Gunvor celebrated victory by swiftly binning her then boyfriend. No less blunt was the resignation letter dispatched shortly afterwards to the ministry. Her cheer-leading colleagues' disappointment was soon upgraded to embittered alienation when, in an interview with leading tabloid *Blick*, she described herself as 'overqualified' for her old job.

Blick had earlier declared Gunvor their artist of the year, and as the Eurovision final approached, the association between the pair grew ever closer. It was *Blick* for whom Gunvor posed with her new boyfriend ('With Michi it was love at first sight!' she gushed, flashing the ring he had given her on Valentine's Day), *Blick* again who bagged the exclusive on Gunvor's new job as a PA to her manager, Rolf Egli ('I'm so lucky: which other singers can stand on the stage and at the same time see behind the window blinds of the music industry?!')

Eager and indiscreet, Gunvor was a tabloid interviewer's dream subject; by April the fresh-faced Swiss everygirl was an almost daily fixture in *Blick*'s colourful pages. Proudly welcoming its photographer into her new flat, 'a romantic three-room oasis in Bern, with garden and mini pool', the singer confided that she'd jumped a long queue of potential buyers 'because the owners are fans of mine'. *Blick*'s readers knew her favourite designers, her little sister's name, Michi's golf handicap. They knew of her cocksure ambition ('the people who selected me for Birmingham will buy my record – of course

I'll be in the charts'), and her gigglingly confessed consumerist extravagance ('I like kir royal, Versace, my black Lancia – and I'm a shoe fetishist!'). If all this seemed sweetly inauspicious, then so did the paper's chortling coverage of 'Gunvor's most embarrassing moment', when the year before the singer's dress had fallen off during a church-hall performance of *Miss Saigon*.

As a licensed purveyor of Alpine tittle-tattle, it is tempting to imagine the editor of *Blick* dutifully processing approved press releases from the ministry of gossip; not for this well-ordered, sternly bureaucratic nation the loose-cannon nastiness of our tabloid press. But as diplomats, refugees and visiting motorists have long been aware, it never pays to second-guess the Swiss. It's as well to remember that the cradle of civic obedience is also the country that less than 100 years ago prosecuted a dog for conspiracy to murder. As Churchill nearly said about something else, Switzerland is a riddle wrapped in a mystery inside an enigma, stuffed up the back of a cuckoo clock and punted into the fondue.

With the benefit of hindsight and an enormous internet archive, it's possible to detect subtle portents of the astonishingly brutal assault *Blick* was preparing to launch against Gunvor. Almost every profile, questionnaire and interview they published was snidely embedded with undermining revelations: that the singer had proactively begun marketing her Eurovision release amongst work colleagues, 'already selling five copies'; that the sponsorship she frequently boasted of securing had yet to extend beyond four pairs of Fogal socks and a discounted Nokia phone; that in a celebrity general-knowledge quiz, Gunvor had failed to name the incumbent Swiss president.

With Eurovision less than two weeks away, *Blick* turned up the gas. '150,000Fr debts!' yelled their front-page splash. 'The vulture of bankruptcy circles over Gunvor!' Over page after gleeful page the details of her ruinous extravagance were laid bare: the 20,000SFr she still owed for her Lancia, the water bed, and above all, the shoes. In a single visit to the Nobel footwear emporium in Bern, Gunvor had acquired shoes and leather accessories to the value of 3,530SFr (which may be more familiar to you as £1,500). And all without paying: 'When I asked for a financial guarantee to secure the goods on thirty-day credit,' said Nobel's manager, 'she just told me, "I am Gunvor," and walked out.' Two months after the credit deadline, the shop contacted Gunvor's management to insist on full payment or the return of all purchases. A few days later an anonymous gentleman scurried in, dropped two bags on the Nobel counter and scurried out. Inside, the manager found several pairs of graphically abused shoes and a note: 'Unfortunately my new puppy has a taste for footwear,' wrote Gunvor, 'and the leather jacket is currently in my sister's possession. As for the Divina boots, with all the exposure I've given them you should be paying me!'

By hallowed tabloid tradition, *Blick* had forewarned Gunvor of their destructive revelations, offering to soft-pedal on the more lurid details should she oblige them with a quote or two. The singer later recalled tearfully begging the paper to hold fire until after Eurovision, and the 'responsibility to their readers' that they regretfully explained made this impossible. So it was that the story came embellished with the self-flagellatory whimperings of its victim: 'I needed dresses for my appearances, and there was a new home to furnish . . . I made some big mistakes, but I now want to pay back all my debts.' Ralf Egli, fighting the first of many rearguard actions, told *Blick* that his client had signed an agreement with a civic-appointed auditor, handing over responsibility for her finances. The story was rounded off with a quote from the defiant May Gun: 'I will always stand by my daughter.'

It's tempting to imagine a Swiss citizen could suffer no shame greater than that of ruin through financial imprudence, but Gunvor set off for Birmingham grimly aware that worse – a lot worse – was still to come. The details *Blick* had withheld under the deal brokered to secure her craven co-operation would emerge sooner or later, and with Gunvor's participation in the world's most widely watched cultural event now just days away, it was always going to be sooner.

'"When Gunvor let her blouse slip open," said erotic photographer Juerg Wyss, 59, "all inhibitions disappeared!"' Thus read the caption below one of the many sanitised 'hot sex photos' with which *Blick* illustrated its sensational 3 May lead, one whose lavish prurience would teach me the German for crotchless knickers. The events Wyss described had taken place over eighteen months previously, yet being Swiss, the raddled pornographer was able to confirm that he had taken precisely 1,878 photographs of Gunvor, then an unknown secretary. 'She said she wanted to be a model in case the music didn't work out,' read a slack-jawed nation as its muesli congealed. 'Gunvor had definite erotic talent – and after it was over she sang for me.'

Blick had evidently been sitting on this story for months; it's likely that the profoundly odious Wyss had approached them straight after Gunvor's triumph at the qualifiers. All the inane at-home puff-pieces they'd run had successfully established the singer as the nation's lilywhite sweetheart; their association with her followed the classic build-them-up, knock-them-down tabloid parabola.

So shocking were the revelations that some feared Switzerland would be expelled from Eurovision. One worried paper contacted the EBU, securing an assurance that an artist's private life was of no bureaucratic concern. 'As long as the song is less than three minutes long,' said an EBU spokeswoman, 'we don't care who sings it.' No doubt she'd said as much to the rather larger number of journalists keen to establish the official position on Israeli entrant Dana International, the extravagantly cleavaged transsexual whose presence – and subsequent victory – would confine the Gunvor-gate fall-out to Switzerland's well-guarded borders.

The day after, *Blick* carried Gunvor's account of her evening in Herr Wyss's glamorous studio (his garage). 'I met this man at a bar,' she said. 'He said he was a friend of Claudia Schiffer, and that I would be perfect for a jeans advertisement he had been commissioned to photograph. At the studio he said he would need to see my back for the advert, and then . . . well, Adam and Eve also came naked into the world.'

On the morning of the final, after months of careful scene-setting and ground preparation, *Blick* triumphantly let loose the devastating final salvo of Operation Gunvor. The headline: 'Our Euro girl – lady of pleasure in uptown brothel!' It was the most appalling work of Eurovision sabotage since an Oslo gentleman's outfitter rummaged through his braces drawer muttering, 'Well, if it's a *really* stretchy pair you're after, Mr Teigen . . .'

In the mere act of taking to the National Indoor Arena stage that evening, Gunvor proved herself a woman of extraordinary mettle. In a quiet year, perhaps it would have been too much to ask; mercifully, the 1998 contest had needed no help from her to prove itself the most controversial Eurovision in decades. Dana International arrived in Birmingham with death threats from Israel's outraged ultra-orthodox fanatics ringing in her neatly sculpted ears; she was installed in the city's only bullet-proof hotel room, and outside it was chaperoned by armed guards. The speculation around this dainty creation was predictably repetitive. Had she ever been a man? Yes. Could she actually sing? No, but we didn't know that yet, and even when we did it wouldn't stop her winning. What did Ireland's doe-eyed country girl think of this hormone-hungry castrato who had hijacked her name? Not much: the voice behind *All Kinds of Everything* had herself shaved two years off her age at the 1970 Eurovision, and performed there under a name she hadn't born with. If Yaron Cohen had done his homework properly, the 1998 Eurovision title would have been awarded to Rosemary International.

To Gunvor's advantage, the few press-moths not drawn to Dana International's billion-watt presence flittered instead around schlager-clown Guildo Horn, a balding, velveteen twerp whose overbearing tomfoolery proved of tireless fascination to the German-speaking press. In astounding consequence, few non-Swiss guests and commentators seemed aware of the stinking, fly-blown scandals piling up outside Gunvor's dressing room. Even Terry Wogan maintained a tactful silence; perhaps as co-compere that year he felt constrained to rein in the *schadenfreude*.

It would be unfair, though, to over-estimate these consolations. Five months before, 400,000 of her countrymen had cheerfully nominated Gunvor as the sweet-voiced bearer of their Eurovision flame; now all those, and seven million others, were tuning in to gawp at a bankrupt topless model who had 'fulfilled male desires around the clock' at two Bern massage parlours. Her career in the private booths of the Roman Bath and Bolero 'sauna clubs' had in fact lasted no more than three weeks back at the end of 1996, yet the managers of both establishments proved able to dredge up fond and detailed accounts of their former employee.

'Gunvor was a natural,' said one, 'she made a lot of money here.' 'The guests really enjoyed it when she sang for them,' recalled the other, 'naked, as God created her.' This time, there was of course no quote from the singer. 'And what does Gunvor have to say to these latest revelations?' smirked *Blick* in the final paragraph. '"We have no comment," says her manager Rolf Egli.'

The horribly depressing truth that emerged later was this: having billed her a monstrous 33,000SFr for his professional services, the ever thoughtful Juerg Wyss suggested a remunerative solution to the tearful Gunvor. 'He actually drove me to the Roman Bath,' she would reveal. 'It was December – I was singing in the church in the early evening, then going off to the sauna clubs . . . I told my mother all about it on Christmas Day.'

Gunvor was out fifth on the Birmingham stage, wearing a dress that proved this latest and most awful revelation had caught her off-guard. Elementary image management demanded something chaste and demure; instead, here she was in a slash-thighed, sheer-chested blood-red number, one of the raciest outfits yet seen on a Eurovision stage. 'Gunvor in *that* dress,' ran one online reminiscence. 'She rehearsed before the Press Conference, and we noticed it was transparent – you could see her dark underwear.' In Andreas-vision, it seems worse than that: either those are rosebuds embroidered on the fabric, or she isn't wearing a bra. Whichever, it wasn't helping her case.

Looking a little distracted, but less nervous than many rival performers, Gunvor somehow summons up a capable performance. Muted, yes – she doesn't work herself up to the Gloria Gaynor levels of furious defiance scaled in her post-victory reprise at the qualifier – but in tune and in time. 'Her singing wasn't completely clean,' said a former Swiss contestant. Said another: 'The gloss in Gunvor's eyes was missing for me.' But in saying so to *Blick*, both rather undermined their own critical significance. To my eyes, and certainly my ears, *Lass' Ihn*'s chief disadvantage as a Eurosong was less to do with Gunvor's performance than with beardy Egon's indulgently ruminative violin solo.

Four slots after Gunvor, the contest, as a spectacle, is over. By then we've already had Dana International's approximate disco warbling, and the cavorting histrionics that compel Guildo Horn to scale the scoreboard gantry and leap off-stage to pump his groin at some poor old dear in the front row – oh, look: it's Katie Boyle.

Guildo's presence – and solid seventh place – was brokered on the dark side of democracy. This was the first year of near universal televoting, in both national qualifiers and the final proper: Herr Horn's selection as Germany's representative was due less to his lamely appalling song than a vote-Guildo campaign stirred up by DJs of the 'I'm a loony, me' school. The nation's extensive community of non-ironists were appalled and ashamed, expressing fears – or hopes – that in failing to understand why it was funny to call your backing group the Orthopaedic Stockings ('It's because they support me'), the televoters of rival nations would send Guildo home without a point. In response, Guildo's studenty fanbase pledged to cross borders in order to cast their televotes for Germany, an oath widely held responsible for the maximum points awarded to him by Holland and Switzerland. Those Germans with memories of their 1933 general election should have known better than anyone that giving people the vote doesn't guarantee they'll use it wisely.

Terry introduces the pre-interval show – an orchestral

medley, which the audience can't know is the last live music that will ever be played on a Eurovision stage, though if you'd announced that as the colliery band struck up there might have been cheers. Ulrika Jonsson takes charge of the voting, and does so without passing comment on Gunvor's unfolding fate – not even when fellow stragglers Greece, to uncouth audience jeers, bag the only points they'll get (that'll be twelve) from Cyprus. Nor are there any sightings of her in the Dana-dominated green room; it's only as I watch the parrot-feathered Ms International step back on-stage to a household cavalry fanfare (boom: we've just blasted through the camp barrier) that the grim resonance of Gunvor's fate tolls out. Somehow, her nul points had seemed almost pre-ordained, the logically dismal conclusion of all that's gone before. But of course it wasn't – going out to perform *Lass' Ihn*, she'd have been thinking: I can still turn this round. A good performance here, a decent score, and I can go home with my head held high. Sod it, I might even win. That'll show the bastards.

'Zero points and rock-bottom for Switzerland,' mourned a Zurich broadsheet the next morning. 'A debacle, which happened last thirty-one years ago in Vienna.' The more considered press were blaming the result on their nation's isolationism: 'We're not in the EU – no one loves us,' was the heading above one editorial.

Blick, of course, spun it rather differently: 'At the end, Gunvor stood there naked.' 'Thank heavens we have better ambassadors for our nation,' announced the Christian Democrats' press spokesman, going on to namecheck a list of Swiss cyclists who two months later were all thrown out of the Tour de France in the race's worst ever drug scandal.

When Gunvor landed at Zurich airport the following afternoon, a huge press crowd lay in wait, along with a handful of fans holding aloft bottles of champagne. 'For *her*?' responded one to a journalist. 'Don't be ridiculous – this is for Egon!' The violinist and Rolf pushed their trolleys through the arrivals-hall ruck, dispensing dutiful thoughts on their nation's status as 'friendless outsiders in a united Europe'; Gunvor, with her mother but minus Michi (the tabloids had already been linking the singer with Damian, one of her backing vocalists), eventually emerged to mumble a token civility before being sped away in a waiting car. 'No sign of her vamp behaviour,' crowed *Blick*, 'just a scared young deer!'

Ditched by Michi, Gunvor moved back to her mother's flat and considered signing up for the army. But not for long: three days later, having consulted the hapless, hopeless Rolf on how best to resurrect her showbiz career, she appeared on a TV chat-show to set the record straight. It was not a success. Recklessly attempting to put an upbeat gloss on her sauna-club career, she claimed to a startled host to have enjoyed the experience: 'My boyfriend had just left me, and I was having a lot of one-night stands. I wanted to be a rebel, to prove I had no inhibitions. Having sex with married men at these clubs was not unpleasant.' When asked why in that case she'd lasted only three weeks, Gunvor responded that the management had sacked her 'for exceeding the time limit with clients'. 'In other words,' concluded next morning's *Blick*, 'her men were enjoying more sex than they had paid for!'

The result at Birmingham had already spawned the odd works-better-in-German joke (What's the difference between Gunvor and ladybird? The ladybird has more points); the three million Swiss who played the national card game Jass were abbreviating a void round as 'a Gunvor'. The non-*Blick* media had proved generally compassionate – many papers referred to her by default as 'poor Gunvor' – but after her disastrous, sympathy-sapping chat-show performance, the gloves came off.

One paper ran an interview with an unnamed associate who claimed the lyrics to *Lass' Ihn* were inspired by the night Gunvor came home early to find her boyfriend in bed with another man. The Roman Bath manager came forward to deny sacking Gunvor on the grounds she had stated: 'It was three days before this girl took her first client,' he now remembered, 'and we asked her to leave because she did not correspond to our concept of beauty.' Just three weeks before, the worst crisis

Gunvor had faced involved a jocular reprimand from Rolf for dyeing her hair without his permission. Now here she was, being publicly branded too ugly to shag old men in a massage parlour.

The feeding frenzy was now gnawing her down to the bone. On 24 May the papers reported that Gunvor and a male associate had been ejected from a Bern nightclub, having racially abused a Spanish waiter and refused to pay their drinks bill. 'I don't understand her attitude,' said the Rock'n Eat's deputy manager. 'We had Bonnie Tyler in once, and she was no trouble.' On 28 May, two policemen who pulled a black Lancia over found that its infamous driver possessed only a learner's licence; four days afterwards it emerged that Gunvor had escaped from a similar situation weeks before using a full permit borrowed with menaces from one of her Eurovision backing singers. 'Gunvor said that if I didn't co-operate, she wouldn't let me go to Birmingham,' said Sandra Heusser. 'Now I want nothing more to do with her.'

For certain sections of Swiss society, this documentation-related motoring infringement was the unforgivable last straw. Tabloid voyeurism made way for broadsheet indignation: 'No money, no underwear, no driving licence,' began one editorial, 'the Birmingham Nullnummer is a Barbie of bad taste, infecting us all with the trash virus.' The considered journal *Weltwoche* ran a 150-line article on 'the Gunvor phenomenon': 'the story of a publicity addict who has become a national celebrity, though not in the way she had hoped'.

At this point Gunvor would have been well advised to essay a little dignified silence. But she was never well advised. Rolf, clearly a graduate of the 'no such thing as bad publicity' school of PR, proudly announced that Gunvor had turned down an offer from *Playboy*, thereby encouraging 'sex king' Patrik Stoeckli to nab some cheap column inches by promising Gunvor a 500,000SFr contract to make five porn films. Soon after, Rolf put her up for another chat-show, where in a sob-racked interview she confessed that Juerg Wyss had compelled her to perform a sexual act upon him before their photo shoot.

The host waited for her shoulders to stop shaking, then barked, 'So was that oral, or a hand job?'

By late June Gunvor had lost so much weight that she was compelled to deny whispers of an eating disorder, and – when the press began to rumour it – a suicide attempt. Yet all the while Rolf was plotting her comeback. In the middle of July Gunvor fulfilled her first post-Eurovision public engagement, firing the starter's pistol at the Davos Uphill Inline Skating final. A week later, her manager announced that Gunvor's new single would be released to coincide with a major concert at the Zurich Civic Centre on 24 July.

Extraordinarily, the gig was organised in co-operation with *Blick*, who promoted it on an eager daily basis. 'After tears at the television: *Blick* lets Gunvor sing!' One can only hope she understood that in doing so, the paper was merely hosing her name down prior to dragging it back through the mud. Perhaps, then, there was some grim satisfaction for her in the concert's crushing commercial failure. 'Gunvor and a sophisticated light and laser show – 1,300 tickets already sold!' trumpeted *Blick* on 23 July, but, in fact, of the crowd that half-filled the hall the night afterwards, all but 114 had been let in for free. Loud and heartfelt cheers greeted Gunvor's rendition of *Lass' Ihn*, though these trickled to polite applause as she ran through a cover of Bryan Adam's *Everything I Do . . .* and followed this with *My Way*, in French. The finale was her new single, the Egon-penned *Money Makes*, whose opening chords released a snowfall of 'Gunvor dollars' on the mildly curious audience. Some picked up on the bravely jocular reference to her ongoing financial troubles, but few cared: *Money Makes* joined *Lass' Ihn* in failing to make the Swiss charts.

By the end of the summer, Gunvor was touring the provinces with her mum and a tape deck, doing twenty-minute karaoke-style slots in 'sausage tents' at rural beer festivals. A journalist from highbrow weekly *Das Magazin* compiled an almost unbearably melancholic diary of a week spent in her company on this demeaning circuit. Gunvor emerges as a damp-eyed picture of total isolation, either ignored by half-drunk audiences or assaulted with hostile jeers and whistles. Her nails are bitten to the quick; she conducts a local-radio interview as if each question 'was a tooth being pulled without anaesthetic'. When her mother erects a table and stocks it with CDs and T-shirts, the boorish inebriates who wander up are interested only in having their bare thighs autographed: 'Fighting against the tears, Gunvor does as they demand.' A quiet, polite chap who then approaches her identifies himself as an evangelist, offering to save her soul.

The deepest depths are plumbed at a local football-stadium engagement, where she's obliged to sing *Happy Birthday* to a leering skinhead as his friends wave a banner that reads, 'GUNVOR – YOU HOT SOW!' 'People now just see me as a joke, a cheap joke,' she blankly tells the journalist afterwards. 'I'm more than ashamed. I hate myself.'

Autumn incorporated another Rolf-plotted relaunch as a cabaret performer, one so disastrously ineffectual that hardly anyone noticed. Soon after, veteran film-maker Paul Riniker made contact: the eventual consequence was a documentary entitled *Gunvor – A Media History*, compiled from three weeks of footage and broadcast prime-time, on the main state channel, just before Christmas.

'I've made forty-six documentaries,' complained Riniker at the press launch, 'but this was my most difficult. Gunvor didn't want to say anything – my questions were usually longer than her answers.' Riniker decided this reticence was the result of Gunvor's immaturity, though I'd be more tempted to point the finger at his insistence on taking her back to the Birmingham National Indoor Arena for the film's opening sequence. Four months after Eurovision, there she is weeping alone on an empty stage.

'It was a terrible feeling,' she said in a later press interview. 'Afterwards I spoke to no one for weeks, and prayed to God to let an airplane fall on me.' The week before she'd walked out of a chat-show after the host introduced her as 'a tart'.

A year on from Eurovision, she was still single, living at home, and struggling to see off her creditors with an eighteen-hour working day that encompassed office temping and tap-dance instruction. But Rolf was still on the scene, telling anyone who'd listen that Gunvor would soon be back like they'd never seen her before. In May she appeared on TV, with straightened hair and a sombre white trouser suit, singing an 'ethno ballad' that would be her third and final single. 'Eurovision and all that is in the past,' she told the host afterwards. 'I have sung away the pain.'

Rolf had pre-released *Land of Fantasy* under an assumed name to sidestep prejudgement, but it hardly helped. 'For the third time in one year the singer has a new image,' said one of the few critics to pass comment, 'but the Gunvor brand has already been smashed beyond repair.' Two years too late, Rolf found himself a client short.

Gunvor took a job in telesales, with after-hours earnings still largely derived from clicky toe-heel instruction; even at a reduced booking rate of 800SFr few live-music venues expressed interest, and her vocal performances were restricted to no-fee charity concerts. In a rare interview she downgraded her showbiz ambitions, expressing a hope to sing at 'big hotels', but by Christmas 1999 found herself doing matinées as a tap-dancing harlequin at Zurich's Circus Conelli. A year later, by now PA to a customer-service manager, she suddenly released her debut CD, 'From A to Z', with a chin-in-hands cover photo that revived her girl-next-door pre-Eurovision image. 'Does anyone still remember Gunvor?' ran a rare review. Negligible sales provided the answer.

In March 2001, a court in Bern found Juerg Wyss guilty of sexual offences against minors, living off immoral earnings, extortion, drink-driving and failing to provide a blood test. No commentators appeared to find his thirty-month sentence inadequate, though plenty grumbled at the 2,000SFr awarded in damages to one of the plaintiffs, a Ms G. Guggisberg. Such sentiments were perhaps behind the story that *Blick* ran three months later, headlined 'Gunvor again in the sex environment'.

A retread of their two-year-old scoops – split-crotch pants, 'diseased purchase behaviour' – the piece was freshened up with the questionable testimony of a 'Michelle', who claimed to have recently worked with Gunvor in a Zurich brothel. 'She told me this sideline of hers had to be kept secret, which was why she always wore a wig.' The story's half-hearted tone aptly reflected its subject's waning tabloid appeal: *Blick* was poking around the cemetery of its victims' reputations, kicking corpses in the hope that one might twitch. Hers didn't. When in 2004 Gunvor finally filed for bankruptcy, *Blick* satisfied itself with a single paragraph headed, 'Singer with sex past goes broke'.

These days Gunvor works as a marketing coordinator for an international food company, unsuccessfully auditioning for the odd musical, accepting weekend bookings to entertain wedding guests. Her last recorded public pronouncement came after Switzerland managed the unprecedented feat of scoring nul points at the 2004 Eurovision semi-final, the abysmal nadir of a run of post-Gunvor form that has seen them fail to finish higher than twentieth, relegated every time they've competed. 'We Swizzerians just have to accept that we do not have a lot of friends in Europe,' she said. If the way they treat their own is anything to go by, you can hardly blame us.

24 May 2003
Skonto Olympic Arena, Riga
Jemini
United Kingdom
Cry Baby

The two-carriage Sprinter strains desperately towards its modest design tolerances, running scared through the bedrizzled badlands. Embankments dense with upturned sofas, stations brutalised beyond identification, mossy asbestos lean-tos and cooling towers: head against rattling window, I watch the post-industrial north-west slide and flick drearily by. It's the last leg of a journey that began at the Skonto Arena in the Latvian capital on a Saturday very nearly two years before, when ORF's commentator, adopting the throaty, sensationalist tone of a voiceover artist flogging a Judas Priest compilation on MTV Europe, welcomed two blond youngsters on to the stage with a roar: 'Jemini – *aus Liverpool*!'

The gaps between wet-bricked terraces diminish; the train slows. These streets produced the greatest talents in popular music history, and a football club that has raised aloft the European Cup as often as all its English rivals combined. Marry the twin elements of this gilded civic heritage and enter a

European pop contest: surely the opposition might as well not bother turning up. How, how, could the seeds of Eurovision disaster have been planted here?

I was in a Spanish hotel room that night in 2003, but preoccupied by a sink full of lathery underpants and a vocally restless donkey out in the back yard, I never even turned the telly on. Events in Riga were only brought to my attention at breakfast the following morning, by a German couple I'd got talking to at dinner.

'I am sorry for UK,' said the husband, looking anything but.

'Ooro-vision,' explained his wife, her face pouches taut with painfully restrained amusement. 'Zero points!'

I'd subsequently read and heard many accounts of the two minutes, forty-nine seconds that followed the ORF chap's dramatic introduction, but witnessed no more than a website snippet until Andreas entered my life. Even forewarned, the experience proved more literally agonising than any previous Eurovision encounter.

In their pre-performance filmette, Gemma Abbey and Chris Cromby seemed the winning essence of chirpy Scousedom, merrily interacting with Riga's stunt-cyclists and skateboarders. A handsome pair, too, whichever way you looked at them – as the rowdy audience cheers faded and the camera swept up to the festival of flesh that was Gemma's rear aspect, stubbled faces from Bucharest to Ballymurphy must have creased in unwholesome lust. The frontal view revealed once the flamenco guitarist had wound up his intro was no disappointment either; if, at that point, a Latvian technician had elbowed his coffee into the PA fuse box, we'd all remember *Cry Baby* as a pleasantly choreographed instrumental. Instead, when Gemma parted those delicate, glistening lips, what came out was the worst noise heard on a Eurovision stage in the contest's forty-seven-year history.

So raw and tender is this memory that dredging it up as the train eases into its terminus causes a peculiar shrinkage of the neck, as if my shoulders are in vain reflex trying to cover my ears. But it's too late. The sound is in my head, and now here come the moving pictures to go with it; perhaps they will never leave. In a moment that lays vicious waste to the theory that it is always possible to judge a nul-pointer with the sound turned off, Gemma launches her voice a good half an octave shy of the urgent bass line that is her sole accompaniment. A continent puckers in agony; it's like having your dental cavities plugged with wire wool. No aerial splits or bar stools, no daft trousers or sex scandals – this is a straightforward case of nil by mouth.

Those pretty eyes dart and flicker, betraying an awareness that something is terribly, terribly awry; yet in trying to find her way back to the elusive melody, Gemma sets off in the wrong direction. For thirty toe-curling, tone-curdling seconds 500 million Europeans listen through hand-muffled ears as that young voice soars and swoops through a mercilessly exposed musical landscape, not so much off-key as off-keyboard, a desperate cat's chorus howled through spreading cracks in a fixed smile. It's only when Chris joins in that an approximation of tonal authority is restored. He does his best to erase the memory of what we have just endured, bouncing manically around, grinning his little Scouse head off, shouting 'C'mon, Latvia!' between verses. Not too little, perhaps, but much too late.

Only five times has the UK finished outside the top ten, but as drunkenly wayward applause gives way to footage of Ukraine's Olexandr duking it out with the trams of Riga in a yellow Porsche, even Terry Wogan must be aware that la Royaume Uni has just witnessed a performance certain to trump Nicki French's portentously titled *Don't Play That Song Again*, 16th in 2000, as its worst ever. By the time Lorraine Kelly appears two-thirds of the way through the voting to deliver the results of the UK tele-jury, the crash-and-burn Doomsday scenario is already beckoning. Her gentle voice steeled with Dunkirk spirit, Lorraine defiantly raises a half-empty glass of fizz and rasps, 'But we're still determined to have a wonderful night!'

My phone rings as I step on to the Lime Street platform. It's Jemini's manager, Alan McCarthy, calling as agreed. 'I'm in a black Jag,' he says, endowing both nouns with a throaty Scouse denouement, 'just out near the taxis.'

Relief that the pair still enjoyed professional representation had not survived my second conversation with Alan. 'You've got to take their current circumstances into account,' he'd begun, reporting back on attempts to persuade his clients to agree to a meeting: having inaugurated his relationship with the pair deep in the post-Riga depths, he was clearly cutting their cloth accordingly. 'Gemma's working in a car showroom, and the lad's in a clothes shop, so their first question was: how much is he paying?' Alarm melted into something approaching pity as Alan then answered this awkward enquiry himself. 'If you were happy to come up to Liverpool, a couple of hundred quid should swing it.'

'We are Merseysound,' stated the stark homepage of Alan's management company. 'WHO ARE YOU?' Here I am, in a city of grudge-bearing finger-pointers, trying to loosen reluctant tongues with cash. Tightening my grip on the ten sweaty twenties stuffed deep in my coat pocket I scan the taxi rank for the author of this unsettling challenge, and the decaying gangster mobile suggested by his description. A hand waves in tentative welcome from the only black car without a yellow light on its roof. A Jaguar it is, but a spotless convertible of very recent vintage.

A dapper, lightly bearded chap of late middle years with a diamond stud in his left lobe, the Alan McCarthy who drives me into a gated dockside development shares nothing with the lairy chancer of my imagination. On the short journey from Lime Street he'd described Merseysound as almost a hobby, a colourful escape from his evidently very successful day jobs as a sales-technique guru and 'contract negotiator'. 'A million dollars always seems to be the magic figure,' said Alan of this latter role, one that sees him travel the world brokering deals between component suppliers and manufacturers. 'If I can squeeze a contract above that level, there's a cut in it for me.'

Welcoming me into a plush marina pied-à-terre – after a life spent in Liverpool his family has recently relocated to the Midlands – Alan proves himself significantly more charming than must be typical in his line of work. Over cans of bitter we discuss at fond length our shared love of the Beatles, during which it emerges that Simon O'Brien, a friend of mine mentioned in relation to his domestic proximity to John Lennon's Quarry Bank school, is Alan's brother-in-law. When the entryphone buzzes, it's almost an unwanted intrusion.

After many unsettling encounters with shadows of a distant televised youth, it's odd to shake hands with such perfectly preserved nul-pointers. Fresh of face and bright of eye, Gemma's simple comeliness is undiminished; give or take a little extra forehead on display beneath those artfully distressed fringe spikes, the Chris who bounds up to greet me is the one who leapt about the Skonto Arena. Less than two years have elapsed since that devastating night in Latvia – is it really fair to pick away at a scar that might not yet have healed? The new bulge in Alan's wallet assures me it is.

Chris and Gemma accept a lager each and sit on the sofa facing out across the fat brown Mersey mudflats; Alan and I take our places on its opposite twin. 'Well, OK,' I begin, awkwardly uncertain how to tackle the novelty of a nul-point pair, but also aware that the meter's already running. 'So, um, what was the musical background in your families?'

Their voluble response to this feeble opener correctly suggests that in terms of words per quid, I'll do pretty well for myself in the hours ahead. Chris talks engagingly of a recent discovery that his father had once worked the Liverpool clubs as a compere, with a sideline in Sinatra/Elvis covers; Gemma fondly recalls her mother's vocal performance on that doyen of talent shows, *Opportunity Knocks*. 'And I always used to watch Eurovision as a kid,' she adds, unprompted. 'I remember asking my mum how you got in to do it, to represent your country, and it's just weird that we ended up doing it.'

Chris lays no claim to a similar heritage. 'Well, I cried my eyes out when Sonia came second,' he giggles, 'but then she was a Scouser.' Later, it emerges that he didn't realise Cliff and Lulu were already established stars when they appeared at Eurovision. But then why should he? *Devil Woman* came out six years before Chris was born; even in 1993, when Sonia had him in tears, he was only eleven. Having lived all their young lives in the era of Terry-tainted teasing, these two are simply too young to remember a time when Eurovision was taken seriously.

The pair met at a local variety-theatre stage school, the Starlite near Everton, and by thirteen they were touring Liverpool's pubs and clubs with the academy's kids' roadshow. 'We were doing Motown covers, and all the big showstoppers,' says Chris, 'playing gigs every weekend, for two years. You can't beat that sort of experience. Plus Gem and I became best mates.' I'd always assumed theirs was a combination manufactured purely for Eurovision; watching them titter and nudge each other in childhood reminiscence, it's clear that their long friendship would have been a comfort in the aftermath of Riga – Seyyal Taner and Locomotif aside, Jemini are the only non-solo nul-pointers. (Friendship is all it was: long before he confirms it with a rundown of the clubs that are his regular hangouts, it's apparent that Chris is not a ladies' man. As one of four brothers raised in a terraced house in the Dingle – one of the toughest suburbs in a city that hosts many – his must have been a challenging adolescence.)

They put their first band together having left college at sixteen: 'Chris, me and this other girl,' remembers Gemma, 'working with loads of songwriters, and doing our own stuff for a while, putting showcases on and doing gigs.' Having rather stupidly not yet decoded its 'Gem and I' derivation, I ask if they were then known as Jemini; Chris embarks on a merry, boisterously Scouse saga that begins with him sitting on a fridge, then somehow breaking it, and naming the band Tricity in its honour.

As a threesome they gigged around the north-west, earning enough to buy their own gear, but the search for more lucrative employment drove Gemma to fulfil solo residences at holiday parks, crowned by a two-week stint at a resort in Lanzarote. 'Top place: five-star,' she says, a little defensively.

By late 2002, both now nineteen and established as a duo, the pair took it as just a workaday session job – 'another day, another song', in Gemma's words – when Martin Isherwood phoned one evening to ask their help in recording 'an idea he'd had for Eurovision'. They'd worked on Isherwood projects many times before: as a multi-tasker who combined studio work and band promotion with a conspicuous role as head of music at Paul McCartney's Liverpool Institute of Performing Arts, he was a major player in the regional pop scene. Isherwood had some years previously become the first student in the land to complete a degree in songwriting and sound recording; by 2003, his compositions had already made the final stages of *A Song for Europe* three times. The melody for *Cry Baby* had come to him on a train journey from Manchester to Liverpool; arriving at Lime Street he'd run straight into a phone box, dialled home and hummed the tune into his answer machine.

'It was all a bit rushed,' remembers Gemma. 'The deadline for entries was the next afternoon, so we had to do it all in a day, from scratch.' What did they think of it? The two exchange a silent, shifty glance. 'We thought it was a bit cheesy, really,' mumbles Gemma; clearly the song encapsulated by its promoters as 'a slice of pure, infectious, disco-driven pop' didn't really do it for her, and two years on she's finally allowed to say so.

'I remember when we got in the car after the session,' says Chris, 'I said, how did that go again? And we couldn't remember. To be honest we didn't think about the song again until Martin called back in February to tell us we were down to the last eight.'

'Oh my God,' says Gemma, widening her eyes in exhilarated recollection. 'That was an *amazing* moment.' Whisking through the first radio-based elimination, on 2 March they found themselves live in the BBC studio, waiting in the wings as Terry Wogan introduced *Cry Baby* as one of the four *Song For Europe* finalists.

The BBC had invited along the UK's three most recent winners, and it's significant that only one of these had carried off the title in Chris and Gemma's lifetime. Perhaps significant too was their backstage encounter with Katrina Leskanich. 'She said Eurovision was the worst thing she had ever done in her life,' says Chris, with a humourless, thanks-for-that smile. My attempts to defend Katrina, with mention of that pride-pummelling pre-vote rendition of *Ding Dinge Dong* at the 1998 Swiss qualifier, prove counterproductive – the pair nod flatly, clearly thinking: What, and that's worse than a sodding car showroom?

'That was a good time, the best time,' says Chris, fiddling with a thigh pocket on his baggy combat trousers. 'Those *X-Factor* and *Pop Idol* shows, it builds up for weeks, but all this has happened to us in days.' Gemma shakes her head – I notice only now that her hair is appreciably darker than before – still awed at the fame and opportunity so abruptly foisted upon them, and perhaps at the shocking brutality with which it was all snatched away. 'We thought that was it, we really did. We thought we were made.' A Scouser isn't often lost for words; I drain my ale as their gaze settles out of the window behind me, somewhere out there amongst the estuary mud and gasometers.

Seeing his young charges in distress, Alan embarks on a long, soothing treatise upon Eurovision's commercial and artistic irrelevance in the MTV world, making all the right noises about festivals of kitsch. 'Yeah,' says Chris, still scanning the desolate horizon, 'but you still want to win it.'

In the breathless two months that followed *A Song For Europe*, Jemini went on the road to support *Pop Idol* star Darius, lip-synched *Cry Baby* on *CD:UK* and *Top of the Pops*, hit the studio to record an album for post-Eurovision release and signed up with Atomic Kitten's management company (in the Reykjavik-esque city-village that Liverpool clearly is, I'm hardly surprised to learn of Chris's pre-existing friendship with the band).

Arriving in Riga to take on the hapless buffoons that a lifetime of Woganism had groomed them to expect, they must have felt almost over-prepared. Certainly some accounts reveal a degree of cockiness amongst their entourage: a reporter from a Merseyside weekly was ordered by the duo's PR Mike Cockayne to tell his readers to start planning their wardrobes for a Liverpool-hosted Eurovision 2004. 'We've got the best song and the best act,' their manager Martin O'Shea told a press conference. 'We're going to win.' Checking in at their hotel, Gemma and Chris would have stood there watching the likes of Jostein Hasselgård and Karmen Stavec shuffle about and thought: Any of you lot got a good-luck message from Sir Paul McCartney to stick on the dressing-room mirror?

Blithe self-confidence did not survive the first rehearsal. 'It just didn't feel right,' says Gemma, shifting about a bit on the sofa. 'The backing track seemed to come out wrong, the sound was all weird. But the manager said it would be fine, not to worry, and you don't want to moan or get negative.' The pair's response was to lock themselves away in their room, rehearsing remorselessly in the six days that remained, skipping the parties and clubs and evidently failing to establish themselves as part of the Eurovision family. When I ask if they made any friends in Riga, Chris says, 'Yeah: the BBC production crew were great.'

As the final approached, the things that were supposed to be getting better got worse. Gemma's dress was a £15,000 backless, bottomless, semi-frontless wisp of red fabric intended, as one paper said, 'to get a big photo of the wearer in the *Daily Star*', but when it arrived, she was appalled. And still is: 'The designer had literally cut the arse right out of it,' she squeals, as outraged as a Liver Bird goosed on the Empire dance floor. 'I told the manager there was no way I was going on TV like that, with my bum cheeks hanging right out for everyone.' The consequence was a dispiriting tour of Riga's boutiques in search of modesty-preserving hot pants in the correct shade of glittery scarlet. When – to universal astonishment – a researcher came up trumps, Chris spoilt the celebrations by asking if someone could sort him out now: he'd forgotten to pack a shirt for the final.

No less inept were the managerial team's attempts at spin-doctoring and story-planting. The press didn't bother to print their ambitious assertion that Jemini's hotel-room purdah was the unwanted consequence of mass fan hysteria; when the *Sun* did run one of their confections, it neutered an account of Gemma's supposed harassment by lust-crazed faux lesbians tATu with inverted-comma qualifications. The Russian teenagers and their management had almost idly whipped up a storm of hype, successfully convincing reporters and petrified EBU officials that their performance was to incorporate simulated acts of Sapphic love, and unsimulated nudity. 'Let's just see if they can sing live,' Chris told the press, as its unkinder members would remind him twenty-four hours later.

Confronted with the crushing might of the tATu PR machine, and the lavish extravaganza that was their stage show, Gemma and Chris began to accept that the UK delegation had both underestimated the opposition and failed to grasp the Eurovision shift from songcraft to showmanship. 'Some people told us we needed a gimmick, you know, like Bucks Fizz and their skirts,' says Chris, 'but the manager was saying no, the song will do it, all you have to do is smile and enjoy yourselves.'

A nagging fear that they might have neglected the non-musical side of their performance swelled into malignant misgiving at the last rehearsal. 'tATu unveiled this amazing routine, all these bits of the stage started moving about and everything,' Chris mutters. 'We had no idea you could do that sort of stuff. Our stage show was just the crappiest nothing. Everyone else had all these amazing lights and all that, and we just had this sad little graphic of rain and clouds, like a shit memorial service.'

Gemma nods eagerly. 'And then the Irish lot came up to us and said: "Where's your ear things?" We looked around and realised everyone else had these little ear monitors, so they could hear themselves above the backing track. But the BBC said it was down to our management to provide them, and the management said it should be the BBC, so we never got any.'

Alan tuts theatrically, then sighs. 'They're only about 100 quid a pop.'

'And then Terry Wogan comes up,' says Chris, with an almost deranged smile, 'and he goes: "You know, with the Iraq war you're not going to get any points."' Perhaps that's Gaelic for 'good luck'.

Tactfully sensing that I'm now about to discuss Eurovision's ugliest vocal apocalypse with its perpetrator, Alan leaps to his feet and offers refills: there are no refusals. This stage of almost every nul-point conversation has required an alcoholic prelude; how grateful my innards will be that this is the last.

Dabbing lager froth off her top lip, Gemma nobly takes the stand. 'As soon as I started I just knew it wasn't right,' she says, looking me straight in the slightly red face. 'Martin explained to me afterwards why I couldn't keep the pitch, that there was something missing in the track, and of course the monitors, but I've only watched it back once, and that was awful: I whacked the sound right off.' Chris idly manipulates an earlobe, saying nothing; Gemma's going to have to get through this alone. 'I mean, all the crappy graphics we had, you just get on with that, but the sound . . .' Alan and I nod slowly. 'I wouldn't have minded about the nul points if I'd sung the best I'd ever sung, but because I sang . . . *wrong* at the beginning, terrible in fact, that's what puts me off it, that's why I don't like watching it.'

I want to stop her now, but she seems oddly keen to get it all out. 'All week I'd been worried about it, I would go back to the room on my own, and just sing, and sing, and sing, because something wasn't right, and I thought, maybe I'm just not getting it, maybe it's me . . .'

'Yeah, it was you,' Chris might have blurted into the pregnant pause that follows, but instead he just takes on board maybe a quarter of a pint of lager.

Weeks later, turning up a rogue domestic cache of Andreas-labelled DVDs – I have well over 100 scattered about behind tellies and under computers – I find one marked 'UK '03'. It's the *Song For Europe* final, and giving it a spin a gratifying truth becomes belatedly apparent: Gemma Abbey can sing, and sing beautifully. 'Love, love's not enough, I need your trust, but you don't try any more . . .' Hearing her sonorous tones, I wonder how on earth anyone, from me upwards, could ever have thought otherwise. Tone deaf she'd hardly have got into the Starlite variety academy down Limekiln Lane, let alone been offered a Eurosong by the big cheese at Paul McCartney's academy. It was those silly monitors all along: I've forced a gentle young woman to confess to a crime she'd never committed.

Stepping off the Skonto Arena stage to a rowdily enthusiastic reception, 'one of the best of the night', the misgivings stockpiled during their performance were joyously discarded. 'The crowd were so brilliant and behind us, we thought we'd done really well,' says Gemma. 'I asked the manager about the dodgy bits and he didn't know what I was talking about – the crowd was making so much noise he hadn't noticed.'

Sandwiched between the backing musicians and their management on one of the green room's cloud-shaped sofas, Jemini felt their adrenalined anticipation decay into bemusement, then disbelief, as the votes came in. 'After all the cheers and applause it just didn't make sense,' says Chris, looking as if it still doesn't. 'We were thinking, We must get a vote, someone's got to give us a vote soon. It just went on and on and on . . .' He wrinkles his nose at the dusk-shrouded world outside, then expels a bleak laugh. 'About halfway through I went outside for a cigarette.'

This obligatory nul-point comforter was followed by greedy indulgence in the world's best-loved bringer of solace when Chris came back in to find *Cry Baby* still stalled on the line. 'Every time we didn't get a vote, we had a drink. So obviously by the end – hah! – we were absolutely hammered.'

'I love the voting,' Martin Isherwood had told the press weeks before. 'It's like watching a World Cup penalty shoot-out.' Slumped dismally in front of his telly (fear of flying kept him away from Riga), Martin might, with reference to his nation's record in the latter, have reflected on the grim aptness of this analogy.

Later, Chris and Gemma made all the right noises about the enhanced publicity benefits of a truly abysmal result. 'Getting nothing is the best result if you can't win,' Gemma ambitiously maintained to London radio station LBC. 'Nul points is better than six or seven,' said Chris. 'It's what people remember.' But backstage in the Skonto, there was only horrified shock, and feverish alcoholic efforts to blunt its impact.

Moments after the Slovenian jury had confirmed Jemini's historic infamy (and indeed Turkey's debut triumph), a BBC delegate emerged to inform waiting journalists that the pair would be coming out to answer questions once they'd composed themselves. For Chris, this was not a straightforward process. 'I found this massive room that was set up for the after-show party, with a big swimming pool in the middle and all these kind of motorised swans going round,' he says; there's nothing forced in the cacophonous merriment the pair now emit, and which Alan and I are powerless not to amplify. 'I just jumped straight in with this flag I had and climbed up the nearest swan, and I'm standing up on it waving a big Union Jack . . .'

'Everyone else is all like calm and collected, having a little glass or two,' says Gemma when at length she's able to, 'and there's us, completely bladdered, dancing about, flags everywhere . . .' My laughter is underpinned with an odd surge of pride: unedifying and unsophisticated as it may be, this is the British way. How splendid if Chris had conducted his interviews from that swan's back; as a compromise, the Union Jack was still in his fist as he dutifully lowered himself on to the cloud sofa.

The shellshocked managerial team's initial spin on the disaster, as relayed by the pair with an articulate efficiency that belied their wine intake, was a simple heads-held-high, strength-in-adversity job; the gathered journalists nodded and scribbled in sympathetic silence. The tactics quickly shifted, though, when after the interviews Martin O'Shea returned to the Jemini dressing room and found it in vandalised ruin. 'The door was kicked in, the walls were smashed,' he was quickly telling journalists. 'It was specifically targeted.'

As he spoke, Martin Isherwood's family trooped by with Union Jacks at half mast. 'I'll tell you what tomorrow's headline should be,' bellowed one with a flag wedged in her topknot, '"Tony Blair – nul points!"'

Thus was born the international conspiracy theory, first

espoused by Terry Wogan the day before, which would form the case for the defence. Jemini had paid a terrible price for their government's conspicuous prominence as a founder-member of the coalition of the willing; Eurovision had created its latest political martyrs. When the sound-monitor issue was wheeled out, it had been repackaged to suit: there were now loud hints of mixing-desk sabotage, and certainly no mention of the petty internal wrangling that had deprived the pair of an in-ear solution.

'We were naïve to think politics wouldn't come into it,' says Chris, with Gemma adding that though she doesn't feel any resentment, it's a shame that people felt they couldn't vote on the music.

But even as I purse my lips into a tight smile of empathy, I'm thinking: Oh, come off it. So intolerable was the aural distress inflicted of *Cry Baby*'s opening minute, you could have delivered it from the back of a nude and whimpering Donald Rumsfeld and still come away with nothing. It's also worth pointing out that of the twenty-six nations competing that night, precisely half were fully paid-up supporters of Operation Enduring Freedom.

No, our disastrous meltdown was precipitated by years of ratcheting complacency. In most rival nations, pre-selection remained a prime-time showcase; by 2003, *A Song for Europe* had been consigned to the Sunday mid-afternoon graveyard. Coming third that Friday evening in 1989, my friend Jane had picked up 47,664 votes – more than Jemini captured in their triumph.

Turkey secured their first victory by sending in an artist who had sold four million albums and duetted with Ricky Martin and Jose Carreras; what did we honestly expect from a pair who had yet to release a record and whose most significant professional engagement was as support act to a *Pop Idol* reject? 'We were just two Scousers, out there trying to do our best for our country, but having a laugh while doing it,' says Chris, and when he does so it all slots into place: we've become the game here-for-the-beer part-timers who have been Terry's targets for all these years, turning up without shirts, too green to grasp the technical requirements, then too tight to meet them, out-thought, out-spent and out-performed by the opposition, but, what the heck, having a giggle while we're at it. We didn't know the score, so we didn't get one.

Our indifference, and Jemini's associated disaster, was the inevitable consequence of a cultural distillation that had over the decades boiled Eurovision down from an exalted international competition to two hours of patronising, chortlesome xenophobia. As the acknowledged motherland of pop, we had nothing to gain by competing in earnest at this daft artistic irrelevance. Chris recalls music-biz elders telling him how they'd cringed when *Save All Your Kisses For Me* won: as early as 1976, Eurovision success was for many Britons a cause for shame rather than celebration. Everyone knew we'd win every year if we made that effort, but like Man U in the League Cup, to be seen making that effort would represent an intolerable loss of face. So like Man U, we'd become the arrogant bastards everyone else wanted to see come horribly, messily unstuck.

The dismissive sneering was apparent even in the agonised autopsies that would fill the comment pages in days ahead. 'How was the UK beaten by Austria's entry,' asked the *Independent*, 'an ecological protest song containing the lyrics "Little rabbits have short noses, and kittens soft paws"?' In similar vein, the *Guardian* called Austria's Alf Poier 'an apparent cretin surrounded by toy animals'.

We'd been at it since 1960, when a British reviewer described Italy's Renato Rascel as 'a short fat man with big ears'. Ignorance and its sidekick xenophobia have been drawing weary corrections from the BBC's continental broadcast brethren almost every year since: Mr Pete Murray, there is no such principality as Monte Cristo; not every Greek male is called Zorba, Mr Terry Wogan. And what kind of message were we sending out by entrusting the 1967 commentary duties to Rolf Harris?

If the rest of Europe was punishing us, it wasn't for getting in bed with the Yanks so much as what we'd caught off them in consequence. When Chris told a Riga press conference that he'd never even heard of Latvia until winning *A Song For Europe*, there was no trace of shame in the bumptious chuckle that followed.

And for too long we'd been trading on past Eurovision glories, looking back to Sandie Shaw, to Lulu; even, once the second bottle's open, to Brotherhood of Man. From the sixties to the eighties we'd been the contest's top performers, but anyone who studied the form would have known how virulently the rot had set in thereafter: down to third in the nineties, and twenty-third since. In the previous twenty years, even Norway had won more Eurovisions.

It was no better in the big wide pop world outside Eurovision. In 1980, British acts filled half the places in the year-end German top-twenty singles chart; twenty years later that was down to two. Having been proudly responsible for very nearly a third of all US music sales in 1986, by the time Jemini set off for Riga, UK performers accounted for less than 0.3 per cent of the American market.

Five months after the first Eurovision Song Contest, the Suez crisis had offered the humiliating evidence that Britain could no longer consider itself a geo-political superpower; the hard lesson of Eurovision 2003 bestowed the same fate on our delusions of pop supremacy. Back in Liverpool, Sir Paul and his academy chums would soon be contemplating a grim symmetry: the feted birthplace of world-conquering British pop had now doubled as its tawdry mausoleum.

The soul-searching, though, had not yet begun in earnest: as a hungover Chris discovered at the Riga airport newsstands the following afternoon, the British press generally prefer to shoot first, and ask questions later. 'He kept reading out this terrible personal stuff,' says Gemma, 'and I kept begging him to stop.' But he didn't, until she was reduced to tears by a review that included the phrase 'a voice that could curdle cream'.

'I've kept everything,' says Chris, with the grudge-hoarding obsessiveness peculiar to his civic brethren, 'even the worst of it.' Of which there was plenty. Jemini were 'nul-points pop flops'; *Cry Baby* was routinely preceded with the likes of 'Euro-disaster' and even, less than a week on, 'the now notorious'. Girls Aloud manager and future *X-Factor* judge Louis Walsh called the performance 'a disgrace, the worst I've ever heard. It was like somebody went into Boots, found the first person they saw behind the counter and asked them if they could sing. They said no, but they were picked anyway.' The *Guardian* summarised *Cry Baby* as 'bloody awful', and even nice Cheryl Baker, who'd been there along with the rest of Bucks Fizz to congratulate Jemini after their qualifying triumph, called their entry 'a bad Eurovision song', whilst tactfully attributing Gemma's wayward vocals to 'nerves on the night'. There was none of that traditionally British sympathy for the underdog – after half a century as Eurovision's overdogs, we just couldn't find it in ourselves.

Doorstepped outside his Liverpool home, Martin Isherwood backed the line being energetically disseminated by Terry Wogan, who was now openly attributing the result to 'post-Iraq backlash'. 'The song was great and the performance was fantastic,' Isherwood stoutly maintained, inciting one paper to introduce him as 'the man responsible for the worst British entry in forty-eight years'. 'But politically we're out on a limb at the moment, and as a country I think we paid the price last night.'

Abroad, the gloating was widespread: this was Wogan-payback time. Germany's *Bild* talked of 'sulking in the home of pop', and Austrian paper *Der Standard* poured scorn on the 'casualty of war theories'; 'Poms caned in Eurovision,' ran one predictable Australian headline. Most damning of all, despite or perhaps because of its reluctant, conciliatory tone, was the testimony of a J. Teigen from Oslo: 'I know I'm in no position to say it, and it makes me a little sad, but they were a bit out of tune.'

Already dumped by their management – Martin O'Shea somehow convinced the press an extended stay in Riga was necessary to pursue his investigations into sabotage and vandalism – Jemini arrived alone back at Manchester airport, enjoyed a quick embrace with their families and were promptly whisked away to a pre-arranged gig in a Birmingham pub. 'Then it was off to London for days of interviews on TV and radio – madness, absolute madness,' says Gemma. It's hard to square the nonchalance of her tone with the task in hand: facing down the media vultures alone, without moral or professional support. 'We had each other. And we just really wanted our say, because the press had had theirs. You couldn't shut us up.'

Peddling their say – Iraq war with a sound-monitor garnish – helped fill in the growing gaps between gigs. Those they did play, though, were apparently well attended and good natured. 'People came because they wanted to see if we were crap, if we could sing,' smiles Gemma, 'and when they found out that we weren't, and we could, everyone came up and shook our hands.'

'We needed to prove that we went to Eurovision for a reason, that the public voted us to go there,' says Chris, doughtily. 'That we were . . . good.'

A pair of twenty-one year olds, abruptly yanked aboard the celebrity merry-go-round and viciously booted off: one can only stand and applaud the unblinking, defiant chutzpah with which Jemini got up and dusted themselves down. There were occasional Kalvik-lite confrontations – cheeky cries of 'nul points!' rang out as Chris walked into a local film preview – but the pair's very public resilience disarmed bullies in the press and on the streets. 'You'd see groups of lads point and stare, and you'd think, Oh aye, here we go,' says Chris. 'Then they'd come up, all polite, and ask for a photo.' After internal deliberation I decide not to share with Chris the following quotation from gay-culture monthly *Attitude*: 'I have spent many a Saturday night following Jemini's Chris Cromby around Liverpool's bars, pinching myself that I am within spunking distance of a living, breathing ESC entrant.'

And there was a moment, a few dizzying days, when the phoenix poked its beak tantalisingly from the smouldering Riga ashes. *Cry Baby* had been released on the day of the final, and when the singles chart came out on 7 June, there it was at number fifteen. The day after, when Chris's mates from Atomic Kitten phoned to tell him 'to keep taking it on the chin', he was able to idly mention that Jemini had just leapfrogged their latest release.

Gemma and Chris waited for an excited management to summon them back to the studio; their half-finished album was still nominally scheduled for an autumn release ('We're thinking of calling it *Nul Points,*' confided Chris to one interviewer). But the call didn't come, and their absence from the following week's chart meant it never would.

There were still engagements of sorts: in the middle of June a wealthy businessman flew them to Geneva to play at his son's eighteenth birthday party. ('That was the first time I ever saw a bottle of proper champagne,' sighs Chris, who walked out of the event with a purloined litre of vodka 'shoved down the back of my pants'.) But by the end of the summer, the gigs had dried to a trickle of Euro-camp charity events in gay pubs and transvestite revue bars; the last on-stage sighting of Jemini was at the 2003 Halloween Spooktacular in New Brighton.

What little they'd earnt from *Cry Baby*'s sales was locked up in a still-unresolved dispute with their former management, and to squeeze the last pennies from the compromised Jemini brand, the pair were obliged to endure modestly rewarded TV humiliation: in a kids'-telly gunge tank, or as the butt of a Harry Hill joke. Sometimes things went too far. When an unkind TV journalist invited Chris to comment on the clearly groundless rumour that Jemini would be supplying backing vocals at the next *Song for Europe*, he snapped back, 'If we won an Oscar, we'd still just be "those guys who scored nul points".'

So didn't they turn anything down? 'If you can laugh at yourself it helps, and we laugh at ourselves more than anyone,' says Gemma, doing just that, almost recklessly. 'We usually took whatever we were offered.' There was no one to tell them not to until Alan turned up.

In the aftermath of Riga, a Scottish psychologist advised Jemini in print to 'get out there with smiles on their faces': with predictable reference to Eddie the Eagle, he said that if the pair portrayed themselves as plucky losers who didn't take things too seriously, 'the record-buying public would respond to them'. But though pity might earn you a pat on the back or a pint at the bar, successfully milking it for much more is a tall order outside the domain of charity. The British reward only those underdogs prepared to get up on their hind legs and dance: if Jemini were going to coax a few last quid out of their humiliation, they'd have to relive it. Don't tell me that what people want to see on Eddie the Eagle's face is a smile. It's bloodied slush and half a pair of bottle-bottom specs.

By Christmas, they weren't even being asked to prostitute their dignity. 'For six months we'd been trying and trying and trying to get Jemini going,' Gemma sighs, 'and that's when you have to say: well, maybe not now, maybe there'll be another time.' The last of the three entries in jeminionline.com's guestbook ('We wuz robbed! Woooo!') is dated November 2003; by the start of 2004 Gemma was manning the reception desk at a Mercedes showroom, with Chris a menswear sales assistant at a store in the city centre.

But as Finn Kalvik has found out, a monumental Eurovision disaster tends to linger on the cultural horizon. 'Just this month there's a guy come up to me in the shop,' says Chris, 'and he says, "You don't half remind me of that bloke from Jemini." When I told him I was he almost dropped on the floor, and I said, "Well, you know, we've all got to pay the bills."' Gemma resigned from the showroom after a customer recognised her, thus inducing colleagues into a light-hearted but quickly unbearable campaign of themed banter; the dyed hair is intended to forestall any similar unpleasantness blighting her current job, selling membership subscriptions at a Manchester health and fitness club.

I later learn of Gemma's Porsche-driving new boyfriend, which may explain her comparative lack of enthusiasm for whatever pickings remain to be scavenged from the tomb of Jemini (notwithstanding the £100 of mine she'll shortly be trousering). Twice Chris taps his nose and mentions 'something we're doing together in September', but Gemma's nod lacks conviction and enthusiasm, and when I ask if it's a comeback she responds with a hollow laugh: whatever it is or was, by November nothing's happened that I've noticed.

Though he dwells with touching sincerity on their personal and professional relationship, one senses that Chris – self-evidently the more fame-driven of the pair, and the one who emerged from Riga with his vocal reputation intact – would happily go it alone. The modest limit of Gemma's current ambition is 'maybe a bit of musical theatre'. ('How can you make a comeback,' she says, 'when you were never there in the first place?') Chris, for his part, eagerly talks of the 'indie pop' solo material he's been working on: 'I was in the studio last night, in fact.' Recalling his most recent – and perhaps most belittling – tabloid appearance, the tone is one of tickled delight. 'A couple of months back I was outside the shop having a smoke, and a chat on my phone, when I see this guy with a big lens over the road . . . And there it is in the *Sunday Star*: "Is this the call that Jemini Chris has been waiting for all this time?"'

'Yeah,' says Alan, drily. 'The Samaritans.'

Everybody laughs, long and loud: no quarter is given or expected in the merciless goading that is a widely enjoyed Liverpudlian pastime. There's more of the same when Gemma interrupts Chris's excited discussion of his last broadcast appearance to inform us of the relevant show's title: *The 50 Most Embarrassing TV Moments*.

We drain beers; Alan slaps his thighs and rises. He's arranged for the two of us to meet Simon O'Brien for a drink, and to my slight surprise the artists formerly known as Jemini express a desire to drive us there. 'Simon O'Brien who lives out in Woolton?' asks Gemma as we file out of Alan's apartment; following confirmation she recalls waitressing in a café he runs.

A minute later we're all squeezed into Gemma's Ford Ka, zipping out of the marina car park beneath the ominous concrete rocket of a Mersey Tunnel ventilation shaft. From the passenger seat Alan calls out the landmarks as we swish through the wet, black city: Penny Lane, Strawberry Fields, the school that was once called Quarry Bank. Perhaps inspired, Chris leans forward beside me to embark on a proud résumé of Jemini's achievements. 'To this day I still think, Hang on, we've done the Eurovision Song Contest, we've done *Top of the Pops*, we had a number fifteen single and we're still only twenty-two.'

'I'm twenty-three,' murmurs Gemma, the spectacles she wears to drive pressed very close to the rainy windscreen.

'I bet we're the only UK Eurovision act most people could name from the last five years,' Chris persists, rather more stridently. 'Even when I'm dead, people will remember Jemini. Maybe our performance wasn't that great, but at least we've come away with . . . we've got our . . .' He slowly settles back in his seat, as if suffering a slow puncture. 'Dignity' and 'intact' were clearly the intended follow-up words, but even in full defiant flow Chris can't quite bring himself to make this ambitious claim.

To fill the awkward silence that follows, I ask if they'll be watching the forthcoming Eurovision final. 'Dunno,' murmurs Gemma guardedly, yanking on the handbrake outside a pub, its etched-glass windows packed tight with silhouetted heads.

'I've got to watch it,' says Chris, as Alan steps out into a puddle with a half-stifled imprecation. 'I'm intrigued now, always will be. I think if I watch, I can in some strange way influence the votes.' Chris squirms out; I follow; he relocates himself in the front passenger seat. 'And that way,' he says, holding a hand through the window which I grasp and shake, 'I can make sure that no one scores nul points again.'

Two weeks later, peering at the scoreboard through a swaying forest of flags in Kiev's Palace of Sport, I'm concentrating very hard on doing precisely that.

21 May 2005
Palace of Sport, Kiev

'Don't mock,' chides the BBC Breakfast presenter, smiling archly from the flat screen that presides over the Heathrow departure gate, 'but Eurovision's here again.' Well, we clearly haven't learnt our lesson. When the heavily pregnant Jordan very nearly pipped Javine Hylton at *A Song for Europe* the month before my trip to Liverpool, the British flirted with the light-entertainment equivalent of sending a Church of the Militant Elvis MEP off to Brussels. It was an ugly lack of respect, made uglier by the lazy arrogance of our top-table status: as one of the EBU's 'big four', we were exempt from the semi-final, which the night before had put paid to Eurovision founder-members Belgium and Holland, the once all-conquering Ireland and a dozen others.

No mockery at least from the fellow passengers seated around me, all en route to the Ukraine for one reason and all charged with excited anticipation. The vaguely familiar young chap on my right blurtingly reveals himself as an ITV showbiz reporter: 'You know what I've got in here?' he asks, tapping the box on the seat beside him with a face like Christmas morning. '*Javine's boots*! I'm on a footwear-for-the-final mercy dash!' This revelation rouses the sombre middle-aged gent to my right to lean across with animated entreaties for a peek; young master ITV looks left and right before slipping the lid off for a quick flash of burgundy leather.

As we file aboard, another unlikely Eurovision enthusiast in a crumpled trenchcoat turns to me: 'So how many have you done, then?' I don't need to ask what he means, but when I tell him this is my first he sighs dreamily. 'Ah . . . mine was Malmo, '92. Michael Ball, Johnny Logan. Well, you're in for something special.'

But then we all are: in a nostalgic return to the age of homespun Eurovision innocence, the age of 'Où est Harrogate', we're off into the unknown. Beyond an association with reactor-core meltdown and butter-stuffed breasts of chicken, I was heading to Kiev unburdened with intelligent expectation. When my eleven-year-old son had mentioned the previous evening that my destination was the capital of Europe's largest country, I'd almost choked in shame.

Counterbalancing the Chernobyl Prejudgement was proving rather more of a challenge than I'd hoped. My seat-pocket copy of *What's on Kyiv* introduces itself with an editorial that begins: 'For many years, Kyiv was perceived as an uninteresting hovel.' No attendant 'but' could ever be big enough to make up the ground lost there. And consulting the email print-out that confirms my reservation for two nights at the Hotel Bratislava, I discover a footnote warning guests that 'there will be no Hot Water at the hotel for the period 7-20 June'.

Three hours later my ITV friend is helpfully fast-tracking me through the bespoke Eurovision lane at Kiev arrivals, and thence, across a sun-warmed car park lavishly bedecked with commemorative banners, on to the coach that's shuttling us to the Palace of Sport. Through a window ominously crazed by the impact of some hefty projectile, I watch the traffic and street furniture spool bumpily by: Moskviches, ex-military lorries hauling trailers of vast logs, a rusted multilingual sign alerting passers-by to the nearby presence of the Exhibition of National Economic Achievements.

Pine forests give way to decaying ranks of apartment blocks

faced with oversized beige bath tiles; sallow youths in hooded tracksuits stare down from the ramshackle balconies. Atop a distant hill stands a gargantuan metal woman, her lofted sword shimmering mightily; long before I discover the Monument to the Motherland dates only from 1981, it's apparent that here is a country with an oppressively recent Soviet past.

Still, it's warm, bright and, as we rumble into the city centre, almost overbearingly green. Between the blocks, lilac trees and chestnuts blossom in extravagant profusion, and only now, right in the middle of town, do I understand the Nazis' extraordinary plans to scrape off the Ukraine's fertile black topsoil and freight it back to the fatherland. How shameful that Stalin's brutally enforced agricultural collectivisation should induce famines that in 1933 and 1947 would cost three million lives in this land of plenty, and how unimaginably tragic that a further eight million Ukrainians were to perish during the significant conflict between these dates, a toll higher than that suffered even by Germany.

With a history like that, and the direct links to it severed only months before by the 'orange revolution' that expelled a Soviet-throwback regime, it's easy to understand why every lamppost in town has been annexed by a huge, green Eurovision 2005 banner. For Ukraine's fledgling pro-Western democracy, the contest was a powerful symbol of European unity, imbued with all the weighty political significance of the Marcel-model original. And then some. In November 2004, with the orange revolution at its most critical juncture, reigning Eurovision champion Ruslana Lizhichko appeared in Kiev's Independence Square to announce her own chosen protest against the fraudulent election result that had brought matters to a head. As the British were toying idly with the chortlesome prospect of sending a heavily pregnant, tone-deaf glamour model to represent them at the 2005 contest, the 2004 winner was embarking on a hunger strike.

When Viktor Yushchenko first sat down at the presidential desk on the morning of 23 January 2005, he got out the photo of his kids, labelled the stapler STOLEN FROM VIK'S OFFICE and then immediately announced a determination to seize with both hands the opportunity handed to Ukraine by Ruslana's victory in Turkey. Eurovision's executive supervisor Svante Stockselius, no doubt accustomed to being met at the airport by a bored culture-ministry factotum, must have been modestly astounded to find his routine progress meeting two weeks afterwards upgraded to a full-on state visit. President Yushchenko grabbed Svante's hand for the photographers and emotionally declared that the forthcoming contest was more than the dawning of a new cultural era; hosting 'the biggest event in Ukrainian history' would allow the nation to entertain and educate 400 million fellow Europeans, and so move closer towards the goal of EU membership. Was it an accident that within two years of staging the Eurovision final, both Estonia and Latvia found themselves amongst the newest stars on the EU flag? Or that only eight months after the Istanbul final, Turkey's application was being considered rather more carefully? 'Any events that contribute to the integration of Ukraine into Europe are important and sacred,' quavered the president, fixing the gingery Swedish bureaucrat beside him with a flinty stare. 'At the EBU you do things that diplomats cannot and will not do. We are soldiers on your side.'

'*Douze points!*' Svante might have responded.

'Awakening' was selected as the 2005 contest's motto (regrettably pipping 'Ukraine: Setting Europe's Heart on Fire!'), and the president backed up his portentous words by allocating to the contest a hefty chunk of the state TV broadcaster's annual budget. The nation's Eurovision entry, dubiously victorious at a national selection final it hadn't actually qualified for, was a blaringly pro-Viktor revolutionary anthem composed and performed by GreenJolly, three plump and nerdish DJs best known for their previous endeavours in 'comedy reggae'. 'No to falsification, yes to Yuschenko.' Get down!

The coach hisses to a halt outside the mighty hulk of mid-sixties Communism that is the Palace of Sport, lavishly swathed in green and guarded by an absurd surfeit of policemen in vast peaked caps. The ITV man runs off with Javine's boots, and following many mimed exchanges with grumpy, clueless big-hats, and some inefficient blundering amongst the outside-broadcast lorries (one from the BBC; three alone from Swedish national broadcaster SVT) I wind up in the accreditation tent. After an hour of photography, data entry and telephone calls, my face emerges from the laminator in the centre of an orange card rather than the blue press pass I'd been promised by email.

'What does orange mean?' I ask the jolly girl who threads a chain through the pass and hangs it round my neck.

'See? It reads here.'

I read there. FAN, it says.

A fan? A *fan*? The Wogan cloven hoof pops out: I'm not walking about for forty-eight hours declaring my strident neck-bound allegiance to one of the cultural world's least esteemed communities.

It's only when I'm struggling excitedly through the tent's plastic flaps with a hefty armful of complimentary merchandise that I accept the authenticity of that laminated label. I could in theory make my life a lot easier by folding, squashing and wedging all these pens and clocks and umbrellas into the lime-green messenger bag, but I just can't bring myself to despoil them so. And how, I wonder, could I even fleetingly have contemplated using this lovely Eurovision Awakening carrier bag for my dirty socks and pants? Oh, I'm a fan all right.

Indeed it's becoming plain that almost all the foreigners on this side of the security cordon are mixing business and pleasure: in a refreshing departure from the weary cynicism that journalists strive to master, all the blue-badges around are chattering breathlessly, eyes wide. Greece, oh yes, still number one for me! Very unlucky Iceland I think. And this Portugal girl who faints in semi-final – too, too funny! But of course also sad.

An enormous proportion are men trying to look younger than they are, accreditations slung across tightly T-shirted chests, sunglasses propped on carefully gelled heads: if you're a gay journalist, Eurovision is the Oscars. The day before I'd read that the official Eurovision nightclub was packed with husband-fishing Ukrainian women wondering what they were doing wrong. By the same token, I've already given up hope of finding a bar anywhere near the Palace of Sport that's likely to be showing the following afternoon's FA Cup final.

I'm grateful to Andy Roberts, an occasional contributor to *Attitude* magazine, for nobly endeavouring to explain why by the age of twelve he was dancing around to chubby Yugoslavian divas using his dressing-gown cord as a feather boa. 'Eurovision is the Lady Di of international competition,' he emailed me some months later. 'At the end of three hours I feel head-fucked but contented, as if I'd just shagged a fit relative.' Perhaps it's just as well that Marcel Bezençon died in 1981.

Outside the security cordon I bundle myself and my belongings into the Lada at the head of the cab queue. After some fruitless key action and a weary oath, the driver leans out of his open window and shouts to the cabbies behind; a moment later we're being push-started past the courtesy coaches. The Lada bucks into life and then we're thudding and rattling through the traffic, the inrushing wind blowing the driver's fag ash straight into my eyes. Reaching down for my window winder, I find only a greasy hole in the hand-painted door trim.

We judder to a halt outside a careworn suburban high-rise with many Cyrillic letters missing from the sign flickering atop its scabbed, off-white superstructure in the early-evening gloom. 'Bratislava,' says the driver, before writing down a figure for the fare, which seems reasonable enough until I'm standing at a metro ticket office the morning after, being asked to pay precisely one hundredth that amount for a trip back into town.

In six stops, my journey from Darnytsia station offers the complete post-Soviet experience, a lingering portrait of a nation caught between Intervision past and Eurovision future. Our spartan, broad-beamed carriage is incongruously crowded with commercial exhortations that slather the walls and scroll across advertising monitors retro-fitted to the ceiling, ordering the heavy-eyed strap-hangers beneath to lose weight, invest in a cameraphone or, most regularly, to LEARN ENGLISH AND BE AU

PAIR! At one point a middle-aged woman carrying two buckets gets on, robotically dictates some spiel and then walks the length of the carriage failing to interest us in her wares, which as she passes I note are tiny cardboard packets each containing a single sticking plaster.

I'd provisionally arranged to meet two people in Kiev, and a text from one of them buzzes against my hip as I wander past bench-bound, Saturday-morning beer enthusiasts whilst failing to find the old town and its loudly trumpeted cosily historic ambience. It's Zhenya, a Kiev-based friend-of-a-friend, apologising for his unexpected absence from the city: 'Unfortunately I've take strong order from boss about urgent business trip,' he reports, going on to wish both the UK and Ukraine 'big luck in contest tonight'. Before retrousering my phone I give my other intended contact a call; like its predecessors, it goes unanswered. Andreas, fantastically, had vaulted the nationality barrier to bag himself a place in the Monaco delegation, and it was rather a blow to discover on arriving that the principality's first ESC entry since 1979 hadn't made it through the semi-final. Perhaps he'd already gone home; perhaps you couldn't get reception behind the locked door of a Sport Palace lavatory.

That this is the city's big day, its Olympics, its Expo, becomes obvious well before I'm in sight of that green-swaddled auditorium. The day before, every street corner had been dotted with headscarved old dears in long coats and dirty trainers, condemned by the end of the Soviet jobs-for-all era to hawk a tragic selection of goods from spring onions to kittens; no sign of their tone-lowering presence this morning. The shop windows gleam, and in the bright sun it looks as if the church domes have been regilded overnight. Coming from a nation of Eurovision boo-boys, I still can't quite believe what hosting the final means to these people.

I've been wondering what my fan ID actually entitles me to, other than a lingering sense of embarrassment and the right to share a Portaloo with 10,000 dumpling-reared policemen, and inside the Palace of Sport compound I find out that it isn't a ticket for the final. Fighting my way to the box office through the hordes of pestering touts who have unmysteriously been allowed through the ring of steel, I discover the cheapest remaining tickets ambitiously priced at the thick end of a hundred quid. That's more than I've ever outlaid to access any live event, and I've been to a World Cup. Then again, I reason whilst assembling a vast pile of notes on the counter, if tonight turns out to be even half as much fun as watching Scotland lose to Costa Rica I won't be complaining.

There are four hours to go, and I spend two of them on a bench by the stage door, eating half a pound of smoked ham and receiving cup-final text updates from kindly minded sources back home. Just after halftime there's an abrupt media scrum as the artists emerge from their final rehearsal. My nul-points radar bleeps into life: as the parade of tiny, blinged-up dollies files slowly out, I examine each lavishly hand-painted face in turn, willing them all to betray no fear or weakness. But watching them work the snappers, pouting, waving, bending down to dangle their hair extensions at a puppy, I'm instead affected by the heart-rending pointlessness of all this eager excitement.

As Jemini's failure and Ruslana's fur-cloaked, whip-cracking triumph had proven, in the televote era Eurovision was all about the show, not the actors. In the Bratislava's Formica-panelled lobby I'd watched a BBC World interview with Bill Martin, co-composer of *Puppet on a String* and *Congratulations*. 'Right up to the eighties all the big songwriters would enter,' he sighed, 'but these days Eurovision is just a choreographic bonanza.' How sad to look at those little women with their bleached and brilliant smiles and know that for almost all, as for my more recent nul-pointers, this would be it: the beginning, middle and end of their celebrity careers.

Meandering through the throng that mills about the corporate tents and stalls in the Palace of Sport forecourt, I'm at last brought face to flag-painted face with Eurovision's fanbase: after all my impersonal online contact with ESC obsessives, it's disarming to be so suddenly engulfed by such a huge, happy throng of them. But what an extraordinary assortment. Scanning the sea of horned helmets, mauve wigs and greasy-fringed bespectacled squints, I crudely split my Euro-mates into three groups, by motto: 'I'm mad, me', 'I'm gay, me' and 'Measured from the tip of her sword, Kiev's Monument to the Motherland is the world's fourth-tallest sculpted figure'.

A human beer bottle trailing a wheeled crate of free samples waddles swiftly past, pursued by a gigantically fat flag-carrying Norwegian squeezed into a pink satin biker suit. This isn't the gay Oscars, I realise, but the gay World Cup, a chance for men in pink biker suits to plumb the depths of public drunkenness with the national flag draped round their shoulders. ('Where else can you support Britain without getting spat on or arrested?' slurs a man I later meet in the hot-dog queue.)

Clanking a couple of brewed freebies into my messenger bag I wander up to a trio of quiet men in little plastic Union Jack bowler hats. 'It's just a great experience,' says the youngest, in pancake-flat Lancastrian, when I ask him to encapsulate the contest's appeal. 'You know, a laugh.' He shares his first Eurovision memory with Chris Cromby – Sonia in 1993 – but a rather more grizzled associate volunteers a CV that goes right back to a place in the Brighton stalls the night that ABBA took the crown.

The smug tone with which I announce that the UK jury failed to award *Waterloo* a single point proves ill-advised. 'Well, that's right,' he says, realigning his bowler, 'and neither did Italy, Belgium, Greece or Monaco.' It's the sort of mild-mannered monomania I've only really experienced face to face with motorhome-dwelling followers of the Tour de France.

I ask them who's going to win, and receive three top-five predictions, each delivered with the quick-fire, cocksure authority of a racing punter. Querying the United Kingdom's absence from the list, I'm treated to looks of withering disdain. 'A *Popstars* reject?' sneers one. 'Haven't we learnt our lesson?'

'Javine was so flat in the rehearsal we hid our flags under the seat,' says his young friend. 'And now we're hearing she's got a sore throat. We'll be lucky if we get a point.' Oh no.

Please don't say that. Maybe she can't sing without her lucky shoes.

There are many Greeks, Turks and Scandinavians about, but I'm greatly surprised at the predominance of Union Jacks. 'Well, there were 20,000 of us at the Athens Olympics,' says middle-aged Brummie Joan, after I inveigle myself rather clumsily into her flag-faced coterie. 'More than any other visiting supporters, I was told.' She's been here for a remarkable two weeks, sight-seeing with a diligence that has seen her visit every station on the metro ('It's magic: you can go ten stops for the price of a pee back home!), yet isn't quite sure why she's here at all. 'I suppose it's a chance to see a different way of life,' is her unconvincing justification. Surveying Joan's friends, with their George-Cross afro wigs and red-blue beards, I'm imagining there's a bit of a Barmy Army thing going on here, the impulse that encourages otherwise stolid Middle Englanders to rise up from Henman Hill and head off to plant the flag in foreign fields.

I'm planning a rueful, disappointed nod when a man wearing a small inflatable bulldog on his head leans over Joan with a thoughtful expression. 'It's just nice to be here with all these other countries,' he says, angling his head at a nearby rosy-cheeked Swede, flag painted inside a heart on either cheek, who's happily waltzing with a similarly decorated British counterpart. By the time we're all shuffling into the Palace of Sport, I'm infused with a warm, fraternal idealism. Turk arm-in-arm with Greek, gay with straight, Brit with . . . um (Excuse me, what's that flag on your forehead? Great – thanks) Belarusian: here we are, Marcel, fifty years on and still breaking down barriers and borders through the international language of funny music.

Aided by the beer, which I'm surprised to find on sale in bold abundance, inside the Palace of Sport lobby this tolerant goodwill is being celebrated with raucous abandon. Beneath the boxer's-mansion chandeliers and soaring ruched drapes, dozens of drum-battering Montenegrans are paying ear-bleeding tribute to Ukraine's president and its principal football team,

Dinamo Kiev. The many locals in attendance respond with enthusiastic but unintelligible chants of their own, and soon it's an ale-slopping, red-faced, vocal free-for-all.

Somewhere in the cacophony a PA announcer is trying to make herself heard, but she's given up long before the general realisation sinks in that the show is about to start with no one yet in their seats. A full-scale crowd surge is underway when I sprint towards my recommended entrance, one which carries me helplessly past the shrugging stewards and into the vast, stagy darkness of the auditorium. Men in headphones are running around in yelping panic, tapping fingers on wristwatches, pushing people up staircases and failing to reanimate the crowd-control personnel. I'm right up against the side of the multi-level stage, in a flabby, multinational conga of flag-hugging inebriates, when a giant screen above is filled with swirling graphics and the *Te Deum* fanfare blasts ceremonially around the hall. The men in headphones sag; this sorry shambles is now going out live to 400 million homes.

Lights flare into sudden life and there's last year's winner Ruslana just above us, doing her *Xena: Warrior Princess* thing, only this time with a flame thrower. Our proximity to its satanic muzzle sparks off a sudden retreat, so sudden that the tall Slavic chap beside me cops a glancing blow as a boom-mounted camera strafes our skulls. In the mêlée thus unleashed we're rather roughly rounded up by a fluorescent-vested snatch squad, and as the young comperes step out to a reception of deranged cheers I'm being shouldered up a staircase whose numbering bears no relation to what's on my ticket. But a small horde of leather-clad Magyar gypsies is already stomping on to the stage; I spot a space, tread on a lot of toes, and a moment later I'm wedged in a modest sliver of half-seat left between the encroachments of a bollard-thighed, flag-cheeked local and two stout red-faces who are swaying, cheering and – oh my, is that a tear? – generally surrendering themselves to the performance now ending. 'Och, this is just *too much*!' shouts one to the other amidst thunderous applause.

Breathless and dishevelled, I endeavour to take stock. Twelve rows up and stage left, beyond the heavily compromised hip room this is a great seat – that much is plain from the ominous preponderance of squat, tuxedoed gangland types and their unsmiling, stick-like blonde companions, all owners of feet I now deeply regret stamping on. Beyond and all around it's dark, and huge, and chantingly boisterous, more like a fight crowd were it not for that pink Norwegian running up and down the lower aisles with his nation's flag hoist high.

OK – there's the scoreboard, here's my bag, there's the beer in it, and here's the programme . . . Oh, butter my arse: Javine's on next! I just don't feel ready for this. The hosts – he in black tie, she ruffled up in mauve chiffon like a big-box Easter egg – step out again, deliver some unintelligible staged quip in their please-to-welcome-all English, and then here's that young woman in those shoes. 'Oh God,' comes a rearward stage mutter, 'here we go.'

I watch Javine and her modest coterie of dancers shimmy and shuffle, and hear her repeat the bhangra-flavoured song's title (touch my fie-YAH!') a great many times. It's an unambitious spectacle by contemporary Eurovision standards, but is that enough to guarantee a points embargo? As she strikes and holds her final pose and the Union Jacks flutter out all around the four-square, industrial auditorium, I begin to fear that it may be. More so when the downbeat critics behind swiftly damn her performance with the very faintest of praise. 'Well,' drones one, 'at least she was in tune.'

'Ish,' adds a dismal companion.

No time for a post-mortem. Distracted by a new and burgeoning fear that my seat is about to be reclaimed by Kiev's hardest man, I'm only aware that the full-figured Maltese soprano and her Disney ballad have been and gone when an overheard coo from my right-hand neighbour ('Oooh, this looks interesting!') alerts me to the on-stage presence of half a dozen Romanians wielding angle grinders.

And so it marches unflaggingly onwards, this confusion of noise, light and spangled, frenzied choreography. My Scottish neighbours' swaying enthusiasm is banging me against the

Ukrainian on every off-beat; the Brits behind are inadvertently tickling my ears with their Union Jacks. Slow down! Even the between-act pauses offer no respite, as the scene-shifters toil with practised urgency, rolling away oil drums, hoisting amps and drum kits into split-level position, almost losing control of a huge grand piano they're wheeling at speed down a ramp. The pub-glam Norwegians, the boldly ethnic Turks . . . and there's Norman Bates's mother in a wicker rocking-chair, belabouring a lap-mounted drum of improbable diameter as beside her a topless man screams, 'Let's make love!' At last – the true spirit of Eurovision (the Moldovans responsible will come home a handy sixth).

A dozen songs or so in I flick through the programme and establish that the opening Hungarian entry is one of just five to lack an English element – clearly a boon to the Scotsmen, who I note with astonishment are singing along to every word, but surely rather an insult to the inclusive spirit of Eurovision. And as tickled as Marcel would surely have been to see the Euro ousting the dollar as the Ukraine's street-preferred foreign currency, it would hardly have atoned for his disappointment at the end of bilingual Eurovision compering. Farewell Royaume Uni, and though it was only ever there in spirit, farewell nul points.

More big drums, a couple of pole dancers, a lot of shouts of 'Hey!' and an air violinist . . . it sounds both bad and funny, but from this distance at least, it isn't. Indeed the overall impression, beyond the overblown theatricality, is one of honed professionalism. I'd learnt that U2 had already bought up the 2005 Eurovision stage-set for their forthcoming tour; it's not easy to imagine the Stones or David Bowie competing to acquire the mirror-ball technology of Eurovisions past. The contest, perhaps Europe in general, has squeezed out the last traces of parochial idiosyncrasy in its drive towards polished, metropolitan competence. We don't do silly any more: no more accordion reggae, no more brace-twanging and aerial splits, no more joke Skodas or 8-0 mismatches at the European Championships. I probably shouldn't be as gladdened as I am by the appearance of the national-hero Klitschko brothers during a brief halfway interval. 'Eh-ooro-vizzion eace seemlah to barksing,' intones white-suited Vladimir, displaying all the expressive articulacy we've come to expect from experienced heavyweights.

'Of course,' replies Vitali, 'but let us hope there are tonight no nackouts!' Yes, let's. Really.

I get talking to the Scotsmen during this soothingly inept lull. We get as far as sharing our fears for Javine before a huge army of horned helmets stands to attention in the facing grandstand and begins to clap in robotic unison. 'Ah, now this isn't bad,' confides the nearest Scotsman when the Swedish smoothie on-stage starts up, 'but the one that came second in their national final was a *cracker*.'

The moment he's departed the stage, the chap to my left, along with perhaps two-thirds of the auditorium, leaps to his feet and embarks on a rolling roar that doesn't let up for three minutes. Halfway through it my pocket buzzes. It's a text from Zhenya: 'Do you agree, GreenJolly not bad?' I wish I could. Though it's hard to make anything out above the throat-shredding singalong beside me, the Ukrainians clearly aren't going to win. They're chubby, middle-aged and male, and what little I can hear of their dirge-like plod-rap goes in one ringing ear and straight out the other. 'Good luck!' I text back.

A toneless schlager-metal shambles composed by the man who (along with Julio Iglesias's songwriting team) gave us Nicole's *Ein Bisschen Frieden*, Germany's entry painfully activates the nul-point alarm that's now embedded deep in my skull. The Scotsmen and I exchange pained expressions, and looking around there isn't a single German flag being waved in Gracia's honour. Come to think of it, I haven't spotted a single French tricolour, either – if there's a common theme that unites the Brits, Scandis, Greeks, Turks and ex-Warsaw Pacters who have commandeered this place, it's that we're all from Europe's peripheries, born the wrong side of the track that runs from Berlin to Paris (change at Brussels).

Events of the previous hour have confirmed that the strange

alchemy by which a winning Eurosong is forged remains to me an unfathomable enigma, but these days I'm poking about the bottom of the Eurovision barrel with the practised sagacity of a tea-leaf reader. Sorting the wheat from the chaff is beyond me, but I can confidently declare Gracia the chaff de la chaff. 'Wasn't that awful?' says a voice from behind with undisguised glee. A year ago I'd have turned round to join in the laughter; now I just sit there, thinking, Get on the phone, good people of Austria, and help out your old mates in their hour of need. All I ask is that tonight no one goes home empty-handed.

Suddenly all the scary fat gangsters and their teenage blondes vault to attention. 'It's the Russians,' hisses a Scotsman. So efficiently has the Awakening theme been pushed, it's easy to forget that a fifth of the Ukrainian population is of Russian origin, and that when the discredited election was rerun, Yushchenko triumphed by a margin of just 8 per cent. On the way here from the metro station I'd passed a small demonstration, shunted away by police down a sidestreet: 'Europe – GreenJolly is not Ukraine!' read one banner. The big Ukrainian beside me is not alone in whistling and jeering; for a horrid moment it seems that Svante Stockselius's worst fears are about to be realised in Eurovision-fuelled civil unrest. And that's before I find out what Natalya Podolskaya is singing about. 'You think you're having fun,' reads my nearest Scotsman from his programme at the end of three tense minutes, 'till a child shoots your gun.'

A trio of bouncy blonde Bosnians put us back on track with a bit of pseudo-ABBA; when they go off my neighbour leans back with a big smile and blares, 'Aw, too much! I wish I had a pair of tits.'

'You have,' deadpans his friend.

After the worst run of results in Eurovision history, Switzerland has called in that Estonian girl group; two pretty-boy Latvians (get off those stools, boys, I shriek silently, then cheer as they do), a pointy-faced, bored-looking Frenchwoman and suddenly it's all over.

There's some kind of floor show incorporating a contortionist and more of the over-sized percussion that is the evening's theme, but I can't look: my overloaded visual cortex has almost shut down. Instead I liberate one of the two half-litres of complimentary beer from my Eurovision satchel, hack it open with a key and offer the Scotsmen a swig they graciously decline. 'Greece will walk it, but I'd love to see the big Maltese girl do well,' says the nearest in response to my request for a final prediction. Greece? Beyond a lot of flags being waved somewhere to our left, I can't remember them at all. And was that Maltese flesh-hill really so special? To hold my Eurovision own I idly invoke her similarly diva-sized compatriot from 1998, year Gunvor. 'Same woman,' says a Scotsman, sounding a little disappointed in me.

The brown bottle in my hand is empty when Vladimir Klitschko comes back on in his white suit to bang a little gong. 'You cannart vote no more!' he cries, a little reedily.

'Well, here we go,' murmurs my neighbour, chewing a fleshy lip. The gigantic flat-screen scoreboard comes to life, sparking an involuntary beer-churning clench deep in my abdomen.

'Khallo, Vienna!' shrieks a compere, and after an exchange of stilted pleasantries, it begins. Nichts for Germany, nowt for Javine – in fact, consulting the animated point-totals as we head off to the headquarters of Lithuania Television, zilch for anyone west of Salzburg.

'Obviously a lot of Slavic expats in Austria,' mutters a voice from behind; the results that unfold will later inspire some commentators to suggest the retrograde step of splitting Eurovision in two.

Twenty-four nations qualified for the final, but with the unsuccessful semi-finalists now also enfranchised, this is the most gruelling vote-a-thon in Eurovision's fifty years. Vilnius, Lisbon, Monaco (go Andreas!) . . . after Minsk, a Scotsman wearily informs me that we still have thirty-four capitals to visit. 'Is this really worth an hour and a half of primetime television?' he sighs rhetorically; when my second beer comes out, they both hold out plastic cups with expressions of frail exasperation.

But the complicit huff of boredom I attempt to expel comes

out as a half-stifled dry retch. It does so because with five – '. . . and Turkey, twelve points!' – with six voting rounds complete, the bottom of the scoreboard is mired in a horrible, deathly stasis. Monaco has sorted Germany out with a couple of points (half their eventual total), and with Greece yet to vote Cyprus are hardly going to be left to die on the start line (so traditional is the twelve points from Athens that when they're announced, Constantinos unfurls a pre-prepared 'thank you Hellas' banner in the green room).

Rather more of a challenge, though, to imagine who can be relied on to rescue the two old enemies grovelling pointless beside them. The prospect of seeing the French strung up by their feet from the drivel monument may be a consolation-in-waiting for some of my countrymen, but as first Iceland, then Belgium, then Estonia fail to offer either *Touch My Fire* or *Chacun Pense à Soi* even a single point, I can't count myself amongst them.

The Scotsmen only have eyes for the top of the scoreboard – as well they might, given the unfolding prescience of their predictions – but as the Finnish fail to include the words 'United Kingdom' or 'France' in their address to the Palace of Sport, I'm including the words 'come on', 'please' and 'pissed-up elk-shaggers' in my muttered equivalent. We're beginning to run out of juries. Say it ain't so, people of Andorra. A minute on, it ain't: with practised diplomatic aplomb, they chuck five points over their northern border (followed by twelve – almost half Spain's final total – to the south). And then there was one.

Can this really be happening? Scrolling back through three kaleidoscopic hours of carnival mania I try and bring up a mental screen-grab of Javine Hylton; all I get is strappy boots and distant dance moves, bathed in dim orange light. What I need is the look in her eye, to see what she's made of. Would she take it on the chin, or in the teeth? Was she a Kojo or a Kalvik? A Seyyal or a Celia?

We're halfway through the Bulgarian voting; at this stage that's enough to rule out any points from them. Why does 'Javine' have to share so many letters with 'Jemini'? I snatch up the programme and flick through to her biography on the United Kingdom page. 'Controversial exit from the hit show *Popstars: The Rivals* . . . devastated . . . six months out of the limelight . . .' My scalp tautens. She's got form! But . . . but maybe that isn't such a bad thing. Jahn's fallow year in Jerusalem with The Lions of Judea, the injuries that put paid to Kojo's keepy-uppy career, Seyyal's rise and fall from Brynner and Bronson to photo-love stories – all those who'd emerged from the nul-points wreckage with the fewest open wounds had been previously inoculated against future professional disappointment.

Goodnight Sofia, hello Dublin. It's Dana! Give us a break, Rosemary: I'm not asking for all kinds of everything, just any kind of something. Bosnia, one point; Greece, two points; Switzerland, three points. Sagging in my seat, I vacantly survey the Greek flags already being hoisted in triumph. All those violent sensory recollections seem to drain away. So this is it, then. Unbidden, a scene takes vivid shape in my hollowed head: there I am, ringing a bell marked 'Hylton' outside a flat in Ladbroke Grove, West London.

Could Javine make a career out of her disaster, as Jahn Teigen had done, or reinvent herself so effectively, à la Daníel, that her countrymen would forget it ever happened? At twenty-three, might she settle into Remedios-model self-imposed exile, pending a glorious metamorphosis into majestic diva-hood a decade and a half later? Or just knuckle down to a workaday career in bread-and-butter entertainment, like Tor or the Ov?

Norway four, Romania five, Israel six. I find I'm grateful for that UK meltdown at Riga 2003: two short years on, the lake of tabloid bile could hardly have been refilled. What am I saying? It's going to be concentrated by bitter experience into a viscous puddle of black spite: countries don't come much nicer than Norway, and look what they did to Finn Kalvik three years on from *Mil Etter Mil*. I see Javine open the door, unkempt head bowed, then cravenly count out the 100 quid I've handed her as my voice recorder starts running: 'So you're, um, backstage at the Palace of Sport, the scores are coming in . . .'

'Denmark, 7 points.' Would I get the Wilfried brush-off, or would she simply vanish like Thomas and poor Çetin? Was there – by the grace of all that is Benny, please no – some Gunvorian cupboard full of skeletons waiting to tumble out on me? Ten years on there'd be a divorce, perhaps a forsaken child, certainly an improbable venture or two. A naturopathic brewery, the teachings of Prem Rawat, an aquatic archery range on the Grand Union canal. I let my dull gaze fall to the programme biography. Maybe – well, what have we got? – maybe she'd be asked to reprise her triumph as Nala in the West End production of *The Lion King*; maybe she'd find productive solace in her mother's collection of soul and reggae albums. Or maybe I'd just find myself being punted back down Ladbroke Grove by burgundy-boot power.

What a strange privilege to meet the extraordinary people I'd met, to uncover the wayward sagas of those I hadn't. Yet cheering as it was to have restored some reputations, to have scrubbed off a little of the stubborn nul-points stigma, the fearsome emotional toll had left me exhausted. The highs had been a little too high, and the lows much too low; I was grateful it was over. But I only realise quite how grateful when the gentle voice of Ireland's 1970 Eurovision winner, amplified to a godlike boom, blasts out around Kiev's Palace of Sport: 'United Kingdom, eight points.'

A travesty in the contest's grand tradition, a shameless, love-blind expatriate vote harvest. As I haul myself upright hoisting both arms wanly aloft, somehow that makes it all the sweeter.